Sokołowski masterfully leads us through the historic and market forces that have shaped cogeneration's role in the energy sector, and the legal and policy approaches governing its use to the current day. Although the focus is on cogeneration, his analysis provides ample food for thought in assessing the role of other forms of generation in today's environment.
– Stephen G. Burns, Former Chairman, U.S. Nuclear Regulatory Commission, United States

This is a most welcome book on CHP and its development from a legal perspective in Europe. It presents a much-needed comprehensive legal overview of what is happening at each Member State level. It will be a sourcebook for those working on CHP into the future and there is an exciting range of conclusions on CHP to consider now and into the future in terms of EU law and policy formulation!
– Raphael J. Heffron, Professor of Global Energy Law and Sustainability and Jean Monnet Professor in the Just Transition to a Low-Carbon Economy, Centre for Energy, Petroleum and Mineral Law and Policy, University of Dundee, United Kingdom

With this book, Maciej M. Sokołowski provides the first comprehensive academic review of the regulation of combined heat and power in Europe. His book takes a critical look at the achievements in CHP policy and regulation so far, and the regulatory toolbox developed. It also looks ahead and provides for some insights as to the future of CHP regulation.
– Catherine Banet, Associate Professor, Scandinavian Institute of Maritime Law, Petroleum and Energy Law Department, Vice-Dean for International Relations of the Faculty of Law, University of Oslo, Norway

Sokołowski-sensei, an excellent European energy expert based in Japan, delivers a well-done guidebook on an increasingly important area of EU law: cogeneration – a technology focused upon in his book from different angles, i.e. national, pan-European, and global, tracked thoroughly in the past and current laws and policies, equipped with telling scenarios for its future development.
– Katsuhiro Shoji, Professor of European Union Law with a Jean Monnet Chair ad personam, Director of the Jean Monnet Centre of Excellence, Keio University, Japan

Cogeneration harnesses heat from industry to produce electricity, reducing the need to rely on fossil fuels. Although the concept is simple, it is no easy task to understand the complex regulatory issues involved in expanding cogeneration. Maciej M. Sokołowski provides an enlightening and invaluable guide to this complex terrain.
– Daniel Farber, The Sho Sato Professor of Law, Faculty Director of the Center for Law, Energy, and the Environment, University of California, Berkeley, United States

By writing a comprehensive book on a complex theme, as combined heat and power is, Maciej Sokołowski has once again proven that he is a 'talented gentleman who could wear the professor's hat' as once Professor Żmijewski (1949–2015), our great Polish top-energy expert, called him.

– *Rafał Czaja, President of the Prof. Krzysztof Żmijewski Association for Efficiency, Poland*

European Law on Combined Heat and Power

This book provides an analysis of the European policy approach to combined heat and power (CHP), a highly efficient technology used by all EU Member States for the needs of generating electricity and heat.

European Law on Combined Heat and Power carries out an assessment of the European legal and policy measures on CHP, evaluating how it has changed over the years through progress and decline in specific member states. Over the course of the book, Sokołowski explores all aspects of CHP, examining the types of measures used to steer the growth of cogeneration in the EU and the policies and regulatory tools that have influenced its development. He also assesses the specific role of CHP in the liberalisation of the internal energy market and EU action on climate and sustainability. Finally, by delivering his notions of "cogenatives", "cogenmunities", or "Micro-Collective-Flexible-Smart-High-Efficiency cogeneration", Sokołowski considers how the new EU energy package – "Clean energy for all Europeans" – will shape future developments.

This book will be of great interest to students and scholars of energy law and regulation, combined heat and power and energy efficiency, as well as policy makers and energy experts working in the CHP sector.

Maciej M. Sokołowski is a Doctor of Law and a Visiting Research Fellow at the University of Tokyo, and a Visiting Associate Professor at Keio University, Japan. He is also associated with the Faculty of Law and Administration at the University of Warsaw, Poland.

Routledge Research in Energy Law and Regulation

Regulation in the European Electricity Sector
Maciej M. Sokołowski

Law and Green Energy Policies
Roy Partain

Nuclear Energy Regulation, Risk and The Environment
Abdullah Al Faruque

Local Content Oil and Gas Law in Africa
Lessons from Nigeria and Beyond
Pereowei Subai

Host Government Agreements and the Law in the Energy Sector
The case of Azerbaijan and Turkey
Hakan Sahin

Iraq's Oil and Gas Industry
The Legal and Contractual Framework
Janan Al-Asady

The Development of Iran's Upstream Oil and Gas Industry
The Potential Role of New Concession Contracts
Mahmoud Fard Kardel

European Law on Combined Heat and Power
Maciej M. Sokołowski

For more information about this series, please visit: www.routledge.com/Routledge-Research-in-Energy-Law-and-Regulation/book-series/RRELR

European Law on Combined Heat and Power

Maciej M. Sokołowski

First published 2020 by Routledge

2 Park Square, Milton Park, Abingdon, Oxon OX14 4RN

605 Third Avenue, New York, NY 10017

Routledge is an imprint of the Taylor & Francis Group, an informa business

First issued in paperback 2021

© 2020 Maciej M. Sokołowski

The right of Maciej M. Sokołowski to be identified as author of this work has been asserted by him in accordance with sections 77 and 78 of the Copyright, Designs and Patents Act 1988.

All rights reserved. No part of this book may be reprinted or reproduced or utilised in any form or by any electronic, mechanical, or other means, now known or hereafter invented, including photocopying and recording, or in any information storage or retrieval system, without permission in writing from the publishers.

Trademark notice: Product or corporate names may be trademarks or registered trademarks, and are used only for identification and explanation without intent to infringe.

Publisher's Note

The publisher has gone to great lengths to ensure the quality of thisreprint but points out that some imperfections in the original copies may beapparent.

British Library Cataloguing-in-Publication Data
A catalogue record for this book is available from the British Library

Library of Congress Cataloging-in-Publication Data
Names: Sokołowski, Maciej M., author.
Title: European law on combined heat and power / Maciej M. Sokołowski.
Description: Abingdon, Oxon ; New York, NY : Routledge, 2020. | Series: Routledge research in energy law and regulation | Includes bibliographical references and index. | Provided by publisher.
Identifiers: LCCN 2019051810 (print) | LCCN 2019051811 (ebook) | ISBN 9780367440237 (hardback) | ISBN 9781003007111 (ebook)
Subjects: LCSH: Cogeneration of electric power and heat–Law and legislation–European Union countries.
Classification: LCC KJE6758 .S67 2020 (print) | LCC KJE6758 (ebook) | DDC 343.2409/2–dc23
LC record available at https://lccn.loc.gov/2019051810
LC ebook record available at https://lccn.loc.gov/2019051811

ISBN: 978-0-367-44023-7 (hbk)
ISBN: 978-1-03-217273-6 (pbk)
DOI: 10.4324/9781003007111

Typeset in Goudy
by Swales & Willis, Exeter, Devon, UK

Contents

List of figures	viii
List of tables	ix
Foreword	xii
Preface	xiii
Acknowledgements	xv
List of abbreviations	xvii

1	Introduction: more heat, more power, less energy	1
2	First policy actions on combined heat and power	20
3	Cogeneration and the EU energy market reform	55
4	CHP in the EU climate action	99
5	European CHP: the EU countries review	141
6	Cogenclusion: cogeneration in conclusion	197
	Index	242

Figures

5.1	Scale of CHP in the European Union (EU-28)	142
6.1	Main EU legislation on CHP in the four energy areas of impact	215
6.2	Main EU legislation on CHP within the European legislative packages	216
6.3	Biggest share of fuel used in CHP in the European Union (EU-28) in 2016	221

Tables

1.1	Overview of operating energy efficiencies (yearly averages) of European natural-gas-fired combustion units	12
2.1	Production of electricity and heat in cogeneration in the European Union (EU-15) between 1994–1998	27
2.2	CHP installed capacity in the European Union (EU-15) between 1994–1998	28
2.3	Heat produced in CHP in the European Union (EU-15) between 1994–1998	29
2.4	Fuel used in cogeneration in the European Union (EU-15) in 1998	30
3.1	Support schemes for CHP in the EU-27	73
3.2	Measures to promote cogeneration in the EU-27	78
3.3	Overview of barriers to realising CHP potential in the EU-27	81
3.4	Overview of the effects of the CHP Directive	83
3.5	Commission's key to the rating of policy effects on the developments of CHP	84
4.1	Selected CHP techniques to increase energy efficiency	104
4.2	Emissions produced by CCGT CHP units	105
4.3	Selected BAT-AEELs for combustion units	106
4.4	Commission's scenarios for amending regulatory framework on CHP	120
4.5	Commission's extreme scenarios of amending the regulatory framework on CHP	121
5.1	CHP portfolio of Finland between 1994–2016	144
5.2	Fuel used in cogeneration in Finland between 1998–2016	144
5.3	CHP portfolio of France between 1994–2016	145
5.4	Fuel used in cogeneration in France between 1998–2016	146
5.5	CHP portfolio of Germany between 1994–2016	147
5.6	Fuel used in cogeneration in Germany between 1998–2016	148
5.7	CHP portfolio of Italy between 1994–2016	149
5.8	Fuel used in cogeneration in Italy between 1998–2016	149
5.9	CHP portfolio of the Netherlands between 1994–2016	150

x Tables

5.10	Fuel used in cogeneration in the Netherlands between 1998–2016	150
5.11	CHP portfolio of Poland between 2005–2016	152
5.12	Fuel used in cogeneration in Poland between 2005–2016	152
5.13	CHP portfolio of Spain between 1994–2016	153
5.14	Fuel used in cogeneration in Spain between 1998–2016	154
5.15	CHP portfolio of the United Kingdom between 1994–2016	155
5.16	Fuel used in cogeneration in the United Kingdom between 1998–2016	155
5.17	CHP portfolio of Austria between 1994–2016	157
5.18	Fuel used in cogeneration in Austria between 1998–2016	157
5.19	CHP portfolio of Belgium between 1994–2016	158
5.20	Fuel used in cogeneration in Belgium between 1998–2016	159
5.21	CHP portfolio of Bulgaria between 2005–2016	160
5.22	Fuel used in cogeneration in Bulgaria between 2005–2016	161
5.23	CHP portfolio of the Czech Republic between 2005–2016	162
5.24	Fuel used in cogeneration in the Czech Republic between 2005–2016	162
5.25	CHP portfolio of Denmark between 1994–2016	163
5.26	Fuel used in cogeneration in Denmark between 1998–2016	164
5.27	CHP portfolio of Hungary between 2005–2016	165
5.28	Fuel used in cogeneration in Hungary between 2005–2016	165
5.29	CHP portfolio of Portugal between 1994–2016	166
5.30	Fuel used in cogeneration in Portugal between 1998–2016	166
5.31	CHP portfolio of Romania between 2005–2016	167
5.32	Fuel used in cogeneration in Romania between 2005–2016	167
5.33	CHP portfolio of Slovakia between 2005–2016	168
5.34	Fuel used in cogeneration in Slovakia between 2005–2016	169
5.35	CHP portfolio of Sweden between 1994–2016	170
5.36	Fuel used in cogeneration in Sweden between 1998–2016	170
5.37	CHP portfolio of Croatia between 2009–2016	171
5.38	Fuel used in cogeneration in Croatia between 2009–2016	172
5.39	CHP portfolio of Cyprus between 2005–2016	173
5.40	Fuel used in cogeneration in Cyprus between 2005–2016	173
5.41	CHP portfolio of Estonia between 2005–2016	174
5.42	Fuel used in cogeneration in Estonia between 2005–2016	174
5.43	CHP portfolio of Greece between 1994–2016	175
5.44	Fuel used in cogeneration in Greece between 1998–2016	176
5.45	CHP portfolio of Ireland between 1994–2016	177
5.46	Fuel used in cogeneration in Ireland between 1998–2016	177
5.47	CHP portfolio of Latvia between 2005–2016	178
5.48	Fuel used in cogeneration in Latvia between 2005–2016	178
5.49	CHP portfolio of Lithuania between 2005–2016	179
5.50	Fuel used in cogeneration in Lithuania between 2005–2016	180
5.51	CHP portfolio of Luxembourg between 1994–2016	181

5.52	Fuel used in cogeneration in Luxembourg between 1998–2016	181
5.53	CHP portfolio of Malta between 2005–2016	182
5.54	Fuel used in cogeneration in Malta between 2005–2016	182
5.55	CHP portfolio of Slovenia between 2005–2016	183
5.56	Fuel used in cogeneration in Slovenia between 2005–2016	183
6.1	Production of electricity and heat in cogeneration in the European Union in 2016–2017 (EU-28)	218
6.2	Fuel used in cogeneration in the European Union (EU-28) in 2016	220

Foreword

Cogeneration is an old energy technology remembering the era of Mr Edison and Mr Tesla. For more than a hundred years it has been continuously powering energy sectors worldwide, coming through storms and various ups and downs when combined heat and power (CHP) was governed by different interests of the industry or policymakers. Moving towards the 2020s CHP is still finding its own space in more and more competitive, changing energy markets. "A willow in the wind", a Japanese proverb says. However, cogeneration has changed, is changing, and will change.

The highlighted continuity and change are the two flywheels of *European Law on Combined Heat and Power*, the book by Maciej M. Sokołowski. Its Author, *Maciej-san* is a heedful observer, asking the right questions, supplying good answers. This allows the cogeneration to be analysed deeply and broadly in his study. The analysis follows the history of the CHP's development – well-presented from a regulatory point of view – within the European energy market reform and climate action, where CHP is clearly reviewed in all the Member States of the European Union (EU-28). The book also offers certain remarks transcending the European ground (e.g. reaching the US legislation) and thought-provoking comments concerning the global, universal values of CHP.

These are just a few topics raised by *Maciej-san*. There is much more inside. Hence, anyone seeking knowledge about cogeneration, how it was regulated in the past, how it should be regulated, what kind of policy tools have piloted its development, and other matters related to laws and policies on CHP – should reach for this book. Just like in combined heat and power – all these issues are combined here, in *European Law on Combined Heat and Power*.

Professor Nobuo Tanaka
Chairman of the Sasakawa Peace Foundation
former Executive Director of the International Energy Agency

Preface

Combined heat and power, CHP, or cogeneration (seldom, co-generation) refers to a process of joint production of energy – usually heat and electricity. CHP is an old technology, reminiscent of early developments of electricity in the nineteenth century. During subsequent periods it recorded ups and downs, growth and decline, with a comeback in the 1970, when its energy efficiency was noticed in Europe and the USA as one of the tools of tackling the oil crisis. In Europe, it has fallen on a fertile soil of the rationalisation of energy usage (which was a platform for cogeneration) until further developments of regulatory framework dedicated to energy efficiency. This included the CHP Directive, the Energy Services Directive, and the Energy Efficiency Directive being covered by legislation on the liberalisation of the energy market, renewable energy sources, and emission of greenhouse gases.

My encounters with this legislation while carrying out research on energy efficiency, my activity in the Public Board for Reduction of Emissions, study visits to power plants and district heating facilities, research stays in Sweden and Switzerland, and project engagement (e.g. "Inno-Heat – Innovation in District Heating" financed under the South Baltic Programme 2007–2013) have increased my personal interest in CHP. My interest stemmed from several factors, one of them being the efficiency of CHP and its use of the cheapest fuel – cheapest, because it is not used but saved. Other factors include CHP's local character (where heat is delivered to neighbouring areas), the possibility of applying cogeneration at a small, or micro scale by individuals (prosumers), and using CHP as a source of renewable energy. To some degree, this study has a personal motivation, as I come from Poland – a country where district heating is a well-established technology and CHP is widely-applied. Thereby, cogeneration (or *kogeneracja* in Polish) is something natural to me.

When writing this book, I had dozens of questions in my mind. I list a few of them below: how has combined heat and power changed in the EU over the years? Where has the cogeneration capacity increased, and where has it dropped? What type of measures have been used to steer the development of cogeneration in the EU? How have the policies and regulatory tools brought by the EU legislation influenced this sector? What kind of a role has CHP' been performing in the liberalisation of the internal energy market and the EU action on climate and sustainability? How will the new EU energy package – "Clean energy for all Europeans" shape it? These, as well as other questions have "powered" this book.

I really do hope that my work provides answers to questions enclosed in the framework of analysis of the European legal environment on cogeneration. To do so, I share with the readers the results of my research on CHP, my knowledge, comments, remarks, clarifications, and interpretations; I also share my assessments of different regulatory approaches, policies, laws, and regulatory tools adopted at the European and national levels by the EU Member States for the needs of CHP. Hopefully, it is enough to provide a clear description of European law on cogeneration – any mistakes are mine. The judgement whether I managed to achieve this goal I leave to my readers.

Maciej M. Sokołowski

Acknowledgements

This book would not have been possible without the combined help of several people. Among them I list *Professor Fumio Shimpo* and *Professor Jun Arima* for all the help they offered during my research stay in Japan (Keio University and University of Tokyo) where I delved into the regulatory matrix of European and Japanese energy sectors (this work was completed during a research stay in Japan under the Mobility Plus funding received from the Ministry of Science and Higher Education of Poland). I am deeply grateful to *Shimpo-sensei* for introducing me to the realm of artificial intelligence and robotics. To *Arima-sensei* I owe many thanks for sagacious talks on global, European, and Asian climate-energy policies as well as history during the Katowice COP24 and here in Tokyo.

Moreover, I would like to express my deep appreciation and gratitude to *Professor Marek Wierzbowski* of the Faculty of Law and Administration, University of Warsaw. By sharing his experiences from UC Berkeley School of Law he taught me how to examine the regulatory approach offered to the energy sector by the state. This knowledge was extremely useful during my work on the topic discussed in "European Law on Combined Heat and Power". I am also thankful for his continuous and unwavering support. Similar thanks for a firm support go to *Professor Kurt Deketelaere* of KU Leuven – "Mr University" – thank you for all the links you have made.

Furthermore, this book takes as much as possible from an important period in my professional and academic life – the cooperation with *Professor Krzysztof Żmijewski* (1949–2015) – an energy titan and champion of energy efficiency, a European strategist and Polish patriot, a manager, scientist and poet, a boss and teacher, a friend. In the course of writing this book, I often wondered what *Professor Żmijewski* would say about a given issue, how he would write it, what he would compare it to. It is a great pity that he is no longer with us.

I also owe many thanks to reviewers of this book for their caring remarks and valuable recommendations. I dedicate my deepest thanks to *Nobuo Tanaka-sensei* for writing a Foreword to my book. I am extremely grateful for all the words of endorsement offered by the notable colleagues:

Professor Catherine Banet of University of Oslo, *Honourable Stephen G. Burns*, a former Chairman of the Nuclear Regulatory Commission, *Professor Dan Farber* of UC Berkeley, *President Rafał Czaja* of the Prof. Krzysztof Żmijewski Association for Efficiency, *Professor Raphael J. Heffron* of University of Dundee, and *Professor Katsuhiro Shoji* of Keio University. I am also very grateful for the support offered by *Professor Kim Talus* of the Tulane Center for Energy Law, by devoting his precious time to reading the initial manuscript of this work and commenting on it. I wish to express my special thanks to my right-hand men from the University of Warsaw: *Jakub Sokołowski* from the Faculty of Economics, for our discussions on the energy statistics analysed in this study; and colleagues from the Faculty of Law and Administration – *Paweł Piwowar* for an injection of motivation during our academic stay in China where I visited China University of Political Science and Law, and *Marek Grzywacz* for good talks on energy on the roads of California to reach UC Berkeley and University of San Francisco.

Furthermore, I am grateful to *Professor David G. Litt, Kimie Hatakeyama*, and *Katsutoshi Hori* from Keio University, the *Kotani family, Umemoto Yasuo, Michał Haruki Yamazaki*, as well as *Ichiro Sugisawa-sensei* and all the colleagues from *Karate Ichibukai dōjō* – for the kindness, help, and advice they have given me and my family during our stay in Japan. We are honoured to call them friends.

Finally, I also thank my dad, *Professor Marek Sokołowski* for all his real-world advice and frank interest in this book. Last, but not least, I am truly grateful to my dear wife *Kinga* and daughter *Felicja* for their time and energy – they are real heroes of this work.

Maciej M. Sokołowski

List of abbreviations

AD_i	annual activity data of fuels i
i.e.	*id est* [that is]
AT	Austria
BAT	Best Available Techniques
BAT-AEELs	energy efficiency levels associated with the Best Available Techniques
BE	Belgium
BG	Bulgaria
Btu	British thermal units
CCGT	combined-cycle gas turbine
CEE	Central and Eastern Europe
cf.	*confer* [compare with]
CFR	Code of Federal Regulations
CHP	combined heat and power
CODE	Cogeneration Observatory and Dissemination Europe
COGEN Europe	European Association for the Promotion of Cogeneration
CO_2	carbon dioxide
CO_2/TJ	carbon dioxide per terajoule
Commission	Commission of the European Communities/from 1 December 2009 Commission of the European Union
Council	Council of the European Communities/from 1 November 1993 Council of the European Union
CY	Cyprus
CZ	Czech Republic
DC Cir.	US Court of Appeals for the District of Columbia Circuit
DDR	*Deutsche Demokratische Republik* [German Democratic Republic, East Germany]
DE	Germany
DGEMP	*Direction Générale de l'Energie et des Matières Premières* [General Directorate for Energy and Raw Materials]
DH	district heating

xviii *List of abbreviations*

DH & C	district heating and cooling
DK	Denmark
DM	*Deutsche Mark*
DOE	US Department of Energy
DSO	Distribution System Operator
e.g.	for example
ECU	European Currency Unit
ed.	editor
edn	edition
eds	editors
EE	Estonia
EF_i	emission factors of fuels *i*
EIA	US Energy Information Administration
EL	Greece
Em_{CHP}	annual emissions of the cogeneration
Em_{FGC}	process emissions from flue gas cleaning
EPA	US Environmental Protection Agency
ES	Spain
ETA	Energy Tax Act of 1978
EU	European Union
EUA	European Emission Allowances
EU ETS	European Union Emission Trading System
EUR	euro (€)
FERC	Federal Energy Regulatory Commission
FI	Finland
FPR	First Progress Report
FR	France
FUA	Power Plant and Industrial Fuel Use Act of 1978
GBP	pound sterling
GHG	greenhouse gas
GW	gigawatt
GW_e	gigawatt electrical
h/yr	hours per year
HFO	heavy fuel oil
HR	Croatia
HU	Hungary
IAEA	International Atomic Energy Agency
IE	Ireland
IED	Industrial Emissions Directive
IGCC	integrated gasification combined cycle
INPP	Ignalina Nuclear Power Plant
IT	Italy
kW	kilowatt
kW_e	kilowatt electrical
LCP Directive	Large Combustion Plants Directive

LNG	liquefied natural gas
LT	Lithuania
LU	Luxembourg
LV	Latvia
mg	milligram
Mt	megatonne
MT	Malta
Mtoe	million tonnes of oil equivalent
MW	megawatt
MW_e	megawatt electrical
MWh	megawatt hour
MW_t	megawatt thermal
n.d.	no date
n/a	not applicable
NA	no relevant specific information available
NCV_i	net calorific values of fuels i expressed
NECP	National Energy and Climate Plan
NECPA	National Energy Conservation Policy Act
NGPA	Natural Gas Policy Act of 1978
NL	Netherlands
Nm^3	normal cubic meter
No	number
NO_x	nitrogen oxides
OECD	Organisation for Economic Co-operation and Development
OJ	Official Journal
OTA	US Congress Office of Technology Assessment
PHARE	Poland and Hungary: Assistance for Restructuring their Economies
PJ	petajoule
PL	Poland
PRIMES	Price-Induced Market Equilibrium System
PT	Portugal
Pub. L.	public law
PURPA	Public Utilities Regulatory Policies Act
RED	First Renewable Energy Directive
RED II	Second Renewable Energy Directive
Rep.	Republic
RES	Renewable Energy Sources
RES Directive	Renewable Energy Sources Directive
RO	Romania
RWC	Renewable-Waste-Cogeneration
SAVE	Specific Actions for Vigorous Energy Efficiency programme
SE	Sweden

List of abbreviations

SEA	*Slovenská Energetická Agentúra* [Slovak Energy Agency]
Sec.	Section
SEP	*Samenwerkende Elektriciteits-Productiebedrijven*
SI	Slovenia
SK	Slovakia
SMEs	small and medium-sized enterprises
SPR	Second Progress Report
Stat.	United States Statutes at Large
t	tonne
TACIS	Technical Assistance to the Commonwealth of Independent States
TJ/Nm^3	terajoule per normal cubic meter
TJ/t	terajoule per tonne
TPA	Third Party Access
TSO	Transmission System Operator
TWh	terawatt hour
UK	United Kingdom
UNFCCC	United Nations Framework Convention on Climate Change
US	United States
VEAG	*Vereinigte Energiewerke AG (Aktiengesellschaft)*
vol.	volume
WEC	World Energy Council

1 Introduction
More heat, more power, less energy

"Promoting combined heat and power production (CHP or co-generation) is considered an important part of the Community energy policy for improving energy efficiency. CHP also plays a crucial role in helping meet the commitments of reducing greenhouse gas emissions", as reported by the Eurostat (2001, p. 2) almost 20 years ago. "CHP is good engineering, good economics and good business" informs the UK branch of transnational water-waste-energy company Veolia (n.d.). "Cogeneration helps consumers and businesses to take control over their energy future by making them the active beneficiaries of an integrated energy system and rewarding them for the benefits they bring to the system" declares COGEN Europe (n.d). Cogeneration offers efficiency, environmental, economic, and reliability benefits – enumerates the US Environmental Protection Agency (n.d. a). Cogeneration represents "a series of proven, reliable and cost-effective technologies that are already making an important contribution to meeting global heat and electricity demand" – assures the International Energy Agency (2009, p. 11).

The aforementioned quotations briefly highlight some basic features of combined heat and power, sketching the main fields related to cogeneration which are presented, juxtaposed, and examined in this book. Among them, a special position is granted to energy efficiency – on which the reciprocal benefits of CHP are built (e.g. producing more heat and more electricity using less energy, as highlgted in the title of this part of the book). Those issues – put into a regulatory framework created by the European policies and law on CHP – are analysed in the following chapters of this study (the outcome of my research work). Before moving on, I describe its main elements, explain the research methods used, and outline its scope in the two subchapters below.

Research and methodology

This book is the result of research on the European regulatory approach to combined heat and power. CHP is an efficient technology used by the EU's Member States for the needs of generating electricity and heat (and, although still less widespread, production of cool, see Werner 2017, p. 619). The amount of generation varies between different scales, ranging from dozens of GW, TWh, or PJ (which describe the large sector), for example, in Germany, Italy, or Poland), to just a few units (e.g. in Malta or Cyprus). Apart from some basic information on cogeneration – its name, definitions, and classifications as presented in this Introduction – the book discusses past and current regulatory framework on CHP in the EU. The analysis is extended by some remarks on other legal systems (mainly the US, with PURPA [Public Utilities Regulatory Policies Act] as a tool to develop CHP).

However, the main research elements of the book cover the assessment of the European legal and policy measures on cogeneration. My book presents cogeneration from different angles; after the past European (1970s–1990s) experiences and foreign developments (the US), it evaluates the steps conducted by the EU with respect to cogeneration as an element of two main pillars of the European energy sector: energy liberalisation and climate action. The book shows the development of combined heat and power with its regulatory framework, with additional remarks on how this sector contributes to the EU climate-energy agenda and energy market reform. Special attention is given to European law and policy on competition and state aid, renewable energy sources, reduction of emission, and energy efficiency where cogeneration plays a vital role.

My book tries to cover combined heat and power in a comprehensive way – that is why different research methods are applied. Notwithstanding how wide and deep the conducted research is, this book does not exhaust the topic of law and policies on CHP in the EU. However, it will hopefully contribute to further discussions and research on cogeneration – an old solution open to new improvements, and adaptable to changing conditions of the electricity, and heating and cooling markets.

Research assumptions

The research in my book is based on the research assumptions deriving from its title. They are as follows: to present, discuss, analyse, and evaluate the European regulatory framework along with relevant laws and policies of the EU-28 as a whole, and of its Member States individually. Those laws and policies include both the legislation created and implemented in Europe over the years and the solutions offered for the future; in short – the European legal environment which has been established for the needs of cogeneration in the EU.

These research assumptions trigger the questions on the European law and policies on combined heat and power. Here, five groups of research questions can be elaborated on:

(i) how did the development of combined heat and power begin? How was it steered by different countries? What legal attitude was offered for this sector in the early developments of the European Community?

(ii) how has this regulatory approach to CHP evolved during consecutive years of the European integration? How has it been influenced by the liberalisation of the internal energy market? What kind of legal and policy measures and regulatory tools have been implemented to promote development of CHP in the EU? How has this been driven at the European and national level by policies and law?
(iii) what impact has the European climate action had on legal environment for cogeneration? What impact is it having now? What impact will it have in the future? How has the CHP sector changed under its legal framework? How is it changing? How will it change?
(iv) what is the approach of the EU Member States to combined heat and power? How has this industry developed in each Member State? What kind of regulatory measures have been dedicated at the national level to support CHP? How have the countries' policies promoted the usage of cogeneration in their energy mixes?
(v) where is the European cogeneration in the current EU legal nexus? How have the recent policies and laws adopted at the European level shaped CHP and how will they affect it in the coming years?

Methods applied

To delve into these matters, present and analyse them thoroughly, and summarise them properly the following approaches, distinguished in the methodology of research work, have been applied. A point of reference for this book is European law and national legislations of the Member States (EU-28) along with correlated policies, both pan-European and national, influenced by the international policy and law framework (like the Kyoto Protocol, the US legislation, etc.). This book tries to keep the timeline of the development of cogeneration throughout its history, maintaining the relation: past – present – future. In this regard it describes and evaluates the early policy approach offered for CHP in Europe, presenting the attitude (law, policies, programmes, measures, regulatory tools etc.) of European countries towards this sector before and during the 1970s–1990s.

The core of the discussion in this book is based on two legal acts adopted at the EU level. These are the CHP Directive (Directive 2004/8/EC) and the Energy Efficiency Directive (2012/27/EU), with recent amendments. Both are as important for this book as they have been (and are) significant for the development of cogeneration in the European Union. Naturally, as they are just elements of a wider and more complex legal nexus determining the situation of combined heat and power in Europe, other EU legislation is also discussed. This includes, *inter alia*, the liberalisation agenda of the internal energy market with its three key directives on electricity (Directive 96/92/EC, Directive 2003/54/EC, and Directive 2009/72/EC), the regulatory regime for industrial emissions in Europe as well as the EU ETS and legal issues related to CO_2 and renewable energy sources. They are the fundaments of the Climate and Energy Package along with its pre- and post-regulatory framework. With respect to the latter, it is crucial to add the Clean Energy Package to this list.

The analysed legislation is accompanied by the evaluation of many strategic documents, which indirectly or directly influenced the European law-making process (e.g. COM, SWD documents). Other policy and working papers were also evaluated: those developed by the EU, by international bodies such as the Organisation of Economic Cooperation and Development (OECD), or by organisations connected with CHP industry, like the European Association for the Promotion of Cogeneration (COGEN Europe). When a legislative process is examined, the specific European documents influencing the law-making process are discussed. This concerns the statements of the Commission, the Council, the Parliament, the Committee of the Regions, and the Economic and Social Committee.

Furthermore, the book's considerations are rooted in the literature on cogeneration, energy and environmental law, and public law regulation, including my own previous works on these matters. Here, a special place is given to my studies on public law regulation in the energy sector. In the EU I find it as a balancing act, keeping the central place on the axis of the state's influence on the market, promoting and strengthening competition, i.e. keeping a market-base attitude, or ensuring public policy interests (like energy security), and environment protection, facilitated under European conditions by regulators of the *day-watchman* type (see Sokołowski 2018, 2017, 2016, 2013, cf. C. Pereira Rolim 2019; Cameron & Heffron 2016; Wierzbowski 2014; Talus 2013; Sokołowski & Stankiewicz 2011; Freiberg 2010, Prosser 2010; Barton 2006; Peeters & Deketelaere 2006; Walaszek-Pyzioł 2002; Ogus 1994).

This matrix influences the approach (methods) applied under the legal methodology in this book. Like combined heat and power, one may combine them in two correlated categories of approaches: (i) dogmatic and comparative, (ii) empirical and interdisciplinary. The former is used to analyse legislation on cogeneration, along with tools and measures adopted in the framework of public law regulation or contractual relations of participants of the energy market. Moreover, this method enables one to highlight the substance of law (as well as its structure, for example, when a legal interpretation is needed) shaping the legal situation of CHP units operating in the European Union. This wider perspective implies the application of comparative method, needed to delve into and juxtapose the legislation adopted in the area of CHP at the European and national level – by each Member State.

The second category, of empirical and interdisciplinary approaches enables one to show and evaluate the basis for a legal discussion about cogeneration, as part of the energy sector. Therefore, the empirical approach adduces numerous data on CHP such as the volume of electricity and heat produced by cogeneration, the installed capacity, or its share in electricity generation. The statistics provided mainly by Eurostat (supplemented by other data delivered by Member States or derived from other sources) allow me to depict the past and current conditions of cogeneration in the EU, and to forecast its situation in the coming years. Moreover, the interdisciplinary method is necessary to explain the features of technology and the economics of operating CHP in the energy market – "being like the two sails of 'Cogeneration' – the CHP-vessel moved on the sea of market by the winds of law and currents of policies", as *Professor Krzysztof Żmijewski* once told me. Nevertheless, as my book is of predominantly a legal nature, this is an auxiliary method – necessary for better understanding of legislation, polices, and measures dedicated to cogeneration in the European Union.

Finally, just like "and" in combined heat *and* power, the two groups of approaches are joined by a historical method. Used in terms of the development of the CHP sector and applied with respect to legislation and policies at the European and national level (Member States), the historical method allows us to follow CHP as a process influenced by a nexus of laws and regulatory measures.

The structure of the book

The issues which stand behind the common denominator of this book – the European law on cogeneration, are presented in this book in six chapters. In Chapter 1, apart from the already offered research assumptions and applied methods, I provide some basic comments on combined heat and power, its features and its role in the energy sector. This refers to definitions, classifications, and divisions which describe and categorise cogeneration. I also explain the difference between energy efficiency and energy savings, evaluate matters related to technologies applied in the CHP industry while juxtaposing their efficiency, and address the environmental and economic matters related to CHP.

In Chapter 2, I highlight the history of development of cogeneration and discuss the first policies and legislation on CHP. This chapter includes a review of combined heat and power in Western as well as Central and Eastern Europe. It also presents an examination of the European action on the rational use of energy (the 1970s–1980s) bringing the framework for Renewable-Waste-Cogeneration auto-producers and financial programmes which covered CHP (the Joule, Thermie, and SAVE programmes) in the 1980s and 1990s. Additionally, I deliver remarks on the US regulatory approach to combined heat with PURPA (1978) as its cornerstone.

Chapter 3 shows how cogeneration was influenced during different stages of the European energy market reform, being tracked from the zero phase of energy liberalisation, through the First and Second Energy Package, to the Third Energy Package. As well as the assessment of the approach applied to CHP in each package, I also analyse such issues as the regime on public utilities' procurement with respect to production of electricity and heat, and the 1997 strategy on CHP, with the proposal of an 18% goal for cogeneration in the total gross electricity generation of 2010. Moreover, I delve into the CHP Directive considering it from a perspective of energy market reform, outlining its regulatory tools, and presenting the assessment of the directive's role in the development of combined heat and power in the EU, which I see as a "soft failure".

To complete the market deliberations of Chapter 3, Chapter 4 examines CHP as an element of the EU climate action, embedded in the energy efficiency pillar of the European climate-energy policy. This part of the book analyse combined heat and power in the legislation on emissions (both the regime on industrial emissions as well as the EU Emission Trading System) and the correlations between regulatory approach dedicated to CHP and renewable energy sources. Continuing the theme of cogeneration in the climate-energy policy of the EU, I evaluate the legal environment for enhancing energy efficiency and searching for a place for CHP within it. The analysis covers the CHP Directive, the Energy Services Directive, the Action Plan for energy efficiency of 2006, and the Energy Efficiency Directive of 2012.

As readers may notice, the regulatory tools established under the CHP Directive are divided in this book between Chapters 3 and 4. Despite close links between liberalisation and climate pillars of the European energy policy (which, to some degree, may blur the boundaries between them), some categorisation of these measures is possible (or even necessary for better understanding of the EU actions regarding the internal energy market, energy efficiency, and cogeneration). The two definitions adopted in the CHP Directive (Article 3) may be useful for the needs of distinguishing these measures: "cogeneration" (i.e. "the simultaneous generation in one process of thermal energy and electrical and/or mechanical energy" and "high efficiency cogeneration" (i.e. cogeneration meeting the criteria of Annex III).[1]

Hence, the tools in relation to which a greater emphasis is placed on high-efficiency cogeneration, are discussed in Chapter 4 of this book, while those which address cogeneration in general are analysed mainly in Chapter 3. Noticing this emphasis may be problematic because the CHP Directive is not very consequent in discerning them.[2] Therefore, what is needed is an interpretation using the internal legal systematics of the directive – where the systematics of a legal act is considered, how the provisions are titled, grouped, or placed within the directive (see Eek 1965, pp. 114–115; Wróblewski 1992, p. 102). With the help of this interpretation, and by using the titles of those articles of the CHP Directive, which reflect the previously mentioned emphasis, one may manage to divide these measures into topics covered in Chapters 3 and 4 of this book. Consequently, the

Introduction 7

fields covered by Article 7 "Support schemes", Article 8 "Electricity grid system and tariff issues", and Article 9 "Administrative procedures" are analysed in Chapter 3, whereas Article 5 "Guarantee of origin of electricity from high-efficiency cogeneration" and Article 6 "National potentials for high-efficiency cogeneration" are discussed in Chapter 4.

The evaluation of the European regulatory regime on CHP provided in Chapters 3 and 4 is complemented and extended by the review of individual countries. I elaborate on it in Chapter 5 of this book, where I outline the three main categories of markets for cogeneration by using a classic division of big – medium – small. As a result, the EU-28 is divided into these three categories in a balanced way: eight Member States are tagged as big CHP players, while ten EU countries are labelled as medium, and ten as small CHP sectors. For each of the reviewed countries a short description of past and recent developments of cogeneration is prepared. This covers several aspects: the regulatory framework and the statistics on CHP electricity generation, the share of CHP in total gross electricity generation, total CHP installed capacity in electricity, total CHP installed capacity in heat, and total heat produced in CHP aggregated in the selected time-frames.

Last but not least, Chapter 6 brings *cogenclusion* – a conclusion on cogeneration with its development in the European regulatory environment. It starts from the examination of the current legal nexus on combined heat and power. Herein, the analysis covers the Energy Efficiency Directive in its current version (as amended in 2018 and 2019 by the Regulation on the Energy Union), the Fourth Electricity Directive, and the Third Electricity Regulation. Additionally, in Chapter 6 I evaluate the recent legislation on renewables (RED II) and the last revision of the EU ETS with their regulatory impact on combined heat and power.

Moreover, Chapter 6 evaluates the overall European regulatory approach to CHP. For that, I gather legislation and policies on cogeneration, with regulatory measures and tools to support and promote combined heat and power in one *regulatory box*. It is a joint category (gathering European laws and policies) which I present to describe CHP in the European law. Apart from the legislation, I also summarise recent statistics on CHP (for 2016 and 2017). It is necessary to show current state-of-the-art cogeneration in the EU and summarise the review delivered in Chapter 5.

Finally, in Chapter 6 the overall impact of the European law on combined heat and power is evaluated. At this point, I recapitulate the examined issues together with the most important findings of the book. Wherever necessary, the additional clarification and explanations are provided. In the last part of the book I trace cogeneration in two dimensions: past and future. I discuss former but still applicable regulatory approaches and measures dedicated to CHP. I also sketch the possible future of the legal framework on CHP in the EU, addressing such issues as cogeneration cooperatives/cogeneration communities (*cogenatives/cogenmunities*), or Micro-Collective-Flexible-Smart-High-Efficiency cogeneration – *MCFlexSHE CHP*.

The importance of cogeneration

The names: CHP, combined heat and power, or cogeneration, each individually, and all together reflect a joint process – usually production of heat and generation of electricity. "Usually" because the simultaneous production of electricity and heat in a single process covers steam and/or hot water, although in general cogeneration can also refer to any process that generates two (or more) products (Rosen & Koohi-Fayegh 2016, p. 49, see Yang & Guo 2010; Havelský 1999). Sometimes – mainly with respect to heat, cool, and power – the name "trigeneration" is used to describe this process (see Al-Sulaiman, Hamdullahpur, & Dincer 2011; Kavvadias & Maroulis 2010).

Such approach is also distinguished in law. One such example is the Directive 2012/27/EU on energy efficiency, which defines cogeneration as "the simultaneous generation in one process of thermal energy and electrical or mechanical energy" and so simply reflects the combination of generating heat – thermal energy and power – electricity. An earlier directive (2004/8/EC) included a very similar definition, having just a slightly different wording of its last element, i.e. "electrical and/or mechanical energy".

Combining classifications and divisions

There are many different classifications and divisions applied to combined heat and power (see Westner & Madlener 2011). With this in mind, one may define the production process as a criterion, dividing cogeneration plants into "topping cycle" and "bottoming cycle" (Rezaie & Rosen 2012, pp. 4–5, see Hinrichs & Kleinbach 2002, pp. 377–378). In the topping cycle, electricity is produced in a turbine generator, while high-pressure steam or exhaust gases are used for heating; in the bottoming cycle, steam (coming from another industrial process) is used in a pressure steam turbine to generate electricity (Rezaie & Rosen 2012, pp. 4–5). This focus on technology can be presented in many ways, among which steam and turbines, reciprocating engines (engine-CHP), combined-cycle gas turbines (CCGT), micro-turbines and Stirling engines, as well as fuel cells and other decentralised mini-/micro-CHP applications are listed (Westner & Madlener 2011, p. 5304).

The scale may be a legal category too. As defined in Directive 2012/27/EU, a "small-scale cogeneration unit" (a "cogeneration unit" being "a unit that is able to operate in cogeneration mode") is a unit with installed capacity below 1 MW_e, whereas a "micro-cogeneration unit" must have the capacity below 50 kW_e. The scale is also broadly used in different studies on combined heat and power. Westner and Madlener (2011) refer to "three typical size classes" of CHP, i.e. "small-scale" (capacity under 2 MW$_e$), "medium-scale CHP (capacity between 2 MW$_e$ – 100 MW$_e$), and large-scale CHP (more than 100 MW$_e$ installed).

Moreover, one may discuss the cogeneration systems denoting "utility cogeneration", "industrial cogeneration", and cogeneration used for other purposes (Rezaie & Rosen 2012, p. 5, see Boyce 2002, pp. 25, 32, cf. Westner & Madlener 2011, p. 5304).[3] In such classification, utility cogeneration is usually based on large units connected to district energy systems which are often owned, or co-owned by local governments. Industrial cogeneration is represented by industrial facilities such as paper, glass, or textiles producers generating heat and power in addition to their main activities. The last of the above-mentioned categories (i.e. other cogeneration) is related to such objectives of using cogeneration in desalination facilities, where electricity is cogenerated with desalinated seawater (see Rezaie & Rosen 2012, p. 5).[4] In these systems, the wasted thermal energy (usually coming from an electricity producing device such as a heat engine, for example, a diesel-engine or a turbine using steam or gas), is used for the heating needs (like space and water heating, industrial process heating) it can also be used as a thermal energy source for another element of the system (Kanoglu & Dincer 2009, p. 76). What distinguishes cogeneration from other technologies and processes (from conventional systems producing either electricity or heat, or from simple heat recovery strategies), is "cascading" of energy use, from high- to low-temperature (Kanoglu & Dincer 2009, p. 76; OTA 1983, p. 3).

Cogeneration and energy efficiency

Cogeneration, if well-designed – by using waste heat recovery to capture the heat created as a coproduct in the electricity generation – is characterised by a significant growth in the efficiency of fuel used (Thomas 2010, p. viii). Usually, the total system efficiency of CHP accounts for 60 to 80%, with some systems reaching 90%, as reported by the EPA (n.d.b). The ability to increase the efficiency of fuel used in combined production of electricity and heat is one of the main strengths of cogeneration – its "principal technical advantage" (Kanoglu & Dincer 2009, p. 76). That is because higher energy efficiency results in lower usage of energy for a given process in a way comparable to energy saving appliances and equipment (Rezaie & Rosen 2012, p. 2). This feature of cogeneration is also a key element of legal definitions established at the European level. This concerns "high-efficiency cogeneration" ("cogeneration units shall provide primary energy savings ... of at least 10% compared with the references for separate production of heat and electricity") or "efficient district heating and cooling" ("a district heating or cooling system using at least 50% renewable energy, 50% waste heat, 75% cogenerated heat or 50% of

10 *Introduction*

a combination of such energy and heat"),[5] as listed in Directive 2012/27/EU.

Although "energy efficiency" and "energy savings" are often treated as synonyms, there is a difference between these two terms (see Commission 2011). The following citation from the Impact Assessment of Energy Efficiency Plan 2011 reflects this matter well:

> "[e]nergy efficiency" means that we use less energy inputs while maintaining an equivalent level of economic activity or service. "Energy savings" is an absolute decrease of energy consumption and can be done through increased energy efficiency, behaviour changes or even decreased economic activities. Examples of energy savings without efficiency improvements are heating a room less in winter, using the car less, or enabling energy saving modes on a computer.
>
> (Commission 2011, pp. 7–8)

Generally speaking, though, improvements in energy efficiency do not automatically scale down the overall reduction of energy consumption (at a macro scale) – even if products and processes are more energy efficient, the total national final energy consumption can grow (see Commission 2011, pp. 7–8). However, at a micro scale of individual installation the improved energy efficiency (as in a CHP installation) gives a lower total fuel consumption than would be necessary to generate heat and power separately (Campbell, Lee, & Wright 1980, p. 1). In the case of separate production, a significant volume of energy released in the combustion of fuel becomes lost and, so, useless (Ouellette et al. 2014, p. 15).[6] In a thermal power plant (for example, coal-fired or nuclear power plant), the energy content of fuel (e.g. coal, uranium) goes through the several processes. First, fuel is converted to heat (it takes the form of steam or hot gas); second, heat is converted to mechanical energy (in the form of a rotating shaft); and finally, mechanical energy is converted to electricity (Rosen 1998, p. 164), with efficiency accounting for around 30–40%.[7] In the cogeneration system, heat from a turbine-generator (which uses fuel to make the turbine work), becomes useful thermal energy (e.g. process steam), and not waste heat (Kanoglu & Dincer 2009, p. 76, see Benelmir & Feidt 1998). Energy contained in the first process is used to produce energy in the second one, which reduces the volume of energy lost (released uselessly to the environment) and increases the overall efficiency of the cogeneration system (Ouellette et al. 2014, p. 15). In effect, from the same primary energy source, both electrical (or mechanical) and thermal energy are produced (OTA 1983, p. 3).

Despite the fact that different types of CHP units generate electricity and steam in different proportions (i.e. the electricity to heat ratio, which describes the relative proportions of electrical and thermal energy produced in cogeneration (Kanoglu & Dincer 2009, p. 76), their scale of energy efficiency is much bigger than that of conventional power plants producing electricity and heat separately. Among CHP applications there are plenty of different installations, ranging from large industrial CHP units, through urban district heating systems based on local power stations (see Werner 2017, p. 619),[8] to small domestic systems providing electricity, hot water, and heat locally (Breeze 2017, p. 7). New technologies make combined heat and power cost-effective at smaller scales (with electrical rated power below 1 MW_e), so in practice both electricity and heat can be produced for neighbourhoods or even individuals (Rosen, Le, & Dincer 2005, p. 147; Chicco & Mancarella 2008, p. 410).

The same diversity concerns the structure of fuel used in cogeneration, which may be of conventional or renewable character, as fuels like oil, coal, natural gas, liquefied gas, biomass or solar energy can be used in CHP (Çakir, Çomakli, & Yüksel 2012, p. 196, see Raj, Iniyan, & Goic 2011). Nevertheless, combined heat and power represents integrated energy systems, where its size and type should be selected to match the thermal and electrical demands as closely as possible. Cogeneration systems can satisfy or follow electrical or thermal base-loads, or can cover peak demand for electricity or heat; they can also be used for energy storage needs (Rosen 1998, p. 165) and deliver heat for air and water heating (to individuals, business, institutions, etc.), where large quantities of heat at relatively low temperatures are needed. Those systems can also fulfil the needs of industrial processes such as chemical and metal processing, manufacturing, mining, or agriculture, which require heat at a range of different temperatures (Rosen 2008, p. 172).

Due to its relatively high total energy efficiency, CHP has attracted increased attention because of environmental and economic aspects connected with enhanced efficiency (Dotzauer, Holmström, & Ravn 1999, p. 738). Nevertheless, one should also note its electrical efficiency performance.[9] Table 1.1 provides an overview of the operating net electrical efficiencies presented together with operating net total fuel utilisation ratios (Lecomte et al. 2017, p. 552).

Summarising this data, the authors of an EU reference document for Best Available Techniques on large combustion power plants emphasise that despite the fact that "[c]ogeneration ... reduces the electrical efficiency of the plant, ... the increase in total fuel utilisation may offset this decrease if the cogeneration heat demand is stable and at the envisaged design point" (Lecomte et al. 2017, p. 553, cf. Åberg 2014). The growth of total energy efficiency implies a decline in fuel used. In the case of cogeneration, this leads to between 3% to 20% points of primary energy saved in comparison with separate production of electricity and heat, as calculated by Lecomte et al. (2017, pp. 71, 258). For thermal installations using conventional fuels like coal, under some conditions, this can result in the reduction of the emission of greenhouse gases even by 50%, while the

12 Introduction

Table 1.1 Overview of operating energy efficiencies (yearly averages) of European natural-gas-fired combustion units

Type	combustion plant rated thermal input [MW$_t$]	commissioning year	operating net electrical efficiency	operating net total fuel utilisation
gas boiler – not CHP	180–800	1959–1992	16–34%	16–34%
gas boiler – CHP	36–427	1970–2001	0–38%	26–95%
simple cycle gas turbine	140–430	1987–2008	20–39.5%	20–39.5%
simple cycle spark-ignited or dual fuel engines – CHP	15–42	1995–2010	39–45%	56–95%
combined-cycle gas turbine – not CHP	235–2030	1992–2011	33.2–57.8%	33.2–57.8%
combined-cycle gas turbine – CHP (50 – 600 MW$_t$)	57–500	1992–2009	22.8–46%	44–94.5%
combined-cycle gas turbine – CHP (> 600 MW$_t$)	670–991	1998–2011	22.8–46%	44–94.5%

Source: Lecomte et al. 2017, p. 553.

same energy (thermal and electrical) services are provided (Kanoglu & Dincer 2009, p. 76). This may be especially important in those countries where electricity is generated mainly from fossil energy sources (Chicco & Mancarella 2008, p. 410). Among the conditions required to reach lower emissions in this way, an annual operation of the heat sink and power production meeting the consumption should last as long as possible in a year (Lecomte et al. 2017, p. 258).[10]

The environmental issues (emissions) related to costs of emission allowances, together with economic matters related to reduced fuel usage, may result in some advantages of cogeneration over the separate production of electricity and heat, allowing CHP to be the preferred option (Kanoglu & Dincer 2009, p. 76, cf. Hinnells 2008, p. 4525). Sometimes, though, certain optimisations for CHP systems (e.g. regarding the operational costs), are needed (see Casisi et al. 2019), as cogeneration can save money when the installed capacity matches the local heat demand – both are equally big. However, CHP may not be feasible if the demand for residual heat or steam is too low (Lecomte et al. 2017, p. 71, see van der Does 1996, p. 50). Nevertheless, case studies demonstrated that significant reductions of the amounts of energy resources (needed to meet a given energy demand) together with lower environmental emissions can be

Introduction   13

achieved, when the increased energy-utilisation efficiency is reached by applying cogeneration in the energy sector, at a regional or national level (see Dincer & Rosen 1998).

Furthermore, regarding the economics of cogeneration, Joskow and Jones (1983) have provided a simple model (industrial cogeneration), where the four main conclusions were discussed. For better understanding, they are divided into five main points. Let us quote them here more broadly, as they present those complex issues in a clear way:

1. ... Cogeneration [is] an economical investment only if the value of the electricity produced is greater than the incremental capital and operating costs. Observations that electricity can be produced via cogeneration with lower net heat rates than heat rates associated with central station electricity production do not necessarily imply that cogeneration is economical. Energy savings from cogeneration simply do not imply economic savings.
2. The economics of cogeneration are very sensitive to absolute and relative values for fuel costs and electricity costs.[11] Where electricity prices are relatively low, it is less likely that cogeneration will be economical. Where electricity prices are high relative to fossil fuel prices, it is more likely that cogeneration will be economical. ...
3. The economics of cogeneration depends critically on the technical characteristics of the industrial plants where it will be used. Industrial processes with long-base steam load durations are most likely to find cogeneration economical.[12]
4. Although the scale of industrial firms is important, there is no simple "minimum scale" for economical cogeneration. The scale at which cogeneration becomes economical depends on several technical and economic parameters, especially capital costs, operating costs, and electricity prices.
5. Different cogeneration technologies imply very different amounts of electricity production for any particular level of process steam cogenerated. Estimates of the amount of electricity that can be economically produced using cogeneration must carefully determine which particular technology is most economical.[13]

(Joskow & Jones 1983, pp. 20–21)

According to the authors, the foregoing model "provides a simple useful framework for the appropriate evaluation of economical cogeneration opportunities and public policies – electricity pricing policies and tax policies – designed to promote economical cogeneration opportunities" (Joskow & Jones 1983, p. 21). Although it has some limitations (e.g. environmental issues, administrative barriers), the Joskow-Jones' model highlights some basic elements of the economics of cogeneration. It also addresses an important public element of the CHP jigsaw – the one driving

14 Introduction

this book. In utilising the potential of combined heat and power a lot depends on the regulatory framework created for the needs of this technology. Therefore, let us now move on and follow this theme throughout the next five chapters of this book.

Notes

1. Annex III of Directive 2004/8/EC.
2. For example, pursuant to Article 9(1) of the CHP Directive, Member States had to evaluate, *inter alia*, the procedures applicable to high-efficiency cogeneration, while this evaluation was to be made with a view of reducing the barriers for the growth in cogeneration.
3. Westner & Madlener (2011, p. 5304) when reviewing the many different classifications of CHP provide examples from literature where the following categories are distinguished: "industrial CHP", "district heating", "small-scale CHP", and "trigeneration", or "industrial CHP", "commercial/institutional CHP", and "district heating and cooling".
4. Rezaie & Rosen (2012, p. 5) quote desalination as a good example of using cogeneration from electricity generators and the distillation unit's brine heater. As these installations are both operated by high-pressure steam, using it for simultaneously producing electricity and desalinated water, reduces fuel consumption. These kinds of facilities are common in the Middle East and North Africa (see El-Nashar 2001), but they also operate in other parts of the world, for example, in Asia (see Wu, Hu, & Gao 2013).
5. This way, the assessment of the performance of new power plants and the refurbishment of older units requires evaluating the effective shares of different energy sources in supplying the final customer (Carpaneto, Lazzeroni & Repetto 2015, p. 714).
6. A single generation meets thermodynamic and technical limitations when a working fluid, like steam or gas, loses its usefulness by reaching the pressure and temperature which prevent the use of the required energy; as a result, the energy that remains in this steam is lost, simply released to the environment (Ouellette et al. 2014, p. 15).
7. For example, the average coal power plant efficiency in Europe is 35% (Alves Dias et al. 2018, p. 8) and 32% in the USA (EIA 2018). The highest coal power plant efficiency exceeds 45%, for example, Unit 3 of Nordjylland Power Station (*Nordjyllandsværket*) in Denmark which, despite being a CHP installation, has a net electrical efficiency of 47% reported without the production of heat; when heat is produced the efficiency increases significantly (see Peltier 2010; Santoianni 2015; cf. Chapter 4 of this book).
8. Among major district heating systems listed by Werner (2017, p. 619), CHP units are used, *inter alia*, in Beijing, Berlin, Bucharest, Copenhagen, Helsinki, Kiev, New York, Milan, Moscow, Seoul, Sofia, Stockholm, Warsaw or Vienna.
9. The different types of energy efficiency are clearly explained by EPA (2015, p. A1):

> the efficiency of electricity generation in power-only systems is determined by the relationship between net electrical output and the amount of fuel used for the power generation. Heat rate, the term often used to express efficiency in such power generation systems, is represented in terms of Btus of fuel consumed per kWh of electricity generated. However, CHP plants produce useable heat as well as electricity. In CHP systems, the total CHP

efficiency seeks to capture the energy content of both electricity and usable steam and is the net electrical output plus the net useful thermal output of the CHP system divided by the fuel consumed in the production of electricity and steam.

10 Lecomte et al. (2017, p. 258) highlight the possibility of bigger CO_2 production by cogeneration than the separate production of the same amount of heat and power in certain separate power plants. As they report:

> [i]f the heat sink or power consumption with combined products (during summer months heat consumption is mostly used for a relatively small amount of hot water production only) are not available, it might be possible that the annual thermal utilisation efficiency of the "combined heat and power plant" (annual efficiency factor) compares unfavourably with the temporary (six-monthly) production of heat in a separate boiler combined with the separate power production in a power plant producing electricity only. In this case, the CHP plant might produce more CO_2 for the production of the same amount of heat and power than the production in separate plants, for example, heat in a gas-fired boiler and power in a high-efficiency power plant.

11 Viklund & Karlsson (2015, pp. 195–196), on the basis of the results from the scenarios where the district heating system is based on CHP, report that:

> [a] low electricity price affects the system by favoring excess heat use in the DH system since the profit to reduce the use of fuels in the heat production exceeds the profit of the otherwise produced and sold electricity and the reduced use of electricity in the DC system. A high electricity price on the other hand, favors heat use in the DC system. When the electricity price is intermediate the trend for the optimal systems solution for heat use is not that clear; how-ever, the combination of an intermediate electricity price and a low or intermediate biofuel price favors heat use in the DH system, whereas the combination of an intermediate electricity price and a high biomass price favors heat use in the DC system.

12 As Joskow & Jones (1983, pp. 20–21) list

> [i]ndustrial firms with large peak steam loads are more likely to find cogeneration economical because of the scale economies associated with boilers and turbine/generator sets. Industries such as pulp and paper, chemicals, and petroleum refining often have plants with these characteristics. Many other manufacturing sectors do not. As a result, empirical analyses of cogeneration opportunities must focus on particular manufacturing sectors with careful consideration of steam load duration and the magnitude of peak steam loads.

13 Joskow & Jones (1983, p. 21) discuss here the technologies of high electricity generation rates such as diesels and gas turbines, emphasising their sensitiveness (in terms of their economic costs and benefits) to changes in fuel and electricity prices.

References

Åberg, M. 2014, "Investigating the impact of heat demand reductions on Swedish district heating production using a set of typical system models", *Applied Energy*, 118, pp. 246–257.

Al-Sulaiman, F.A., Hamdullahpur, F., & Dincer, I. 2011, "Trigeneration: a comprehensive review based on prime movers", *International Journal of Energy Research*, 35(3), pp. 233–258.

Alves Dias, P., Kanellopoulos, K., Medarac, H., Kapetaki, Z., Miranda-Barbosa, E., Shortall, R., Czako, V., Telsnig, T., Vazquez-Hernandez, C., Lacal Arántegui, R., Nijs, W., Gonzalez Aparicio, I., Trombetti, M., Mandras, G., Peteves, E., & Tzimas, E. 2018, *EU coal regions: opportunities and challenges ahead*, Publications Office of the European Union, Luxembourg.

Barton, B. 2006, "The theoretical context of regulation", in *Regulating energy and natural resources*, eds B. Barton, A. Lucas, L. Barrera-Hernández, & A. Rønne, Oxford University Press, Oxford, pp. 11–33.

Benelmir, R., & Feidt, M. 1998, "Energy cogeneration systems and energy management strategy", *Energy Conversion and Management*, 39(16–18), pp. 1791–1802.

Boyce, M.P. 2002, *Handbook for cogeneration and combined cycle power plants*, New York, NY: ASME Press.

Breeze, P. 2017, *Combined Heat and Power*, Elsevier – Academic Press, London.

C. Pereira Rolim, M.J. 2019, *Reconciling energy, the environment and sustainable development: the role of law and regulation*, Alphen aan den Rijn: Kluwer Law International.

Çakir, U., Çomakli, K., & Yüksel, F. 2012, "The role of cogeneration systems in sustainability of energy", *Energy Conversion and Management*, 63, pp. 196–202.

Cameron, P.D., & Heffron, R.J. (eds) 2016, *Legal aspects of EU energy regulation: the consolidation of energy law across Europe*, 2nd edn, Oxford University Press, Oxford.

Campbell, J.J.J., Lee, J.C., & Wright, D.E. 1980, "Coal-fired, closed-cycle, gas turbine cogeneration systems", *Turbo Expo: power for land, sea, and air*, 1B General, American Society of Mechanical Engineers, New York, NY, pp. 1–13. Available from: doi: 10.1115/80-GT-156 [27 February 2019].

Casisi, M., Costanzo, S., Pinamonti, P., & Reini, M. 2019, "Two-level evolutionary multi-objective optimization of a district heating system with distributed cogeneration", *Energies*, 12(1), 114, pp. 1–23. Available from: doi:10.3390/en12010114 [27 February 2019].

Chicco, G., & Mancarella, P. 2008, "Assessment of the greenhouse gas emissions from cogeneration and trigeneration systems. Part I: models and indicators", *Energy*, 33(3), pp. 410–417.

COGEN Europe n.d., *Our vision*. Available from: https://www.cogeneurope.eu/about/our-vision [14 September 2019].

Commission. 2011, *Commission staff working document: Impact Assessment accompanying document to the communication from the Commission to the European Parliament, the Council, the European Economic and Social Committee and the Committee of the Regions – Commission staff working document. Energy Efficiency Plan 2011*, SEC (2011) 277 final, 8 March 2011.

Dincer, I., & Rosen, M.A. 1998, "A worldwide perspective on energy, environment and sustainable development", *International Journal of Energy Research*, 22(15), pp. 1305–1321.

Directive 2003/54/EC of the European Parliament and of the Council of 26 June 2003 concerning common rules for the internal market in electricity and repealing Directive 96/92/EC, OJ L 176, 15 July 2003.

Directive 2004/8/EC of the European Parliament and of the Council of 11 February 2004 on the promotion of cogeneration based on a useful heat demand in the internal energy market and amending Directive 92/42/EEC, OJ L 52, 21 February 2004.

Directive 2009/72/EC of the European Parliament and of the Council of 13 July 2009 Concerning common rules for the internal market in electricity and repealing Directive 2003/54/EC, OJ L 211, 14 August 2009.

Directive 2012/27/EU of the European Parliament and of the Council of 25 October 2012 on energy efficiency, amending Directives 2009/125/EC and 2010/30/EU and repealing Directives 2004/8/EC and 2006/32/EC, OJ L 315, 14 November 2012.

Directive 96/92/EC of the European Parliament and of the Council of 19 December 1996 concerning common rules for the internal market in electricity, OJ L 27, 30 January 1997.

Dotzauer, E., Holmström, K., & Ravn, H.F. 1999, "Optimal unit commitment and economic dispatch of cogeneration systems with a storage", *Proceedings of the 13th Power Systems Computation Conference 1999*, Trondheim, pp. 738–744.

Eek, H. 1965, *The Swedish conflict of laws*, Nijhoff, the Hague.

EIA. 2018, *Table 8.1 Average operating heat rate for selected energy sources*. Available from: https://www.eia.gov/electricity/annual/html/epa_08_01.html [27 February 2019].

El-Nashar, A.M. 2001, "Cogeneration for power and desalination – state of the art review", *Desalination*, 134(1–3), pp. 7–28.

EPA. 2015, *Catalog of CHP technologies. Appendix A: expressing CHP efficiency*. Available from: https://www.epa.gov/sites/production/files/2015-07/documents/catalog_of_chp_technologies_appendix_a_expressing_chp_efficiency.pdf [27 February 2019].

EPA. n.d. a, *CHP benefits*. Available from: https://www.epa.gov/chp/chp-benefits [27 February 2019].

EPA. n.d. b, *Methods for calculating CHP efficiency: total system efficiency*. Available from: https://www.epa.gov/chp/methods-calculating-chp-efficiency [27 February 2019].

Eurostat. 2001, *Combined heat and power production (CHP) in the EU. Summary of statistics*, Office for Official Publications of the European Communities, Luxembourg.

Freiberg, A. 2010, *The tools of regulation*, Federation Press, Sydney.

Havelský, V. 1999, "Energetic efficiency of cogeneration systems for combined heat, cold and power production", *International Journal of Refrigeration*, 22(6), pp. 479–485.

Hinnells, M. 2008, "Combined heat and power in industry and buildings", *Energy Policy*, 36(12), pp. 4522–4526.

Hinrichs, R.A., & Kleinbach, M. 2002, *Energy, its use and the environment*, Brook/Cole, Boston, MA.

IEA. 2009, *Cogeneration and district energy: sustainable energy technologies for today... and tomorrow*, OECD Publishing, Paris, https://doi.org/10.1787/9789264077171-en.

Joskow, P.L., & Jones, D.R. 1983, "The simple economics of industrial cogeneration", *The Energy Journal*, 4(1), pp. 1–22.

Kanoglu, M., & Dincer, I. 2009, "Performance assessment of cogeneration plants", *Energy Conversion and Management*, 50(1), pp. 76–81.

Kavvadias, K.C., & Maroulis, Z.B. 2010, "Multi-objective optimization of a trigeneration plant", *Energy Policy*, 38(2), pp. 945–954.

Lecomte, T., de, F., la Fuente, J.F., Neuwahl, F., Canova, M., Pinasseau, A., Jankov, I., Brinkmann, T., Roudier, S., & Delgado Sancho, L. 2017, *Best Available Techniques (BAT) reference document for Large Combustion Plants*, Publications Office of the European Union, Luxembourg.

Ogus, A.I. 1994, *Regulation: legal form and economic theory*, Oxford University Press, Oxford.

OTA. 1983, *Industrial and commercial cogeneration*, OTA-E-192, US Government Printing Office, Washington, DC.

Ouellette, A., Rowe, A., Sopinka, A., & Wild, P. 2014, "Achieving emissions reduction through oil sands cogeneration in Alberta's deregulated electricity market", *Energy Policy*, 71, pp. 13–21.

Peeters, M., & Deketelaere, K. (eds) 2006, *EU climate change policy: the challenge of new regulatory initiatives*, Edward Elgar Publishing, Cheltenham.

Peltier, R. 2010, *Plant efficiency: begin with the right definitions*, 2 January 2010, POWER. Available from: https://www.powermag.com/plant-efficiency-begin-with-the-right-definitions/?pagenum=3 [27 February 2019].

Prosser, T. 2010, *The regulatory enterprise: government, regulation, and legitimacy*, Oxford University Press, Oxford.

Raj, N.T., Iniyan, S., & Goic, R. 2011, "A review of renewable energy based cogeneration technologies", *Renewable and Sustainable Energy Reviews*, 15(8), 2011, pp. 3640–3648.

Rezaie, B., & Rosen, M.A. 2012, "District heating and cooling: review of technology and potential enhancements", *Applied Energy*, 93, pp. 2–10.

Rosen, M.A. 1998, "Reductions in energy use and environmental emissions achievable with utility-based cogeneration: simplified illustrations for Ontario", *Applied Energy*, 61(3), pp. 163–174.

Rosen, M.A. 2008, "Allocating carbon dioxide emissions from cogeneration systems: descriptions of selected output-based methods", *Journal of Cleaner Production*, 16(2), pp. 171–177.

Rosen, M.A., & Koohi-Fayegh, S. 2016, *Cogeneration and district energy systems: modelling, analysis and optimization*, Institution of Engineering & Technology, London.

Rosen, M.A., Le, M.N., & Dincer, I. 2005, "Efficiency analysis of a cogeneration and district energy system", *Applied Thermal Engineering*, 25(1), pp. 147–159.

Santoianni, D. 2015, *Setting the benchmark: the world's most efficient coal-fired power plants*, 15 April 2015, World Coal Association. Available from: https://www.worldcoal.org/setting-benchmark-worlds-most-efficient-coal-fired-power-plants [27 February 2019].

Sokołowski, M.M. 2013, "Rozważania o istocie współczesnej regulacji" [Considerations on the essence of modern regulation], in *Regulacja – innowacja w sektorze energetycznym* [Regulation – innovation in the energy sector], ed. A. Walaszek-Pyzioł, C. H. Beck, Warsaw, pp. 309–329.

Sokołowski, M.M. 2016, *Regulation in the European electricity sector*, Routledge, Abingdon and New York, NY.

Sokołowski, M.M. 2017, "Aksjologia europejskiego prawa energetycznego" [Axiology of European energy law], in *Aksjologia prawa administracyjnego* [Axiology of administrative law], ed. J. Zimmermann, 2, Wolters Kluwer Polska, Warsaw, pp. 633–646.

Sokołowski, M.M. 2018, "Regulatory dilemma: between deregulation and overregulation", in *Prawo administracyjne wobec współczesnych wyzwań. Księga jubileuszowa dedykowana profesorowi Markowi Wierzbowskiemu* [Administrative law facing contemporary challenges: Jubilee anniversary publication dedicated to Professor Marek Wierzbowski], eds J. Jagielski, D. Kijowski, M. Grzywacz, C.H. Beck, Warsaw, pp. 591–598.

Sokołowski, M.M., & Stankiewicz, R. 2011, "Ku instytucjonalizacji europejskiej regulacji sektorowej: wnioski płynące z analizy ram ustrojowych Agencji do Spraw Współpracy Organów Regulacji Energetyki" [Towards the institutionalisation of European sectoral regulation: the conclusions of the analysis of the Institutional Framework of the Agency for the Cooperation of Energy Regulators], in 3 of *Problemy prawa polskiego i obcego w ujęciu historycznym, praktycznym i teoretycznym* [Problems of Polish and foreign law in historical, practical, and theoretical contexts], eds B.T. Bieńkowska, D. Szafrański, C.H. Beck, Warsaw, pp. 223–243.

Talus, K. 2013, *EU energy law and policy: a critical account*, Oxford University Press, Oxford.

Thomas, D.H. 2010, *Energy efficiency through combined heat and power or cogeneration*, Nova Science Publishers, New York, NY.

van der Does, T. 1996, "Fuel cell co-generation: the future of co-generation", *Journal of Power Sources*, 61(1–2), pp. 49–51.

Veolia. n.d. *Combined Heat Power – what we do*. Available from: https://www.veolia.co.uk/combined-heat-power/about-us/what-we-do [27 February 2019].

Viklund, S.B., & Karlsson, M. 2015, "Industrial excess heat use: systems analysis and CO2 emissions reduction", *Applied Energy*, 152, pp. 189–197.

Walaszek-Pyzioł, A. 2002, *Energia i prawo* [Energy and law], LexisNexis, Warsaw.

Werner, S. 2017, "International review of district heating and cooling", *Energy*, 137, pp. 617–631.

Westner, G., & Madlener, R. 2011, "Development of cogeneration in Germany: a mean-variance portfolio analysis of individual technology's prospects in view of the new regulatory framework", *Energy*, 36(8), pp. 5301–5313.

Wierzbowski, M. 2014, "Współpraca niezależnych organów administracji publicznej" [Cooperation of independent administrative authorities], *Ruch Prawniczy, Ekonomiczny i Socjologiczny* [Journal of Law, Economics and Sociology], 76(2), pp. 231–235.

Wróblewski, J. 1992, *The judicial application of law*, eds Z. Bańkowski & N. MacCormick, Kluwer Academic Publishers, Dordrecht.

Wu, L., Hu, Y., & Gao, C. 2013, "Optimum design of cogeneration for power and desalination to satisfy the demand of water and power", *Desalination*, 324, pp. 111–117.

Yang, W., & Guo, K. 2010, "Analysis on energy saving for a cool, heat and power cogeneration system with a micro gas turbine", *2010 Asia-Pacific Power and Energy Engineering Conference*, Chengdu, pp. 1–5. Available from: https://doi.org/10.1109/APPEEC.2010.5448339 [27 February 2019].

2 First policy actions on combined heat and power

Combined heat and power is a proven technology as old as the generation of electricity; it first appeared in Europe and the USA in the late 1880s, before the era of transmitting electricity, when industrial facilities generated their own electrical power and often supplied it to nearby communities (Kolanowski 2008, p. 5; EDUCOGEN 2001, p. 7; Caton & Turner 1997, p. 670; OTA 1983, p. 3). As Thomas R. Casten (1999, p. 47) writes "[e]lectric generation began by combining heat and power generation at Thomas Edison's Pearl Street plant in Manhattan". In fact, the inventor's first power plant, built in New York in 1882, was a cogeneration installation (Dincer & Rosen 2007, p. 258).[1] Between the late 1880s and the early 1900s, as the energy services of public utilities were limited in availability and rather unreliable, as well as expensive (usually), an onsite generation selling surpluses nearby[2] was a cheaper and more reliable alternative (OTA 1983, p. 3; Wooster 1983, p. 706). The potential in the use of steam produced along with electricity was quickly noticed by the industry that generated power in these on-site installations; heat was captured there and utilised locally, both in production and for heating (Kolanowski 2008, p. 5; Caton & Turner 1997, p. 670). For instance, in the early 1900s approximately half of the US electricity sector was cogenerated, and by 1902, about 3,600 private and public electric generating systems existed in the USA (Mogk & Lepley 1989, p. 1053).

Nevertheless, very soon the cogeneration sector faced a range of problems. Among them one may find, *inter alia*, the development of alternating current and, as a result, the possibility to economically transmit electricity over longer distances which has removed the need for the generation of electricity from local consumers; reliability of central electric generation and decreasing electricity rates charged by the public utilities (due to the improvements in technology and economies of scale),[3] tax regimes which favoured expenses instead of capital investments, or focusing on their own, main product rather than the side issue as generating heat and power (Mogk & Lepley 1989, p. 1053; Turner 2015, pp. 893–894; Bergmeier 2003, p. 1363). Frank B. Cross (1979, p. 240) calls this the fight with cogeneration, where the energy utilities discouraged the use of CHP by intentionally adjusting rates and construction plans in a way designed to eliminate cogeneration from the market. This changing environment caused a retreat from cogeneration and a progressive switch to services offered by public utilities. Some exceptions were noticed in certain industries such as paper, chemicals, refining, iron, or steels, as they had high demand for steam or/and free by-product fuels (Bergmeier 2003, p. 1363).

In the USA, further weakening of cogeneration was accompanied by the intensification of competitive pressure on the part of electricity generators, switching to natural gas and oil for heating in the 1940s, as well as destroying heating systems during the implementation of urban renewal programmes in the 1950s (Mogk & Lepley 1989, p. 1053). Between 1945 and 1970, the local and state regulatory authorities reinforced the protection of the monopoly status of energy utilities (Charo, Stearns, & Mallory 1986, p. 451). In effect, a share of CHP in the US energy sector declined gradually. W. Dan Turner (2015) gathers statistics which indicate a decrease from around 25% to just 9% of the total electrical power produced in the USA between mid-1950s and the mid-1970s, but Cross (1979, p. 240) refers to lower levels, i.e. over 15% in 1950, and less than 5% in 1973; the same scale seems to be confirmed by Pickel (1982, p. 20), who – by using the Edison Electric Institute's data – reported a drop from 18% in 1941 to less than 4% in 1979. Irrespective of their accuracy, there was a significant decrease in electricity supplied by the CHP units in the USA. Additionally, the drop in electricity production was followed by reduced use of heat produced by cogeneration but here the decrease started later, in the 1960s; before it, the US cogeneration noted a growth in this segment of generated energy (Pickel 1982, pp. 21–22).

The turning point for combined heat and power in the USA was in 1978. It was during the era of the oil crisis when PURPA was adopted with goals of enhancing energy efficiency by, among others, greater use of energy-efficient CHP (Yüzügüllü 2013, p. 51). As in the USA, some Western European countries restarted cogeneration after the oil crisis of the 1970s. However, a range of different factors has steered the development of CHP. They include, *inter alia*, climate, population and its density, fuel prices, competitiveness in the electricity sector, industrial structure, and environmental considerations, with specific issues like large natural gas resources in the Netherlands or an extensive heat distribution network in Denmark (Grohnheit 1999, pp. 20–21; Commission 1997, p. iii). Apart from Denmark, cogeneration for district heating was intensively developed in West Germany and to some extent in France (Commission 1982c, p. 12). Isolated CHP systems existed in the Netherlands as well as in the UK, Belgium, and Italy (Commission 1982c, p. 12). In the early 1970s, cogeneration used in Community industry accounted for 13–14 Mtoe savings annually (Commission 1982c, p. 11). Combined heat and power has also developed in Central and Eastern Europe, with Hungary and Poland (Lund 2014, p. 328) among the leaders. In the following subchapters we will take a closer look at some European countries and their post-war experiences in the development of cogeneration.

Cogeneration and the European experience

The large-scale combined heat and power units have been used for decades in district heating in the Nordic countries as well as Central and Eastern Europe (see Grohnheit 1999, p. 20). Certain European post-war CHP case studies are shown below, giving a general view of the early developments of cogeneration in Europe. They come from Western Europe (EU-15) as well as countries from Central and Eastern Europe which later joined the EU. These early developments are followed-up in Chapter 5 of this book where I review all of the European Member States (EU-28), together with their legislation, policies, and regulatory tools, which have been dedicated to combined heat and power over the years.

Combined heat and power in Western Europe

For instance, in West Germany, the CHP installations were developed by local energy distributors on the basis of their existing heat network and electricity grid (Commission 1997, p. iii). In the 1980s, these systems supplied around 1.4 million dwellings, with 18% of total power capacity provided by CHP plants (Commission 1984b, pp. 74, 77). An extension of district heating was planned under the 1982–1986 federal/*Länder* programme, including a 35% subsidy, with a budget of 493 million ECU; financial grants were also given for the conversion of oil-fired heating systems used in agriculture to district heating (Commission 1982b, Annex 2, p. 5). Apart from these investment aids, grants for constructing/ converting to coal-fired CHP plants and tax write-offs for connecting buildings to district heating were offered under an extended financial framework,[4] aimed at doubling heat supplies from 4 Mtoe in 1980 to 8 Mtoe by 1995 (Commission 1984b, p. 74).

However, some issues coming from the German reunification occurred. The reasons for such a state of affairs could be found among different institutional preconditions for cogeneration systems. With respect to CHP in former East Germany, Hvelplund & Lund (1998, p. 542) enumerate four means of obstructing cogeneration. These were, first, unfavourable payments for the electricity sold to the grid; second, unfavourable rules on payment of reserve capacity; third, an obligation imposed on the regional electricity distributors to purchase a minimum of 70% of electricity from a large eastern German energy company, *Vereinigte Energiewerke AG* (VEAG), and finally, the introduced mechanisms of cross-subsidisation.[5]

In Denmark the development of cogeneration accelerated after the oil crisis; however, even before that, Danish combined heat and power was an important element of the country's energy system, accounting for about 40% of the total electricity generated (Østergaard 2010, p. 2194). The Heat Supply Act of 1979 imposed on Danish municipalities an obligation to designate areas which were to be supplied with district heat produced by central or local CHP units (Möller 2008, p. 470). In practice, the growth of combined heat and power in those areas was driven by the stakeholders of municipal heat network: its managers, local distributors and producers-distributors (Commission 1997, p. iii).[6] At that time, the Danish government wanted to extend the district heating system (cf. Grohnheit 1999, p. 20); in 1979, approximately 30% of Danish households were using district heating (Commission 1984b, pp. 62–63). This was continued in the 1980s under the subsequent policy framework brought by the Danish Energy Plan of 1981. The Plan focused on deeper improvements in the Danish energy industry to achieve a highly structured energy supply system (Commission 1984b, p. 63). To reach the set goals, Denmark offered a system of aid, financing the connection of selected installations to district heating systems.[7]

Towards the end of the 1970s, in the Netherlands CHP was a popular technology used by corporations like Shell, DOW Chemicals, DSM, and others in industries such as paper or food production, which had their own market for heat and electricity (Hekkert, Harmsen, & de Jong 2007, p. 4680). Due to the changes in energy law in the late 1980s, the CHP units were constructed on a number of sites as non-licensed or decentralised capacity, (Verkuyl, Roggenkamp, & Boisseleau 2005 p. 122). Apart from that, the Dutch government provided numerous incentives to develop industrial cogeneration – Blok & Turkenburg (1992, pp. 4–5) list, *inter alia*, investment grants, special energy conservation loans, subsidies for feasibility studies, pro-cogeneration changes in the electricity tariffs, cheap contracts for standby electricity from the utility grid during outages of a CHP unit, a research and development programme on cogeneration, as well as a possibility to deliver electricity from the CHP plants to energy consumers ("open transmission"). In effect, between 1968 and 1988 cogeneration in the Netherlands grew from around 840 MW to 1800 MW, generating respectively more than 10% and 14% of the electricity consumed in the country (Blok & Turkenburg 1992, p. 2).

Other European countries also addressed heating systems with CHP units by different state policies, including granting subsidies. In Italy for example, subsidies of up to 50% were granted for feasibility studies of projects applying renewable energy sources in district heating, and subsidies of up to 30% were provided for district heating systems using CHP (Commission 1982b, Annex 2, p. 9). Further initiatives were offered in Italy in the 1990s, when increased tariffs given to energy-saving plants were established (CIP 6 mechanism) leading to the growth of cogeneration across Italy (Macchi & Poggio 1994, p. 1; ABB 2011, p. 3).[8] Similarly to Italy, grants (50%) for CHP feasibility studies were established in the UK in 1978 (Commission 1984a, p. 32).[9] The industrial cogeneration in Britain was launched against the background of declining CHP capacity between the 1950s and the 1980s (Brown & Minett 1996, pp. 11–12). In the 1980s, the Lead City Scheme was introduced by the government to finance cogeneration in Belfast, Edinburgh, and Leicester, whereas the private sector together with municipalities developed CHP in Sheffield, London, and Newcastle (Babus'Haq & Probert 1996, pp. 50–51). Among other examples of promoting cogeneration, one may mention Belgium where schemes used for the needs of developing gas in the electricity generation were often applied to CHP (Commission 1998, p. 48).

In contrast, some northern Member States, like Ireland, did not perceive CHP and district heating as commercially applicable in the short term at a large scale (Commission 1984b, p. 111). The same situation applies to southern Europe where the heat demand was too small to justify any investment in the capital-intensive heating systems (Grohnheit 1999, p. 21). Despite some progress noted in the CHP leading countries, as the Commission reported (1997, p. 3), between 1974–1990 the penetration of cogeneration in the Community decreased. The fuels used in cogeneration, based primarily on hydrocarbons (mainly heavy oil), kept the capital and operating costs low (Commission 1982c, pp. 11–12). A sharp increase in oil prices, caused by the 1970s oil crisis, together with the competition from the large coal-fired and nuclear power plants producing electricity at relatively stable prices, resulted in a slowdown of the CHP business; this, in the scenario of fuel structure change, faced the high costs of modernisation into new small- or medium-sized, coal-fired units as well as the high interest rates (Commission 1982c, p. 12). For the countries where gas was the main energy source the relation between the price of oil and gas was also a problem (Blok & Turkenburg 1992, p. 3). In effect, just a few new installations have been put into operation, and the existing ones either limited production, or were decommissioned (Commission 1982c, p. 12). As the Commission (1982b, p. 12) admitted, it was a paradox "when rising energy costs have caused a decline in interest in what is nevertheless one of the best ways of saving energy".

In this light, the scale of CHP usage in the EU in the 1990s, has been evaluated as "disappointing" (Commission 1997, p. 3). Only the Netherlands and Denmark oscillated around 40% of electricity produced in cogeneration – Finland which took the 3rd place, accounted for more than 30%; and, in 1994, only 9% of electricity generation in the Community came from cogeneration (Commission 1997, p. 3, 9). In comparison, the total gross electricity capacity in Germany accounted for around 115 GW of power installed, with more than 26 GW of CHP (23% of total installed capacity) which reached only 9% of the total gross electricity generated in 1994 (Commission 1997, p. iv).

CHP in Central and Eastern Europe

When addressing the matter of combined heat and power in Central and Eastern Europe (CEE), one should note an extensive development of cogeneration in post-war Poland. As the Polish Member Committee of the World Energy Council (WEC) reports, the first new heat network supplied by a CHP plant was built in Warsaw in 1953 and new cogeneration plants were constructed there in 1954 and 1961 (cf. Wojdyga & Chorzelski 2017, p. 107); also, starting from the 1950s (with a peak in the 1970s and the 1980s), numerous CHP stations were built in other industrial regions of Poland (Upper Silesia) and in many Polish cities, like Łódź, Kraków, Wrocław, Bydgoszcz, Gdańsk, Gdynia, Elbląg, Szczecin, Gorzów, Białystok, Lublin, or Ostrołęka (WEC 2014, pp. 185–186).[10] The most common units had the capacity or 50–55 MW_e, built in the limits of 120 MW_e and 230 MW_t (WEC 2014, p. 186). As a result of these investments, the share of total electricity produced in cogeneration in Poland increased, reaching respectively 5.7% in 1970 and 8% in 1980 (Marecki 2005, p. 3).

Cogeneration was also mentioned as one of the tools of energy policy for Central and Eastern Europe and its countries during their democratic transformation at the turn of the 1980s and the 1990s. As reported, Bulgaria gave a priority to the increased use of CHP (Commission 1990a, pp. 173–174), Poland predicted a growth in production of heat in combined units, with gas complementing coal for electricity generation in the combined cycle and small-scale cogeneration (Commission 1990a, p. 315, 323). Developing CHP was also recommended for Romania (Commission 1990a, p. v), where the first cogeneration power plants appeared in the 1980s, as an upgrade of the existing units (which produced only electricity) was needed due to the expansion of district heating in the country (Iacobescu & Badescu 2011, p. 270).

However, cogeneration encountered some problems that occurred after the transformation of CEE which, apart from political systems, also touched national economies. In Romania, for example, after the initial growth, the usage of combined heat and power decreased, as in the 1990s the condition of the heat networks run by the local governments deteriorated (due to financial limitations) leading to large heat losses, and many industrial facilities curbed or even finished their operation (Iacobescu & Badescu 2011, p. 273). Before 1989, Romanian industrial sites and major cities were supplied with electricity and heat from large industrial and urban central heating plants, providing around 40% of the total electricity generated in Romania – due to de-industrialisation the electricity generated by CHP has decreased to around 10% (Leca 2015, pp. 6–7). In addition, a market of micro-thermal units for heating for homes emerged in Romania in the 2000s; that was accompanied by mass disconnection of previous users from district heating (Iacobescu & Badescu 2011, p. 273).[11] To tackle these matters the National Strategy[12] was adopted (cf. Benkő et al. 2015, p. 12). Despite this, the disconnection continued between 2006 and 2010; however, in the beginning of 2010 some stabilisation appeared on the district heating market.[13]

Cogeneration in the EU-15 according to the 1990s' statistics

Regardless of the Commission's earlier disappointment related to the development of combined heat and power in the Community, its share in the electricity generation in the EU-15[14] has grown from 205 TWh in 1994 to 271 TWh in 1998, representing a relative increase of 33%, to reach a growth, as percentage of total electricity generation, raising from 9% to almost 11%[15] over the same period (Eurostat 2001, pp. 6–7). Table 2.1 depicts this increase.

As one may observe, in 1998, the biggest generation of electricity in combined heat and power was recorded in the Netherlands, Italy, and Germany, reaching approximately 48 TWh, 45 TWh, and 42 TWh respectively. The fourth and fifth major producers, Denmark and Finland did not reach the 30 TWh barrier, accounting for around 26 TWh and 25 TWh accordingly. The biggest share of CHP usage in the production of electricity in 1998 was noted in Denmark (more than 62%) and the Netherlands (almost 53%). In general, the generation of electricity in CHP between 1994 and 1998 increased in almost all Member States. Interestingly, among these exceptions one may find Germany where cogeneration, in terms of electricity production, decreased from the level reaching 48 TWh in 1994 to about 42 TWh in 1998. Denmark also noted some changes in this respect, recording a drop from more than 29 TWh in 1996 to around 26 TWh in 1998; however, in comparison to 1994 (approximately 22 TWh), it was still bigger.

The EU-15's biggest producers of electricity in CHP also had the biggest capacity installed, both in terms of power and heat. In 1998, the majority of cogeneration units were installed in Germany (around 22 GW in electricity and about 36 GW in heat), Italy (around 9.5 GW in electricity and 23 GW in heat), and the Netherlands (8.5 GW in electricity and almost 17 GW in heat), followed by Denmark (slightly more than 7 GW in electricity and 11 GW in heat) and Finland (over 5 GW in electricity and about 15 GW in heat). With respect to heat capacity France also noted a significant share (nearly 19 GW) surpassing the Netherlands in this regard. The overall EU-15 installed CHP capacity in 1998 accounted for almost 72 GW in heat and 170 GW in power. In terms of 1994's levels, it was an increase by 14% in the power capacity and 13% in the heat capacity. This development was driven by growth recorded in

Table 2.1 Production of electricity and heat in cogeneration in the European Union (EU-15) between 1994–1998

Member State	1994**		1996		1998	
	CHP electricity generation [TWh]	share of CHP in total gross electricity generation	CHP electricity generation [TWh]	share of CHP in total gross electricity generation	CHP electricity generation [TWh]	share of CHP in total gross electricity generation
Belgium	2.44	3.4%	3.00	3.9%	3.41	4.1%
Denmark	21.87	54.5%	29.26	54.6%	25.59	62.3%
Germany	47.75	9.0%	37.82	6.8%	41.77	7.5%
Greece	0.82	2.0%	0.89	2.1%	0.98*	2.1%
Spain	8.54	5.3%	13.39	7.7%	21.92	11.2%
France	8.51	1.8%	9.86	1.9%	12.66	2.5%
Ireland	0.26	1.5%	0.36	1.9%	0.40	1.9%
Italy	26.48	11.4%	31.38	12.9%	44.86	17.3%
Luxembourg	NA	NA	NA	NA	0.32	22.5%
Netherlands	31.54	39.5%	36.41	42.7%	47.84	52.6%
Austria	11.72	21.4%	13.54	24.7%	14.27	24.8%
Portugal	3.11	9.9%	2.85	8.2%	3.29	8.4%
Finland	20.31	30.9%	22.54	32.5%	25.13	35.8%
Sweden	9.26	6.4%	10.24	7.3%	9.54	6.0%
United Kingdom	11.62	3.6%	15.11	4.3%	18.64	5.2%
European Union (EU-15)	**204.23**	**9.0%**	**226.65**	**9.4%**	**270.62**	**10.9%**

* Eurostat estimate.
** German figures are for 1995.
Source: Eurostat 2001.

all Member States, excluding Germany and Portugal, although the latter had a minor impact on the general EU-15 statistics, due to its small scale (in contrast to Germany).

The picture of the Community's 1990s cogeneration should be supplemented with one more statistic. It concerns the heat produced in combined heat and power. Table 2.3 presents the 1994–1998 data on this matter.

The early 1990s leader in the heat generated in cogeneration – Germany, reduced the production of heat in CHP by more than 100 PJ in four years. This major decrease enabled Italy to take the first place as of 1998, almost reaching the barrier of 400 PJ of heat generated in combined heat and power. Germany, producing a little more than 340 PJ, was second. Finland, being third in these statistics, generated almost 270 PJ of heat. Among

28 *First policy actions on combined heat and power*

Table 2.2 CHP installed capacity in the European Union (EU-15) between 1994–1998

Member State	1994[**] electricity [GW]	heat [GW]	1996 electricity [GW]	heat [GW]	1998 electricity [GW]	heat [GW]
Belgium	0.73	3.1	0.63	3.05	0.80	3.19
Denmark	5.21	9.18	5.49	9.58	7.03	11.00
Germany[***]	26.18	46.56	22.54	40.73	22.16	35.87
Greece	0.22	0.55	0.22	0.55	0.26[*]	0.71
Spain	1.53	4.70	2.28	4.28	3.56	5.31
France	2.92	11.19	3.17	11.53	3.49	18.84
Ireland	0.07	0.34	0.08	0.40	0.11	0.46
Italy	6.33	17.51	7.42	19.43	9.52	23.34
Luxembourg	NA	NA	NA	NA	0.10	0.20
Netherlands	6.15	12.05	6.81	13.67	8.50	16.91
Austria	3.25	6.00	3.13	7.26	3.42	7.35
Portugal	0.99	4.19	0.96	4.29	0.97	3.98
Finland	4.09	12.67	4.27	13.72	5.10	14.78
Sweden	2.81	8.48	2.84	9.41	3.21	12.44
United Kingdom	2.52	13.20	3.08	14.95	3.72	15.35
European Union (EU-15)	**62.99**	**149.72**	**62.92**	**152.84**	**71.92**	**169.72**

[*] Eurostat estimate.
[**] German figures are for 1995.
[***] German figures are for gross capacity.
Source: Eurostat 2001.

other major heat producers, one may find the Netherlands and the UK generating respectively about 269 PJ and over 225 PJ from cogeneration.

Finally, the description of the European CHP sector has to include the structure of fuels used in cogeneration. A visible trend was the increase of usage of natural gas, which almost doubled between 1994–1998, and the usage of renewable energy has grown noticeably, whereas solid fuels recorded a decrease (Eurostat 2001, p. 14). The division (into five categories) of fuel consumed in the EU-15 in 1998 is shown in Table 2.4.

The statistics discussed above and below (Tables 2.1–2.4) clearly show that the state-of-the-art cogeneration in Europe in the 1990s was very heterogeneous. One may easily find the leaders of developing combined heat and power (like Denmark, Finland, Germany, or the Netherlands), as well as mark those Member States not giving any real priority to CHP (e.g. Greece or Ireland); although this was not always due to the lack of willingness to support cogeneration. For its development, much depends

Table 2.3 Heat produced in CHP in the European Union (EU-15) between 1994–1998

Member State	CHP heat [PJ] 1994*	1996	1998
Belgium	38.97	32.19	38.03
Denmark	92.39	119.12	119.72
Germany	446.89	362.98	340.76
Greece	5.49	6.61	7.47
Spain	91.51	104.51	141.32
France	116.57	128.79	170.67
Ireland	3.93	5.83	4.86
Italy	253.68	296.27	397.80
Luxembourg	NA	NA	2.20
Netherlands	171.03	206.44	238.77
Austria	79.18	101.64	81.47
Portugal	46.92	48.08	50.80
Finland	256.40	264.24	269.44
Sweden	124.47	138.69	155.75
United Kingdom	174.91	219.02	225.17
European Union (EU-15)	**1,902.32**	**2,034.41**	**2,244.22**

* German figures are for 1995.
Source: Eurostat 2001.

on the conditions affecting its potential. These are, *inter alia*, climate, grid and industrial issues, habits of energy users, and the state of the energy sector (including the state of competition).

Stagnation and decline (1998–2002): how to develop cogeneration?

A year after the elaborated report of Eurostat (2001) was published, the Commission (2002) presented a proposal on the new legislation on combined heat and power. It tried to evaluate a short-range development of cogeneration (1998–2002), also by referring to the material presented by the Eurostat (2001), slightly outdated at that time. Despite treating the figures "with some caution", the Commission managed to provide some general conclusions. In their light:

> [s]ince 1998, the cogeneration sector has reported stagnating or even declining market trends in several EU countries. This lack of progress in promoting new cogeneration [...] to large extent results from the existence of a number of barriers, which hampers the development of cogeneration.
>
> (Commission 2002, p. 7)

Table 2.4 Fuel used in cogeneration in the European Union (EU-15) in 1998

Member State	fuel used for CHP [PJ]	hard coal and lignite	liquid fuels	natural gas	renewables	other fuels*
biggest share: natural gas						
Luxembourg	4.58	NA	0%	100%	NA	NA
Belgium	63.13	6%	12%	72%	8%	2%
Netherlands	561.27	16%	0%	71%	2%	10%
Italy	783.23	1%	15%	68%	NA	16%
Ireland	7.30	31%	7%	55%	0%	7%
Spain	291.87	3%	24%	51%	9%	13%
United Kingdom	370.60	12%	13%	48%	2%	26%
Austria	223.30	12%	14%	46%	16%	12%
France	277.99	7%	13%	38%	33%	9%
biggest share: renewable						
Finland	440.85	27%	2%	24%	43%	3%
Sweden	241.63	12%	16%	5%	55%	12%
biggest share: solid fossil fuels and peat						
Greece	56.61	76%	5%	2%	NA	17%
Germany	606.75	43%	5%	42%	2%	9%
Denmark	364.27	55%	4%	24%	7%	10%
biggest share: liquid fuels						
Portugal	93.92	NA	53%	1%	38%	8%

* Derived gases like refinery gas, coke oven gas, and blast furnace gas make up the majority of the "other fuels".
Source: Eurostat 2001.

These circumstances raise a very basic but fundamental question: how to develop cogeneration? Seemingly simple yet it causes a lot of trouble in finding the right answer, or rather – answers. An attempt to solve it brings forth the need to analyse and consider many factors which determine an operation of CHP (see Chapter 1 of this book). What measures are the most effective to promote the growth of cogeneration? What policy or legal tools should be used? What legal form is the most adequate to support CHP? Which level, national or European, is the right one for the legal or policy approach?

These are just a few issues that are behind the complex matter of developing combined heat and power. The European countries, as well as the European Union as a whole, have significant experience in the development, promotion, and support of CHP. Other countries also enjoy similar experience (e.g. USA). In the next section, I start discussing the main topic of this book: European law and policies on cogeneration. Let us follow them starting from the following subchapter.

The framework for the rational usage of energy and the space for CHP

The potential of cogeneration was first noticed by European policymakers around 50 years ago. As in the USA, its turning point can be placed on the timeline somewhere in the 1970s, when a wider interest in the energy efficiency in Europe was driven by the energy crisis of the 1970s (see Hoerber 2013, p. 148, cf. Lifset 2014, pp. 283–284; Clô 2000, pp. 179–181). In response to the first emerging energy problems, the European leaders, gathered in Paris in October 1972 (Statement from the Paris Summit), urged the institutions of the European Community to elaborate on "an energy policy guaranteeing certain and lasting supplies under satisfactory economic conditions".

This happened almost two years later, after the oil shock caused by the Arab embargo of 1973 (cf. Griffin & Steele 1986, pp. 214–215), when the Commission (1974a) presented a framework for the new energy policy strategy for the Community. Among its aims, a more effective use of energy resources played a vital role being one of the tools "to reduce [Community's] dependence for energy on the rest of the world to the utmost extent possible" (Commission 1974a, p. 1). More efficient use of energy was to lead to an estimated reduction of energy consumption by 10% in 1985. This was combined with a "more rational utilisation of energy", defined as "the reduction of the energy input for the same level of output of useful energy" (Commission 1974a, p. 59),[16] included among those areas of public concern designated to be covered by the Community's incentives for initiating or developing research (Commission 1974b, p. 8).

Apart from the action on research, the Commission called on the public authorities of Member States to prepare and implement measures (e.g. a legal framework, technical norms) aimed at promoting and strengthening rational use of energy. At that time, as a result of energy crises, attention was given to energy resources (so, the primary energy) – the Commission underlined the need for joint action of Member States and the harmonisation of projected measures to prejudice the free movement of goods (energy resources) in the common market (Commission 1974a, p. 60). However, this does not downgrade the importance of the rationalisation of consumption of the final energy, as well as its generation. Among the areas which needed the first actions of the Community, the Commission (1974a, p. 62) listed for example minimising heat losses in new buildings (mainly by using better insulation and energy-efficient appliances), applying heat recovery (both in the housing and industrial sectors), and using "combined production powers" in the energy sector.

The Community's energy saving objective for 1985

In September 1974, the Council – recognising the line drawn during the Paris Summit in 1972 and the previously mentioned energy policy framework offered two years later by the Commission – adopted the guidelines on energy efficiency (cf. Solorio, Mischa, & Popartan 2013, p. 95). With respect to energy demand, the Council (1974a) announced a "reduction of the rate of growth of internal consumption by measures for using energy rationally and economically without jeopardizing social and economic growth objectives", as stated in its resolution. Three months later, in December 1974, another resolution concerning energy efficiency was passed by the Council. Motivated by the growth of prices of energy resources, the Council (1974b) called for improving the energy performance "by reducing losses and gradually eliminating non-essential consumption", providing a field for exchange of information and measures planned at the national and European level to rationalise the use of energy (see Volpe 2012, p. 444).

Moreover, the Council (1974b) adopted a new Community energy saving objective for 1985, i.e. the level of energy consumption which was 15% lower than the level projected by the Commission in January 1973 (see Commission 1974b, p. 3), granting some flexibility for the Member States in reaching this goal on the one hand, and reserving the right to introduce separate, short-term energy savings objectives on the other hand. The background for the 15% reduction goal was a revision of the Commission's energy policy framework for 1985 presented in November 1974 (Commission 1974c), covering a programme for the rational use of energy. As the Commission (1974c, p. 8) explained:

> [t]his programme is to be achieved, on the one hand, by cooperation of Member States in the exchange of information and experience and rigorous analysis of problems and, on the other hand, by the coordination – and as far is necessary by the harmonization – of national measures, at least to the extent necessary for the functioning of the common market. In addition, important results for the economy of energy could be obtained by Community research and development actions, and technical innovation.

The programme was designed to achieve the reduction of energy consumption of the Community (see Knodt 2018, p. 228) – but without hindering the economic and social development in Europe (Commission

1974c, p. 8); in a way, in this approach one can find the foundations for the postulate of zero-energy growth (cf. Jorgenson 1986, p. 8; Stewart 1981, pp. 37–42). Although not fully included in that policy framework, CHP, as high-efficient energy units, fell within its scope. Fortunately, improvements of this situation came very soon. It was the result of the experts' discussions delivered at different levels of the Community.

In the December 1974 document, the Council noted the Commission's idea of bringing together a "Steering and Coordinating Committee for the Rational Utilization of Energy", whose members, being national experts delegated by the Member States, were to exchange information and consult each other on the lessons learnt about the rational use of energy, discussing the general outlines of future measures in this respect. In May 1976, the Council adopted the Commission's proposals on the rational use of energy, including the recommendations for heating, noticing the possibility of achieving substantial short-term energy savings in the heating systems of buildings. One year later, in May 1977, the Commission announced its plans to submit a new series of proposals to the Council. Apart from the energy labels and standards for measuring electric consumption by household devices, the Commission (1977) announced solutions proposed for "the removal of legal or administrative barriers to the development of combined heat and power production". This declaration was realised in the following year – in October 1977 the Council passed its Recommendation 77/714/EEC on advisory bodies to promote combined heat and power (Hopkins 1981, p. 141).

US regulatory benchmark: Public Utility Regulatory Policies Act and beyond

However, the European "broader way" was not as wide as in the USA, where a complex legislation on energy efficiency, including the promotion of combined heat and power (see Yüzügüllü 2013) was established with passing PURPA in 1978. This legislation was a part of the comprehensive action on energy sector. Passed along with the Energy Tax Act of 1978 (ETA), the National Energy Conservation Policy Act (NECPA), the Power Plant and Industrial Fuel Use Act of 1978 (FUA), and the Natural Gas Policy Act of 1978 (NGPA), it created a framework of the National Energy Act of 1978 (Charo, Stearns, & Mallory 1986, p. 449). All of the above-mentioned Acts, except ETA, concerned the strengthening of cogeneration, including the elimination of institutional barriers to its development; FUA prohibited electric utilities and major industries from using oil or natural gas as the primary fuel in any new installations, at the same time authorising the conversion to other fuels where feasible; NGPA gave power to the Federal Energy Regulatory Commission (FERC) to exempt some CHP units from the provisions on incremental pricing;

NECPA provided grants for CHP projects, and last but not least, PURPA created a legal environment for the promotion of cooperation between public utilities and the cogeneration sector (Charo, Stearns, & Mallory 1986, pp. 449–450).[17]

The major issues tackled by PURPA were energy conservation and energy efficiency, which were to be improved by PURPA's legal solutions including those promoting cogeneration (Cudahy 1995, 421). Additionally, it addressed decentralisation of energy production and new small-scale energy technologies – what Fox-Penner (1990, p. 520) calls "a vertical disintegration" brought by this legislation, with a certain role performed by CHP. Sec. 210 of PURPA proves it, as cogeneration is covered there alongside small generators of electricity. From this perspective, PURPA introduced a regulatory regime to promote cogeneration (and electricity production at a smaller scale), where FERC has played an important role, prescribing and revising rules on the purchase of electricity from cogeneration and small generators by the utilities. These rules were to assure that the rates offered by the utilities to purchase electric energy from any qualifying cogeneration (or small generators) were to be "just and reasonable to the electric consumers" and non-discriminatory in reference to those CHP units or small power producers (Sec. 210(b)). Moreover, these rules could not deliver rates exceeding "the incremental cost to the electric utility of alternative electric energy".[18] FERC has also been entitled to facilitate a connection of combined heat and power with small energy sources to the energy utility's grid (by issuing an order), although, as set in Sec. 202 of PURPA, some criteria had to be met, *inter alia*, it had to be "in the public interest", or had to improve energy efficiency, energy conservation, or the reliability of the utility's energy system.

Additionally, after PURPA's entry into force, FERC adopted regulations on electric utilities and qualifying facilities concerning the previously mentioned connection to the grid and electricity purchase along with its regulations on utilities – facilities' arrangements regarding wheeling[19] and the sale of electricity.[20] Those regulations introduced certain obligations imposed upon the electric utilities, which covered, *inter alia*, purchasing electricity from qualifying facilities and selling it to them, connecting these facilities and wheeling electricity from them, as well as a duty to operate simultaneously with the qualifying facility; this framework was supplemented with other requirements and standards, e.g. the standards of a state public utility commission to determine the rate payable to a qualifying facility for electricity (Martin 1983, pp. 164–166). Such legal environment, where federal law and state authorities were engaged, has created uncertainty, a "grey area" which was "used by utilities and regulators to hamper the implementation of the PURPA goals", as reported by Martin (1983, p. 167).

Moreover, soon after its enactment, PURPA was challenged by lawsuits (*FERC v. Mississippi* and *American Electric Power Service Corp. v. FERC*) reaching high court's instances, including the Supreme Court, but the verdicts affirmed PURPA's provisions (Charo, Stearns, & Mallory 1986, pp. 454–455). However, these court cases delayed the implementation of PURPA in many states – only 16 states met the deadline to implement the regulations within one year after they entered into force, and the partial legal coverage lasted until January 1986 when all states adopted the necessary rules (Charo, Stearns, & Mallory 1986, p. 460). As a result of those delays, in the short run, it was hard to assess the overall impact of PURPA on the qualified facilities, including cogeneration; however, using the statistics of the US Department of Energy (DOE), provided by Charo, Stearns & Mallory (1986, pp. 461–462), a growth in the CHP projects can be noted – it increased by more than 16% in 1984, reaching more than 3,600 potential plants in 1985 and contributing about 7% of the US electricity production capacity at the end of 1984.[21]

European cooperative and informative approach

In comparison to the US experiences, with the passing of Recommendation 77/714/EEC, the Community officially acknowledged (no more and no less) a role performed by CHP in enhancing energy efficiency, or in "a more rational use of energy", as it was called in the 1970s. By encouraging Member States to establish expert bodies to promote CHP (Gochenour 2001, p. 18), the Community has addressed the matter of cogeneration at the European level in a broader way for the first time (cf. Van Oostvoorn et al., 2003, p. 5) – the panels were responsible for giving opinions on incentives that could support CHP in accordance with the Community law on competition and state aid, as set in Article 92 of the Treaty establishing the European Economic Community.

Besides, the Council (1977) noticed comprehensive problems of different character (economic, technical, legal) faced by CHP (together with the difficulties of using residual heat in the industry, electricity sector, as well as in the remote systems of heat supply). Solving them required both local, regional, and national action; to find remedies for the local and regional level, the Council proposed a top-down approach, encouraging the exchange of information on the matters related to CHP usage (and residual heat), with cooperation at the national and Community level. To tackle these issues, the Council (1977) recommended developing the expert dialogue on CHP. It paved the way for the already-mentioned advisory panels aimed at discussing all the measures necessary to increase the energy efficiency in supplying heat.[22]

One of the listed measures was "making greater use of combined heat and power production"; however, the Council also addressed the issues of concentrating the generation of heat or increasing the thermal efficiency of power units (by using residual heat produced there). In practice, the measures to increase energy efficiency in the heating industry could cover general issues, like strengthening the collaboration between energy producers and industrial consumers of heat, reviewing (but also eliminating) legal, administrative, and price barriers in the development of CHP, and providing better information to small and medium-sized industrial enterprises, as well as specific steps such as reserving the sites where industrial facilities and CHP plants could be built in proximity (Council 1977).

The role of the Member States (apart from establishing the previously discussed advisory panels) was to initiate and promote technical and economic research to identify new remote heat supplies and promote the development of existing district and industrial heating systems. The research was to be "economically viable", and the promotion of heating system conducted "where justified" (Council 1977). Finally, in its 1977 statement, the Council suggested to the Member States that they should inform the Commission regularly about any measures taken in this field, and present any results achieved or envisaged on the basis of these measures.

The Community's initial programmes on combined heat and power

In the 1980s, the Commission recognised cogeneration as a formidable mean of saving energy, reaching 30–44% of energy savings in comparison to the separate generation of the same volume of heat and electricity (1982c, p. 11). Because of its high energy conversion efficiency, a wider use of CHP in the Community could have led to saving an extra 10 Mtoe in primary energy if the industrial cogeneration capacity was doubled (Commission 1986, p. 13). As it was declared "[a]chieving this aim will demand a resolute policy approach in view of the present obstacles in most Community countries to any extension in CHP such as the terms for taking surplus electricity or for obtaining emergency power" (Commission 1986, p. 13).

Nevertheless, the cogeneration itself was to change. As it was based on conventional technologies, mainly oil as the fuel, it was exposed to the effects of rapid price jumps on the oil markets, like those during the oil crisis of the 1970s (cf. Bohi 1991; McKay & Rabl 1985). These circumstances made it necessary to establish new priorities for CHP, particularly for larger units. They were based on three main directions: the reduction of used oil products, growth in the alternative energy sources and the promotion of waste-to-energy (both waste heat[23] and waste as a fuel), as well as the adoption of technologies with higher energy performance (Commission 1982c, p. 14). Apart from that, the Commission

(1982c, p. 14) insisted on providing heat systems and cogeneration with an "institutional innovation", promoted with the use of different legal and administrative means, including new policies established for the heat market (technological innovation was its benchmark).

In February 1982 the Commission (1982a) presented its action programme on the investments in the rational use of energy, covering measures to overcome the obstacles hindering those kinds of investments. Among the tools for improving the "general context in which decisions to invest in the rational use of energy are taken", an interesting postulate on decentralising the decision-making process was included (Commission 1982a, p. 24). In many points it matches with the development of CHP, where the local and regional approach is needed. As the Commission (1982a, p. 24) reported, the local and regional communities are particularly well-suited to:

(i) suggest[ing] ways of adapting aid schemes to local conditions (environment, climate, consumers' habits);
(ii) helping to work out energy balances;
(iii) informing local authorities, firms, and individuals of the action open to them, and setting up education and information programmes aimed at the public and heads of industry with the support of local authorities, the general public and people engaged in the occupations and trades concerned;
(iv) list[ing] the resources which are not properly exploited (natural resources, heat, etc.);
(v) encourage[ing] the exploitation of [the] local alternative energy resources (biomass, solar energy, geothermal energy and small heads of water);
(vi) encourage[ing] local transport projects and better use of equipment, and generally any measures likely to reduce wastage;
(vii) tak[ing] steps to promote projects to recover heat, to set up and extend district heating networks and to recycle energy-rich materials.

This framework provided a fertile ground for further action with respect to cogeneration. It stems from its character and features. CHP is related to local conditions of environment, climate, consumers' habits it can fulfil local energy needs, it has the possibility to use local energy resources like biomass, wastes, or geothermal energy, and finally, it acts locally, cooperates with local authorities, companies, and individuals, sets up education and information campaigns, etc. In this context, the Commission (1982a, p. 25) encouraged Member States to open their markets for private capital, giving more freedom for the implementation of private projects in the field of cogeneration as well as electricity.

Moreover, in 1986 the Community adopted its new energy policy objectives for 1995 (Council 1986), setting horizontal goals with energy savings and the rational use of energy among them, where improving energy efficiency was qualified as one of the "balanced solutions as regards energy and the environment". In addition, the Community's sectoral objectives on energy were established (see Haghighi 2007, p. 61), with the focus on energy efficiency among them. As the Council decided, the efficiency of final energy in demand per unit of gross national product was to be improved by 1995 by at least 20%. Despite being only indicative guidelines, the goals' quantitative nature could support the evaluation of the convergence and cohesion of the energy policies of Member States between 1986 and 1995, as the Council (1986) underlined.

Renewable-Waste-Cogeneration auto-producers

This pro-efficiency approach resulted in greater consideration of CHP in the Community's policy. Cogeneration, addressed by the Community briefly in the mid-1980s (see Commission 1986), found broader coverage in November 1988, when the Council adopted its Recommendation 88/611/EEC. Dedicated to the promotion of cooperation between public utilities and auto-producers of electricity, Recommendation 88/611/EEC included the Council's focus on CHP driven by its shared potential[24] of making "an important contribution to the achievement of the Community's 1995 energy policy objectives". Within this scope, cogeneration was grouped together with renewable energy sources and waste energy in the category of RWC auto-producers (Renewable-Waste-Cogeneration) for which the Council intended to provide a regulatory environment (Gochenour 2001, p. 18). To strengthen the position of RWC auto-producers, the Council (1988) called on the Member States to establish the conditions for their cooperation with public utilities, including the quantity and price of electricity exchange. In this context, the Member States were advised to prepare the criteria for a standard contract between RWC auto-producers and public utilities, as the profitability of auto-production depended on the conditions of cooperation between these entities, which, along with the national law and administrative procedures, could hinder the development of RWC auto-generation (Council 1988).

The right direction for breaking up the monopolistic structure of the energy market, introducing new technologies in the sector, as well as promoting highly-efficient and local sources, was limited by the public approach that was still preferred at the Community level. The Council (1988) recommended that the Member States should, first, oblige their public utilities to offer the purchase of electricity generated by the RWC auto-producers, providing that this did not hinder a "smooth economic operation" of the public power plants, and second, that auto-production should be allowed until a "public interest [was] not ... infringed [being] impeded neither by legal and administrative provisions nor by conditions imposed by the public utilities". Regardless of this public priority, Recommendation 88/611/EEC gave a field for obtaining reimbursement for electricity sold by the RWC auto-producers to the public grid, designed to be as "transparent as possible". This was to be related, *inter alia*, to the average supply costs avoided by the public utilities in the long term, being linked to the savings made by these utilities in the costs of fuel, and guaranteeing the RWC auto-producers an extra reimbursement so far as they allowed the public grid to save the investment costs associated with the generation or purchase of electricity[25] (Council 1988).

The approach offered by the Council (1988) was to be introduced either at a contract level, i.e. voluntarily, by the concerned parties themselves (RWC auto-producer and the public utility), or by a Member State, with the use of legal or administrative tools; the Community's countries were to report to the Commission the progress reached on the matter of this cooperation after three years, in 1991. Apart from that, voluntary environmental agreements could be used as measures to develop cogeneration in the Community (cf. ten Brink 2017; van Dril 2005). Under this framework certain actions to promote CHP were conducted in various Member States: the Netherlands and Ireland developed industrial cogeneration, Denmark offered conversion of district heating installations to CHP), Italy increased auto-production (Commission 1992, p. 10).

However, some experts (Mors 1991, p. 66) noted the lack of incentives to allow the independent sources of electricity supply (like CHP in industry) access to the distribution grid of energy utilities. Even the Commission (1990b, p. 22) itself announced the targeting of commercial and structural obstacles to the development of energy production in cogeneration; if any such obstacles appeared, the Member States would have been requested to tackle them. Moreover, a legislative action on CHP was planned to be delivered in the first half of 1992 (Commission 1990b, p. 32). Finally, cogeneration – declared "[a] vital source of energy savings" – received financial support at the Community level (Commission 1990b, p. 22) at the turn of the 1980s and 1990s. This was done through the Community's action where the specific financial programmes were to play a crucial role.

The Joule, Thermie, and SAVE programmes

In May 1988, the Commission published a review of the energy policies of the Member States. Its axis was the evaluation of the Community's energy objectives for 1995. This report revealed difficulties in reaching the 20% saving by 1995. Between 1973 and 1982 energy efficiency in the Community was improved by 20%, in contrast to around 2% between

1982 and 1986; the past positive development slowed down drastically, not continuing in the direction set for 1995, making the achievement of the 20% savings in the final energy demand "unlikely" (Commission 1988, pp. 4–5). "If no new policy measures are introduced at Community and/or national level it now seems to be clear that the achievement of a minimum 20% energy efficiency improvement by 1995 will not be realized", the Commission (1988, p. 6) assessed. In response to this call, the Community quite soon elaborated on new financial initiatives. These were, among others, the Joule, Thermie, and SAVE programmes (see Paterson 1993).

Motivated by the goal of strengthening the scientific and technological capacity of industry in Europe, and enhancing its competitiveness in the world the Council (1989a) established the Joule (Joint Opportunities for Unconventional or Long-term Energy supply) programme by passing the Decision 89/236/EEC. The programme could be linked with a bigger energy policy agenda offered in the 1980s by the Community when, *inter alia*, Regulation 3640/85/EEC on the promotion, by financial support, of demonstration projects and industrial pilot projects in the energy field, was adopted (see Morris, Boehm, & Geller 1991, p. 55). Under this Regulation, the Community was able to grant financial support for "demonstration projects", also those leading to substantial energy savings. Among them one could find energy saving applications for the energy industry, which enabled developing solutions for CHP ("[m]ore efficient methods of producing heat and/or electricity for collective use; methods exploiting residual heat in district heating systems; demonstration of new district heating concepts"). Apart from that, Regulation 3640/85/EEC provided a separate space for substituting the use of hydrocarbons in the heating sector.[26]

Granted 122 million ECU, the Joule programme was to develop energy technologies falling within the Community's energy strategy (see Clément et al. 2002; Fraenkel 2006; Gaudiosi 1999; Infield 1994). Its goals included increasing the security of energy supplies by reducing energy imports, "bearing in mind the environment" ("a research effort to reduce significantly nuisance and pollution caused by the production and use of energy"). This involved, among others, increasing the capacity of renewable energy sources and improving energy efficiency together with the rationalisation of energy usage. The way to achieve the assumed goals was seen in techniques, processes, products, and models developed and made available for the needs of the Community's energy and environmental agenda.

The Joule programme covered shared financing (50% as a rule) of the costs incurred while conducting activities by many of the programme's participants selected in an official call: enterprises, research institutions, universities, as well as individuals, or a partnership of these entities, if formed in the Community. Exceptionally, 100% of additional costs involved in the realisation of selected project were incurred by universities and research institutions.

Another Community initiative to support energy efficiency was the Thermie programme (Council 1990). Rooted in the philosophy of "no relaxation of efforts to diversify the Community's energy supply and improve energy efficiency" expressed in a preamble to Council Regulation No 2008/90, the programme began supporting the development of innovative energy technologies because of their economic and social benefits,[27] but also environmental welfare. With respect to the latter, energy technology had "a key role to play in meeting the ecological challenge by increasing energy efficiency, developing new and renewable sources and ensuring the clean use of solid fuels" (Council 1990).

The Thermie programme, with 350 million ECU deemed necessary for its implementation between 1990 and 1992, started financing projects aimed at advancing, implementing, and/or promoting innovative energy technologies within four areas: the rational use of energy, renewable energy sources, solid fuels, and hydrocarbons. Financial support under the programme was set at the maximum level of 40% of the eligible cost for the innovatory projects,[28] or 35% in case of dissemination projects.[29] It could also be granted for developing cogeneration – CHP was broadly covered by the first of above mentioned areas, i.e. the rational use of energy, defined as leading "to substantial energy savings". Within this area, four other categories (sectors) were distinguished ("buildings", "industry", "energy industry, electricity and heat", and "transport"); cogeneration projects could be financed under two of them ("buildings" together with "industry, electricity and heat"). These were the actions aimed at enhancing the energy efficiency in buildings by a more efficient use of heat from CHP plants, projects applying small-scale cogeneration, as well as initiatives designed to produce heat and electricity in a more effective way.

Just over a year after the Thermie initiative (October 1991), the SAVE (Specific Actions for Vigorous Energy Efficiency) programme was established. By referring to Decision 89/364/EEC (Council 1989b) it combined, but also broadened, the financial framework for enhancing energy efficiency, including cogeneration. Having a five-year timeline, its implementation was estimated at 35 million ECU, with four categories of actions on energy efficiency financed under it. These were the technical assessments of data needed to define technical standards and specifications as well as three types of measures: first, to support Member States in the development or creation of energy efficiency infrastructure; second, to create an information network to promote the coordination of national, Community, and international activities on energy efficiency (and to assess their impact); third, to implement the programme for improving the efficiency of electricity use as set by Decision 89/364/EEC. The last measure expressed the previously mentioned fusion of an earlier Community's action on energy efficiency, by providing financing in five areas related to enhancing energy efficiency: consumer information,[30] technical advice,[31] the efficiency of electrical appliances and equipment,[32] demonstration,[33] and studies and other support activities.[34] The level of funding for those areas differed: conducting technical assessment was fully financed by the Community, the first and second group of measures were granted 30% – 50% funding (the rest could be paid either by Member States, public-private partnership, or solely privately funded) – exceptionally this level could reach 60%, whereas the third category of measures (those listed in Decision 89/364/EEC) was to be financed at a level determined individually, depending on the type of each measure.

These areas, being quite broad in their approach to energy efficiency gave possibilities for financing projects focused on cogeneration (due to its pro-energy-efficiency nature). Nevertheless, CHP was also directly addressed by the SAVE programme. As previously mentioned, the programme granted support to development or creation of energy efficiency infrastructure. Apart from training and information activities dedicated to the final energy consumers, it included supporting pilot projects for which the Annex to Decision 91/565/EEC was the benchmark. It was because of the Annex's nature – it attached an "[i]llustrative, non-limitative list of sectoral pilot projects" on energy efficiency to the Council Decision (1991). The exemplary list contained the following initiatives:

1. Pilot studies on least cost planning and demand side management;
2. Feasibility studies on cogeneration projects involving institutional or organizational innovations;
3. Sectoral targeting and monitoring of energy efficiency;
4. Sectoral audits;
5. Pilot projects in the transport sector, e.g. improving traffic flow in towns, toll systems, etc.;
6. Pilot projects on third-party financing within the framework of the European network for third-party financing (Community participation in the direct financing of an investment is ruled out).

Cogeneration, addressed directly with respect to feasibility studies of CHP projects, could also be financed within other pro-energy-efficiency areas listed in the SAVE programme. The assessments aimed at defining technical standards specifications, and measures to develop or create the infrastructure energy efficiency, and establishing the information network could also cover the action on CHP. Additionally, some areas for improving the efficiency of electricity, recognised by Decision 89/364/EEC, could be used for the needs of promoting CHP (e.g. consumer information on electricity produced in cogeneration; the same applies to demonstration, studies and other support activities referring to electricity generated in CHP).

Evaluation of the 1990s' financial initiatives on cogeneration

The financial initiatives, discussed in the section above, gave more possibilities for gathering extra resources for building the capacity of cogeneration in the Community. In 1991, the contracts financed under the Joule programme were summarised by the Commission; actions on CHP were also included in this list.[35] Four years later the Commission (1995b) assessed the application of the Thermie programme (which completed the Joule programme's focus on a basic research with market implementation). Although it was a quite an early evaluation (some projects, supported in 1994, have just started), the programme's direct results were regarded as "satisfactory", with a "potentially sizeable" impact on energy supply and demand, having an environmental impact (with respect to the rationalisation of energy usage and support of renewable energy sources), being "very significant if a replication rate close to the potential rate is achieved", and being "particularly significant" for the economic development and international cooperation[36] (Commission 1995b, pp. 1a–1b).

On the one hand, the steps taken in the framework of the Thermie programme showed how CHP could be successfully applied – many of the actions concerned Central and Eastern Europe, as having "a big potential for converting heat only boiler systems to cogeneration systems in district heating, and for small decentralised cogeneration schemes" (Commission 1995b, p. 39). Moreover, initiatives such as PHARE and TACIS covered the activities promoting energy efficiency and CHP in Central and Eastern European Countries and the New Independent States (Commission 1997, p. 5); in Eastern Europe the pro-cogeneration move was steered by a big potential for converting heat systems to cogeneration systems in district heating, and for small decentralised CHP (Commission 1995b, p. 39).

On the other hand, despite including CHP among the Community's main sectorial areas of interest (as in the SAVE programme),[37] the reality has shown low interest in cogeneration projects (cf. Michaelowa 1998, p. 154). This was regardless of the Commission's (1995a, p. 14) declarations to continue the pilot actions in these fields (also with respect to cogeneration) to establish a more comprehensive approach and to delve into specific issues of the main areas (e.g. "how to overcome the barriers to cogeneration"). In fact, between 1991 and 1994 cogeneration accounted only for a 6% share of the programme's funding, where a few direct projects on cogeneration (i.e. 12 out of 203 in total) were conducted under the SAVE programme (Commission 1995a, pp. 23–24).

It is not without significance that the projects implemented in the field of cogeneration in the 1990s were conducted in the already changing legal environment. The Community, or the European Union, established in 1993 with the entry into force of the Maastricht Treaty, driven by the spirit of liberalisation, launched the first stage of the energy market reform. Covering electricity and gas, it also concerned heat, and cogeneration.

Notes

1 In the same year Consolidated Edison bought the New York Steam Company and entered the district heating sector (Wooster 1983, p. 706).
2 The surpluses were usually sold in the same block, which gave rise to the term "block plant" (Wooster 1983, p. 706).
3 This was possible in 1903 with the application of a turbogenerator in the energy industry (Charo, Stearns, & Mallory 1986, p. 450). As Claire A. Wooster (1983, p. 707) writes:

> [t]hese new units could send steam through a turbine to produce mechanical energy that then was converted into electricity by a directly connected generator. This development produced huge economies in electric power generation, but also reduced the quality of the steam emerging as a waste product.

4 The Third Revision of the Energy Programme adopted by the federal government in November 1981 provided new financial support of 1–2 billion DM over five years for the development of district heating, with federal and lander governments paying half of the share (Commission 1984b, p. 74).
5 VEAG, which owned and managed almost all electricity generation and transmission in former East Germany, was controlled by western Germany energy companies, including the second largest German energy company, i.e. Preussen-Electra (Hvelplund & Lund 1998, pp. 542–543). Regarding the third and fourth issue, as Hvelplund and Lund (1998) outline:

> [the West] German power companies and the DDR Government obliged the East German power distribution companies to buy at least 70% of their electricity sales from the company organizing the centralized and brown coal based power production VEAG. In this way the market of independent power production was limited. ...
> In the ... agreement from January 1996 between the regional governments, the central government and the power companies cross subsidization mechanisms were established as "barriers to entry" against independent power producers, for instance decentralized cogeneration based power production. In this agreement the German minister of industry stated, that VEAG was allowed to use 150 million DM annually to lower the prices in competitive market segments. The 150 million DM came from customers from market segments with no price competition.

6 One may also find some criticism related to the development of Danish CHP. This concerns the direction chosen by the government. According to Henrik Lund (1999, p. 118) "the expansion of decentralized cogeneration was delayed for several years because the potential was considered too small to motivate development".
7 For example, the connection of glasshouses to district heating systems was supported with certain aid in Denmark (Commission 1982b, Annex, p. 4).
8 For example, in a study on the Italian pulp and paper industry Comodi et al. (2013, p. 342) proves that 55 of 61 Italian CHP plants surveyed by them were installed from 1991 to 2010, so after the introduction of the first incentive mechanism (1992).
9 Maximum 10,000 GBP, offered under the Energy Survey Scheme.

10 To show the scale of the development of combined heat and power in Poland, let us mention two examples, Łódź and Upper Silesia. In Łódź, the first CHP plant Łódź I was built in 1959 (modernisation of old power plant), and three new big CHP plants were constructed in 1961 (Łódź II), 1968 (Łódź III), and 1977 (Łódź IV); new CHP plants were also built in Upper Silesia (Bielsko I, Bielsko II and Katowice), and numerous power plants were upgraded to cogeneration, e.g. Szombierki, Chorzów, Zabrze, Będzin, or Miechowice (WEC 2014, p. 186).

11 By referring to COGEN Romania's statistics, Flavius Iacobescu & Viorel Badescu (2011, p. 275) summarised that:

> [i]n 2002 in Romania were in operation 184 DH systems, which provided heat for 2,696,000 apartments. From a total of 57.6 TWh of electricity produced in 2003 about 16% were produced by cogeneration. (…)
> Between 2003 and 2004 over 40 DH systems were switched off. In 2004 the vast majority of localities with less than 20,000 inhabitants were no longer provided with DH systems (…). In the same year, the number of larger localities provided with DH was 129 (i.e. 70% of the 184 systems operating in 2002). About 60% of these heating systems were assisted by cogeneration systems.

12 It was the "National Strategy on the heating supply of localities through district generation and distribution systems".

13 Iacobescu & Badescu (2011, p. 275) record that during the period of 2006–2010 581,000 apartments (21% of households) have been disconnected from the district heating in Romania, but this process slowed in the beginning of 2010, with 92 district heating systems operated (serving about 5,500,000 people, i.e. 24% of Romania population), including 20 representing cogeneration.

14 Austria, Finland, and Sweden acceded to the European Union on 1 January 1995.

15 10.9% (Eurostat 2001, p. 7).

16 As the Commission (1974, p. 59) explained, "the reduction of the utilisation of useful energy is not intended; this energy being necessary for economic and social development. On the contrary, our concern is with the better use of available energy".

17 Charo, Stearns, and Mallory (1986, p. 453) review the major obstacle to cogeneration (along with small energy generators), which were to be removed by PURPA, i.e.:

1) the unwillingness of utilities to purchase the electric output of cogenerators and small power producers,
2) the likelihood that utilities would charge discriminatorily high rates for the back-up power required by these producers, and
3) the risk that cogenerators and small producers which provide electricity to a utility's grid would be subjected to regulation as an electric utility.

18 The PURPA's Sec. 210d defined "incremental cost of alternative electric energy" as "the cost to the electric utility of the electric energy which, but for the purchase from [a qualifying] cogenerator or small power producer, such utility would generate or purchase from another source".

19 "Wheeling", as Martin (1983, p. 161) explains, is the transfer of electricity by a utility from the producer of the electricity to another utility that is buying the power from the producer. If the producer is not within the area of service of the purchasing utility, FERC may order a utility between the producer and purchaser to wheel, or transfer, the power to the purchaser.

20 18 CFR §§ 292.301–292.308, 1982.

46 *First policy actions on combined heat and power*

21 For example, between 1980–1983, approximately half of the filings came from California. Florida, Tennesse, and Virginia were behind it, although they were not as developed in these terms (two-thirds of total submissions were from California, Florida, Tennesse, and Virginia combined), and with respect to a rated capacity, Texas and Massachusetts together with California were to produce two-thirds of the total capacity offered by these new energy producers (Charo, Stearns, & Mallory 1986, p. 462).
22 The advisory panels were to cooperate with each other at the Community level, mainly by exchanging their experiences; the Commission was to organise this process (Council 1977).
23 The Commission (1982c, p. 14) emphasised the need for finding financial solutions for using waste heat, which requires heat to be transported over long distances and stored for an extended period of time.
24 Shared with the use of residual heat.
25 The reimbursement amount depended on how regular the generation of electricity by the auto-producer was, especially during peaks (Council 1988).
26 The list of eligible areas of application under Regulation 3640/85/EC included demonstration projects in the field of heat transmission, distribution, and storage of heat produced mainly from energy sources other than hydrocarbons. This covered:

- [h]eat transmission over medium and long distances in industry and district heating systems;
- [m]ore efficient and more economic heat-distribution techniques;
- [n]ew heat-storage techniques (daily, weekly, and seasonal accumulators) in industry and district heating systems;
- [d]emonstration of new demand-management methods in district heating systems.

27 As the Council (1990) highlighted, "the promotion of projects for exploiting the indigenous energy potential of the regions, particularly less-developed regions, will help to strengthen the economic and social cohesion of the Community".
28 According to Article 2(2)(a) of Council Regulation (EEC) No 2008/90 the "innovatory projects" were:

> projects designed to advance or implement innovatory techniques, processes or products for which the research and development stage has for the most part been completed, or new applications of established techniques, processes or products ... [being] designed to prove the technical and economic viability of new technologies by applying them on a sufficiently large scale for the first time.

29 As defined in Article 2(2)(b) of Council Regulation (EEC) No 2008/90 the "dissemination projects" were:

> projects designed to promote with a view to their broader utilization within the Community, either under different economic or geographical conditions or with technical modifications, innovatory techniques, processes or products which have already been applied once but, owing to residual risk, have not yet penetrated the market.

30 Consumer information covered:

    -   action to improve the quality and availability of information to electricity consumers and equipment specifiers concerning the efficiency of electrical appliances and equipment and their efficient use;
    -   provision of information by electricity distributors, consumer organizations and, where appropriate, by governments, including more detailed information about tariffs, metering and accounts;
    -   most effective use of all media for disseminating information;
    -   provision by manufacturers of data relating to appliance and equipment efficiency, including improvement of the labelling system;
    -   use of appropriate databases;
    -   adoption of directives by the competent authorities, in this context, regarding the provision of information to the consumer.

    (Council 1989b)

31 Technical advice, understood as "[a]ction to ensure that technical advice on the purchase, installation and use of the most efficient electrical appliances and equipment is readily available to electricity consumers", included:

    -   action by electricity distributors, consumer organizations and Member State governments to ensure that advice is available to consumers on the purchase, installation and use of the most efficient electrical appliances and equipment possible;
    -   action by professional institutions concerned with the specification and installation of electrical equipment to ensure that their members are adequately informed on the efficient use of electricity, the aim being to safeguard consumer interests while protecting the interests of the Community as a whole.

    (Council 1989b)

32 The efficiency of electrical appliances and equipment, together with the action to improve the market share of the most energy-efficient products covered:

    -   the establishment of cooperation between manufacturers to improve the efficiency of appliances and equipment and in particular the fitting of thermostats to all electrical equipment with a heating element;
    -   efforts to increase the market penetration of efficient appliances and equipment including examination of the potential of selective financial intervention and particularly of third-party financing;
    -   action by official authorities to ensure that, in all activities which they are responsible for and in all buildings they own or occupy, including street-lighting, electrical appliances and equipment are of high efficiency and efficiently operated;
    -   examination by the Commission of how it can promote the effectiveness of the Programme at Community level, to supplement the activities of the Member States under the Programme both by coordination and by promoting harmonization of product information regarding the (energy) performance of appliances and equipment and the development of European product standards on performance and energy consumption;
    -   examination of the possibilities for electronic control of domestic and industrial electricity consumption, by use of remote reading and control microprocessors;
    -   examination of a more comprehensive system of metering and signalling that would be more accessible to the consumer, enabling him to act promptly in cases of excessive consumption.

    (Council 1989b)

48 *First policy actions on combined heat and power*

33 Demonstration, as defined by the Council (1989b), was an "[a]ction in conjunction, where necessary, with other existing programmes, to ensure that the demonstration of new, more efficient appliances, equipment and technologies is adequately supported, and that information thereon is disseminated throughout the Community".
34 These were the actions "to analyse factors determining the efficiency of electricity use and to identify areas in which additional measures might effectively be taken; other studies and information seminars".
35 Among them one can mention such projects as "Simulation and control of fast transients in process and utility systems", "European wind power integration study: the Dutch contribution", or "Biomass turbine for cogeneration (BTC) — Assessment study and pilot project" (see Commission 1991, pp. 91, 229, 403).
36 It was the result of the following considerations:

- the direct investments of the Community in advanced and efficient technologies having an impact on industrial "competitivity";
- the promotion and dissemination of technologies and information about these technologies throughout the Community, including the less-favoured regions, directly affecting economic and social cohesion;
- the setting-up of an industrial network for international cooperation between large companies and especially SMEs [small and medium-sized enterprises] which, by virtue of the Thermie programme, have had access to advanced technologies;
- the strengthening of cooperation with third countries specifically through associated measures and more particularly with the Eastern European countries, whose energy potential is a matter of prime concern in tomorrow's European energy scenario.

(Commission 1995, p. 1b)

37 Among them, apart from cogeneration were: education and training, integrated resource planning, transport, buildings, as well as monitoring and targeting (Commission 1995a, p. 14).

References

American Electric Power Service Corp. v. FERC [American Electric Power Service Corporation, et al., Petitioners, v. Federal Energy Regulatory Commission, Respondent, Elizabethtown Gas Company, American Paper Institute, Inc., Brooklyn Union Gasco., Occidental Geothermal, inc., Intervenors], 675 F.2d 1226, DC Cir., 1982.

ABB. 2011, *Italy: energy efficiency report*. Available from: www04.abb.com/global/seitp/seitp202.nsf/0/1d7e77cc97ad7390c1257912002e9dff/$file/Italy_EnergyEfficiencyReport.pdf [27 February 2019].

Babus'Haq, R.F., & Probert, S.D. 1996, "Combined heat-and-power implementation in the UK: past, present and prospective developments", *Applied Energy*, 53(1–2), pp. 47–76.

Benkő, I., Járy, K., Molnár, J., Péter, E., Lorek, S., & Trotta, G. 2015, *Consumers and energy efficiency – country report Romania: an inventory of policies, business and civil society initiatives, focusing on heating, hot water and the use of electricity*, EUFORIE – European Futures for Energy Efficiency. doi:10.13140/RG.2.2.20600.65287 [27 February 2019].

Bergmeier, M. 2003, "The history of waste energy recovery in Germany since 1920", *Energy*, 28, pp. 1359–1374.

Blok, K., & Turkenburg, W.C. 1992, "Past and future of industrial cogeneration in the Netherlands", *American Society of Mechanical Engineers 1992 International Gas Turbine and Aeroengine Congress and Exposition*, Cologne, pp. V004T10A019–V004T10A019.

Bohi, D.R. 1991, "On the macroeconomic effects of energy price shocks", *Resources and Energy*, 13(2), pp. 145–162.

ten Brink, P., ed., 2017, *Voluntary environmental agreements: process, practice and future use*, Routledge, Abingdon and New York, NY.

Brown, K., & Minett, S. 1996, "History of CHP developments and current trends", *Applied Energy*, 53(1–2), pp. 11–22.

Casten, T.R. 1999, "Myths of electric regulation: looking at the future of energy through entrepreneurial eyes", *The Electricity Journal*, 12(9), pp. 45–53.

Caton, J.A., & Turner, W.D. 1997, "Cogeneration", in *CRC handbook of energy efficiency*, eds F. Kreith & R.E. West, CRC Press, Boca Raton, FL, pp. 669–683.

Charo, R.A., Stearns, L.R., & Mallory, K.L. 1986, "Alternative energy power production: the impact of the public utility regulatory policy act", *Columbia Journal of Environmental Law*, 11(2), pp. 447–494.

Clément, A., McCullen, P., Falcão, A., Fiorentino, A., Gardner, F., Hammarlund, K., Lemonis, G., Lewis, T., Nielsen, K., Petroncini, S., Pontes, M.T., Schild, P., Sjöström, B.-O., Sørensen, H.C., & Thorpe, T. 2012, "Wave energy in Europe: current status and perspectives", *Renewable and Sustainable Energy Reviews*, 6(5), pp. 405–431.

Clô, A. 2000, *Oil economics and policy*, Kluwer Academic Publishers, Boston, MA.

Commission. 1974a, *Towards a new energy policy strategy for the European Community. Communication and proposals from the Commission to the Council*, COM (74) 550 final/2, 26 June 1974.

Commission. 1974b, *Energy for Europe: research and development. Communication of the Commission to the Council*, SEC (74) 2592 final, 17 July 1974.

Commission. 1974c, *Community energy policy objectives for 1985. Communication from the Commission to the Council*, COM (74) 1960 final, 27 November 1974.

Commission. 1977, *Communication from the Commission to the Council: community action programme for the rational use of energy (RUE) – 2d series of legislative proposals*, COM(77) 185 final, 25 May 1977.

Commission. 1982a, *Investment in the rational use of energy. Communication from the Commission to the Council*, COM (82) 24 final, 10 February 1982.

Commission. 1982b, *Review of Member States' energy policy programmes and progress towards 1990 objectives*, COM (82) 326 final, 10 June 1982.

Commission. 1982c, *Assessment report on the community demonstration programmes in the fields of energy saving and alternative energy sources*, COM (82) 324 final/2, 11 June 1982.

Commission. 1984a, *Comparison of energy saving programmes of EC Member States. Communication from the Commission to the Council*, COM (84) 36 final, 2 February 1984.

Commission. 1984b, *Review of Member States' energy policies. Communication from the Commission to the Council*, COM (84) 88 final, 29 February 1984.

Commission. 1986, *Towards a European policy for energy efficiency in industrial firms. Communication from the Commission to the Council. Council Resolution on improving* energy efficiency in industrial firms in the Member States, COM (86) 264 final, 16 May 1986.

Commission. 1988, *The main findings of the Commission's review of Member States' energy policies. The 1995 Community energy objectives. Communication from the Commission*, vol. I, COM (88) 174 final, 3 May 1988.

Commission. 1990a, *Promotion and development of energy cooperation between EEC and Central and East European countries. Final report, vol. 1, Proposals for cooperation*, July 1990.

Commission. 1990b, *Proposal for a Council Decision concerning the promotion of energy efficiency in the Community*, COM (90) 365 final, 13 November 1990.

Commission. 1991, *Joule programme 1989-1992. Catalogue of contracts of the joint opportunities for unconventional or longer-term energies*, Office for Official Publications of the European Communities, Luxembourg.

Commission. 1992, *Report from the Commission to the Council on the progress on cooperation between public utilities and auto-producers of electricity*, SEC (92) 1411 final, 22 July 1992.

Commission. 1995a, *Communication from the Commission concerning the promotion of energy efficiency in the European Union (SAVE II Programme). Proposal for a Council Decision concerning a multi-annual programme for the promotion of energy efficiency in the Community – SAVE II*, COM (95) 225 final, 31 May 1995.

Commission. 1995b, *Commission report on the application of Council Regulation 2008/90 of 29 June 1990. Assessment of the Thermie programme*, COM (95) 665 final, 15 December 1995.

Commission. 1997, *Communication from the Commission to the Council, the European Parliament, the Economic and Social Committee and the Committee of the Regions. A community strategy to promote combined heat and power (CHP) and to dismantle barriers to its development*, COM (97) 514 final, 15 October 1997.

Commission. 1998, *Report from the Commission. The market for solid fuels in the Community in 1997 and the outlook for 1998*, SEC (98) 2144 final, 16 December 1998.

Commission. 2002, *Directive of the European Parliament and of the Council on the promotion of cogeneration based on a useful heat demand in the internal energy market*, COM (2002) 415 final, 22 July 2002.

Comodi, G., Cioccolanti, L., Pelagalli, L., Renzi, M., Vagni, S., & Caresana, F. 2013, "A survey of cogeneration in the Italian pulp and paper sector", *Applied Thermal Engineering*, 54(1), pp. 336–344.

Council. 1974a, Council Resolution of 17 September 1974 concerning a new energy policy strategy for the Community, OJ C 153, 9 July 1975.

Council. 1974b, Council Resolution of 17 December 1974 on a Community action programme on the rational utilization of energy, OJ C 153, 9 July 1975.

Council. 1976, 76/493/EEC: Council Recommendation of 4 May 1976 on the rational use of energy in the heating systems of existing buildings, OJ L 140, 28 May 1976.

Council. 1977, 77/714/EEC: Council Recommendation of 25 October 1977 on the creation in the Member States of advisory bodies or committees to promote combined heat and power production and the exploitation of residual heat, OJ L 295, 18 November 1977.

Council. 1985, Council Regulation (EEC) No 3640/85 of 20 December 1985 on the promotion, by financial support, of demonstration projects and industrial pilot projects in the energy field, OJ L 350, 27 December 1985.

Council. 1986, Council Resolution of 16 September 1986 concerning new Community energy policy objectives for 1995 and convergence of the policies of the Member States, OJ C 241, 25 September 1986.
Council. 1988, 88/611/EEC: Council Recommendation of 8 November 1988 to promote cooperation between public utilities and auto-producers of electricity, OJ L 335, 7 December 1988.
Council. 1989a, 89/236/EEC: Council Decision of 14 March 1989 on a specific research and technological development programme in the field of energy – non-nuclear energies and rational use of energy – 1989 to 1992 (Joule), OJ L 98, 11 April 1989.
Council. 1989b, 89/364/EEC: Council Decision of 5 June 1989 on a Community action programme for improving the efficiency of electricity use, OJ L 157, 9 June 1989.
Council. 1990, Council Regulation (EEC) No 2008/90 of 29 June 1990 concerning the promotion of energy technology in Europe (Thermie programme), OJ L 185, 17 July 1990.
Council. 1991, 91/565/EEC: Council Decision of 29 October 1991 concerning the promotion of energy efficiency in the Community (SAVE programme), OJ L 307, 8 November 1991.
Cross, F.B. 1979, "Cogeneration: its potential and incentives for development", *Harvard Environmental Law Review*, 3, pp. 236–250.
Cudahy, R.D. 1995, "PURPA: the intersection of competition and regulatory policy", *Energy Law Journal*, 16(2), pp. 419–440.
Dincer, I., & Rosen, M.A. 2007, *EXERGY: energy, environment and sustainable development*, Elsevier, Oxford.
van Dril, A.W.N. 2005, "Using the benchmarking covenant for allocating emission allowances: are we still moving ahead?", in *The handbook of environmental voluntary agreements*, ed. E. Croci, Springer, Dordrecht, pp. 365–380.
EDUCOGEN. 2001, *The European educational tool on cogeneration*, 2nd edn. Available from: http://hacchp.gr/wp-content/uploads/2017/03/EDUCOGEN_Tool.pdf [27 February 2019].
Energy Tax Act, Pub. L. 95 – 618, 92 Stat. 3174, 1978.
Eurostat. 2001, *Combined heat and power production (CHP) in the EU. Summary of statistics*, Office for Official Publications of the European Communities, Luxembourg.
FERC v. *Mississippi*, 456 US 742, 1982.
Fox-Penner, P.S. 1990, "Cogeneration after PURPA: energy conservation and industry structure", *The Journal of Law and Economy*, 33(2), pp. 517–552.
Fraenkel, P.L. 2006, "Tidal current energy technologies", *Ibis*, 148, pp. 145–151.
Gaudiosi, G. 1999, "Offshore wind energy prospects", *Renewable Energy*, 16(1–4), pp. 828–834.
Gochenour, C. 2001, *District energy trends, issues, and opportunities: the role of the World Bank*, World Bank, Washington, DC.
Griffin, J.M., & Steele, H.B. 1986, *Energy economics and policy*, 2nd edn, Academic Press, Orlando, FL.
Grohnheit, P.E. 1999, *Energy policy responses to the climate change challenge: the consistency of European CHP, renewables and energy efficiency policies*, Risø-R-1147(EN), Risø National Laboratory, Roskilde.
Haghighi, S.S. 2007, *Energy security: the external legal relations of the European Union with major oil- and gas- supplying countries*, Hart Publishing, Oxford and Portland, OR.

Hekkert, M.P., Hekkert, R.H., & de Jong, A. 2007, "Explaining the rapid diffusion of Dutch cogeneration by innovation system functioning", *Energy Policy*, 35(9), pp. 4677–4687.

Hoerber, T.C. 2013, *The origins of energy and environmental policy in Europe: the beginnings of a European environmental conscience*, Routledge, Abingdon and New York, NY.

Hopkins, M. 1981, *Policy formation in the European Communities: a bibliographic guide to Community documentation 1958–1978*, Mansell, London.

Hvelplund, F., & Lund, H. 1998, "Rebuilding without restructuring the energy system in east Germany", *Energy Policy*, 26(7), pp. 535–546.

Iacobescu, F., & Badescu, V. 2011, "Metamorphoses of cogeneration-based district heating in Romania: a case study", *Energy Policy*, 39(1), pp. 269–280.

Infield, D.G. 1994, "Wind diesel design and the role of short term flywheel energy storage", *Renewable Energy*, 5(1–4), pp. 618–625.

Jorgenson, D.W. 1986, "The great transition: energy and economic change", *The Energy Journal*, 7(3), pp. 1–13.

Knodt, M. 2018, "EU energy policy", in *Handbook of European policies: interpretive approaches to the EU*, eds H. Heinelt & S. Münch, Edward Elgar Publishing, Cheltenham, pp. 224–240.

Kolanowski, B.F. 2008, *Small-scale cogeneration handbook*, 3rd edn, Fairmont Press, Lilburn, GA.

Leca, A. 2015, "Romania needs a strategy for thermal energy", *Management & Marketing. Challenges for the Knowledge Society*, 10(1), pp. 3–11.

Lifset, R. 2014, "Environmentalism and the electrical energy crisis", in *American energy policy in the 1970s*, ed. R. Lifset, University of Oklahoma Press, Norman, pp. 283–302.

Lund, H. 1999, "Implementation of energy-conservation policies: the case of electric heating conversion in Denmark", *Applied Energy*, 64, pp. 117–127.

Lund, P.D. 2014, "Integrated green energy approaches", in *Green energy economies: the search for clean and renewable energy*, eds J. Byrne & Y.D. Wang, Routledge, Abingdon and New York, NY, pp. 324–348.

Macchi, E., & Poggio, A. 1994, "A cogeneration plant based on a steam injection gas turbine with recovery of the water injected: design criteria and initial operating experience", *American Society of Mechanical Engineers 1994 International Gas Turbine and Aeroengine Congress and Exposition*, vol. 4, *Heat transfer; electric power; industrial and cogeneration*, the Hague. doi:10.1115/94-GT-017 [27 February 2019].

Marecki, J. 2005, "Skojarzone wytwarzanie ciepła i energii elektrycznej" [Combined heat and power generation], *Wokół Energetyki* [Around Energy Sector], 1. Available from: www.cire.pl/pliki/2/Skojarzone_wytwarzanie.pdf [27 February 2019].

Martin, S.A. 1983, "Problems with PURPA: the need for state legislation to encourage cogeneration and small power production", *Boston College Environmental Affairs Law Review*, 11(1), pp. 149–202.

McKay, M.E., & Rabl, A. 1985, "A case study on cogeneration", *Energy*, 10(6), pp. 707–720.

Michaelowa, A. 1998, "Impact of interest groups on EU climate policy", *European Environment*, 8(5), pp. 152–160.

Mogk, J.E., & Lepley, F.J., Jr. 1989, "PURPA and the evolving regulation of cogeneration – a guide for prospective cogenerators focusing on the greater Detroit resource recovery facility", *Wayne Law Review*, 35(3), pp. 1051–1111.

Möller, B. 2008, "A heat atlas for demand and supply management in Denmark", *Management of Environmental Quality: An International Journal*, 19 (4), pp. 467–479.

Morris, B., Boehm, K., & Geller, M. 1991, *European Community 1991/92*, 3rd edn, Macmillan, London.

Mors, M. 1991, "The economics of policies to stabilize or reduce greenhouse gas emissions: the case of CO_2", *Economic Papers*, 87, pp. 1–113.

National Energy Conservation Policy Act, Pub. L. 95 – 619, 92 Stat. 3026, 1978.

Natural Gas Policy Act, Pub. L. 95 – 621, 92 Stat. 3350, 1978.

Østergaard, P.A. 2010, "Regulation strategies of cogeneration of heat and power (CHP) plants and electricity transit in Denmark", *Energy*, 35, pp. 2194–2202.

OTA. 1983, *Industrial and Commercial cogeneration*, OTA-E-192 US Government Printing Office, Washington, DC.

Paterson, M. 1993, "The politics of climate change after UNCED", *Environmental Politics*, 2(4), pp. 174–190.

Pickel, F.H. 1982, *Cogeneration and utility planning*, MIT EL82-015. Massachusetts Institute of Technology Energy Laboratory, Cambridge, MA.

Power Plant and Industrial Fuel Use Act, Pub. L. 95 – 620, 92 Stat. 3289, 1978.

Public Utility Regulatory Policies Act, Pub. L. 95 – 617, 92 Stat. 3117, 1978.

Solorio, I., Mischa, M., & Popartan, L. 2013, "The European energy policy and its 'green dimension': discursive hegemony and policy variations in the greening of energy policy", in *Sustainable development and governance in Europe*, eds T. C. Hoerber & P.M. Barnes, Routledge, Abingdon and New York, NY, pp. 91–105.

Statement from the Paris Summit, Bulletin of the European Communities No 10, October 1972.

Stewart, H.B. 1981, *Transitional energy policy 1980–2030: alternative nuclear technologies*, Pergamon Press, New York, NY.

Treaty establishing the European Economic Community, signed in Rome, 25 March 1957.

Turner, W.D. 2015, "Cogeneration", in *Energy efficiency and renewable energy handbook*, eds D.Y. Goswami & F. Kreith, 2nd edn., Chapman and Hall/CRC, Baton Rouge, LA, pp. 891–938.

Van Oostvoorn, F., Millet, B., Simus, P., Bayer, W., Sletbjerg, M., Gronfors, K., Schollin, M., Kloots, J., Boeng, A., Parish, A., Offermann, J., Palsson, O., Gardner, A., Nischkauer, H., Livrieri, A., Garcia Montes, J., Guedelha, M., Capros, P., Rijkers, F.A.M., Bernsen, E., Madsen, K., Sorensen, E., Ranalli, L., Yerro, G., & Minett, S. 2003, *CHP Statistics and impacts of the gas directive on the future development of CHP in Europe (CHP STAGAS)*. Available from: https://www.ecn.nl/publicaties/PdfFetch.aspx?nr=ECN-C--03-123 [27 February 2019].

Verkuyl, O., Roggenkamp, M.M., & Boisseleau, F. 2005, "The liberalisation of the electricity sector in the Netherlands and the role of the APX", in *The regulation of power exchanges in Europe*, eds M.M. Roggenkamp & F. Boisseleau, Intersentia, Antwerp and Oxford, pp. 119–148.

Volpe, F. 2012, "Energy saving and energy efficiency: an unsustainable confusion", in *International environmental law: contemporary concerns and challenges*, ed. V. Sancin, GV Založba, Ljubljana, pp. 443–458.

WEC. 2014, *Energy sector of the world and Poland: beginnings, development, present state*, 2nd edn. Available from: https://dokumen.tips/documents/energy-sector-of-the-world-and-poland-energy-sector-of-the-world-and-poland.html [27 February 2019].

Wojdyga, K., & Chorzelski, M. 2017, "Chances for Polish district heating systems", *Energy Procedia*, 116, pp. 106–118.

Wooster, C.A. 1983, "Cogeneration: revival through legislation?", *Dickinson Law Review*, 87, pp. 705–777

Yüzügüllü, E. 2013, *Synergies for sustainable energy*, Artech House, Boston, MA.

3 Cogeneration and the EU energy market reform

Before the 1990s the Community's energy sector was based on national and state-owned monopolies, granted (formally or actually) exclusive powers with respect to energy purchase, its import and export, or energy infrastructure (Jones 2010, p. 1; Sokołowski 2016, pp. 40–41). Therefore, it was rather the structure of national energy industries, than a joint Community's platform. Being reminiscent of a "traditional paradigm" (Cameron 2007, p. 8) in which the energy industry was a strategic asset for national economy, the state monopolies had broad powers; in the electricity sector they held control over the synchronised grid, provided generation, transmission, and distribution of electricity (Sokołowski 2016, p. 41). It was an anti-competitive environment which reacted poorly to changes and approached consumers wrongly. This started to change in the 1980s, with the United Kingdom as the forerunner of the liberalisation movement.

In the UK, a conservative government headed by Margaret Thatcher, driven by the neo-liberal thinking and works of F.A. Hayek and other representatives of the "Austrian School" (see Teeble 2013, p. 12; Burczak 2009, p. 1), introduced a broad policy of the privatisation and liberalisation of state-owned industries, including the energy sector (Pearson & Watson 2012, p. 33). In the cabinet reorganisation of September 1981, Nigel Lawson – a proponent of the privatisation strategy that became the axis of Thatcher's programme – was appointed the Secretary of State for Energy (Pearson & Watson 2012, p. 7). As he declared during the parliamentary debate on the new oil and gas legislation in January 1982:

> the proper business of Government is not the government of business. No industrial corporation should be owned and controlled by the State unless there is a positive and specific reason for such an arrangement.
>
> (UK Parliament 1982)

The British government did not find this specific reason in the energy industry. After oil and gas, the electricity sector was also to be addressed by the cabinet. The works on the liberalisation started after the 1987 elections; the Electricity Act was passed in 1989, and the privatisation started in 1990 (under the new conservative government led by John Major) with the sale of regional electricity companies (Pearson & Watson 2012, pp. 10–12) along with the division of the Central Electricity Generating Board into four companies of which three were sold to the general public soon after (Newbery & Pollitt 1997, p. 270). An electricity pool was established and the entry into the generation market was liberalised (Newbery & Pollitt 1997, p. 275).

The UK's energy market reform has been a benchmark for continental Europe. The liberalisation of the electricity market could be a chance for the development of cogeneration. It opened the sector for new entrants, giving possibilities for investments to new entities, also those of a smaller, local scale. The liberalised electricity sector, with unbundled generation, distribution, and transmission was favourable for the development of cogeneration (Commission 1997b, p. iii). This was noticed by the other Member States even before the market liberalisation was conducted at the European level with the use of subsequent energy packages.

In this light, the continental Europe has its own achievements in the market liberalisation regarding cogeneration. For example with passing the Electricity Act in 1989, the Netherlands established a new framework for the electricity market, aimed, among others, at increasing competition and separating generation from distribution (Commission 1990, Sec. 2.29). After consultations with the distribution companies, *Samenwerkende Elektriciteits-Productiebedrijven* (SEP) – the Dutch energy joint venture owned by large energy generators (see Roggenkamp & Boisseleau 2005, p. 20) – had to elaborate on an electricity plan on supply development, which should propose a policy on decentralised generation based on cogeneration and renewable energy sources. These kinds of sources (if smaller, i.e. below 25 MW) built and operated by distributors were also exempted from SEP's approval, and when the approval was required (for larger sources), SEP had to include the guidelines on the development of decentralised capacity, as set in the previously mentioned electricity plan (Commission 1990, Sec. 2.30).

The individual actions of the Member States were accompanied by the Community's approach aimed at tackling exclusive powers of the monopolies. At the turn of the 1980s and 1990s it was the Commission which took the steps to overcome the monopolies, starting from telecoms, then moving to the energy sector (Sokołowski 2016, p. 41). Due to the lack of the Member States' consent on energy market liberalisation agreed at the Community level, in the early 1990s the Commission used the competition law as an alternative, launching the antitrust proceedings against eight Member States to eliminate the harm to competition and free movement of goods caused by monopolies in their energy sectors, both electricity and gas (Jones 2010, p. 2).

Nevertheless, a more complex action on the energy sector was to come very soon – its regulatory scope also affected cogeneration. A study based on the methodology of the Cecchini report (Comission 1988) showed that integrating the internal gas and electricity markets could result in significant savings in the electricity sector, which, among others, would come from the development of CHP (Commission 1992, p. 3). Seen in this light, the energy market reform could contribute to the growth of CHP. This was to happen in the 1990s.

Zero-phase of energy liberalisation and the First Energy Package

A market reform programme launched by the Community in the 1980s was linked with the establishment of the internal energy market: first, in 1986, a document vital for European integration – "the Single European Act" – was issued (see Ehlermann 1987; Toth 1986), and two years later the Commission (1988) presented the main objectives for the establishment of the internal energy market (Sokołowski 2016, pp. 1–2, p. 99). However, a future reform aimed at regulating both electricity and gas, started relatively innocuously, targeting transparency and cross-border transit at the beginning, then moving to utilities' procurement and upstream licensing which were related to practices more harmful to the energy market (Talus 2013, p. 40).[1]

Production of electricity and heat in the regime on public utilities' procurement

In this zero-phase (or pre-package, i.e. before the era of energy packages which started in 1996), only one of the Directives established by the Community concerned generation of electricity and heat. It was Directive 93/38/EEC (see Rillaerts 1999, p. 14). Driven by the need to open-up the market in the water, energy, transport, and telecommunications sectors,[2] together with ensuring a fair balance in applying the rules on procurement, it replaced the previous Directive 90/531/EEC and harmonised the review procedures for contracts in these four sectors (Kierkegaard 2006, p. 32, see Piggin, Young, & McLaughlin 1999, p. 288).[3] This concerned, *inter alia*, energy activities related to infrastructure providing services to the public including the production and delivery of electricity, gas, or heat.

Initially excluded from the Community's rules on procurement (due to their diversity and the complexity of their status) public utility entities operating in the four sectors were addressed by the European law step-by-step, and the original exclusion has been partially compensated by providing specific procurement rules for them (Verdeaux 2003, p. 721). This happened with the enactment of Directive 90/531/EEC which managed to solve the matter of complex utility status by being applied to public actors that exercised one of the activities in these sectors, i.e. to the public authorities, public undertakings, or entities being granted the special or exclusive rights (see Bovis 2005, pp. 91–92). The latter meant powers deriving either from authorisation made by a competent authority of the Member State, law, or administrative action, which – as a result – reserved the exploitation of these activities to one or more entities; a contracting entity was considered to enjoy these type of rights particularly when it supplied the network (with electricity or heat but also drinking water or gas) operated by the entity benefiting from special or exclusive rights.

Directive 93/38/EEC established a regulatory system with procurement duties imposed on those entities when awarding supply, works or service contracts. However, some exemptions from this system were provided, too. With respect to electricity, it concerned those supplies to grids which offered a service to the public by a contracting entity, other than a public authority, where the production of electricity was conducted for other needs than the activities covered by Directive 93/38/EEC and the scale of this delivery was limited.[4] A similar approach was given to heat, where exempted heat was to be produced as "the unavoidable consequence of carrying on an activity", conducted at a smaller scale.[5] In both cases, to mark the activities irrelevant for the purposes of the Directive, Article 2(2) was a reference (i.e. activities other than those referred to were not falling under the scope of the Directive).[6]

In 1994, Directive 93/38/EEC was amended to align it with the World Trade Organisation's Agreement on Government Procurement (Talus 2013, p. 40), and in 2004 a new regulatory framework on procurement was enacted, with utilities within its scope. The move of 1994 coincided with an intense policy discussion on changes in the energy market in the 1990s (Sokołowski, pp. 99–100) which led to the adoption of new legislation in 1996 and 1998. These were the two Directives aimed at liberalising the electricity (96/92/EC) and gas (98/30/EC) sectors in the European Union.

Cogeneration and the models for the energy market: the First Electricity Directive

This first chapter of the energy market reform did not omit cogeneration. In its Green Paper on the European Union's energy policy (see Pointvogl 2009, p. 5708), the Commission (1995a, pp. 48, 60) assessed that the development of CHP would depend on the expansion of the gas network, as the share of gas (fuel) would increase in cogeneration (together with the growth of gas usage in the electricity sector). This was correlated with the prevailing European trend of growing penetration of electricity and gas (Commission 1995c, p. 13). Discussing the European energy outlook up to the year 2020 in another policy document (White Paper), the Commission (1995c, p. 13) predicted growth in the production of heat from decentralised cogeneration plants.

Nevertheless, the most important point of the White Paper concerning CHP was related to a declaration to elaborate on a Community strategy to promote cogeneration and district heating (Commission 1995c, p. 34, cf. Michaelowa 1998, p. 157). Two kinds of issues were set as its main goals. First, the strategy was to ensure the cooperation between the Community, Member States, utilities, and consumers of electricity and heat; second, it had to eliminate barriers to the development of CHP (Commission 1995c, p. 34). According to an indicative work programme established in the White Paper, the strategy was to be ready in 1997. Before it was completed, a new regulatory pillar of the European energy legislation was constructed. It was the First Electricity Directive, i.e. Directive 96/92/EC being a part of the First Energy Package (see Talus & Aalto 2017, p. 16; Pepermans 2019).

On a way to the First Energy Package, the matter of different models for the energy market was discussed (cf. Glachant 2016, p. 674). Among different analysis one may find a Working paper created by the Commission in March 1995. This document (Commission 1995b), prepared in response to the Council's request (1994),[7] addressed the market opening in the electricity sector with a focus on the electricity systems based on negotiated Third Party Access and Single Buyer models (see Sokołowski 2016, pp. 29–30). Among the areas included in the Commission's analysis (1995b), was the position of RWC producers on the electricity market with respect to the need for simultaneous authorisation in the tender systems. As the Commission evaluated (1995b, p. 30), the RWC producers theoretically could have joined tenders for new capacities only in those cases where they were not auto-producers; however, except hydropower, RWC faced problems related to high production costs, so continuing operation "in a tendering climate of sharp competition" would have been very hard for them.

A separate point of the assessment concerned cogeneration and a justification to exclude it from the competitive tendering. Its highest overall efficiency (an advantage of the CHP producers) was contrasted with the competition in two markets: electricity and heat (Grohnheit 1999, p. 99), where "[i]n no case they can afford to lose one of these outlets as this would erode their whole economic base" (Commission 1995b, pp. 30–31). Therefore:

> RWC-producers could in theory be included in tendering procedures, but this would not sufficiently satisfy the political need to support these environmentally benign production facilities. Therefore, to meet this demand RWC-producers will also require a parallel authorisation ... [t]o redress the imbalance between authorisation and tender procedures ... even under tendering systems ... to strengthen competitive forces.
>
> (Commission 1995b, pp. 34, 37)

At the time of this discussion, the draft of the new legislation on the internal energy market has already been revealed. Nevertheless, cogeneration was addressed there only briefly. It was recognised as one of the areas needing the intervention of the Member States which had "a legitimate interest in retaining a certain freedom of action as regards the nature of electricity production capacities, for reasons of energy policy and security of supply" (Commission 1992a, p. 15). For this reason, a possible priority for using cogeneration smaller than 25 MW was proposed (the same priority was offered to renewable energy sources, and those energy installations fired by waste). This approach was repeated in the draft Article 13(4) of the proposal of the Directive on the internal market in electricity. It granted the priority for these three types of installations having less than 25 MW of power installed (including cogeneration) when dispatching the generating unit by the TSO (Transmission System Operator) in its area of operation.

"These interventions shall be at national level in the first instance", the Commission declared when drafting the new legislation (1992, p. 16), seeing the possibility to extend them progressively at the Community level (cf. Grohnheit & Gram Mortensen 2003, p. 819). This kind of attitude to promote CHP was implemented in the First Electricity Directive. Instead of granting the priority, as in the draft (Commission 1992), Member States could require that system operators give priority to cogeneration when dispatching generating installations (Sokołowski 2016, pp. 101–102). This softer version of the previous approach to cogeneration (as well as renewables and generators using waste) concerned both the TSO (Article 8(3)), and the Distribution System Operator (DSO), as stated in Article 11(3) of Directive 96/92/EC.[8] In practice, this was moving the intervention regarding the cogeneration to the Member State's level, leaving it to their decision, as predicted in 1992.

The Strategy on CHP (1997)

Despite this softer approach to cogeneration which derived from the First Electricity Directive, the issue of providing CHP with a more comprehensive approach reached the Community's top level a few years later, when, in 1997, the previously announced Strategy on CHP was adopted. However, the Strategy (Commission 1997b, p. 10) confirmed the indirect role which the European Union would perform with regard to cogeneration (both the coordination and the support of promotion), defining the Member States as the appropriate actors to promote and support CHP. It was a step towards providing cogeneration with a clearer position in the EU energy market (cf. Pilavachi 2000, pp. 1427–1428) and a move "to ensure that the benefits which CHP can bring, in terms of energy saving, cost-effective environmental improvement and sustainable development, are fully achieved" (Commission 1997b, p. 9).

Apart from presenting previous developments and the potential of combined heat and power, the Strategy listed the barriers to the growth of cogeneration capacity in the EU (cf. Jörß et al. 2003, p. 132; van der Does 1996, pp. 49–50).[9] Regardless of the heterogeneous nature of the situation on combined heat and power in the Member States, resulting in different barriers (in different economies) arising from a variety of factors, such as the structure of the energy system or the nature of the demand for electricity and heat (see Khabdullin et al. 2017, p. 540), etc., some general categories of issues hindering the development of CHP were listed in the Strategy (Commission 1997b, pp. 6–7). There were three groups of problems, including: economic barriers (*inter alia*, low remuneration for cogenerated electricity, high prices for back-up grid electricity in case of unavailability of the CHP unit, high rates for input fuels together with the unpredictability of energy prices; hence the difficulties in financing CHP systems), regulatory barriers (time-consuming bureaucracy, expensive procedures to obtain operating licences, etc.), and institutional barriers (e.g. problems with connecting a CHP plant to the network, delays and lack of transparency in obtaining necessary permits). As it was concluded:

> it seems that many of the important barriers to the development of CHP in Europe result from the relationship between cogenerators and electricity production utilities. Obstacles to free access to the grid, inadequate payments for sales of surplus capacity to the grid and high tariffs for stand-by and top-up supplies are key factors impeding the penetration of CHP even in a partly liberalised European Energy market.
>
> (Commission 1997b, p. 7)

The latter factor (i.e. incomplete liberalisation) was highlighted in the Strategy with the use of examples from different Member States. The evaluation of the energy sectors with a strong dominance of the existing utilities, like in France or Italy, revealed that they distorted the economics, making it unattractive (unprofitable) for CHP to enter the market, whereas in the liberalised markets (or rather, almost liberalised, like the UK in the mid-1990s where the market reform was almost completed)[10] many of the "artificial barriers" to the development of combined heat and power have been overcome or their negative effects have been mitigated (Commission 1997b, p. 7).

Despite noticing these issues, the Strategy provided a rather non-regulatory approach to the development of cogeneration in the European Union. The Community left the promotion of combined heat and power to the Member States' consideration. For example, early in 1997, the Commission (1997a, p. 7) indicated the promotion of third-party financing as a "way of accelerating the introduction of cogeneration". However, this development could also be steered by financial sources distributed from the European level. In this context, the Strategy reviewed the financial funds which were to be offered under the 5th Framework programme for different initiatives in the field of CHP. The plans connected with the EU's greater interest in the cogeneration were to be implemented with the use of the already-known programmes (their extensions), like the Joule-Thermie, SAVE, or ALTENER (see Flin 2010, pp. 88–90). First, in terms of the technological development such actions as improving the conversion of efficiency, increasing reliability, lowering emissions, developing the cost effective mini (below 30 kW$_e$) and micro-CHP units (as low as 0.5 kW$_e$) or CHP applications for the high temperature industries as well as cogeneration powered by biomass, low heating value fuels and other mixed fuels were included in CHP (the Joule-Thermie) (Commission 1997b, p. 12). Second, with respect to developing the capacity of CHP in the European energy market, these were the continuations of the SAVE and ALTENER programmes which were to provide a growth in CHP units (especially the SAVE II programme).[11]

What must be highlighted, are the ideas for reaching an increase in cogeneration capacity. Those plans were ambitious. In the Strategy on CHP the Commission presented a possibility of making the 9% share of combined heat and power in the total gross electricity generation twice as big (see van Gerwen 2003, p. 369; Michaelowa 1998, p. 157). The "visionary" target of reaching at least 18% of cogeneration by 2010 (Hammons 2011, p. 263, see Lazaro, Millan, & Peral 2006, p. 163) was presented as "realistically achievable" (Commission 1997b, p. 10, see Verbruggen 2005, p. 37). Apart from doubling the 1990s cogeneration capacity (67 GW producing 204 TWh of electricity),[12] this required a growth in the yearly load factor (by 30%), as well as actions on the part of the Member States, which were called on to eliminate various obstacles preventing the development of cogeneration in their energy systems (Commission 1997b, p. 10). Again, it referred the decision to the Member States, which should implement the assumptions expressed in the Strategy at their national levels.

The 18% goal for cogeneration in electricity production also had its environmental dimension – discussed in Chapter 4 of this book. However, what should be emphasised at this point, is the impact of the energy market reform that could lead to even greater achievements with respect to CO_2 emissions. By doubling the CHP use in the Community by 2010, a reduction of over 65 Mt CO_2 yearly was expected, although the potential for cogeneration in the Community's energy sector was much bigger (see Commission 2000b, p. 66). "[W]ith the right framework in the liberalised market it has been estimated that CHP could triple by 2010 leading to an additional reduction of CO_2 of around 65 Mt per year", as declared in the Green Paper on the European strategy for energy security (Commission 2000b, p. 66). At the same time, this assumption was a call for the further growth in cogeneration which could entail extra reduction of emissions.

The First Energy Package: no adequate regulatory capacity to move towards CHP

Achieving the set goals required "the right" approach. Has the regulatory framework established in the first phase of the liberalisation of the European energy market met this condition? On the one hand, when looking at the EU energy policy through the prism of electricity market reform, driven by the First Electricity Directive as well as Strategy on CHP, one should notice their rather positive overall impact on cogeneration.[13]

Besides their current effects, some follow-up actions were introduced. For example, the Commission (1997b, p. 15) addressed the need to monitor the influence of the energy market reform on combined heat and power, and if needed, to introduce the measures necessary to prevent the negative effects. This was related to the positive and negative effects of price reductions, which could result in lower costs of input fuels on the one hand, and lower electricity prices for generators of electricity in CHP on the other hand (Commission 1997b, p. 15; Heinen 2001, p. 84). Moreover, "[o]ne of the principal remaining barriers to CHP in the liberalised markets is the failure of energy prices to reflect the cost of environmental externalities", as assessed in the Strategy (Commission 1997b, p. 15). To tackle this matter, a soft action, i.e. monitoring of the impact of new rules on CHP (when introduced) was proposed, together with applying other (but not specified) "appropriate measures to prevent negative effects" (Commission 1997b, p. 15).[14]

On the other hand, the gas pillar of the First Energy Package – Directive 98/30/EC (First Gas Directive) – adopted one and a half years after the First Electricity Directive, i.e. in June 1998 – contained certain provisions blocking the development of cogeneration (cf. Bianco 2018, pp. 154–155). Under its Article 18(2), Member States had the possibility to exclude CHP units from access to the internal gas market. It was a measure of a threshold which could be imposed on cogeneration with respect to its eligibility for having the legal capacity of entering the natural gas transactions. In contrast, the gas-fired electricity generators (not combined units) were not covered by this possible restriction, regardless of their annual consumption level. The reason for this was explicitly presented in Directive 98/30/EC. If needed, to "safeguard the balance of … electricity market", Member States could introduce this type of limitation related to combined heat and power. The Commission was to be notified of such actions.

Concluding the situation of cogeneration, covered by the scope of the First Energy Package, one should notice the intention to improve the situation of CHP in the European Union by concretising and advancing it to some extent with the use of the initial legislation, dedicated action programmes equipped with financial sources, and a strategy on CHP.

However, the 1990s agenda on cogeneration also contains some inconsistency in action (see Grohnheit & Gram Mortensen 2003, p. 819), as exemplified by the First Gas Directive which, in fact, introduced barriers to the development of combined heat and power in the Community; the same barriers which were to be removed, as mentioned in the Strategy on CHP.

What derives from this analysis is the unfinished construction of the single energy market in the EU. This legal environment had no adequate regulatory capacity to move on the development of cogeneration at the Community's level. A change was needed, and the new impetus for the European energy sector, including cogeneration, was to come with the advent of the twenty-first century.

From the Second to the Third Energy Package via other initiatives

In August 2003, a new phase of the EU energy market reform entered into force, just 20 days after the official publication of a new regulatory framework on electricity and gas established by Directive 2003/54/EC (the Second Electricity Directive) and Directive 2003/55/EC (the Second Gas Directive); this time both were adopted simultaneously. They derived from a proposal put forward by the Commission in 2001 which was aimed at removing several weaknesses in the existing legal environment to achieve a fully operational internal market for gas and electricity in the EU (Commission 2001b, p. 6). To reach completion of the internal energy market and take the full advantage of its benefits, new measures were offered, i.e. quantitative proposals related to a degree (percentage) of the market opening, and qualitative proposals focused on the access to energy infrastructure, unbundling, consumer protection, or regulatory authorities (Sokołowski 2016, p. 110, see Zimmermann & Talus 2008).

Towards the Second Energy Package: combined heat and power in the 2001 proposal

Cogeneration was also one of the fields addressed in the 2001 proposal, presented mainly in the section on the environmental consequences of energy market opening. As the Commission emphasised "competition may mean that electricity from new and less developed energy sources (e.g. renewables and combined heat and power) becomes less attractive", so a transition to "a cleaner fuel mix in the electricity production" could be hindered (Commission 2001b, p. 22). To tackle this issue, the existing provisions of the First Electricity Directive[15] together with the Strategy on CHP and the Action Plan on energy efficiency were recalled. The latter, adopted in 2000, offered an outline of policies and measures for the removal of barriers which blocked the economic potential for energy efficiency improvement (Commission 2000a). The Action Plan emphasised the need for including the issue of enhancing energy efficiency, wherever possible, in the European policies and programmes without significant changes to the original intent of the initiative, as in the case of regional and urban policies and programmes, such as the Regional Development and Cohesion Funds, giving priority to investments in energy-efficient and innovative technologies such as cogeneration (Commission 2000a, p. 7).[16]

In its proposal of 2001, the Commission (2001b, p. 41) declared that "a fully opened market needs an internalisation of external costs to ensure a true level playing field". This assumed the support of initiatives such as CO_2 taxation, strict rules on state aid, tools to enhance demand-side management, as well as any measures to promote cogeneration and renewables facing "a competitive disadvantage as long as external costs are not fully integrated" (Commission 2001b, p. 41). However, neither renewable energy sources nor cogeneration were directly covered by the Commission's proposal. One exception was a draft amendment of Article 5 of the First Electricity Directive, which stated that Member States, when granting authorisations for the construction of energy sources, were to establish certain criteria, including energy efficiency or the nature of primary sources. However, it was still an indirect way of dealing with combined heat and power.[17]

Nevertheless, at that time, the Commission (2001b, p. 24) expressed its will to elaborate on new proposals with respect to promoting cogeneration (it was intended to happen in 2002). In this context, one should also note here an earlier proposal on CHP provided by the Action Plan on energy efficiency of 2000 (cf. Filippini, Hunt, & Zorić 2014, p. 74; Geller et al. 2006, pp. 566–567). It was an initiative requiring new plants to apply cogeneration where feasible, an approach which was to be introduced in the revision of Directive 88/609/EEC (a former LCP Directive) aimed at establishing a new system on emissions from large combustion plant (Commission 2000a, p. 10). This was not the only one change in the regulatory framework which was to cover CHP. Moreover, as declared by the Commission (2000, p. 11), the amended Directive 93/76/EEC (SAVE) was to be extended to address combined heat and power.

The Commission's proposal was further discussed by the European Parliament (2002) which, among many changes, insisted on separating the Commission's proposal into two separate legal acts on electricity and gas.[18] Some of the Parliament's amendments were very forward-looking e.g. a new recital of the preamble to Directive 96/92/EC was proposed (18), showing a clear urge for supporting cogeneration in the EU. As stated there:

> [t]he Commission, the European Parliament and the Member States should take a decision as soon as possible on a Directive on the promotion of combined heat and power and a Directive on energy and

electricity saving measures. These should set Community and national targets, with decisions on the most appropriate mechanism for achieving these targets being left to Member States. These Directives should come into force in parallel with the opening of the market.

(European Parliament 2002b)

With self-explanatory justification (European Parliament 2002a), it was a very pro-cogeneration approach, drawing a complex policy agenda on CHP, including the introduction of new legislation and setting the policy goals on the European and national levels of cogeneration along with the tools for reaching them. Other amendments offered by the Parliament confirmed this attitude. In this light, the European Parliament (2002b) proposed the introduction of minimum information in the energy bills sent and in all the advertising and promotional materials delivered to final consumers – the percentage production from CHP units was to be included there,[19] exempting certain entities using micro CHP from authorisation procedures,[20] and addressing the cost of connecting new cogeneration units to the grid (they were to be "objective, transparent and non-discriminatory").[21]

In June 2002, the Commission delivered a new version of the proposed legislation. First, it addressed the Parliament's call to elaborate on the proposals on cogeneration. As the Commission declared (2002a, p. 10), "[w]hilst it is the intention of the Commission to come forward this year with the proposal on combined heat and power ... a Directive is not the place to call on the Commission to present proposals". Second, the last one of the listed Parliament's postulates was approved by the Commission, and with some modifications it appeared in the new version of the draft. The non-discriminatory connection was maintained; however, the specific characteristics together with the costs and benefits of connecting renewables and CHP units were addressed in the new wording of Article 22(1g) of Directive 96/92/EC. The emphasis was put on energy regulation, with a necessity to establish regulatory authority (or authorities) responsible for the energy market. Among its powers was (at least) to contentiously monitor the energy market "to ensure non-discrimination, effective competition and the efficient functioning of the market" (Commission 2002a, pp. 7–8). One of the areas to be covered by the aforementioned monitoring was connecting new producers to the grid, where "the terms, conditions and tariffs" had to be "objective, transparent and non-discriminatory, in particular taking full account of the benefits of the various renewable energy sources technologies, distributed generation and combined heat and power" (Commission 2002a, p. 31). Especially the tariffs (if harmonised) could have been of importance for increasing the use of CHP in the EU (see Hendriks & Blok 1996, p. 734).

As the splitting of the initial proposal into two separate legal acts, as suggested by the Parliament, was soon favoured by the Council (2002,

2003), it evolved into a legislative package, "a set of interdependent or related legal acts viewed or organised as a unit" (Sokołowski 2016, pp. 37–39). In a relatively natural way, cogeneration was included in the draft Directive on electricity,[22] and it was almost the end of the legislative process which led to the adoption of the Second Energy Package in June 2003. The draft became Directive 2003/54/EC (the Second Electricity Directive) accompanied by Directive 2003/55/EC (the Second Gas Directive).

Electricity Directives (Second and Third) and Energy Taxation Directive – rules for CHP

When assessing the legal regime brought for combined heat and power by the Second Energy Package, one should make a note of the soft approach for addressing CHP there. For example, cogeneration was named in the preamble to the Second Electricity Directive as the "new capacity" (for the needs of tendering procedure, launched if enough generation capacity is not built under the authorisation procedure). In practice, it did not have a great significance, as this was just an example of the technology that could be used for the needs of tenders contributing to the security of supply (which were more of an exception than a rule – as they concerned extreme situations of threat to energy security). Additionally, the Second Electricity Directive maintained some of the solutions provided by Directive 96/92/EC. Like in the First Electricity Directive, Member States could voluntarily give the priority to the CHP installations dealing with the system operators, as stated in Articles 11(3) and 14(4) of Directive 2003/54/EC.[23]

Apart from these examples of the soft regulatory attitude to cogeneration (cf. Cseres 2008, p. 86), one may also find stricter approach (but still more of an exception than a rule). With the necessity to designate an independent regulatory authority (being responsible for ensuring non-discriminatory treatment of different market players), the promotion of cogeneration was strengthened by the monitoring duties of energy regulators that were obliged to cover, *inter alia*, the terms, conditions and tariffs for connecting new producers of electricity, including CHP units, to the grid (Sokołowski 2016, pp. 129–132). Pursuant to Article 23 (1)(f) of the Second Electricity Directive, this monitoring had to include the costs and benefits of combined heat and power, listed together with renewables and distributed producers, as in the draft legislation.

In 2009, the internal energy market entered another phase of reform. This happened with the adoption of the Third Energy Package, with Directive 2009/72/EC (Third Electricity Directive) as part of it (see Eikeland 2011; Nowak 2010; Swora 2010). Aimed at reaching the state of "[a] well-functioning internal market in electricity [that] should provide producers with the appropriate incentives for investing in new power generation, including in electricity from renewable energy sources", the Third Electricity

68 *Cogeneration and the EU energy market reform*

Directive (see Chapter 6, also including the terms of its force) has not extended the regulatory framework on cogeneration, and in some elements it limited it (cf. Elżanowski 2011, p. 143). For example, despite enhancing the position of the energy regulators (Sokołowski 2016, pp. 162–165, cf. De Somer 2012, pp. 97–98), the monitoring of the conditions for connecting new CHP installations is not actually mentioned in Directive 2009/72/EC.

Moreover, the Directive treats it rather as a part of other general categories. CHP can be denoted by such definitions as "producers" ("a natural or legal person generating electricity") or "renewable energy sources" (if electricity is produced in CHP unit using renewable non-fossil energy sources like biomass[24] or geothermal[25]). However, in the Third Electricity Directive one may also find some provisions which directly address combined heat and power. These few examples concern a certain approach to the dispatching generators where the Member States may decide about granting priority to CHP (exactly like in the Second Electricity Directive). Here, this matter is covered by Articles 15(3) and 25(4) of Directive 2009/72/EC.

Among the initiatives that have been promoting the use of combined heat and power one should also mention legislation separate from the Energy Packages. The matter of energy taxation with Directive 2003/96/EC (Energy Taxation Directive) could be listed among them (see Gvozdenac et al. 2017, p. 270; Sibilio, Roselli, & Sasso 2010, p. 328). Its legal regime, directed towards the proper functioning of the internal energy market in the EU by introducing minimum levels of taxation at Community level for energy products (including electricity, natural gas, and coal),[26] offers pro-cogeneration treatment. It concerns the possibility to "apply certain … exemptions or reduced levels of taxation, where that will not be detrimental to the proper functioning of the internal market and will not result in distortions of competition" – these reliefs ("preferential treatment") could be applied particularly to CHP, as highlighted in Recitals 24 and 25 of the preamble to the Energy Taxation Directive. Due to this approach, under its Article 15, Member States may introduce full or partial exemptions or reductions regarding the tax level with respect to both energy used for the needs of generation in CHP units (energy products and electricity), as well as energy (electricity) produced in "environmentally-friendly" (high-efficiency) cogeneration.

Nevertheless, since 2004, cogeneration has already been operating under a new regulatory regime being covered by the provisions of a separate legislation. How much has changed for this element of the energy market under this framework? The next subchapter delves into this matter.

CHP Directive on the internal market's service

In the early 2000s, the idea to adopt a legislation dedicated to the promotion of CHP was outlined by the Commission. Its benchmark was

Directive 2001/77/EC (RES Directive) with legal solutions to enhance the position of renewable energy sources on the internal energy market (see Rowlands 2005). Among its "market tools" discussed in the initial concept, one may find the network issues (access and cost of connection) as well as administrative procedures related to combined heat and power (Commission 2001b, p. 12). The proposed legislation was to be cohesive with a general EU campaign on energy efficiency (see Chapter 4 of this book), to some degree using the tools based on the measures applied to the promotion of the development of renewables brought by Directive 2001/77/EC (see Kanellakis, Martinopoulos, & Zachariadis 2013, p. 1023).

The proposal on a regulatory framework on CHP was elaborated on in 2002. Driven by "the need for reinforced efforts to promote high-efficiency cogeneration in the internal energy market", it sought to influence the liberalisation agenda with specific provisions covering cogeneration (Commission 2002b, p. 2). The following declaration highlights the recalled approach:

> [t]his Directive [on CHP] will create the necessary legislative framework whereby efforts at all levels can be concentrated on promoting high-efficiency cogeneration. The Directive will serve as a means to reduce the current market uncertainty surrounding cogeneration and provide important stimuli for cogeneration in individual Member States by establishing a coherent Community framework. ... Legislative action at Community level will ensure that a set of common principles for the promotion of cogeneration is developed. ... [The] common principles for high-efficiency cogeneration can also ensure that financial support for cogeneration is prioritised in such a way that support is allocated to the most efficient production.
> (Commission 2002b, p. 19)

As a consequence, the proposed regulatory framework was to create a legal environment for the development of CHP which could facilitate the installation and proper operation of cogeneration plants where there was (or was expected) a useful heat demand – as the progress related to the assumed 18% target for cogeneration was not satisfactory (Commission 2002b, p. 3). Paradoxically, the 18% target was just a benchmark, being an indicative goal for the EU as a whole. The failure to achieve it did not have any negative legal consequences.

The assumptions of the proposal: the framework to facilitate the increase of cogeneration

Difficulties with the development of cogeneration (apart from the differences in potential, as discussed further on) resulted from the existence of barriers which hindered its growth. The Commission (2002b, pp. 5–6) categorised them into four groups: first, high prices of fuels; second, access to the electricity market; third, higher costs of CHP installations, and finally, the operating hours of cogeneration.[27] Cogeneration, seen through those groups, faced problems due to its smaller capacity in comparison with the incumbent electricity utilities (see Collier 2002, p. 184). Hence, it could not exploit the effect of scale when competing with them, both for the needs of purchasing fuels, as well as optimising production, e.g. in terms of maintenance or investment. Finally, the condition of market liberalisation and the state of competition on the market impeded the increase of cogeneration capacity, as CHP units noticed issues related to accessing the market and being connected to grid. Especially the lack of grid access and unfair conditions for exchanging power were harmful obstacles for combined heat and power, being very destructive for this industry (see Energy Charter Secretariat 2002, p. 9; Verbruggen 2008, p. 3070). However, as some reported, "[t]he greatest threat to cogeneration remains ... with the prospects of low electricity prices, which would defer most investments in new generating capacity" (Energy Charter Secretariat 2002, p. 9).

All things considered, the offered framework on cogeneration was to facilitate the increase of CHP in the Community, tackling the recorded problems by bringing a common Community's approach, the regulatory regime based on unified definitions and methodologies. The following assumption was behind it – the support of combined heat and power was to be linked with "an economically justified heat demand", where the generated electricity and produced heat had to meet real energy demand (Commission 2002b, p. 3). As highlighted in the proposal:

> [t]he electricity can be transmitted into a market place and sold where it is needed, the heat however cannot easily by transported or stored, and therefore the cogeneration process must be based in time and place of a real need for heat. The real need for useful heat is the cornerstone of efficient cogeneration, because if the produced heat is not meeting a real demand the advantages of cogeneration disappear. Furthermore, the promotion of cogeneration should not lead to encouragement of increased heat consumption.
>
> (Commission 2002b, pp. 2–3)

So the promotion of cogeneration itself had to be efficient, eliminating the waste of not used, overproduced energy. This "double efficiency rule" or "efficiency in promotion" was a general precondition for developing new rules for increasing the use of combined heat and power in the Community. The aim was to support CHP wherever the economically justified potential occurred, measured with the help of a definition of "useful heat" and the efficiency criteria annexed to the drafted legislation. The "double efficiency" derived from different conditions influencing the development of combined heat and power in the EU Member States. Climate varies among the Member States, ranging from the cold North to the warm South of Europe (see Moreci, Ciulla, & Brano 2016, Olsson, Hajabdollahi, Ganjehkaviri Jaafar 2015, Wetterlund & Söderström, 2015, cf. Spinoni et al. 2018; Isaac & van Vuuren 2009; Lough, Wigley, & Palutikof 1983); thus, the share of cogeneration has been very diverse, from a minor to a major scale. The same concerns the situation of the industry, where different branches, with different potential for using heat, existed. The sum of these conditions had an impact on the usage of CHP, leading to elaboration on three areas where CHP could be used: industrial applications, central heating applications, and agricultural applications,[28] along with setting a direction for promoting cogeneration where it is possible and reasonable (see Commission 2002b, p. 4). Therefore, the Commission's legislative initiative was not aimed at ensuring "the same level of penetration of cogeneration in all Member States [but was] ... to promote cogeneration wherever an economically justified potential is identified" (Commission 2002b, p. 4).

The promotion – having a financial dimension, too ("vital for cogeneration") and strengthened by the regulatory certainty – was to make space for CHP on the internal energy market, as the internal energy market of the 2000s was not completed being in the "transitional phase of the liberalisation process ... where internalisation of external costs is not reflected in energy prices" (Commission 2002b, p. 3). This was to mitigate a likely adverse impact of liberalisation on cogeneration (cf. Magnusson 2016), where the high capital costs of district heating together with lower cost-effectiveness (a result of removing the guaranteed customer base), introduced uncertainty about recovering the incurred investment costs (Energy Charter Secretariat 2002, p. 36).

However, in this context, the possible support had to meet the conditions of the liberalised energy market, where certain former practices and national policy instruments could be disqualified, e.g. central planning favouring specific installations, purchase obligations to take excess electricity, or some favourable tariff schemes which might not be suitable (Energy Charter Secretariat 2002, p. 9). Without prejudging their compliance or non-compliance with the rules of liberalised energy market, among other ways of promoting cogeneration one may list the environmental policies backing high efficiency energy solutions, minimum efficiency requirements, or taxation (Energy Charter Secretariat 2002, p. 35).

These factors fell under the scope of the short-term aims of the proposed legislation, where the CHP Directive was to respond to the needs of both the existing and future CHP capacity in the Community. The first one was to be consolidated, the latter (the new high-efficiency cogeneration) was to be promoted in the framework of the internal energy market of the EU (Commission 2002b, p. 3, see Badami et al. 2014, p. 255). Besides the short-term goals, the medium- and long-term goals, also distinguished in the draft legislation, were corelated with the energy market reform. It was due to the assumed results of the proposed CHP Directive which – by developing cogeneration – were to diversify and improve the Community's energy system, strengthen the competition of electricity production (by allowing new CHP producers to enter the market), and create opportunities for cooperation between different energy stakeholders (see Commission 2002b, pp. 3–6).

To improve the situation of cogeneration on the internal energy market, in its proposal for the new legislation, the Commission (2002b, p. 5) urged on the introduction of provisions on the principles for the interaction between CHP generators and the operators of electricity grid, as well as the establishment of a framework for evaluating the administrative procedures, with a view to reduce the administrative burdens hampering the development of combined heat and power in the EU. These solutions were reflected in the final version of the CHP Directive (2004/8/EC) which was passed in February 2004. They echo the very first provisions of the Directive, calling for a larger market share in the European energy sector. "It is ... necessary to take measures to ensure that the potential [of cogeneration] is better exploited within the framework of the internal energy market", as declared in Recital 1 of the preamble of Directive 2004/8/EC, simultaneously praising the energy efficiency of the combined production of heat and power for its positive contribution to the energy security and competition in the energy market of the EU (cf. Ferreira et al. 2012, p. 148).

The regulatory regime of the CHP Directive: a catalogue of tools

Let us discuss those of the listed measures which ensure better exploitation of CHP in the internal electricity market, taking into consideration the research assumptions made in Chapter 1 of this book. The analysis starts with the first measure mentioned there – the support schemes (systems of support). They were specific legal solutions that could be established by the Member States in their national legislation to promote the development of cogeneration either by granting it additional financial sources or removing fiscal burdens.

The aim of the support was to assure market confidence for CHP investors, and, as a result, lead to growth in combined heat and power in the EU.[29] This also derives from Recital 30 of the preamble to the CHP Directive, where creating "a stabile economical and administrative environment for investments in new cogeneration installations" – so a framework with stable ("avoiding frequent changes") support schemes established for a period of at least four years – had to lead to it. In practice, cogeneration could be supported by different means (cf. Moreira, Monteiro, & Ferreira 2007, p. 5749). These could be, for instance, investment aid, tax exemptions or reductions, certificates, and direct price schemes used during the era of the CHP Directive for supporting cogeneration in the EU.

Table 3.1 Support schemes for CHP in the EU-27

Member States	feed-in tariff/guaranteed purchase price	certificate scheme	energy tax exemption	business tax exemption	accelerated fiscal allowance for investment	capital grants
type of support	operational	operational	operational	operational	investment	investment
indicate range of value	15–80 EUR per MWh	~40 EUR per MWh	2–12 EUR per MWh (electricity produced)	minor	5%–10% of investment costs	10%–50% of investment
Austria						x
Belgium		x			x	x
Bulgaria	x					
Cyprus	x					x
Czech Republic	x					x
Denmark	x			x		x
Estonia	x					
Finland			x			
France	x		x	x	x	x
Germany	x		x			x
Greece	x					x
Hungary	x					
Ireland					x	x

(Continued)

Table 3.1 (Cont.)

Member States	support measures feed-in tariff/guaranteed purchase price type of support operational indicate range of value 15–80 EUR per MWh	certificate scheme operational ~ 40 EUR per MWh	energy tax exemption operational 2–12 EUR per MWh (electricity produced)	business tax exemption operational minor	accelerated fiscal allowance for investment investment 5%–10% of investment costs	capital grants investment 10%–50% of investment
Italy		x*	x			x
Latvia	x					x
Lithuania	x					x
Luxembourg	x					x
Malta						
Netherlands			x			x
Poland		x			x	x
Portugal	x					x
Romania						
Slovakia	x					x
Slovenia	x		x			x
Spain	x					x
Sweden			x			
UK	x		x	x	x	x

* CHP qualified as eligible for certificate schemes enhancing energy efficiency (white certificates).
Source: Commission 2011b, p. 87.

Cogeneration and the EU energy market reform 75

The support systems established by the Member States were subjected to the Commission's evaluation. Pursuant to Article 7(3) of the CHP Directive, the Commission had to elaborate on "a well-documented analysis on experience gained with the application and coexistence of the different support mechanisms". This was to include such matters as cost-effectiveness of these systems, the national potential of cogeneration in each Member State, and an overall assessment of a given way of promoting cogeneration (see Moreira, Monteiro, & Ferreira 2007, p. 5749). Herein, let us again refer to the following parts of this book, as the evaluation published by the Commission (2014a, 2014b) is discussed together with national reports of the selected Member States in Chapter 5.

Nevertheless, some general conclusion on the systems of support of cogeneration should be made at this point. What emerges from the review carried out by the Commission (2011) is a distinct diversity of the support systems used by the Member States. The systems varied in many aspects, including the selection of supported technologies and fuels, size of capacities, etc. The background for this situation were the different levels of ambition as well as the ways in which Member States interpreted the CHP Directive; hence, the EU system for supporting cogeneration was rather "a patchwork of national legislation" than a common framework (Commission 2011b, p. 86). Among the measures chosen to support CHP, the most popular way was applying capital grants (investment aid) and introducing feed-in tariff or guaranteed purchase price schemes (operational aid). The first method has been introduced by 20 Member States, the second was implemented in 17 of them (out of EU-27). With respect to their characteristics, the capital grants have been aimed at specific technologies or applications (especially innovative),[30] whereas the tariff/pricing schemes have been linked to the price of electricity delivered to the grid, like in the feed-in tariff, or the electricity market price, as in the price premium scheme – offering either a fixed price (feed-in tariff) for this delivery or a fixed bonus (price premium) on the market price of electricity (see Commission 2011b, pp. 88, 90). The capital grants have been an advantage where the investment barrier hindered CHP from entering the market, while the tariff/pricing schemes have been mitigating operational risks like fuel costs (Commission 2011b, pp. 90–91).

Another operational way of supporting combined heat and power has been providing them with a dedicated certificate scheme.[31] In this support system, electricity suppliers have been obliged to obtain a certain share of cogeneration certificates (either directly – bought from the CHP operators, or indirectly – purchased on the certificate market) and then to submit them to the energy market regulator (or pay a buy-out fee) in order to fulfil their duty (Commission 2011b, p. 89). To maintain their effectiveness, these types of systems require a regulatory approach. As the revenue from the certificates provides an additional income for cogeneration allowing for the improvement of their operational performance, maintaining the certificate price required such actions as regulating the level of supply, introducing the floor and ceiling prices, and/or providing the targets for cogeneration (market share) (Commission 2011b, p. 89).

Finally, the development of cogeneration has been promoted with the help of tax and fiscal mechanisms like tax deduction or accelerated fiscal allowances for investments (see preceding subchapter and comments on Energy Taxation Directive). The schemes with operational character (tax exemptions) provided mitigation of fuel price risks. These types of measures tended to be "fairly resilient to political change, and therefore more secure than e.g. feed-in tariffs", however, as the Commission (2011b, p. 91) reported, they have been "rarely considered the decisive driver of the CHP market".

In terms of practical implementation, the support was to be in a line with the Community guidelines on State aid for the environmental protection (in 2004 the guidelines from 2001 were still in force). With respect to their main rules (Commission 2001a), when establishing the support schemes for promoting cogeneration the Member States had to link them with the economically justifiable demand for heat and cooling.[32] The eligible investments in CHP could be given the aid amounting to the basic rate of 40% of eligible cost. This required "particularly high conversion efficiency" allowing the reduction of energy consumption or the production of energy less damaging to environment (also in terms of the fuel used).[33] These conditions also determined the operating aid for the CHP units.[34] It could be granted when the costs of producing electricity power or heat exceed its market price (the decision whether the aid was essential was based on the costs and revenue resulting from the production and sale of electricity or heat); it referred to the entities distributing electricity and heat to the public which could be the beneficiaries of this type of aid.

The second element of the market agenda offered for cogeneration in Directive 2004/8/EC concerned access to the grid (cf. Lazaro, Millan, & Peral 2006, p. 163). The CHP Directive linked this matter with the provisions of Directive 2001/77/EC and Directive 2003/54/EC facilitating the connection to the grid.[35] CHP Directive fell short of the approach taken in Directive 2001/77/EC (see Talus 2013, p. 194). While the Directive on renewables from 2001 encouraged to "provide for priority access to the grid system of electricity produced from renewable energy sources", the CHP Directive called for facilitating the access to the grid for "electricity produced from high-efficiency cogeneration from small scale and micro cogeneration units" (see Kilkis & Kilkis 2007). In both cases, these were the technological characteristics of electricity generators that determined the possible support (Ropenus, Jacobsen, & Schröder 2011, p. 1950), and in both cases, this approach was weaker rather than stronger (as it was not a real obligation but just a possibility).

The same soft way of dealing with the access to the grid for cogeneration derived from the way in which the CHP Directive tried to solve the matter of tariffs. Until being qualified as "an eligible customer" in the framework on national legislation implementing provisions on market opening brought by the Second Electricity Directive (Article 21(1)), the Member States pursuant to Article 8(2) of the CHP Directive were obliged to "take the necessary measures to ensure that the tariffs for the purchase of electricity to back-up or top-up electricity generation are set on the basis of published tariffs and terms and conditions". However, the problems with accessing the market encountered by CHP were often anchored in the restrictive market role prescribed to cogeneration, where this attitude fenced off the market entry by setting specific tariffs for the power exchanged between a CHP unit and the grid (Verbruggen 2008, p. 3070). These kinds of market barriers suggest a discussion on the third pillar of energy market reform covering heat and power, i.e. the administrative burdens imposed on cogeneration.

Behind it were the solutions aimed at tackling these administrative barriers. Nevertheless, once again, it was a soft regulatory approach offered for cogeneration. The framework established under Article 9 of the CHP Directive proves it. On its basis the Member States had to evaluate their legislation implementing the procedures for new energy generators, brought by the Second Electricity Directive applied to high-efficiency CHP units.[36] The evaluation had to address the areas related to growth in cogeneration, *inter alia*, any obstacles to the development of combined heat and power, as well as an assessment on the rules on CHP (whether they were "objective, transparent and non-discriminatory"). When conducting it, the focus was to be set for "[t]he specific structure of the cogeneration sector, which includes many small and medium-sized producers".[37]

The reporting activity of the Member States was extended by the provisions enabling them to take some regulatory action at the national level, e.g. elaborating on the possible guidelines in areas related to cogeneration – like the energy efficient design of units, regulatory and non-regulatory barriers, or the improvement of administrative procedures. Still, it was a soft way of dealing with the issue of cogeneration in the European legislation. As in the case of support systems, Directive 2004/8/EC left the way of promoting the use of high-efficiency cogeneration to the decision of each Member State – some of them were more active, some were more passive (see Commission 2011b, p. 75). Table 3.2 reviews this issue.

The Member States have promoted cogeneration with the use of measures addressed in the Directive 2004/8/EC such as encouraging the development of CHP units (with the use of financial support), removing administrative barriers (lowering or removing time costs and expenses), streamlining procedures (e.g. reducing the time and costs of obtaining necessary permits), improving the coordination between administrative bodies, adopting guidelines for the design and authorisation of CHP units, and providing fast-track planning procedures for CHP producers (reducing

Table 3.2 Measures to promote cogeneration in the EU-27

Member State	encouraging	removing barriers	streaming procedures	transparent rules	coordination	guidelines	mediators
Austria	x	?	?	x	x	?	?
Belgium							
Bulgaria	?	x	x	x	x		x
Cyprus	x	x	x	x	?	x	?
Czech Republic							
Denmark	x	x	x	x			
Estonia							
Finland							
France							
Germany							
Greece	?	?	?	?	?		
Hungary	?	x					
Ireland	?	x	x	x	x	x	
Italy	?	?	?	?			
Latvia	?	?	?	?			
Lithuania	?	?	?	?			x
Luxembourg		x	x				
Malta	x	?	x	x	x		x
Netherlands							
Poland							
Portugal							
Romania	x						
Slovakia							
Slovenia	x	x	?	x	?	?	
Spain							x
Sweden			?				
United Kingdom					x	x	x

Source: Commission 2011b, p. 75.

time-costs, minimising investment risks), as well as designating mediators for dispute resolution (Commission 2011b, p. 75).

Introducing those measures was not an obligation imposed on the Member States by the Directive. In fact, the Member States were obliged only to inform about the progress on their activity regarding the administrative procedures for combined heat and power – and to report it ("provide an indication of the stage reached") only where it was "appropriate in the context of national legislation", e.g. in terms of the previously mentioned guidelines. In practice, even such a seemingly unproblematic activity caused problems. As one may find in Table 3.2 some Member States did not provide enough information in their reports prepared under Article 9 of Directive 2004/8/EC (Moya 2013, p. 348).

The regime provided for combined heat and power established by the CHP Directive within the EU liberalisation packages (Second and Third) was to release the potential of the European cogeneration, contributing to the competition in the energy market, enhancing energy efficiency, reduction of emissions, or energy security. How far has it succeeded in promoting cogeneration in Europe? What has been achieved? What has the Directive failed to realise? Let us look for the answers in the subchapter to follow.

Not enough power to power CHP

When summarising the effects of Directive 2004/8/EC the phrase "business as usual" may be useful, as, in fact, little has changed in the CHP business under the rules of the CHP Directive. Cogeneration was supported where it was supposed to be supported. Not having a binding, European goal on combined heat and power, the Member States set (or not) their own CHP goals. Therefore, "CHP has not received the focus that has been given to other policies where mandatory targets exist", making it easy for national governments to "roll back their policy and financial support to the benefit of other priorities (stop and go policies)" (Commission 2011b, p. 83). Under these circumstances, during the early years of the legal environment's existence established by Directive 2004/8/EC, the share of high-efficiency cogeneration in the European Union increased by only 0.5% (Commission 2011a, p. 12). The installed CHP capacity in electricity grew merely by 5 GW, from 95 GW in 2004 to just over 100 GW in 2008;[38] the same applies to electricity produced from combined heat and power: 10.2% in 2004 in comparison to 11% in 2008 (Commission 2011b, p. 92). Moreover, in the given period the share of cogeneration has decreased in some Member State (see Chapter 5 of this book).

"Soft failure" of Directive 2004/8/EC

Besides the lack of concrete national obligations regarding the development of combined heat and power in the EU, it was the soft wording of the

Directive that was identified as one of the main reasons of its ineffectiveness (cf. Frangopoulos 2012). The soft approach, delivered by the CHP Directive, led to its "soft failure". In other words, Directive 2004/8/EC "failed to create the investment security needed, to decrease the burden of the numerous administrative procedures and to create a [level] playing ... field for this technology and its operators" (Commission 2011a, pp. 12–13). The pro-cogeneration measures brought by the Directive have not been effective enough.

First, the guarantees of origin (see Chapter 4) have not been fully operational (as of 2011); second, there has been no evidence that the various support schemes adopted by the Member States have been driven by the CHP Directive; third, the rules on connecting CHP units to the grid varied across the Member States, not providing enough certainty and stability for accessing the energy market; fourthly, the evaluation of administrative procedures on cogeneration has not been completed by all Member States (2011); moreover, very little has been done to implement the results of those evaluations (see Commission 2011a, p. 13). Furthermore, cogeneration was still facing problems blocking its development and hindering the exploitation of the CHP potential. Table 3.3 reports these difficulties.

The barriers, which the Commission (2011b) enumerated on the basis of national reports and other studies (Joint Research Centre, COGEN), have shown that the situation of cogeneration was far from the state the European Union wanted to achieve. Competition from depreciated generation assets (nuclear, large hydro, and old coal plants), high and unstable prices of fuels (see Jörß et al. 2003, p. 166), unstable heat demand (resulting from industrial restructuring and energy efficiency measures), limited access to energy sources (mainly natural gas), problems with accessing the grid (high, non-transparent charges for connection, non-transparent connection conditions), limited financial sources for the renewal of aging units, regulatory and policy uncertainty (complex permit procedures, access to and the future of the systems of support, the uncertainty related to the EU emissions trading scheme), limited heat infrastructure, and insufficient experience in cogeneration were among the factors which hampered the growth of combined heat and power in the EU (Commission 2011b, p. 85).

Furthermore, regardless of the national potential of cogeneration, each Member State recorded some problems with respect to the development of CHP. On the one hand, in many cases the problems which some EU countries had to overcome were not limited to one or two issues. Portugal, Romania, and Bulgaria were facing almost all of the previously mentioned barriers to the development of cogeneration. The situation of combined heat and power in Slovakia was even worse, as all of the identified barriers were present there.[39] On the other hand, countries like Hungary or Sweden noted just one of the issues defined as barriers to the utilisation of their national potential of cogeneration; these were decreasing heat demand

Table 3.3 Overview of barriers to realising CHP potential in the EU-27

Member States	low power prices	high or volatile fuel prices	decreasing heat demand	fuel access	capital access	grid access	complexity of law or regulations	policy uncertainty	lack of capacity
Austria	x							x	x
Belgium		x	x						x
Bulgaria		x	x	x	x	x	x		x
Cyprus			x	x			x		
Czech Republic	x	x		x	x	x		x	
Denmark	x		x						
Estonia		x	x	x				x	
Finland	x	x	x	x			x	x	
France									
Germany	x	x	x	x		x	x	x	
Greece			x	x		x	x		x
Hungary			x						
Ireland		x	x	x		x			x
Italy		x	x			x	x	x	
Latvia	x				x		x		
Lithuania									
Luxembourg		x	x	x	x				
Malta		x	x						x
Netherlands	x	x				x		x	
Poland		x			x	x		x	x
Portugal		x	x	x	x	x	x	x	x

(Continued)

Table 3.3 (Cont.)

Member States	low power prices	high or volatile fuel prices	decreasing heat demand	fuel access	capital access	grid access	complexity of law or regulations	policy uncertainty	lack of capacity
Romania	x	x	x		x	x	x		x
Slovakia	x	x	x	x	x	x	x	x	x
Slovenia					x		x		
Spain	x	x		x	x	x	x		
Sweden		x							
United Kingdom		x	x			x	x	x	x

Source: Commission 2011b, p. 86.

Table 3.4 Overview of the effects of the CHP Directive

Member States	market trend	primary market driver	effect of the CHP Directive
Austria	increasing	ambitious national CO_2 targets drive the switch to natural gas and biomass	1
Belgium	increasing	CHP obligation policy	2
Bulgaria	increasing	CHP feed-in tariff	3
Cyprus	stable	NA	NA
Czech Republic	stable	NA	NA
Denmark	decreasing	NA	NA
Estonia	decreasing	NA	NA
Finland	increasing	industrial and residential heat demand	0
France	stable	NA	NA
Germany	increasing	improving feed-in tariff and building regulation	1
Greece	increasing	feed-in tariff and market liberalisation	2
Hungary	stable	NA	NA
Ireland	increasing	political support	1
Italy	increasing	high electricity prices and improving policy framework	1
Latvia	increasing	feed-in tariff	2
Lithuania	increasing	feed-in tariff	2
Luxembourg	stable	NA	NA
Malta	stable	NA	NA
Netherlands	stable	NA	NA
Poland	stable	NA	NA
Portugal	increasing	feed-in tariff and wider availability of natural gas	2
Romania	increasing	feed-in tariff	3
Slovakia	decreasing	NA	NA
Slovenia	decreasing	NA	NA
Spain	increasing	feed-in tariff and wider availability of natural gas	2
Sweden	increasing	ambitious national CO_2 targets drive the switch to natural gas and biomass	1
United Kingdom	stable	NA	NA

Source: Commission 2011b, p. 91.

84 Cogeneration and the EU energy market reform

Table 3.5 Commission's key to the rating of policy effects on the developments of CHP

rating	policy effect on market activity	alternative	effect of the CHP Directive on policy
0	policy has not contributed to growth in the CHP market	and/or	the introduction of policy was not the result of the Directive
1	policy support has had a slight positive effect on market activity	and	the Directive was not the primary driver for introducing the legislation
2	policy has been a minor contributing factor to decisions to invest in CHP	and	the Directive was not the primary driver for introducing the legislation
3	policy has been one of several factors leading to decisions to invest in CHP	and	the introduction of supportive legislation was partly the result of the Directive
4	policy has offered direct financial value driving decisions to invest in CHP	and	the Directive was the main reason for introducing the support measures
5	financial support has been a "deal maker", and has attracted new parties to the market	and	the Directive was the main reason for introducing the support measures

Source: Commission 2011b, p. 91.

(Hungary)[40] and high or volatile fuel prices (Sweden).[41] Apart from them, two Member States: France and Lithuania, did not find any problems related to the development of cogeneration.[42]

Parenthetically, the last of the national reports was delivered as late as October 2011, so almost five years after the deadline for notifying the Commission (Commission 2011b, p. 83). This confirms the general trend in which the Member States' approach to the CHP Directive and its implementation was rather non-committal or limited – just like the Directive (see Westner & Madlener 2010, p. 7912). The Directive's market effect on CHP remained small, which resulted from its "broad and vague wording and the lack of stringent measures [,] ... obligation [,] or ... concrete guidance for the promotion of CHP" (Commission 2011b, p. 83).

For a better understanding of this table the following key was prepared (see Table 3.5). It juxtaposes the 0–5 grades awarded by the Commission (see Table 3.4) with the market effects of policies on cogeneration and the effect of CHP on these policies.

Inertia of the regulatory action on cogeneration in the EU

As one may observe, the CHP Directive did not have a significant impact on the situation of combined heat and power in any of the Member States, and its overall role in steering the growth and harmonising development of cogeneration in the EU has remained limited (Commission 2011b, p. 92). Neither has the direct financial value offered by the policies motivated decisions to invest in CHP (and the Directive was the main reason for introducing them), nor has the financial support been a "deal maker", attracting new parties to the market due to the Directive and its support tools. Only in Romania and Bulgaria some of the introduced measures on cogeneration were, to a certain extent, the result of the adoption of the CHP Directive (see Chapter 5 of this book, cf. Musatescu, Podasca, Opris 2017, Paroussos, 2016). Hence, the estimated contribution of the Directive 2004/8/EC to the increase of the CHP capacity in the EU was not decisive and rather minor (Commission 2011b, pp. 92–93). According to the Commission's evaluation (2011b, p. 92), "[t]he increase or decrease of CHP capacity was mainly driven by specific national policies and conditions and the CHP Directive often played no or only a marginal role".

Directive 2004/8/EC did not have enough power to *power* CHP. The European action on cogeneration aimed at support schemes, electricity grid system and tariff issues, as well as administrative procedures, was not sufficient to fully exploit the potential of combined heat and power in the EU (see Commission 2011a, p. 13). There has been no clear proof that systems of support stimulate the progress in the development of CHP because of the CHP Directive; the rules on connection have not provided any certainty and stability regarding access to the grid, as the rules introduced by the Member States varied, and, in many cases, have been ineffective; finally, the conducted evaluations of administration procedures on CHP, completed by all Member States, very often have not been implemented (Commission 2011a, p. 13).

The same soft approach applies to the regulatory framework introduced by the Energy Packages, ranging from the First, through the Second, to the Third. Despite addressing combined heat and power, the legal regime established at the European level was rather neutral to CHP – except for anti-cogeneration approaches such as that included in the First Gas Directive. The market pillar of the European energy policy, regulated by the three Energy Packages, recognised cogeneration, although the real support was to be delivered at the national level.

Seemingly, such an approach may not raise any objections. However, in view of the ambitious goals on cogeneration, as well as on energy efficiency – with combined heat and power as one of the tools for enhancing it and using energy in a more efficient way (see Chapter 4 of this book) – contrasted with problems which cogeneration had to face, an effective EU action was needed. Naturally, it required taking into account the principle of subsidiarity (see Grzeszczak 2012, Kersbergen & Verbeek 2004; Marquardt 1994).

There is much to indicate that the actions discussed here were not as effective as they should have been. These juxtaposed circumstances prove that the CHP sector developed only where it could, steered by national

86 *Cogeneration and the EU energy market reform*

efforts. This resulted from the soft nature of the adopted legislation, leading to an inertia of the European action on cogeneration. In effect, it made the European policymakers and the EU institution consider a revision of the policy framework on combined heat and power. However, it took some time before the revised legal regime on cogeneration was established. Changes could have been brought by the climate agenda of the European Union, which has accelerated in the second half of the 2000s. Let us analyse this matter in the next chapter.

Notes

1 This was done by passing six directives: Price Transparency Directive (90/377/EEC), Electricity Transit Directive (90/547/EEC) and Gas Transit Directive (91/296/EEC), Public Procurement (Utilities Remedies) Directive (92/13/ECC) and Public Procurement (Utilities) Directive (93/38/EEC), as well as Hydrocarbons Licensing Directive (94/22/EC).
2 This issue was discussed in the preamble of the Directive. As stated there in Recitals 11 and 12:

> ... among the main reasons why entities operating in these sectors do not purchase on the basis of Community-wide competition is the closed nature of the markets in which they operate, due to the existence of special or exclusive rights granted by the national authorities, concerning the supply to, provision or operation of, networks for providing the service concerned, the exploitation of a given geographical area for a particular purpose, the provision or operation of public telecommunications networks or the provision of public telecommunications services;
> ... the other main reason for the absence of Community-wide competition in these areas results from various ways in which national authorities can influence the behaviour of these entities, including participations in their capital and representation in the entities administrative, managerial or supervisory bodies;

3 The first Community directive on procurement, i.e. on public works (71/305) and public supplies (77/62) had a limited contribution to improving competition, as their scope was narrow – procurement in the water, energy, transport, and telecommunications sectors as well as contracts for services was excluded there; this was changed with the adoption of Directive 90/531/EEC, superseded by Directive 93/38/EEC (Commission 1996, p. 50).
4 According to Directive 93/38/EEC "supply to the public network depends only on the entity's own consumption and has not exceeded 30% of the entity's total production of drinking water or energy, having regard to the average for the preceding three years, including the current year".
5 Similarly as with drinking water and electricity, "supply to the public network is aimed only at the economic exploitation of such production and amounts to not more than 20% of the entity's turnover having regard to the average for the preceding three years, including the current year", as stated in Directive 93/38/EEC.
6 Among the activities covered by Directive 93/38/EEC were:

  (a) the provision or operation of fixed networks intended to provide a service to the public in connection with the production, transport or distribution of:

(i) drinking water; or
(ii) electricity; or
(iii) gas or heat;

or the supply of drinking water, electricity, gas or heat to such networks;

(b) the exploitation of a geographical area for the purpose of:

(i) exploring for, or extracting, oil, gas, coal or other solid fuels; or
(ii) the provision of airport, maritime or inland port or other terminal facilities to carriers by air, sea or inland waterway;

(c) the operation of networks providing a service to the public in the field of transport by railway, automated systems, tramway, trolley bus, bus or cable. ...
(d) the provision or operation of public telecommunications networks or the provision of one or more public telecommunications services.

7 The Council (1994) insisted on analysing "how to open the markets beyond the area of electricity production". This included:

> the question of the possible simultaneous introduction of a negotiated TPA and a so-called single-buyer system. In this context, it is necessary to verify that both approaches, in the spirit of reciprocity, lead to equivalent economic results and, therefore, to a directly comparable level in the opening of markets and to a directly comparable degree of access to electricity markets and that they conform with the provisions of the Treaty.
> (Council 1994)

Apart from that, a separate issue covered cogeneration. The Council (1994) wanted to obtain the result of an examination of "the side-by-side application of both approaches" which had to discuss the following question:

> whether in Member States introducing a tender procedure, power plants destined for export, for autoproduction and independent production, as well as power plants based on CHP and renewable energies, should be permitted by authorization procedures – in parallel to the tender procedures – as well.

8 According to Article 8(3), placed in Chapter IV of Directive 96/92/EC which concerned TSO, "[a] Member State may require the system operator, when dispatching generating installations, to give priority to generating installations using renewable energy sources or waste or producing combined heat and power". Similar provisions referred to DSO (Article 11(3)).
9 A study made by COGEN Europe (1995) was the Strategy's reference point – the Strategy summarised its review of the barriers to the development of cogeneration in the EU Member States.
10 The example of the UK was highlighted in the Strategy, as being below the average in terms of the development of cogeneration, but due to the liberalisation and progressive removal of the market barriers, the country's position was improved (Commission 1997, p. 7).
11 The Strategy listed specific pro-cogeneration initiatives that were to be included in the SAVE II programme. They were the actions to:

- improve awareness of financial solutions and Energy Service Company (ESCO) involvement (e.g. third party financing of CHP projects);

88 Cogeneration and the EU energy market reform

- map the demand for energy services which could be met by CHP;
- determine CHP potentials based on economic, energy and environmental criteria;
- further investigate barriers to CHP and DH & C in the new liberalised energy market and find ways to overcome them, taking into consideration social and economic factors, environmental impact and security of supply;
- disseminate information on CHP and DH & C ...

(Commission 1997, p. 13)

The revised guidelines for SAVE II priorities for 1998 also maintained the possibilities for supporting CHP, including, in the call for proposals, the following activities in terms of cogeneration:

a) [n]on-technological projects assessing the energy savings by CHP plants in industry and in the buildings sector;
b) [a]nalysis of legal, administrative and regulatory obstacles to the expansion of centralised and decentralised CHP and proposals for possible solutions in the new liberalised energy markets in the context of Article 8 of Directive 96/92/EC;
c) [p]ilot actions concerning the introduction of TPF in the CHP sector;
d) [t]ools and methods for analysing the impact of CHP projects and programmes

(Commission 1998, p. 12)

12 As in 1994 according to Eurostat (see Commission 1997, p. iv).
13 According to the Commission (1997a, p. 7) "[i]n a market economy context, in the long run cogeneration is likely to be developed if there are transparent and fair rules with regard to the quantity and price of the electricity produced; and if the new gas contract situation ensures competitiveness".
14 In practice, as the Commission suggested (1997, pp. 15–16), the previously mentioned monitoring could be done by the national committees on CHP, established on the basis of Council Recommendation 77/714/EEC, and supported with statistics on cogeneration gathered by the Member States and elaborated on by Eurostat.
15 These were the already-presented Article 8(3) and Article 11(3) of the First Electricity Directive.
16 As the Commission (2000, p. 7) emphasised, the action on combined heat and power could be more closely coupled with such instruments as voluntary agreements, energy audits, or labelling as well as best practice initiatives introduced by the Member States.
17 This was not an issue for the European Economic and Social Committee (2001) which evaluated the Commission's proposal as an initiative that "respects changes that had already been made to the original Directives" maintaining "[e]xemptions designed to promote the incorporation into the electricity grid of energy from renewables and waste and from cogeneration plants".
18 The motive for dividing the Commission's proposal was justified by two reasons: the first being that the electricity and gas markets were simply different: the second, that the rules for them were established in two separate directives in different phases of implementation (Sokołowski 2016, p. 115).
19 New Article 3(4) of Directive 96/92/EC.
20 It concerned undertakings or domestic premises wishing to generate their own electricity using micro combined CHP or similar technology, as stated in the proposed Article 5(5) of Directive 96/92/EC.
21 Paragraph 5 added to Article 8 of Directive 96/92/EC.
22 Despite using the phrase in "a natural way" one can also image certain areas related to cogeneration which could have been covered by the Directive on gas

(e.g. natural gas as a fuel used in combined heat and power what which could have resulted in separate provisions on CHP units put within the framework of the Directive on gas). Therefore, it was rather "a relatively natural way" of dealing with cogeneration.

23 According to Article 11(3) "[a] Member State may require the system operator, when dispatching generating installations, to give priority to generating installations using renewable energy sources or waste or producing combined heat and power"; similarly "[a] Member State may require the distribution system operator, when dispatching generating installations, to give priority to generating installations using renewable energy sources or waste or producing combined heat and power", as provided in Article 14(4) of the Directive 2003/54/EC.

24 See e.g. Prando et al. 2015.

25 With respect to geothermal CHP units, such installations exist in the EU, e.g. in Austria – Altheim or Bad Blumau, or Germany – Neustadt-Glewe (see Lund & Chiasson 2007, pp. 4–5). In 1999, the Commission published a "Blue book on geothermal resources", where advantages and disadvantages of this type of cogeneration are briefly discussed (see Commission 1999, pp. 26–27).

26 See Recital 3 of the preamble to Directive 2003/96/EC.

27 The matter of operating hours addressed in the Commission's proposal (2002b, p. 6) was related to the technical circumstances linked to operating a CHP unit, where the volume of operating hours is usually lower than the amount of operating hours in a large baseload power plant due to the link between the production of electricity and cogeneration and the real use of heat in the associated installations, not needed e.g. at night, at weekends, or in summer.

28 These three classes are characterised by different temperature of steam or water used. Industrial applications usually require steam or hot water warmer than 140°C, central heating applications need warm water at a temperature between 40°C and 140°C, whereas agricultural applications usually need water colder than 40°C (see Commission 2002b, p. 4).

29 This was linked with the proper operation of the support mechanisms which eventually were to become an element of the harmonised Community framework (see Recital 26 of the preamble to Directive 2004/8/EC).

30 For example, in the Netherlands, grants have been offered for residential micro-CHP; the Czech Republic, Finland, and Ireland have provided grants for biomass cogeneration, while Latvia, Lithuania, and Slovakia have used the EU Structural Funds to modernise their CHP sector (Commission 2011b, p. 90).

31 Sometimes the systems for cogeneration were correlated with renewable (green) certificates or energy efficiency (white) certificates (Commission 2011b, p. 89).

32 See Recital 25 of the preamble to Directive 2004/8/EC.

33 "Conversion efficiency" was defined in the Community guidelines (2001) as:

> the ratio between the quantity of primary energy used to produce a secondary form of energy and the quantity of secondary energy actually produced. It is calculated as follows: electric energy produced + thermal energy produced/energy used.

34 The operating aid granted for the industrial use of CHP (namely, the conditions for granting it) was also a benchmark for delivering the operating aid to the production of energy, where the cost of one unit of energy produced using that technique exceeds the market price of one unit of conventional energy (see Community guidelines 2001).

35 These were the already-analysed Articles 11(3) and 14(4) of Directive 2003/54/EC and Paragraphs 1, 2, and 5 of Article 7 of Directive 2001/77/EC.

90 Cogeneration and the EU energy market reform

36 Pursuant to Article 6(1) of Directive 2003/54/EC Member States had to "adopt an authorisation procedure, which shall be conducted in accordance with objective, transparent and non discriminatory criteria" for the needs of construction of new energy sources.
37 Recital 29 of the preamble to Directive 2004/8/EC.
38 Paradoxically, most of the new production capacity was renewable cogeneration driven not by the CHP Directive but by Directive 2001/77/EC and Directive 2009/28/EC (see Commission 2011b, p. 92)
39 The barriers to the development of cogeneration in Slovakia were compiled in three main groups: technical, financial, and administrative. They covered, *inter alia*, "decrease in industrial production with high demand for energy", "disconnection of customers", "not adapted structure of distribution energy supply systems", insufficient awareness of the technologies used in high-efficiency cogeneration" (technical barriers), "lack of own financial resources", "lack of means in the area of public finance", "lack of guarantees to cover credit resources", "sharp rise in the price of natural gas as the most frequently used fuel in terms of cogeneration resources (financial barriers), or "unhelpful approach of distribution companies", "lack of specialist capacities in the area of environmental protection", "administratively demanding procedures relating to determination and approval of electricity purchase prices" (administrative barriers) – as listed in the Slovakia's report on the potential for high-efficiency cogeneration (SEA, n.d., pp. 54–55).
40 As reported in the Hungarian evaluation of the potential for high-efficiency cogeneration:

> [w]e currently do not see any legislative or regulatory barriers to the spreading of cogeneration [in Hungary], but as economically satisfiable heat demand in one of the largest markets for heat, district heating, is satisfied nearly entirely from cogeneration, further opportunities for growth are very limited.
> (Government of Hungary 2009, p. 4)

41 According to the Swedish report on the potential for high-efficiency cogeneration:

> [t]he price of fossil fuels (coal, natural gas and oil) varies between low and high values. The price of fossil fuels affects the potential for new cogeneration to a certain extent. From this we may conclude that, under the given prerequisites and assumptions, investment in biomass cogeneration will be made in the majority of cases, provided that the heating infrastructure is adequate. In itself, the price of fossil fuels is not a determining factor.
> (Öhrlings PricewaterhouseCoopers 2005, p. 61)

42 As they informed:

> [in France] measures were taken to put in place a legal, fiscal, technical and economic framework to encourage its development. These measures have proved effective, since they are now represented by a large number of cogeneration installations in all sectors of the industry, both tertiary and heating networks, for the entire power range.
> (DGEMP, n.d., p. 6)

> [t]he main barrier to effective development of high-efficiency cogeneration plants in [Lithuania] is the current market price of electricity, which is influenced by the marginal costs of short-term electricity production at the INPP

[Ignalina Nuclear Power Plant]. However, this barrier no longer needs to be taken into account, since the situation will change after 2010, when Lithuania will have fulfilled its obligations regarding the decommissioning of Unit II of the INPP.

In relation to utilization of the cogeneration potential, no technical barriers have been found, apart from the insufficient natural gas pressure in the case of construction of combined cycle systems. ...

After analysing the legislation regulating combined heat and power production, it can be stated that no artificial administrative barriers to combined heat and power production are created and the system for its promotion and support is developed in [Lithuania].

(Ministry of the Economy of the Republic of Lithuania 2005, pp. 7, 60)

References

Badami, M., Camillieri, F., Portoraro, A., & Vigliani, E. 2014, "Energetic and economic assessment of cogeneration plants: A comparative design and experimental condition study", *Energy*, 71, pp. 255–262.
Bianco, V. 2018, "Overview of the Italian natural gas sector", *International Journal of Energy Sector Management*, 12(1), pp. 151–168.
Bovis, C.H. 2005, "Financing services of general interest in the EU: how do public procurement and state aids interact to demarcate between market forces and protection?", *European Law Journal*, 11(1), pp. 79–109.
Bröckl, M., Pesola, A., Vehviläinen, I., Tommila, P., & Oy, G.C. 2011, *Guarantees of origin and eco-labeling of electricity in the Nordic countries*, Gaia Consulting Oy, Copenhagen.
Burczak, T.A. 2009, *Socialism after Hayek*, University of Michigan Press, Ann Arbor, MI.
Cameron, P.D. 2007, Competition in energy markets: law and regulation in the European Union, 2nd edn, Oxford University Press, Oxford.
COGEN Europe. 1995, *The barriers to Combined Heat and Power in Europe*, Brussels.
Collier, U. 2002, "European Union energy policy in a changing climate", in *Environmental policy integration: greening sectoral policies in Europe*, ed. A. Lenschow, Earthscan Publications, London – Sterling, VA, pp. 175–192.
Commission. 1988, *Europe 1992: the overall challenge* [summary of the Cecchini report], SEC (88) 524 final, 13 April 1988.
Commission. 1990, *Inventory of features of the electricity supply sector in the European Community*, Working document XVII/315/90-EN, July 1990.
Commission. 1992, *Proposal for a Council Directive concerning common rules for the internal market in electricity. Proposal for a Council Directive Concerning common rules for the internal market in natural gas*, COM (91) 548 final, 21 February 1992.
Commission. 1995a, *For a European Union energy policy – Green Paper*, COM (94) 659 final/2, 23 February 1995.
Commission. 1995b, *Working paper of the Commission on the organisation of the Internal Electricity Market*, SEC (95) 464 final, 22 March 1995.
Commission. 1995c, *White Paper: an energy policy for the European Union*, COM (95) 682 final, 13 December 1995.
Commission. 1996, *Green Paper. Public procurement in the European Union: Exploring the way forward*, COM (96) 583 final, 27 November 1996.

Commission. 1997a, *Communication from the Commission to the Council, the European Parliament, the Economic and Social Committee and the Committee of the Regions: the energy dimension of climate change*, COM (97) 196 final, 14 May 1997.

Commission. 1997b, *Communication from the Commission to the Council, the European Parliament, the Economic and Social Committee and the Committee of the Regions. A Community strategy to promote combined heat and power (CHP) and to dismantle barriers to its development*, COM (97) 514 final, 15 October 1997.

Commission. 1998, *Communication from the Commission to the Council and the European Parliament. Progress report on the multiannual programme for the promotion of energy efficiency in the Community – SAVE II*, COM (98) 458 final, 17 July 1998.

Commission. 1999, *Blue book on geothermal resources. A strategic plan for the development of European geothermal sector*, Office for Official Publications of the European Communities, Luxembourg.

Commission. 2000a, *Communication from the Commission to the Council, the European Parliament, the Economic and Social Committee and the Committee of the Regions: Action Plan to improve energy efficiency in the European Community*, COM (2000) 247 final, 26 April 2000.

Commission. 2000b, *Green Paper: towards a European strategy for the security of energy supply*, COM (2000) 769 final, 29 November 2000.

Commission. 2001a, Community guidelines on State aid for environmental protection (2001/C 37/03), OJ C 37, 3 February 2001.

Commission. 2001b, *Communication from the Commission to the Council and the European Parliament: completing the internal energy market. Proposal for a Directive of the European Parliament and of the Council amending Directives 96/92/EC and 98/30/EC concerning common rules for the internal market in electricity and natural gas. Proposal for a Regulation of the European Parliament and of the Council on conditions for access to the network for cross-border exchanges in electricity*, COM (2001) 125 final, 13 March 2001.

Commission. 2002a, *Amended proposal for a Directive of the European Parliament and of the Council amending Directives 96/92/EC and 98/30/EC concerning rules for the internal markets in electricity and natural gas. Amended proposal for a Regulation of the European Parliament and of the Council on conditions for access to the network for cross-border exchanges in electricity*, COM (2002) 304 final, 7 June 2002.

Commission. 2002b, *Directive of the European Parliament and of the Council on the promotion of cogeneration based on a useful heat demand in the internal energy market*, COM (2002) 415 final, 22 July 2002.

Commission. 2011a, *Commission staff working paper: Impact Assessment accompanying the document Directive of the European Parliament and of the Council on energy efficiency and amending and subsequently repealing Directives 2004/8/EC and 2006/32/EC*, SEC (2011) 779 final, 22 June 2011.

Commission. 2011b, *Commission staff working paper: annexes to the Impact Assessment accompanying the document Directive of the European Parliament and of the Council on energy efficiency and amending and subsequently repealing Directives 2004/8/EC and 2006/32/EC*, SEC (2011) 779 final, 22 June 2011.

Commission. 2014a, *Commission staff working document: progress report on energy efficiency in the European Union. Accompanying the document Report from the Commission to the European Parliament and the Council: Progress Report on the application of Directive 2006/32/EC on energy end-use efficiency and energy services and on the application of*

Directive 2004/8/EC on the promotion of cogeneration based on a useful heat demand in the internal energy market, SWD (2013) 541 final, 8 January 2014.

Commission. 2014b, *Report from the Commission to the European Parliament and the Council: Progress Report on the application of Directive 2006/32/EC on energy end-use efficiency and energy services and on the application of Directive 2004/8/EC on the promotion of cogeneration based on a useful heat demand in the internal energy market*, COM (2013) 938 final, 8 January 2014.

Council. 2002, 2452nd Council meeting – Transport, Telecommunications and Energy, Luxembourg, 3–4 October 2002.

Council. 2003, Common Position (EC) No 6/2003 of 3 February 2003 adopted by the Council, acting in accordance with the procedure referred to in Article 251 of the Treaty establishing the European Community, with a view to adopting a Directive of the European Parliament and of the Council concerning common rules for the internal market in natural gas and repealing Directive 98/30/EC, OJ C 50E, 4 March 2003.

Council Directive 2003/96/EC of 27 October 2003 restructuring the Community framework for the taxation of energy products and electricity, OJ L 283, 31 October 2003.

Council Directive 71/305/EEC of 26 July 1971 concerning the co-ordination of procedures for the award of public works contracts, OJ L 185/5, 25 August 1971.

Council Directive 77/62/EEC of 21 December 1976 coordinating procedures for the award of public supply contracts, OJ L 13/1, 15 January 1977.

Council Directive 88/609/EEC of 24 November 1988 on the limitation of emissions of certain pollutants into the air from large combustion plants, OJ L 336, 7 December 1988.

Council Directive 90/377/EEC of 29 June 1990 concerning a Community procedure to improve the transparency of gas and electricity prices charged to industrial end-users, OJ L 185, 17 July 1990.

Council Directive 90/547/EEC of 29 October 1990 on the transit of electricity through transmission grids, OJ L 313, 13 November 1990.

Council Directive 91/296/EEC of 31 May 1991 on the transit of natural gas through grids, OJ L 147, 12 June 1991.

Council Directive 92/13/EEC of 25 February 1992 coordinating the laws, regulations and administrative provisions relating to the application of Community rules on the procurement procedures of entities operating in the water, energy, transport and telecommunications sectors, OJ L 76, 23 March 1992.

Council Directive 93/38/EEC of 14 June 1993 coordinating the procurement procedures of entities operating in the water, energy, transport and telecommunications sectors, OJ L 199, 9 August 1993.

Council Directive 93/76/EEC of 13 September 1993 to limit carbon dioxide emissions by improving energy efficiency (SAVE), OJ L 237, 22 August 1993.

Council of the European Communities 1977, 77/714/EEC: Council Recommendation of 25 October 1977 on the creation in the Member States of advisory bodies or committees to promote combined heat and power production and the exploitation of residual heat, OJ L 295, 18 November 1977.

Council of the European Union 1994, 1807th meeting of the Council – Energy, Brussels, 30 November 1994.

Cseres, K. 2008, "What has competition done for consumers in liberalised markets?", *Competition Law Review*, 4(2), pp. 77–121.

De Somer, S. 2012, "The Europeanisation of the law on national independent regulatory authorities from a vertical and horizontal perspective", *Review of European Administrative Law*, 5(2), pp. 93–130.

DGEMP n.d., *System of guarantee of origin. Administrative procedures associated with cogeneration installations*. Available from: https://ec.europa.eu/energy/sites/ener/files/documents/ms_reports_translated.zip [27 February 2019].

Directive 2001/77/EC of the European Parliament and of the Council of 27 September 2001 on the promotion of electricity produced from renewable energy sources in the internal electricity market, OJ L 283, 27 October 2001.

Directive 2003/54/EC of the European Parliament and of the Council of 26 June 2003 concerning common rules for the internal market in electricity and repealing Directive 96/92/EC, OJ L 176, 15 July 2003.

Directive 2003/55/EC of the European Parliament and of the Council of 26 June 2003 concerning common rules for the internal market in natural gas and repealing Directive 98/30/EC, OJ L 176, 15 July 2003.

Directive 2004/8/EC of the European Parliament and of the Council of 11 February 2004 on the promotion of cogeneration based on a useful heat demand in the internal energy market and amending Directive 92/42/EEC, OJ L 52, 21 February 2004.

Directive 2009/28/EC of the European Parliament and of the Council of 23 April 2009 on the promotion of the use of energy from renewable sources and amending and subsequently repealing Directives 2001/77/EC and 2003/30/EC, OJ L 140, 5 June 2009.

Directive 2009/72/EC of the European Parliament and of the Council of 13 July 2009 Concerning common rules for the internal market in electricity and repealing Directive 2003/54/EC, OJ L 211, 14 August 2009.

Directive 96/92/EC of the European Parliament and of the Council of 19 December 1996 concerning common rules for the internal market in electricity, OJ L 27, 30 January 1997.

Directive 98/30/EC of the European Parliament and of the Council of 22 June 1998 concerning common rules for the internal market in natural gas, OJ L 204, 21 July 1998.

Economic and Social Committee 2001, *Opinion of the Economic and Social Committee on the proposal for a Directive of the European Parliament and of the Council amending Directives 96/92/EC and 98/30/EC concerning common rules for the internal market in electricity and natural gas, and the Proposal for a Regulation of the European Parliament and of the Council on conditions for access to the network for cross-border exchanges in electricity*, 17 October 2001, OJ C 36, 8 February 2002.

Ehlermann, C.D. 1987, "The internal market following the Single European Act", *Common Market Law Review*, 24(3), pp. 361–409.

Eikeland, P.O. 2011, "The third internal energy market package: new power relations among Member States, EU institutions and non-state actors?", *JCMS: Journal of Common Market Studies*, 49(2), pp. 243–263.

Elżanowski, F.M. 2011, "The duties of the President of the Polish Energy Regulatory Office in the context of implementing the Third Energy Package", *Yearbook of Antitrust and Regulatory Studies (YARS)*, 4(4), pp. 135–150.

Energy Charter Secretariat 2002, *Impacts of market liberalisation on energy efficiency policies and programmes*. Available from: https://energycharter.org/fileadmin/Docu

mentsMedia/Thematic/Liberalisation_and_Energy_Efficiency_2002_en.pdf [27 February 2019].

European Parliament 2002a, *Report on the proposal for a Directive of the European Parliament and of the Council amending Directives 96/92/EC and 98/30/EC concerning common rules for the internal market in electricity and natural gas*, final A5-0077/2002, 1 March 2002.

European Parliament 2002b, European Parliament legislative resolution on the proposal for a European Parliament and Council Directive amending Directives 96/92/EC and 98/30/EC concerning common rules for the internal market in electricity and natural gas, 13 March 2002, OJ C 47E, 27 February 2003.

Ferreira, A.C.M., Rocha, A.M.A.C., Teixeira, S.F.C.F., Nunes, M.L., & Martins, L.B. 2012, "On solving the profit maximization of small cogeneration systems", in *Computational science and its applications – ICCSA 2012*, eds B. Murgante, O. Gervasi, S. Misra, N. Nedjah, A.M.A.C. Rocha, D. Taniar, & B.O. Apduhan, Springer, Berlin and Heidelberg, pp. 147–158.

Filippini, M., Hunt, L.C., & Zorić, J. 2014, "Impact of energy policy instruments on the estimated level of underlying energy efficiency in the EU residential sector", *Energy Policy*, 69, pp. 73–81.

Flin, D. 2010, *Cogeneration: a user's guide*, The Institution of Engineering and Technology, London.

Frangopoulos, C.A. 2012, "A method to determine the power to heat ratio, the cogenerated electricity and the primary energy savings of cogeneration systems after the European Directive", *Energy*, 45(1), pp. 52–61.

Geller, H., Harrington, P., Rosenfeld, A.H., Tanishima, S., & Unander, F. 2006, "Polices for increasing energy efficiency: thirty years of experience in OECD countries", *Energy Policy*, 34(5), pp. 556–573.

Gerwen van, R.J.F. 2003, "Systems and applications", in *High-temperature solid oxide fuel cells: fundamentals, design and applications*, eds S.C. Singhal & K. Kendall, Elsevier, Oxford, pp. 365–392.

Glachant, J.M. 2016, "Tacking stock of the EU 'Power Target Model'... and steering its future course", *Energy Policy*, 96, pp. 673–679.

Government of Hungary 2009, *Progress towards increasing the share of high-efficiency cogeneration based on useful heat demand in Hungary*. Available from: https://ec.europa.eu/energy/sites/ener/files/documents/ms_reports_translated.zip [27 February 2019].

Grohnheit, P.E. 1999, *Energy policy responses to the climate change challenge: the consistency of European CHP, renewables and energy efficiency policies*, Risø-R-1147(EN), Risø National Laboratory, Roskilde.

Grohnheit, P.E., & Gram Mortensen, B.O. 2003, "Competition in the market for space heating. District heating as the infrastructure for competition among fuels and technologies", *Energy Policy*, 31(9), pp. 817–826.

Grzeszczak, R. 2012, "Executive power in the European Union", *The multi-level and polycentric European Union: legal and political studies*, eds R. Grzeszczak & I.P. Karolewski, Lit, LIT Verlag, Berlin, pp. 77–102.

Gvozdenac, D., Gvozdenac Urošević, B., Menke, C., Urošević, D., & Bangviwat, A. 2017, "High efficiency cogeneration: CHP and non-CHP energy", *Energy*, 135, pp. 269–278.

Hajabdollahi, H., Ganjehkaviri, A., & Jaafar, M.N.M. 2015, "Assessment of new operational strategy in optimization of CCHP plant for different climates using evolutionary algorithms", *Applied Thermal Engineering*, 75, pp. 468–480.

Hammons, T.J. 2011, *Electricity infrastructures in the global marketplace*, InTech, Rijeka.

Heinen, A. 2001, "The interface between electricity liberalization and environmental protection: the German example", in *The liberalization of electricity and natural gas in the European Union*, D. Geradin, Kluwer Law International, the Hague, pp. 81–106.

Hendriks, C., & Blok, K. 1996, "Regulation for combined heat and power in the European Union", *Energy Conversion and Management*, 37(6–8), pp. 729–734.

Isaac, M., & Vuuren, D.P. van, 2009, "Modeling global residential sector energy demand for heating and air conditioning in the context of climate change", Energy Policy, 37(2), pp. 507–521.

Jones, C. 2010, "Introduction", in *The internal energy market: the Third Liberalisation Package*, ed. C. Jones, vol 1 of *EU energy law*, 3rd edn, Claeys & Casteels, Leuven, pp. 1–14.

Jörß, W., Holst Joergensen, B., Loeffler, P., Morthorst, P.E., Uyterlinde, M., van Sambeek, E., & Wehnert, T. 2003, *Decentralised power generation in the liberalised EU energy markets: results from the DECENT research project*, Springer-Verlag, Berlin and Heidelberg.

Kanellakis, M., Martinopoulos, G., & Zachariadis, T. 2013, "European energy policy – a review", *Energy Policy*, 62, pp. 1020–1030.

Kersbergen, K. van, & Verbeek, B. 2004, "Subsidiarity as a principle of governance in the European Union", *Comparative European Politics*, 2(2), pp. 142–162.

Khabdullin, A., Khabdullina, Z., Khabdullina, G., Lauka, D., & Blumberga, D. 2017, "Demand response analysis methodology in district heating system", *Energy Procedia*, 128, pp. 539–543.

Kierkegaard, S.M. 2006, "Going, going, gone! E-procurement in the EU", *International Journal of Computing & Information Sciences*, 4(1), pp. 30–39.

Kilkis, B.I., & Kilkis, S. 2007, "Upgrading EU Directive with rational exergy model", *ASHRAE Transactions*, 113(2), pp. 181–191.

Lazaro, E.C., Millan, A.R., & Peral, P.R. 2006, "Analysis of cogeneration in the present energy framework", *Fuel Processing Technology*, 87(2), pp. 163–168.

Lough, J.M., Wigley, T.M.L., & Palutikof, J.P. 1983, "Climate and climate impact scenarios for Europe in a warmer world", *Journal of Climate and Applied Meteorology*, 22(10), pp. 1673–1684.

Lund, J.W., & Chiasson, A. 2007, "Examples of combined heat and power plants using geothermal energy", *Proceedings European Geothermal Congress 2007*, Unterhaching, pp. 1–7. Available from http://www.geothermal-energy.org/pdf/IGAstandard/EGC/2007/091.pdf [27 February 2019].

Magnusson, D. 2016, "Who brings the heat? – from municipal to diversified ownership in the Swedish district heating market post-liberalization", *Energy Research & Social Science*, 22, pp. 198–209.

Marquardt, P.D. 1994, "Subsidiary and sovereignty in the European Union", *Fordham International Law Journal*, 18(2), pp. 616–640.

Michaelowa, A. 1998, "Impact of interest groups on EU climate policy", *European Environment*, 8(5), pp. 152–160.

Ministry of the Economy of the Republic of Lithuania 2005, *Analysis of high-capacity cogeneration potential in Lithuania and adoption of necessary methodologies or other legal instruments required for full implementation of Directive 2004/8/EC of the European Parliament and of the Council*. Available from: https://ec.europa.eu/energy/sites/ener/files/documents/ms_reports_translated.zip [27 February 2019].

Moreci, E., Ciulla, G., & Brano, V.L. 2016, "Annual heating energy requirements of office buildings in a European climate", *Sustainable Cities and Society*, 20, pp. 81–95.

Moreira, N.A., Monteiro, E., & Ferreira, S. 2007, "Transposition of the EU cogeneration directive: a vision for Portugal", *Energy Policy*, 35(11), pp. 5747–5753.

Moya, J.A. 2013, "Impact of support schemes and barriers in Europe on the evolution of cogeneration", *Energy Policy*, 60, pp. 345–355.

Musatescu, V., Podasca, C., & Opris, I. 2017, "The Romanian state aid policy for promoting electricity produced in high efficiency cogeneration", *European State Aid Law Quarterly (ESTAL)*, 2, pp. 243–262.

Newbery, D., & Pollitt, M. 1997, "The restructuring and privatisation of Britain's CEBG – was it worth it?", *The Journal of Industrial Economics*, 45(3), pp. 269–303.

Nowak, B. 2010, "Energy market of the European union: common or segmented?", *The Electricity Journal*, 23(10), pp. 27–37.

Öhrlings PricewaterhouseCoopers 2005, *An assessment of the potential for high-efficiency cogeneration in Sweden*. Available from: https://ec.europa.eu/energy/sites/ener/files/documents/ms_reports_translated.zip [27 February 2019].

Olsson, L., Wetterlund, E., & Söderström, M. 2015, "Assessing the climate impact of district heating systems with combined heat and power production and industrial excess heat", *Resources, Conservation and Recycling*, 96, pp. 31–39.

Paroussos, L., Mangalagiu, D., Meissner, F., & Jaeger, C. 2016, "The economic cost of a transition to a low-carbon economy: the case of Bulgaria and Romania", *The Journal of Energy and Development*, 42(1/2), pp. 33–66.

Pearson, P., & Watson, J. 2012, *UK Energy Policy 1980 – 2010: a history and lessons to be learnt*, Parliamentary Group for Energy Studies, London. Available from: http://sro.sussex.ac.uk/38852/1/uk-energy-policy.pdf [27 February 2019].

Pepermans, G. 2019, "European energy market liberalization: experiences and challenges", *International Journal of Economic Policy Studies*, 13(1), pp. 3–26.

Piggin, R., Young, K., & McLaughlin, R. 1999, "The current fieldbus standards situation – a European view", *Assembly Automation*, 19(4), pp. 286–289.

Pilavachi, P.A. 2000, "Power generation with gas turbine systems and combined heat and power", *Applied Thermal Engineering*, 20(15–16), pp. 1421–1429.

Pointvogl, A. 2009, "Perceptions, realities, concession – what is driving the integration of European energy policies?", *Energy Policy*, 37(12), pp. 5704–5716.

Prando, D., Renzi, M., Gasparella, A., & Baratieri, M. 2015, "Monitoring of the energy performance of a district heating CHP plant based on biomass boiler and ORC generator", *Applied Thermal Engineering*, 79, pp. 98–107.

Rillaerts, F. 1999, "Concessions in the water sector", *Desalination*, 124(1–3), pp. 13–17.

Roggenkamp, M.M., & Boisseleau, F. 2005, "The liberalisation of the EU electricity market and the role of power exchanges", in *The regulation of power exchanges in Europe*, eds M.M. Roggenkamp & F. Boisseleau, Intersentia, Antwerp and Oxford, pp. 1–30.

Ropenus, S., Jacobsen, H.K., & Schröder, S.T. 2011, "Network regulation and support schemes – how policy interactions affect the integration of distributed generation", *Renewable Energy*, 36(7), pp. 1949–1956.

Rowlands, I.H. 2005, "The European directive on renewable electricity: conflicts and compromises", *Energy Policy*, 33(8), pp. 965–974.

SEA n.d., *Analysis of the national potential of high-efficiency cogeneration in the Slovak Republic*. Available from: https://ec.europa.eu/energy/sites/ener/files/documents/ms_reports_translated.zip [27 February 2019].

Sibilio, S., Roselli, C., & Sasso, M. 2010, "Micropolygeneration applications for mild climate", *Proceedings of the 6th International Conference on Improving Energy Efficiency in Commercial Buildings*, Frankfurt am Main, pp. 325–337.

Single European Act, OJ L 169, 29 June 1987.

Sokołowski, M.M. 2016, *Regulation in the European electricity sector*, Routledge, Abingdon and New York, NY.

Spinoni, J., Vogt, J.V., Barbosa, P., Dosio, A., McCormick, N., Bigano, A., & Füssel, H.M. 2018, "Changes of heating and cooling degree-days in Europe from 1981 to 2100", *International Journal of Climatology*, 38, pp. 191–208.

Swora, M. 2010, "Intelligent grid: unfinished regulation in the Third EU Energy Package", *Journal of Energy & Natural Resources Law*, 28(4), pp. 465–480.

Talus, K. 2013, *EU energy law and policy: a critical account*, Oxford University Press, Oxford.

Talus, K., & Aalto, P. 2017, "Competences in EU energy policy", in *Research handbook on EU energy law and policy*, eds R. Leal-Arcas & J. Wouters, Edward Elgar Publishing, Cheltenham, pp. 15–29.

Teeble, A.J. 2013, *F.A. Hayek*, Bloomsbury Academic, New York, NY and London.

Toth, A.G. 1986, "The legal status of the declarations annexed to the Single European Act", *Common Market Law Review*, 23(4), pp. 803–812.

UK Parliament 1982, *Oil and Gas (Enterprise) Bill*. Available from: https://api.parliament.uk/historic-hansard/commons/1982/jan/19/oil-and-gas-enterprise-bill [27 February 2019].

van der Does, T. 1996, "Fuel cell co-generation: the future of co-generation", *Journal of Power Sources*, 61(1–2), pp. 49–51.

Verbruggen, A. 2005, "CHP (Combined Heat & Power) regulation by the EU for facing the liberalised electricity market", *International Energy Journal*, 6(1) part 3, pp. 29–45.

Verbruggen, A. 2008, "The merit of cogeneration: measuring and rewarding performance", *Energy Policy*, 36, pp. 3069–3076.

Verdeaux, J.-J. 2003, "Public procurement in the European Union and in the United States: a comparative study", *Public Contract Law Journal*, 32(4), pp. 713–738.

Westner, G., & Madlener, R. 2010, "The benefit of regional diversification of cogeneration investments in Europe: a mean-variance portfolio analysis", *Energy Policy*, 38, pp. 7911–7920.

Zimmermann, C.F., & Talus, K. 2008, "Regulation of electricity markets at the EU level", *European Energy and Environmental Law Review*, 17(1), pp. 12–22.

4 CHP in the EU climate action

The entry into force of the Kyoto Protocol in February 2005 was the impulse to boost the climate action. at the European level in a wider way. Two years later, in 2007, the basic assumptions of the EU climate agenda for 2020 were provided; this was the result of "a must" to "adopt the necessary domestic measures and take the lead internationally to ensure that global average temperature increases do not exceed pre-industrial levels by more than 2°C" (Commission 2007, p. 2). The proposed agenda was to cover three identified fields: greenhouse gases, renewable energy sources, and energy efficiency. The EU action was to reduce (greenhouse gases), promote (renewable energy sources), and enhance them (energy efficiency), as the pillars of the climate-energy policy of the EU can be outlined.

At that time, the first percentage assumptions regarding the previously mentioned areas were presented, i.e. the EU "3 x 20%" goals for 2020 concerning the reduction of GHG by at least 20% in comparison to 1990, the increase in the share of renewable capacity by 20%, and the improvement of energy efficiency by 20%; an exception concerned the reduction of emissions which could be decreased by 30%, if an international agreement on climate change has been concluded (cf. Etty et al. 2012, p. 236).[1] In March 2007, the EU leaders gathered at the European Council confirmed this basic framework of the European integrated climate and energy policy, urging the Member States and EU institutions to pursue the action aimed at realising those goals (European Council 2007). This also concerned legal environment. Here, a major change was brought by legislation recognised as the Climate and Energy Package (see Capros et al. 2011; Kulovesi, Morgera, & Muñoz 2011; Wettestad, Eikeland, & Nilsson 2012). Agreed in December 2008 (European Council 2008), the Package was passed and published the next year, establishing a new regulatory framework on the EU policy on energy and climate (see Sokołowski 2016, pp. 38, 39). In October 2014, the European Council established the 2030 climate and energy policy targets of at least 40% GHG emission reduction (from 1990s levels), as well as renewable energy and energy efficiency goals of at least 27%. In

2018, the targets for renewables and energy efficiency were revised and increased, accordingly to at least 32% in terms of a share for renewable energy and to at least 32.5% regarding the improvements in energy efficiency (see Commission n.d. d). Moreover, in December 2015, the first multilateral agreement on climate change covering almost all of the global emissions – the Paris Agreement – has been concluded (see Banet 2017; Commission 2016a).

Has there been a place for cogeneration in this agenda? The answer is: "yes, but ...". Cogeneration has been included in the European regulatory framework for climate (and sustainability and environment) for a long time, much earlier than its appearance in the Climate and Energy Package. Due to its features, first recognised in the 1970s–1980s, combined heat and power has been maintained as a policy option through the 1990s–2000s and, in the twenty-first century, is attracting the attention of European policymakers – although with varied results if any. Despite variations in the current degree of interest in cogeneration, it still enables a better allocation of resources, is an energy-efficient source, and, as a result, can limit CO_2 emission (see Commission 1995, p. 4).

In addition, CHP can, in many ways, be linked to renewable energy sources. Regulating these two areas together has been a European tradition for quite some time. Numerous policy documents and legislation manage them together, providing a similar or fairly similar approach towards both cogeneration and renewables. What can be revealed at this point concerns the road they have followed. The way to the development of CHP has turned towards renewables. However, the space for promoting cogeneration itself is still there. This chapter aims to provide some answers.

"[W]inning the battle against climate change, inside the EU and together with the international community", needed medium and long term strategies; during their preparation the Commission (2005a, pp. 3, 6) placed energy efficiency and energy savings in the centre of any future EU energy strategy.[2] What should be clearly emphasised, is that cogeneration means energy efficiency. However, discussing combined heat and power only by considering energy efficiency would be too simple and – what is worse – very often misleading. Therefore, in the previous chapters, cogeneration was analysed from different angles, put into the framework of initial European policies on combined heat and power or the EU energy market reform. Despite being addressed there too, energy efficiency was rather the background (than the core) in that part of the book. In this context, in this chapter CHP is discussed as an important element of the European Union climate action (as a whole), and a pillar of the EU action on energy efficiency (as an element of the climate action). Hopefully, this "stacking approach",[3] where one issue is placed inside another (climate action – energy efficiency – cogeneration), is sufficiently clear.

In this short introduction, let us remember that the role played by combined heat and power in the European climate agenda derives from its advantages noticed by the EU (see Chapter 2 of this book). CHP has been defined as one of the very few technologies that could offer an important short- or medium- term contribution to the energy efficiency and environmental policies in the European Union (see Commission 1997b, p. 2). Because cogeneration could contribute to meeting the EU Kyoto and post-Kyoto commitment (cf. Anger 2008; Whiteley 2001), it has become an element of the European action on reducing emissions. These two elements, i.e. energy efficiency (as in the initial policies on combined heat and power) and the reduction of emissions (noticeably larger in climate awareness) made the EU willing to significantly increase the share of cogeneration in the European energy mix by 2010 (see Commission 1997a, p. 9).

The latter, linked with the possibilities to develop renewable capacity through and in cogeneration, makes it possible to cap all three pillars of the EU climate-energy policy by combined heat and power. So, the topics mentioned here are discussed in this chapter, starting with the reduction of emissions and the promotion of renewable energy sources, analysed jointly to balance the emphasis presented in the part on energy efficiency – the main strength of cogeneration, widely addressed at the European level.

Cogeneration in the framework on emissions and renewables

Cogeneration has been covered by the European policies and law on emissions for more than 20 years. This concerns both the regulatory framework on industrial emissions, as well as the EU Emission Trading System (EU ETS) established by the European Union for the needs of targeting air quality and climate change. It results from the cogeneration's potential for reducing emissions, driven by its pro-efficiency values. The 1990s' projections calculated the Community's potential for the reduction of emissions (i.e. cost-effective, technical potential) for up to 20% (as of 2010), where around half of the reduction could come from energy sector (generation), being achieved by action on energy efficiency, including the enhancement of cogeneration (Commission 1995, p. 13); or assumed that the possibility of doubling the 9% share of cogeneration usage in electricity (as declared in the 1990s), when considered as replacing old CHP plants, could reduce CO_2 emissions by 150 Mt per year or around 4% of the total CO_2 emissions in the Community in 2010 (Commission 1997b, p. 10).

CHP and industrial emissions

The background outlined led to cogeneration being finally addressed in European legislation on emissions. A significant step on the road to the promotion of cogeneration was made in 1998, when the announced revision of Directive 88/609/EEC was presented, and a new approach to cogeneration was offered by requiring that, where feasible, new plants use cogeneration. The draft revision highlighted bringing "the existing Directive 88/609/EEC into line with recent developments in Community policy on sustainable development" (Commission 1998c, pp. 14–15). For this purpose, it assumed dismantling the barriers hindering combined heat and power, identified in the Strategy on CHP, by introducing the requirement to consider CHP as an option when designing new energy installation (Commission 1998c, p. 8).

The draft legislation changed into law in 2001, when the new LCP Directive (Directive 2001/80/EC) was passed (see Vajda 2016; Kaldellis et al. 2005, p. 512). As declared earlier (see Commission 2000b, p. 10), the new regulatory framework on emissions from large combustion plants supplied the provisions intended to promote combined heat and power in the Community (cf. Streimikiene, Burneikis, & Punys 2005, p. 37). It derived from the pro-efficiency nature of CHP, appreciated in the preamble to the LCP Directive ("[w]here it is feasible the combined production of heat and electricity represents a valuable opportunity for significantly improving overall efficiency in fuel use").[4] In this context, under Article 6 of the LCP Directive, the Member States had to ensure the examination of feasibility (both technical and economic) of implementing cogeneration[5] (see Kliucininkas, Zieniute, & Mockuviene 2005, p. 401); this concerned new power plants, granted licences after November 2002,[6] or combustion plants extended by at least 50 MW (cf. Wojdyga, Chorzelski, & Rożycka-Wrońska 2014, p. 160). If the feasibility was confirmed, such installations were to be developed; however, "bearing in mind the market and the distribution situation" was always a way-out which enabled actions on cogeneration to be stopped in a given power plant. Moreover, higher emission levels (NO_x) were given for efficient gas turbines used in cogeneration.[7]

After 15 years in power, Directive 2001/80/EC was repealed by Directive 2010/75/EU on industrial emissions (IED), as the repeal was postponed to 1 January 2016 (see Hitchin 2011, p. 42). The new Directive omitted previous legal solutions concerning cogeneration, applied after a positive feasibility study – the former Article 6 of the LCP Directive was not included in Directive 2010/75/EU. Nevertheless, what has been kept in the new legal framework on industrial emissions with respect to cogeneration, were the emission levels for NO_x as established by Directive 2001/80/EC. Parenthetically, one should emphasise that the IED attaches a great importance to the emission limit values,[8] being "an essence of the IED and its regulatory system" (Sokołowski 2018, p. 262). A vital role in this system is played by the Best Available Techniques (BAT) which determine the conditions of environmental permits granted under the IED (Sokołowski 2018, p. 262). They cover different areas e.g. common waste water and waste gas

CHP in the EU climate action 103

treatment/management systems in the chemical sector, non-ferrous metals industries, for refining mineral oil and gas (see Ibáñez-Forés, Bovea, & Azapagic 2013; Polders et al. 2012; Yukseler et al. 2017), being passed in the form of separate decisions (Sokołowski 2018, p. 263). One of them, i.e. Decision 2017/1442/EU concerns large combustion plants (2017 LCP BAT conclusions).[9] As all BAT conclusions, this Decision results from the BAT reference document (Sokołowski 2018, p. 263). In this case, it is the 2017 BAT LCP reference document elaborated on by Thierry Lecomte et al. (2017).[10] Both of them – the reference document and the conclusions – repeatedly refer to cogeneration.

In the 2017 BAT LCP reference document, besides being presented in its initial chapters of rather descriptive character,[11] CHP is discussed more broadly in Chapter 3 "General techniques to prevent and/or reduce emissions and consumption" (with detailed comments and case studies provided in the subsequent chapters). CHP is listed there among "General primary techniques to reduce emissions/consumption" (section 3.1.1) and "Techniques to increase energy efficiency" (section 3.2.3), assessed as one of the techniques having "a general positive and global impact on emissions and/or consumption due to … better energy efficiency or to … full integration into the combustion process" (Lecomte et al. 2017, p. 101), and recovering heat lost in energy processes, "to avoid such heat being wasted and to efficiently use the fuel's energy content" (Lecomte et al. 2017, p. 254). These characteristics of combined heat and power, together with its other features, are juxtaposed with certain applications of CHP techniques, as shown in Table 4.1.

The reviewed specific applications, like cogeneration in general (see Celades et al. 2018; Rende et al. 2018, p. 28), are characterised by higher energy efficiency, increased total fuel utilisation, as well as reduced greenhouse gas emissions. The specific values vary among different types and scale of CHP unit. The comparison of emissions from smaller and bigger CCGT CHP units, as reviewed in the 2017 BAT LCP reference document, is presented in Table 4.2.

The techniques and standards addressed in the 2017 BAT LCP reference document are reflected in the 2017 LCP BAT conclusions, formally established by Decision 2017/1442/EU (the 2017 LCP BAT are attached to the Decision in the form of an annex) – in practice, they derive from the reference document.[12] The power of the conclusions is highlighted in Recital 1 of a short preamble to Decision 2017/1442/EU:

> [b]est available techniques (BAT) conclusions are the reference for setting permit conditions for installations covered by Chapter II of Directive 2010/75/EU and competent authorities should set emission limit values which ensure that, under normal operating conditions, emissions do not exceed the emission levels associated with the best available techniques as laid down in the BAT conclusions.

Table 4.1 Selected CHP techniques to increase energy efficiency

technique	achieved environmental benefits	environmental performance and operational data	technical considerations relevant to applicability — new plants	technical considerations relevant to applicability — existing plants	economics
cogeneration (CHP), including district heating (generally)	increased fuel utilisation	high operational experience	when locating a new project, existing steam and hot water needs have to be investigated	very limited, depending on site-specific demands for heat loads	the fuel price might be higher
heat recovery in CHP plants	increased total fuel utilisation	high operational experience	applicable within the constraints associated with the local power and heat demand		NA
flue-gas condenser	increased efficiency/ reduced emissions	high operational experience with cross-media effect recorded: waste water stream generated (condenser blowdown)	applicable to CHP units, provided there is enough demand for low-temperature heat		NA
heat recovery in CHP plants: HFO- and/or gas-oil-fired boilers	increased efficiency	high operational experience; specific CO_2 emission: 370 g/kWh (produced electricity + recoverable heat) when operating on HFO at a total boiler plant efficiency of 80–96%	applicable within the constraints associated with the local power and heat demand		NA
heat accumulation (heat storage)	increased efficiency and decreased NO_X and CO emissions; less use of oil-based peak load boilers when unloading the accumulator	NA	generally applicable		NA

Source: Lecomte et al. 2017, p. 407, 471, 511.

Table 4.2 Emissions produced by CCGT CHP units

type	operating energy efficiency [h/yr]	equivalent full load factor	annual NO$_x$ emission concentrations [mg/Nm^3]	annual CO emission concentrations [mg/Nm^3]	commissioning year	sectors
combined-cycle gas turbinc – CHP (50–600 MW$_t$)	4000	55–93%	< 75	30 <	mid-1990s – 2011	pulp and paper, food and drink, and chemical industries, or energy generation (electricity and district heat)
combined-cycle gas turbine – CHP (> 600 MW$_t$)	4000	> 70%	< 32	< 5	2000–2011	industry (like the chemical sector) or energy generation (electricity and district heat)

Source: Lecomte et al. 2017, p. 570, 571.

Table 4.3 Selected BAT-AEELs for combustion units

type of combustion unit	BAT-AEELs			
	net electrical efficiency		net total fuel utilisation	
	new unit	existing unit	new unit	existing unit
Solid biomass and/or peat boiler	33.5–to > 38%	28–38%	73–99%	73–99%
Gas-oil-fired open-cycle gas turbine	> 33%	25–35.7%	n/a	n/a
Lignite-fired, < 1000 MWt	36.5–40%	31.5–39.5%	75–97%	75–97%
Coal-fired, < 1 000 MWt	36.5–41,5%	32.5–41.5%	75–97%	75–97%
HFO- and/or gas-oil-fired boiler	> 36.4%	35.6–37.4%	80–96%	80–96%
Boiler using liquid process fuels from the chemical industry, including those mixed with HFO, gas oil and/or other liquid fuels	> 36.4%	35.6–37.4%	80–96%	80–96%
Boiler using gaseous process fuels from the chemical industry, including those mixed with natural gas and/or other gaseous fuels	39–42.5%	38–40%	78–95%	78–95%
Gas-oil-fired combined cycle gas turbine	> 40%	33–44%	n/a	n/a
Lignite-fired, ≥ 1 000 MWth	42–44%	33.5–42.5%	75–97%	75–97%
Coal-fired, ≥ 1 000 MWt	45–46%	33.5–44%	75–97%	75–97%
CHP CCGT (combustion of iron and steel process gases)	> 47%	40–48%	60–82%	60–82%
HFO- and/or gas-oil-fired reciprocating engine – combined cycle (combustion of HFO and/or gas oil in reciprocating engines)	> 48%	n/a	n/a	n/a
CHP CCGT, 50–600 MWt (combustion of natural gas)	53–58.5%	46–54%	65–95%	65–95%
CHP CCGT, ≥ 600 MWt (combustion of natural gas)	57–60.5%	50–60%	65–95%	65–95%

Source: the 2017 LCP BAT conclusions.

This approach, together with the necessary reviews and updates of BAT reference documents, makes the legal environment for emission criteria, established in the IED, flexible and binding – so "being 'the reference' does not mean that they have no legal force", as expressed in the aforementioned Recital (Sokołowski 2018, p. 265). In terms of the scope of this power, the 2017 LCP BAT conclusions target three activities from a broad list specified in Annex I of the IED, i.e. combustion of fuels, gasification of coal, and disposal and recovery of waste (Sokołowski 2018,

p. 265, cf. Makowska et al. 2019; Dziok, Grzywacz, & Bochenek 2019). Cogeneration (here we mean large scale cogeneration) falls under the first of them, as the conclusions cover only the combustion of fuels in the installations with a total rated thermal input accounting for at least 50 MW, pursuant to the Chapter III and Annex V of the IED.

For this type of cogeneration, the 2017 LCP BAT conclusions provide a regulatory framework that differs in some points from the other provisions on combustion of fuels. This concerns both the general rules established by the conclusions, like the energy efficiency levels associated with the best available techniques (BAT-AEELs),[13] the monitoring associated with BAT-AEELs,[14] as well as specific emission values introduced for combined heat and power. Table 4.3 reviews some of them.

BAT-AEELs for combined heat and power, set by the 2017 LCP BAT conclusions, either provide general levels for all combustion units of a given type (e.g. coal-fired power plants) supplementing them with separate provisions on combined heat and power,[15] or introduce separate types of cogeneration units, like different categories of CHP CCGT listed in Table 4.3. As one may observe, the latter units (especially combustion of natural gas) reach the highest level of net electrical efficiency, accounting for almost 60%, or even more than that.

When discussing external benchmarking in the public regulation one issue should be mentioned. It is the matter of its precarious nature highlighted by Verbruggen et al. (2013). As they write, except "the difficulties in fixing appropriate efficiency numbers" applying external benchmarks, like in the EU law, weakens the benchmarks because of "the false assumption that any cogenerated power and CCGT power are perfectly comparable and exchangeable any time of the year" (Verbruggen et al. 2013, p. 581). Trying to find a solution, these authors claim that the "[p]ublic regulation needs uncontested defined concepts and indicators, measured by argued, transparent and robust methods" (Verbruggen et al. 2013, p. 581). While agreeing in principle with this statement, it should be emphasised that creating such universal definitions is not easy. Benchmarking delivers adoptable and measurable joint approach (see Ziemele, Cilinskis, & Blumberga 2018). The case study attitude (see e.g. Badami, Gerboni, & Portoraro 2017, pp. 701–702) does not seem to be a real alternative as the problem with harmonisation occurs. A well-discussed, widely consulted, and periodically revised (see Gvozdenac et al. 2017, p. 269) benchmark adapted to market needs, and considering its political assumptions (e.g. related to the support of high-efficiency cogeneration), seems, to some degree, to be a fair option – at least until a better one is not offered.

CHP and EU ETS

Apart from its significance to the European regulatory framework established under the IED, cogeneration has played a vital role in the compliance with the

Kyoto Protocol (Gambini et al. 2019, p. 3), having the capacity to "make a significant contribution to achieving the Kyoto target by reducing emissions" (Commission 1998c, p. 10) – the EU's Kyoto goal.[16] In 2000, its potential equivalent of CO_2 reduction was assessed at 65 Mt of CO_2 which could bring a 1.6% reduction in relation to the 1990 level (Commission 2000c, p. 33). The increased use of cogeneration in some of the Member States (EU-15), was reported as one of the factors contributing to a drop in CO_2 emissions in the energy sector (electricity and heat) between 1990 and 2000 (Commission 2002b, p. 16).[17] Moreover, as discussed in Chapter 3 of this book, "the right framework in the liberalised market" could triple the use of cogeneration in the electricity production, and so lead to an additional reduction of CO_2, estimated as around 65 Mt less in a year (Commission 2000d, p. 66).

Combined heat and power is also an element of the EU ETS, being anchored in Directive 2003/87/EC (EU ETS Directive) as early as 2003, when the system was created (cf. Mortensen 2004).[18] Nevertheless, the issue of CHP was addressed in the EU ETS Directive very briefly (see Cendra de Larragán de 2008, p. 70); the proposals to extend the role of cogeneration, submitted during the legislative process on the Directive, were not contained in the final version of the legislation – this concerns, for example, the initiatives for providing a concrete legal basis for including cogeneration among indirect mechanisms to reduce CO_2 and grant it coverage in the national allocation plans (see European Parliament 2002b).[19] Pursuant to Recital 20 of the preamble to the Directive 2003/87/EC, the Directive itself had to "encourage the use of more energy-efficient technologies, including combined heat and power technology, producing less emissions per unit of output". However, a wider policy agenda on combined heat and power was coming soon. As announced in the same Recital, "the future directive ... on the promotion of cogeneration based on useful heat demand in the internal energy market will specifically promote combined heat and power technology".

The previously mentioned "future directive" was, of course, the CHP Directive (Directive 2004/8/EC). Despite providing a complex legal framework on combined heat and power, the issue of emissions – just like cogeneration in the EU ETS Directive – was addressed there rather sparingly. Under Article 11 of the CHP Directive, the Commission had to review the application of the Directive. This involved reporting on, *inter alia*, the "progress towards realising national potentials for high-efficiency cogeneration" as well as addressing the implications for the European initiatives, including the emission trading under Directive 2003/87/EC, which were related to high-efficiency cogeneration.

In 2009, with the amendment of the EU ETS Directive, by Directive 2009/29/EC, stricter rules for the European regulatory framework on greenhouse gases were adopted. Changes also affected the legal environment for cogeneration related to CO_2 emissions, and it is worth noting that they promoted the use of combined heat and power. Pursuant to Directive 2009/29/EC, cogeneration was enhanced by an exemption from a general rule that began in 2013, i.e. the full auctioning of CO_2 allowances in the EU electricity sector[20] as a method for allocating them within the EU ETS (see Commission 2015, p. 96). The exemption gave a possibility to provide free allowances for district heating and cooling as well as for heating and cooling produced in high-efficiency CHP units. As explained in the preamble to Directive 2009/29/EC (Recital 19), these free allowances were to mitigate the negative effects of competition introduced in the emission trade.[21] Pursuant to Article 10a(4) introduced to the EU ETS Directive by the previously discussed revision of 2009, the free allocation for high efficiency CHP, related to "economically justifiable demand", has to be adjusted linearly on the annual basis, starting from 2013.[22]

The free allowances are aimed at encouraging electricity generators delivering heat to DH or industrial installations to produce electricity in a more efficiency way (Commission 2008, p. 8). Those allowances also address competitiveness of some industries and set the pace for the transition to a low-emission economy in the EU (see Commission 2015, p. 97). Currently, the allowances amount is still (2013–2020) calculated under the Commission's Decision 2011/278/EU (Benchmarking Decision) with the use of a benchmark value based on historical emission. With respect to combined heat and power, high efficiency cogeneration (among technologies and applications such as efficient energy recovery of waste gases, use of biomass, or capture and storage of CO_2) was considered for the needs of the Benchmarking Decision when the starting points for the determination of benchmark values were analysed.

Another revision of the EU ETS Directive was conducted in 2018 with the passing of Directive (EU) 2018/410 followed by Delegated Regulation (EU) 2019/331 which repeals the Benchmarking Decision of 2011 and brings substantial changes in the EU ETS (see Carlén et al. 2019; Woerdman & Nentjes 2019, cf. Calmfors et al. 2019, pp. 76–82). To keep the continuity of the book's structure – as the recent legislative changes are discussed in its final chapter – let us briefly address this revision here. First of all, among a range of changes, one should note the new rules for distribution of free allowances for cogeneration. Second, free allocation for DH is exempted from the decrease of free allowances. Nevertheless, let us leave some space for further comments on this issue in Chapter 6 of the book.

CHP and renewable energy sources

Another pillar of the climate-energy policy of the European Union which influences combined heat and power is the development of renewable energy sources – a recognised and permanently developed policy option promoted by the EU for a long time. Numerous declarations, statements, reports, communications, and legislation, including dedicated legal acts adopted at the European level, clearly indicate how preferable the growth of renewable capacity in the EU is. Three Directives: Directive 2001/77/EC, Directive 2009/28/EC, and the latest, Directive (EU) 2018/2001 were established to support renewable energy sources, and so to realise the European policy with its goals, also steered by the Climate and Energy Package and subsequent framework on sustainability.

The adoption of Directive 2001/77/EC (on the promotion of electricity produced from renewables – RES Directive) intensified the discussion on using renewable heat in the energy sector (Commission 2004, pp. 30–33, cf. Jansen & Uyterlinde 2004). Cogeneration was not directly addressed in this Directive, although to some degree it could be, as in some areas both cogeneration and renewables face similar problems (see Commission 2002a). Nonetheless, a correlation between Directive 2001/77/EC and Directive 2004/8/EC was provided by the latter. To some extent the provisions of Article 9 of the RES Directive apply correspondingly to combined heat and power under Article 8 of the CHP Directive (Bjørnebye 2010, p. 185). This concerned the priority access to the grid and dispatching renewable energy sources, as well as the rules applied to renewables by system operators.

The approach to cogeneration offered by Directive 2001/77/EC was changed with passing two more directives on renewables. Besides focusing on renewable energy sources, the First Renewable Energy Directive (RED) – Directive 2009/28/EC, and the Second Renewable Energy Directive (RED II) – Directive (EU) 2018/2001 address combined heat and power. Apart from a general approach that can be applied to cogeneration due to the possibility of it falling under the scope of a definition of renewables by using "energy from renewable non-fossil sources" in CHP unit,[23] cogeneration is also directly regulated there. For example, pursuant to Article 13(4) of the repealed RED, the Member States, when adopting the measures to increase the share energy from renewable sources in their building sectors, could use the national measures relating to cogeneration (cf. De Rosa, Carragher, & Finn 2018). Other provisions of RED which covered cogeneration were related to the prohibition of double counting of guarantees of origin, established under the CHP Directive for the needs of providing the information on the use of energy produced from renewable sources to the energy customers, as required by Directive 2003/54/EC (see Jansen, Gialoglou, & Egenhofer 2005 p. 22).[24] However, it is difficult to classify this approach as supporting cogeneration (it is more of a pro-consumer approach, as it provides reliable information to energy consumers).

Currently in force, the RED II not only maintains this possibility, but it also extends the provisions on combined heat and power, which do not concern only the references to Directive 2012/27/EU on energy efficiency. For instance, cogeneration is used for the needs of definitions adopted in the Directive (EU) 2018/2001,[25] or to qualify electricity produced from biomass for the needs of the EU 2030 renewable target (32%)[26] and the national renewable energy shares, or for financial support of these type of fuels,[27] as well as the rules for calculating the greenhouse gas impact of biofuels, bioliquids, and their fossil fuel equivalents (Annex V or RED II). In particular, the previously mentioned extension covers renewable energy in heating and cooling (see Braungardt et al. 2019). As in the case of the already-mentioned new rules on the reduction of emissions in the current framework, let us analyse this matter in more detail in Chapter 6 of this book.

***

Concluding on the European approach to the promotion of renewable energy sources and reduction of emission, one should take note of the place of combined heat and power within those approaches. Both regimes have been recognising the role of CHP in the internal energy market of the EU. This was done with the use of different types of regulatory measures, including the introduction of the provisions on feasibility of cogeneration, granting allocation of free allowances for CHP installations, addressing CHP as part of a wider action on non-fossil energy capacity, or providing some exemptions when high-efficiency cogeneration has been applied. However, for both of those approaches, covering combined heat and power was not a number one priority. Therefore, in many aspects CHP is regulated there in a non-complex way (regarding the promotion of CHP use). The pillar of the European climate-energy policy clearly based on cogeneration – fuelled by combined heat and power – is energy efficiency.

Powering European energy efficiency: the CHP Directive and beyond

In the 1990s, CHP was listed among potential areas for the action in energy policy, as any progress in the development of cogeneration could lead to "considerable efficiency improvements" in the Community (Commission 1997a, p. 8), where enhancing energy efficiency was to "lead to a more sustainable energy policy and enhanced security of supply … [playing] a key role in helping the Community to meet its challenging Kyoto target economically", as highlighted in the 1998 policy document on energy efficiency (Commission 1998a).

Therefore, energy efficiency was a form of response to rising energy security and environmental issues (Filippini, Hunt, & Zorić 2014, p. 74). In this respect, as discussed in previous chapters, to increase the use of CHP, the Community's financial programmes were adopted and the Strategy on CHP was delivered (Commission 1997b). In addition, at that time the Commission acknowledged CHP as "critical for energy efficiency", clearly expressing the necessity to promote cogeneration both at the European and national level (Commission 1998a, p. 15).

CHP's contribution to European climate efforts: the way towards high-efficiency cogeneration

Further developments of energy efficiency came with the speeding-up of the European climate change agenda in the twenty-first century. In 2001, the EU Strategy for Sustainable Development prompted a call for a "clear action to reduce energy demand" (Commission 2001a, p. 11). Earlier, in 2000, increasing the use of CHP was listed among the common and coordinated policies and measures on climate change offered in the European Climate Change Programme – an action plan aimed at bringing together all of the relevant stakeholders to cooperate during the preparatory works for common policies to tackle greenhouse gas emissions (Commission 2000a, pp. 5–6, 11).[28] Within the framework of the European Climate Change Programme, the Commission highlighted a set of future measures on four policy-fields. Among them, in the section on energy, combined heat and power was addressed. This was the idea to adopt a separate directive dedicated to the promotion of CHP (see Chapter 3 of this book), sketched in the report on the implementation of the European Climate Change Programme in the following way:

> [t]he Directive should provide a definition of CHP Quality and CHP Certification in order to ensure that incentives are provided only to efficient CHP systems. The Directive should also … contain provisions obliging Member States to set national targets in accordance with the EU-wide CHP target from 1997.
>
> The CHP Directive will cover technologies ranging from small-scale CHP in the residential and tertiary sectors to industrial CHP and CHP with district heating, with special provisions to promote small-scale CHP and renewables CHP.
>
> (Commission 2001b, pp. 11–12)

The proposed legislation was to be integrated with the Community's general campaign on energy efficiency, and the benchmark for its regime was the legal environment established by Directive 2001/77/EC, passed just one month before the Commission's report was published (2001b, p. 12).[29] It was inspired by similar problems which both the renewables and cogeneration faced, *inter alia*, lack of internalisation of external costs, grid uncertainty, or administrative burdens (Commission 2002a, p. 5). This way, it also fell within the European agenda on renewable energy sources. Apart from that, the proposal covered the reduction of emissions, which was intended to become a platform to facilitate the reduction potential of CHP (up to 65 Mt CO_2)[30] identified earlier.

Due to these factors, combined heat and power was listed among the areas to be developed by the EU; not directly, however, as cogeneration itself, but indirectly, as a part of a bigger policy agenda on energy efficiency, corelated with the action on renewable energy sources. As the Commission (2002a, p. 2) emphasised in its proposal for the CHP Directive, "cogeneration is not a target in itself ... but can be an efficient tool"; a tool that enhances energy efficiency and enables achieving certain reduction of CO_2 emissions. A clear reflection of this approach may be found in the medium- and long-term goals of the proposal, where the "cogeneration Directive should serve as a means to create the necessary framework that will ensure that high-efficiency cogeneration alongside other environmentally friendly supply options" (Commission 2002a, p. 3). Less fuel consumed, less CO_2 emitted, and less energy used (or wasted – e.g. due to energy losses) contribute to the EU's agenda on sustainable development; in the same way – i.e. falling under this agenda – one may qualify "[f]acilitation of the link between the population and the territory, mainly in less favorised, isolated or ultraperipherical areas" (Commission 2002a, p. 6). Both, listed among the motives for the political support for high-efficiency CHP, represent the climate-type justification for the promotion of cogeneration and have a clear impact on the adopted provisions of the CHP Directive.

Nevertheless, as all Member States had a possibility to decide on the specific support mechanisms for cogeneration (see Chapter 3 of this book), and some uncertainties regarding the achieved reduction of emissions and exploitation of the CHP potential could occur (see Commission 2001b, p. 12), the proposed Directive had to provide a certain level of the joint approach. Still, it was a soft approach, not involving a specific regulatory action, not strengthened by any concrete obligations and real enforcement. The Member States were to analyse their national potential for combined heat and power (together with evaluating the barriers to the growth of cogeneration), or exchange the experiences of applying various support schemes for cogeneration (see Commission 2002a, p. 5). A more specific idea proposed by the Commission concerned the guarantees of origin for the electricity produced in CHP units.

In 2004, when the CHP Directive was passed, cogeneration received the postulated Community framework established at the EU level. In many ways this concerned high-efficiency cogeneration – a category distinguished among many definitions brought by the Directive (see Chapter 4). This category concerns the Directive's Article 5 and Article 6 which addressed high-efficiency cogeneration directly. Moreover, the category also includes tools devoted to the development of cogeneration (as a whole, and where high-efficiency cogeneration was just an element of a wider action on CHP in general), namely the tools establishing the systems of support, facilitating the grid access, and addressing the administrative procedures on CHP (see Chapter 3 of this book).

Starting with the analysis of the guarantees of origin, one should emphasise that they, in fact, represent reporting schemes (see Lise et al. 2007, p. 5856), and so they derive from the approach to strengthen transparency in the energy market. To enhance the knowledge of energy consumers, enabling them to consciously decide on the purchased electricity and its source (i.e. whether it was produced in high-efficiency cogeneration), the Member States were obliged to introduce such tools as the guarantees of origin for electricity generated in CHP units and a tracking instrument for evidencing the origin of electricity (Gkarakis & Dagoumas 2016, p. 136).[31] The origin, calculated for these needs with a detailed procedure (see Piacentino, Barbaro, & Cardona 2014, p. 882), was to be based on objective, transparent, and non-discriminatory criteria adopted by each Member State, enabling the producers to prove that electricity they sell is produced in high-efficiency CHP units. For this purpose, as provided by Article 5 of Directive 2004/8/EC, each guarantee of origin, apart from such basic information as the date and place of production, had to contain more specific data on electricity and heat. This included: lower calorific value of the fuel source, the use of co-produced heat, the quantity of electricity, and the primary energy savings.[32] The Member States could extend this catalogue with other information, e.g. related to renewable energy, or used fuel.

The system of guarantees of origin adopted in the CHP Directive was steered in an administrative way. The Member States were to supervise it in practice, with the help of other bodies (e.g. regulatory authority, system operator).[33] The supervision was to ensure the accuracy and reliability of guarantees, enabling a pan-European recognition in each Member State. A refusal, as a matter of exception, was possible under Article 5(6) of Directive 2004/8/EC. Pursuant to it, "[a]ny refusal to recognise a guarantee of origin …, in particular for reasons relating to the prevention of fraud, must be based on objective, transparent and non-discriminatory criteria". If a recognition was refused, the Commission could intervene.

Parenthetically, the support schemes should not be confused with the guarantees of origin (cf. Ziębik & Gładysz 2012, 2013). As highlighted in Recital 22 of the preamble to the Directive, "[i]t is important to distinguish guarantees of origin clearly from exchangeable certificates";[34] guarantees were designed to prove the origin of electricity, along with the information on any elements covered by its scope. Therefore, these two different measures, despite having different assumptions and legal bases, are often mistaken and treated as one tool; especially when a quota system (certificate) is selected by a Member State and introduced as the support scheme – it can easily lead to the incorrect perception that a guarantee means a certificate. The same concerns the guarantees of origin and certificates (green certificates) introduced for the needs of renewable energy sources (see Raadal et al. 2012, p. 420).

Moving on to Article 6 of the CHP Directive and the duty imposed on the Member States (to prepare analyses of their potential regarding high-efficiency cogeneration), one should note (yet again) its soft approach. Actually, it was rather just a call for conducting the analysis on cogeneration, than undertaking any real regulatory action.[35] To some degree, the Directive provided a sample for conducting analysis, although much depended on the Member States' attitude. Directive 2004/8/EC sketched only the main elements of the analysis. It was to have a well-documented scientific basis, identify the national potential of high-efficiency cogeneration (together with the availability of fuels and energy resources which could be used in cogeneration), as well as review any barriers to utilisation of this potential. The latter was to cover such matters as barriers related to prices, costs, fuels, grid access, or procedures. Apart from that, the evaluation had to comply with Annex IV to the Directive, which contained the criteria (rather open and ambiguous) for the assessment of the Member States' potential for high-efficiency CHP.[36] As a result, the reports on national evaluations varied significantly (see Commission n.d. c). This is yet another example which confirms the soft nature of the legal solution adopted in the CHP Directive.

Combined heat and power in the Energy Services Directive

However, passing Directive 2004/8/EC was not the end of the road for the European cogeneration. The legal environment on CHP has continued to evolve. In 2006, the promotion of energy efficiency has become the subject of a specific European Union legislative action. Its result was the adoption of Directive 2006/32/EC (Energy Services Directive) which has been under way since 2003 (see Commission 2003). The Directive was driven by the need for improving the energy end-use efficiency and managing the demand for energy. This approach was to have a whole range of positive results. Their assumptions were as follows: the improved energy end-use efficiency could lead to better (economically efficient) exploitation of the potential cost-effective energy savings; the achieved energy savings could reduce the energy dependence of the Community; more energy-efficient technologies could foster European competitiveness and boost innovativeness. "Improved energy end-use efficiency will also contribute to the reduction of primary energy consumption, to the mitigation of CO_2 and other greenhouse gas emissions and thereby to the prevention of dangerous climate change", as emphasised in the preamble to Directive 2006/32/EC (Recital 2).

These improvements could be covered by each Member State with the use of "overall national indicative energy savings target of 9% for the ninth year (2016) of application of [the] Directive" (Article 4 of the Energy Services Directive). As in the case of the tools brought by the CHP Directive, this was a soft regulatory approach. The Directive's target was not mandatory but only indicative (Filippini, Hunt, & Zorić 2014, p. 74). As clearly addressed in Recital 12 of the preamble to Directive 2006/32/EC, "the national energy savings target is indicative in nature and entails no legally enforceable obligation for Member States to achieve it". Again, much depended on the approach preferred by each country and on recognising energy efficiency as a priority, as well as engaging in the implementation of the pro-efficiency tools.[37]

Each national target was to be reached with the help of the previously mentioned tools, the "energy efficiency improvement measures", defined in Article 3(h) of Directive 2006/32/EC as "all actions that normally lead to verifiable and measurable or estimable energy efficiency improvement as formally" named. The way in which the Directive dealt with the energy efficiency improvement measures was in line with the general soft nature of the discussed legislation. Its Annex III included only examples of eligible pro-efficiency tools.[38] In the Annex's part on industry one may find high-efficiency cogeneration as an area in which the energy efficiency measures could be applied to contribute to the realisation of a given national target. Additionally, combined heat and power was also an element of the eligible pro-efficiency measures which could be used in residential and tertiary sectors.[39] However, this does not change the soft approach delivered by the Directive but rather confirms it. Moreover, in this approach little space was left for cogeneration.

Action Plan for energy efficiency (2006)

Combined heat and power was addressed in another policy document of the 2000s, besides Directive 2004/8/EC and Directive 2006/32/EC. It was the Action Plan for energy efficiency presented just a few months after the adoption of the Energy Services Directive (Commission 2006a). Aimed at "maintaining Europe's position as one of the most energy-efficient regions in the world", the Plan brought pro-efficiency policies and measures to accelerate the realisation of the EU savings potential in the annual primary energy consumption, oscillating around 20% by 2020 (Commission 2006a, pp. 3–4). This included the schedule for further steps concerning the development of cogeneration in the European Union. Collected in the scope of implementation and amendment of the CHP Directive they covered:

- ... harmonisation of the calculation methods for high-efficiency CHP (2008–2011);
- [issuing] a mandate for a European Norm ... for certification of chief engineers for CHP plants (2008);
- ... agreement on a harmonised electronic Guarantee of Origin (2007–2009);
- ... stricter requirements for market regulators to promote CHP (2008–2011);
- [proposal] to require Member States to identify heat demand suitable for CHP (2007–2008);
- [requiring] to identify in national potentials waste heat potential (2007–2008);

- ... minimum efficiency requirements for district heating based on new norm (2007–2008);
- [seeking] to adopt a European Norm and a minimum efficiency requirement for micro CHP (2007–2009).

(Commission 2006a, p. 22)

Cogeneration was also covered by the Impact Assessment which accompanied the Action Plan for energy efficiency (Commission 2006b). Two policy options which concerned combined heat and power were included there: "Action 7: 'Off-grid' CHP and other power generation" and "Action 8: Promotion of grid-connected CHP". Both could contribute to energy savings in Europe, enabling the achievement of 16 Mtoe (micro CHP together with other types of off-grid installations, including renewable energy sources) and 14 Mtoe by applying high efficiency CHP (see Commission 2006b, pp. 27–29). However, as acknowledged in the Impact Assessment, the success of implementing the program on the promotion of both small and large scale CHP depended on the reinforcement, *inter alia*, by active programmes on innovation and research on combined heat and power, as well as regulation which could be necessary to implement and develop CHP technologies by the industry (Commission 2006b, p. 29).

Despite being highlighted in the Impact Assessment of the Action Plan for energy efficiency, the call for more regulation with respect to CHP did not have a real impact. However, it can serve as an example of the general approach of the EU concerning combined heat and power as of the 2000s. Summarising this European legislative and policy framework on cogeneration and energy efficiency, offered mainly by Directive 2004/8/EC and Directive 2006/32/EC, one should notice that it was a soft framework (cf. Chapter 3 of this book).

***

Further changes in the field of the European policies and law on cogeneration could have come with the adoption of the Climate and Energy Package (see preceding subchapter). However, despite being one of the key-elements of the Climate and Energy Package (Sokołowski 2016, p. 207), energy efficiency was not treated in the same way as the promotion of renewable energy sources and reduction of emission; their 20% goals for 2020 were confirmed and strengthened by binding legislation, whereas the energy saving goal was non-binding (Ruzzenenti & Bertoldi, p. 149).

Paradoxically, the non-binding 20% savings goal has further emphasised the need for revision of the existing legal environment on energy efficiency and cogeneration. The mid-term evaluations of the CHP Directive and the Energy Services Directive have shown that they were not as supportive as they should have been to reach 20% target on energy savings (see Commission 2011c, p. 5). "[T]heir frequently 'soft' and open wording has not been sufficient to overcome the main barriers to energy efficiency" the Commission (2011c, p. 11) reported. In effect, both Directives failed to achieve their goals. The First, Directive 2006/32/EC has not fully exploited the potential for energy savings in the sectors it addressed;[40] second, Directive 2004/8/EC has not created the required investment security – needed to reduce the administrative burdens and create a playing field for cogeneration and the operators of CHP units (Commission 2011c, pp. 11–13).

Regarding the measures established by Directive 2004/8/EC: the guarantees of origin of electricity from high-efficiency cogeneration and the evaluation of national potentials for high-efficiency cogeneration – their assessment was also negative. Despite the fact that all Member States have adopted their systems of guarantees of origin, those systems have not been fully operational in half of them (Commission 2011c, p. 13). The main issue of national evaluations for high-efficiency cogeneration was their heterogeneity. The deficiencies of these tools emerged from the lack of methods of implementing them, and the absence of defined depth, length, and quality; hence, "[t]he information given [was] not conducive for comparison and [did] not give the detail needed for a comprehensive evaluation of national potentials" (Commission 2011c, p. 13). Moreover, there was no obligation imposed on the Member States to take an effort with respect to the realisation of this potential. Thus, the evaluation was merely statistics, often of an uncertain quality. To improve this situation, an idea of adopting a new legislation on energy efficiency emerged. This happened in 2011, when a draft of a revision of the CHP Directive and the Energy Services Directive was presented (Commission 2011b).

Change in the regulatory regime for cogeneration: the Energy Efficiency Directive (2012)

The main reason for changing the legal environment of energy efficiency in the EU derived from the 2020 non-binding 20% goal on this matter. The estimates provided by the EU have revealed that the European Union would achieve less than half of its goal by 2020 (see Commission 2011b, p. 1). Pursuant to these estimates:

> the EU is not on track to fully realize this cost-effective energy savings. Whilst, the latest business-as-usual scenario ... shows a break in the trend towards ever increasing energy demand, the reduction in the consumption will be only about 9% in 2020. Therefore, if the EU does not double the efforts, it will not reach its 20% target and will not realize all the associated benefits for the economy, society, and environment.
>
> (Commission 2011a, p. 7)[41]

No significant progress towards the realisation of the energy efficiency goal was made, as powering the European energy efficiency did not have enough power in itself. The new regulatory framework aimed at changing this state was to be delivered soon; it took the EU less than a year and a half to adopt the draft proposal published by the Commission in June 2011. However, before moving on to the final version of this legislation, let us focus on the analysis of cogeneration in the Commission's initial proposal – a legislation designed "to make a significant contribution to meeting the EU's 2020 energy efficiency target" (Commission 2011b, p. 1), as a way to answer the aforementioned lack of "significant progress".

Scenarios of amending the legal environment on cogeneration

In the Commission's assumptions, the legal environment for developing cogeneration in the EU had to change, as both Directives which addressed CHP, i.e. 2004/8/EC and 2006/32/EC "failed to fully tap the energy saving potential" (Commission 2011b, p. 2). The idea was to repeal them (except for some provisions of the Energy Services Directive)[42] by a new comprehensive legislation on energy efficiency (a new directive). The new approach included the establishment of the mandatory minimum performance requirements for cogeneration, with an obligatory connection and priority access to the grid guaranteed for high-efficiency CHP, leading to the real deployment of cogeneration, omitted by the CHP Directive (Commission 2011b, p. 4). The other measures offered by the proposal ranged from adopting national heating and cooling plans to develop the potential for high-efficiency generation, to providing the authorisation criteria which were to ensure that all new and substantially modernised power units are equipped with high-efficiency CHP (Commission 2011b, p. 5). The possible scenarios considered in the Impact Assessment of the proposed legislation (Commission 2011c) are shown in Table 4.4.

These measures were to, in particular, ensure the realisation of the economic potential for high-efficiency cogeneration, overcome market barriers, introduce tools to match heat demand with supply from waste heat, strengthen transparency, objectiveness, and non-discrimination, or exchange best practice (see Commission 2011c, pp. 58–59). In general, the measures had to provide the investors with a "certainty as regards the achievement of the EU target and support for energy efficiency improvement measures such as high-efficiency cogeneration" (Commission 2011b, p. 6). As one may notice, the emphasis was put on high-efficiency CHP. This was steered by the desire for better exploitation of the potential of cogeneration for the needs of the EU energy efficiency goal. As a result of applying these measures, such cogeneration was to be developed.

The listed measures on combined heat and power were not the only scenarios analysed during the work on the new legislation. Among the possible alternatives, such options as maintaining the existing regulatory

Table 4.4 Commission's scenarios for amending regulatory framework on CHP

scenario	area for the EU	area for the Member States	effects
mandatory CHP requirement	obligation to apply CHP (whenever there is an appropriate demand for heat nearby) in the new thermal electricity generation capacity	coordination of administrative procedures on the CHP units; measure based on national economic conditions	ensuring a common high ambition level for CHP
mandatory connection and priority access to the grid for CHP	obligatory priority connection or guaranteed access to the grid (and priority dispatch) offered for high-efficiency CHP (to ensure level playing field for cogeneration in electricity markets as well as support distributed for combined heat and power)	correct implementation	ensuring a common EU approach to grid access for high-efficiency CHP (within the limits of reliable operation of the national power grid)
voluntary measures to promote CHP (together with DH & C)	national measures and programmes established by the Member States on the basis of their own evaluation and ambitions, including local and regional initiatives to support combined heat and power	full flexibility at the national level to decide on the pro-CHP measures	the role of CHP in the Member States' future energy systems determined by the applied pro-efficiency measures

Source: Commission 2011c, p. 22.

framework on CHP or removing it completely (with switching to the national action) were discussed (see Commission 2011c, pp. 56–58). Table 4.5 contrasts these two extreme scenarios evaluated in the Impact Assessment of the proposed legislation (Commission 2011c).

Both of these options were rather theories than possibilities. That was because the EU, its institutions, policymakers, and stakeholders really wanted to change the legislation in the field of combined heat and power (as it announced earlier in many policy documents). Maintaining the CHP Directive without any changes meant keeping in force its identified

Table 4.5 Commission's extreme scenarios of amending the regulatory framework on CHP

scenario	area for the EU	area for the Member States	effects
maintaining the unchanged CHP Directive	keeping the regulatory system established under the CHP Directive, i.e. guarantees of origin; a harmonised or alternative methodology for the calculation of the efficiency of CHP (and primary energy savings); periodical reporting on the progress in increasing the share of high-efficiency CHP; the submission of statistics on CHP; the soft way of dealing with the grid access for high-efficiency cogeneration	flexibility in deciding on the need for supporting CHP and measures to support cogeneration; requirement imposed on the Member States to apply a common definition of the type of CHP that needs support	an inefficient promotion of CHP, exploiting the national potentials on CHP in a limited way, a low degree of harmonisation of national approaches
completely removing the CHP Directive	no common framework on cogeneration (no obligatory reporting, the lack of requirements for providing the statistics for CHP sector), no common definitions (e.g. on high-efficiency CHP)	as in the scenario on maintaining the unchanged CHP Directive (see earlier); additionally, the Member States may freely decide on the type of CHP which should be supported; however, these decisions must comply with the rules on state aid in the EU	in a positive scenario – the continuation of the low growth of CHP, or in a negative scenario – a drop in the CHP capacity (with minor macroeconomic impact)

Source: Commission 2011c, p. 21.

drawbacks and limitations, including no clear policy drivers, weak harmonisation, or the inefficiency in the promotion of combined heat and power and exploiting the national potentials on CHP (see Commission 2011c, p. 56). Due to a minor influence on the growth of cogeneration in the EU, deleting the CHP Directive from the European legal environment would either lead to the continuation of the low growth of CHP or result in a decrease of the CHP capacity with small overall impact (see Commission 2011c, p. 58).[43] However, leaving the field already taken by the EU (for the Member States' own approach (so rejecting the existing obligations – even soft – or common definitions, for uncoordinated national frameworks on cogeneration) was even less possible than keeping the existing CHP Directive in force.

Finally, the proposed regulatory framework on combined heat and power had to deal with a formal matter of choosing the right approach for conducting the revisions. This concerned the introduction of a consolidated or dispersed approach when adopting a new law. The first approach included the establishment of one, unified legislation for all sectors, where energy efficiency should be promoted. The second covered keeping separate legal acts for different sectors (as under the rules of the Energy Services Directive and the CHP Directive). To conclude, the first option prevailed; the simplification of law and better coherence of legal solutions were among its reasons (see Commission, 2011c, p. 70). Consequently, "[t]he new legislative proposal would in this way become the general EU legal framework for energy efficiency, encompassing energy saving instruments across all sectors" (Commission 2011c, p. 24).

The joint approach selected to conduct the revision was approved during the EU legislative process. In the opinion of the European Economic and Social Committee (2011) integrating both Directives was particularly beneficial for CHP, helping to achieve a synergy effect and improving the way towards the realisation of set efficiency goals. Naturally, this formal aspect of work on the new regulatory framework for energy efficiency was not the gist of the European action. For example, the second of the European consulting bodies, i.e. the European Committee of the Regions (2011) did not address this issue in its opinion.

However, what was clearly emphasised during the legislative process, were certain deficiencies of the proposal, among them those related to its too soft character, e.g. no binding national objectives for the period before 2014, the limited range of areas in which the pro-efficiency tools could be applied (European Committee of the Regions 2011). Some remarks directly concerned cogeneration. "[T]he scope for Member States to avoid obligations regarding the application of binding measures, and more specifically the mechanisms requiring the introduction of energy efficiency measures and high-efficiency cogeneration development plans" were marked as shortcomings of the draft legislation (European Committee of the Regions 2011). Other issues raised during the legislative process covered, *inter alia*, the introduction of specific measures for selected CHP units (thermal capacity lower than 20 MW), correlation with Directive 2004/8/EC (e.g. in terms of comprehensive assessment of the potential for the application of high-efficiency cogeneration), or the cost-benefit analysis of applying high-efficiency CHP together with extending the list of possible exemptions from the scope of this analysis (see European Parliament 2012).

CHP under the Energy Efficiency Directive (2012 version)

As previously mentioned, after a relatively short legislative process (June 2011–October 2012, publication: November 2012), the Energy Efficiency Directive (2012/27/EU) entered into force in December 2012. The Directive, which adopts the EU joint framework on the promotion of energy efficiency for the needs of the 2020 energy efficiency 20% goal (including the establishment of indicative national energy efficiency targets for 2020, see Zangheri, Economidou, & Labanca 2019), recognises the role performed by cogeneration in reaching the Directive's aims. With respect to the Directive's specific coverage of cogeneration, despite the fact that the Directive repealed the CHP Directive, some of the previous legal measures focused on combined heat and power were sustained and/or modified (e.g. the guarantees of origin).[44] Apart from referring to the existing tools, the Directive adopted two types of other measures to promote combined heat and power. They can be collected in the categories of a softer approach and more concrete regulatory tools. What links them are the definitions introduced by the Directive (see Chapter 1 of this book), especially the one of high-efficiency cogeneration (i.e. cogeneration which, in comparison with separate production of heat and electricity, achieves at least 10% primary energy savings, see Atănăsoae et al. 2018, p. 657), the axis of this legislation, "defined by the energy savings obtained by combined production instead of separate production of heat and electricity".[45]

Regarding the softer measures, one may find, *inter alia*, the calls for establishing the tools to promote cogeneration lower than 20 MW or for reviewing the administrative procedures for small and medium-sized CHP. In terms of the strength of regulatory power and effectiveness encouraging "the introduction of measures and procedures to promote cogeneration installations with a total rated thermal input of less than 20 MW in order to encourage distributed energy generation" (Recital 37 of the preamble to Directive), or considering "[t]he specific structure of the cogeneration ... which ... should be taken into account, especially when reviewing the administrative procedures for obtaining permission to construct cogeneration capacity or associated network" (Recital 40) implies any concrete, measurable duty that must be executed by the Member States.[46] The same approach concerns adopting the policies in favour of high-efficiency CHP at local and regional levels (cf. Jakubcionis & Carlsson 2017, p. 225).[47] In practice, the presented approach leaves the field open for skipping over the implementation, improper implementation, or lack of implementation.

Apart from that, the new European framework for the promotion of energy efficiency also provides more concrete regulatory tools. This concerns those provisions of Directive 2012/27/EU which address the rules for equipping new and modernised CHP installations with high-efficiency cogeneration (Recital 35 and Article 14 (5)) or the duties imposed on the transmission and distribution system operators, i.e. the priority or guaranteed access to the grid for high-efficiency cogeneration (Article 15 (5)). The latter however, was changed in 2019 (see Chapter 6 of this book). Moreover, Directive 2012/27/EU obliges the Member States to conduct a comprehensive assessment regarding their potential for developing high-efficiency cogeneration (Article 14 (1)). Due to the character of the regulatory tools – which differs from the previous approach to cogeneration offered by the past legislation on CHP – let us discuss them in more detail.

"New electricity generation installations and existing installations which are substantially refurbished ... should, subject to a cost-benefit analysis showing a cost-benefit surplus, be equipped with high-efficiency cogeneration units". This statement, expressed in Recital 35 to the preamble of the Energy Efficiency Directive – regardless of how strong/weak the phrase "should" sounds – clearly indicates the willingness of the Member States to comply at the national level. In contrast to the already-mentioned approaches marked as "soft" (Recital 37 and 40) this way of promoting cogeneration is strengthened in Article 14 of the Directive (see Cornelis 2019, pp. 576–577). Pursuant to its Paragraph 5, starting from June 2014,[48] every new and existing, but substantially modernised thermal power installation of a thermal input over 20 MW, is subjected to the cost-benefit analysis of installing high-efficiency CHP. To a certain degree, this analysis resembles the feasibility of applying cogeneration elaborated on in Article 6 of the LCP Directive (cf. a section on emissions and renewables of this chapter). With respect to other installations where cogeneration should be applied after conducting the cost-benefit analysis, this, to some extent, concerns industrial units – the new or noticeably refurbished installations of a similar input (i.e. exceeding 20 MW) which produce waste heat at a useful temperature.[49] Nevertheless, a group of installations is released from this duty. An exemption provided by Article 14(6) of the Energy Efficiency Directive covers, *inter alia*, nuclear power plants (see Leurent et al. 2017).

With respect to practical aspects of conducting the cost-benefit analysis, it should be based on the comparison between installations (both new and refurbished), planned as those generating electricity in a single process and those being high-efficiency CHP – if a given installation will be an electricity-only power plant (or an installation without heat recovery). The analysis should contain a description of the planned and compared installation; this includes such elements as "electrical and thermal capacity, as applicable, fuel type, planned use and the number of planned operating hours annually, location and electricity and thermal demand". An important element of the analysis concerns economic and financial issues – the assessment should be based on real cash flow transactions from investing in the installations and operating them. Finally, the "cost-benefit surplus" determining the decision on installing high-efficiency cogeneration means that "the sum of discounted benefits in the economic and financial

CHP in the EU climate action 125

analysis exceeds the sum of discounted costs" leading to a positive cost-benefit outcome of the project. These and other detailed formal steps regarding the analysis are addressed in Annex IX to the Directive 2012/27/EU.[50] Despite this unification at the European level, one may find the provisions weakening the conducted harmonisation. Under the previously mentioned Annex IX, these are the Member States that decide on the economic analysis, setting the guiding principles for its methodology, assumptions, and time frame.

Apart from the provisions on generation, the Energy Efficiency Directive has influenced the grid and market issues related to high-efficiency combined heat and power – as this regime was changed in 2019 (see Chapter 6 of this book). Under Article 15(5) of the Directive, the rules on access to the grid for high-efficiency cogeneration have been provided (valid until 1 January 2020). These were the obligations which the Member States had to impose on system operators (both transmission and distribution). They include an approach in favour of electricity produced in high-efficiency CHP: a guarantee of transmitting and distributing it, a priority or a guaranteed access to the grid, and a priority dispatch for this type of electricity. To some degree, the limitations of these duties could result from the operational matters related to the reliability and safety of the grid or the secure operation of the national power systems (with respect to dispatching electricity from high-efficiency CHP), although this must be subjected to transparent and non-discriminatory criteria established by the Member States. The same approach has applied to the granted dispatch priorities in the electricity systems.[51]

Moreover, certain specific requirements regarding the grid issues are delivered in Annex XII to the Directive. According to them, the system operators must act transparently and fairly, presenting an open approach to high-efficiency cogeneration. This applies to the costs of technical adjustments of their grids which are necessary to integrate high-efficiency CHP with their systems (the rules regarding this matter have to be established and published by the operators); the information provided to the new producers of electricity from high-efficiency CHP intending to connect to the grid (e.g. complex and detailed estimations of costs related to the connection to the grid, a reasonable and accurate timetable processing the grid application, an indicative schedule for the proposed grid connection), as well as standardised and simplified procedures for the connection of distributed high-efficiency CHP to the grid.

What should be emphasised here, is that the connection to the grid of the new producer of electricity generated in high-efficiency CHP must be accomplished within 24 months. Such a maximum period for the "overall process to become connected" is literally addressed in the Directive's Annex XII. Apart from that, the Directive, in its Article 15(5), encouraged the Member States to provide a separate, simple procedure ("install and inform") for connecting micro-cogeneration ("to simplify and shorten authorisation procedures for individual citizens and installers"). In addition, the facilitation of grid connection could include small-scale, high-efficiency cogeneration units.[52]

Finally, Directive 2012/27/EU, obliges the Member States to conduct a comprehensive assessment regarding their potential for applying high-efficiency cogeneration. The deadline for caring it out and notifying the Commission was set in Article 14(1) for the end of December 2015 (the results of the analyses conducted by the Member States are discussed in the next chapter of the book). In comparison to the analysis of the national potential regulated under Article 6 of the CHP Directive, the one introduced by the Energy Efficiency Directive is intended to be much more detailed than its predecessor; however, as proposed during the legislative process, the Energy Efficiency Directive takes into account the analysis conducted under the CHP Directive.[53]

The analysis has to contain the information included in Annex VIII to the Directive 2012/27/EU. Despite treating high-efficiency cogeneration together with efficient district heating and cooling as general areas for the analysis, what results from the evaluation of Annex VIII is the preponderance of district heating and cooling over cogeneration. Due to the wording of the Annex, the analysis focuses more on this field (or fields, i.e. national heating and cooling potentials). In this context, the matters related to cogeneration, covered by the scope of the analysis, include, *inter alia*: mapping the existing and planned cogeneration installations using cogeneration technologies addressed by the Energy Efficiency Directive; identifying the heating and cooling demand which could be satisfied with the use of high-efficiency cogeneration (including residential micro-cogeneration[54]); or reviewing strategies, policies, and tools (which could be adopted by 2020 and by 2030) including, if applicable, the proposals to increase the cogeneration in heating and cooling as well as in electricity production, together with providing the already-mentioned assessments made under Directive 2004/8/EC.

Last but not least, the assessment elaborated on by the Member States on the basis of Article 14(1) of the Energy Efficiency Directive is not a static document (or, may not be such a document). The dynamics may be provided by the Commission's requesting the Member States to update their assessment (and notify the Commission). The provisions of Directive 2012/27/EU are more concrete than the CHP Directive's Article 6(3). The previous Directive assumed only an ambiguous evaluation of the progress towards increasing the share of high-efficiency CHP made by the Member States on the Commissions' request. The new approach seems to be more definite, and so more effective.

Summarising the framework brought by the Energy Efficiency Directive in 2012, one should notice its dual nature represented by the indicative energy efficiency target, and pro-efficiency binding measures (Geiss 2013, p. 55, cf. Schiavo 2013). Although intended to develop combined heat and power – especially high-efficiency cogeneration, also via the public support (see Article 14(11)), in many ways the Directive has been insufficient to promote the spread of cogeneration and utilise its potential in the EU (Colmenar-Santos et al. 2015, p. 411). For instance, some technologies which could be used in cogeneration, like nuclear CHP, are not tackled by Directive 2012/27/EU (Leurent et al. 2017, p. 146).[55]

Moreover, the Energy Efficiency Directive was adopted under the climate and energy action for 2020 and its 20% goals – having eight years to reach it (2012–2020). Looking ahead into the future, the European Union has adopted new goals for the climate and energy policy for 2030, with energy efficiency covered by at least 27% goal established in 2014 as its element (see Knoop & Lechtenböhmer 2017, p. 1098, cf. Pereira & Pereira Da Silva 2017, p. 1283). Furthermore, a new set of legislative proposals was presented by the Commission in November 2016. The initiative named "Clean Energy Package" offers a new target for improving energy efficiency: 30% in 2030 (Commission 2016b, p. 4) implying the changes to the existing legal environment, including Directive 2012/27/EU. How has the Package revised this Directive? What position has been given to cogeneration within its scope? Comments on these issues, together with the evaluation of the Package, last elements of which were adopted in 2019, are presented in the final chapter of this book (Chapter 6). However, before getting there, let us juxtapose the situation of combined heat and power at the national level (Chapter 5), reviewing the Member States divided into three groups: those where CHP grows, is stable, or decreases.

Notes

1. See Commission (2007), p. 5.
2. Five out of 15 technologies to reduce greenhouse gas emissions identified as "the most promising" were related to energy efficiency (see Pacala & Socolow 2004, p. 970). These were four specific areas "(1) Improved fuel economy of vehicles", "(2) Reduced reliance on cars", "(3) More efficient buildings", and "(4) Improved power plant efficiency", together with a general field of energy efficiency and energy conservation.
3. Stacking as in the case of stacking dolls (or Russian dolls), where wooden dolls of decreasing size are inserted one into another.
4. Recital 13 of the preamble to Directive 2001/80/EC.
5. In the Commission's proposal (1998b, p. 26) the Member States were to ensure that the operators of the installations examine the possibilities of installing CHP units on the sites having a heat requirement.
6. Precisely, these were the plants other than those constructed or operated which were subjected to a full request for a licence before 27 November 2002, provided that the plant is put into operation no later than 27 November 2003.
7. This concerned the gas turbines used in CHP (bigger than 50 MW$_t$ of power installed) having an overall efficiency higher than 75% — they could apply 75 mg/Nm^3 standard for NO$_x$ emissions, instead of 50 mg/Nm^3.

8   Pursuant to Article 3 of the IED, "emission limit value" as defined in point 5 is "mass, expressed in terms of certain specific parameters, concentration and/or level of an emission, which may not be exceeded during one or more periods of time".
9   BAT affects large combustion plants which will have to review their environmental permits within four years, and as a result, by mid-2021, the emission limits established for these plants will have to be in accordance with the requirements of the 2017 LCP BAT conclusions (Sokołowski 2018, p. 260).
10 The document was prepared for the Joint Research Centre — the European Commission's science and knowledge service.
11 These are Chapter 1 "General information on the structure of the sector", together with some parts of Chapter 2 "Processes for energy generation", e.g. 2.1 "Combustion principles" or 2.2 "Common technical combustion processes".
12 For example, among the techniques "to increase the energy efficiency of combustion, gasification and/or IGCC units operated ≥ 1500 h/yr" the following techniques related to cogeneration are listed: heat recovery by cogeneration ("[a]pplicable within the constraints associated with the local heat and power demand ... may be limited in the case of gas compressors with an unpredictable operational heat profile"), CHP readiness ("[o]nly applicable to new units where there is a realistic potential for the future use of heat in the vicinity of the unit"), flue-gas condenser ("[g]enerally applicable to CHP units provided there is enough demand for low-temperature heat"), heat accumulation ("[o]nly applicable to CHP plants ... may be limited in the case of low heat load demand").
13 As stated in "General considerations" of 2017 LCP BAT conclusions, BAT-AEEL is:

> the ratio between the combustion unit's net energy output(s) and the combustion unit's fuel/feedstock energy input at actual unit design. The net energy output(s) is determined at the combustion, gasification, or IGCC unit boundaries, including auxiliary systems (e.g. flue-gas treatment systems), and for the unit operated at full load.

In comparison, BAT-AEEL for cogeneration refer to "the combustion unit operated at full load and tuned to maximise primarily the heat supply and secondarily the remaining power that can be generated" with respect to the net total fuel utilisation BAT-AEEL for CHP and to "the combustion unit generating only electricity at full load" regarding the net electrical efficiency BAT-AEEL.
14 According to BAT2, "a performance test at full load" used for determining the net electrical efficiency and/or the net total fuel utilisation and/or the net mechanical energy efficiency of the gasification, IGCC and/or combustion units, with respect to cogeneration can be enhanced or even substituted by a calculation which uses full load parameters "if for technical reasons the performance test cannot be carried out with the unit operated at full load for the heat supply".
15 For example, as in the case of BAT-AEELs for coal and/or lignite combustion with respect to CHP units one should apply "net electrical efficiency" or "net total fuel utilisation"; this depends on the design of the given cogeneration unit and the nature of the dominant product, i.e. if it is electricity or heat. With respect to HFO- and/or gas-oil-fired reciprocating engine – combined cycle, "net

electrical efficiency" applies to CHP units oriented towards the production of electricity due to their design.

16 Pursuant to the 1997 Kyoto Protocol, a binding legal framework for the global reduction of greenhouse emissions under the United Nations Framework Convention on Climate Change (UNFCCC), the EU-15 has agreed to reduce its emissions by 8% as a whole, in comparison to the first period of the Protocol (2008–12), its parties committed to an average reduction of emissions accounting for 5% below 1990 levels (Commission n.d. a). This target was shared between EU-15 Member States under a binding burden-sharing agreement (Decision 2002/358/EC), and followed along with their own national Kyoto's goals (6% or 8%) by eight out of ten Member States which acceded the EU on 1 May 2004 – all except Cyprus and Malta (Commission 2005b, p. 3).

17 It was the third largest reduction (after, first, chemical industry and, second, manufacturing industries), reaching 55 Mt of CO_2, or 5% (Commission 2002b, p. 16).

18 EU ETS, established in 2003 by Directive 2003/87/EC, was launched in 2005 with its Phase 1 (see Commission n.d. b).

19 In addition, the European Parliament (2002b) proposed extending Article 5 of the EU ETS Directive with provisions on "carbon value of savings achieved through combined heat and power generation investments". As justified in the Report on the proposal:

> CHP (combined heat and power) investments should be encouraged since they are the most efficient way to produce energy on production sites that need both steam and electricity. CHP investments represent a substantial saving of primary energy and hence of CO_2 emissions. The present proposal discourages CHP investments on sites since the emissions from production of electricity and steam would be capped whilst purchased electricity and steam would not. With a view to a harmonised approach, the Commission should establish European Guidance on the Carbon Equivalence of CHP to be used in calculating the benefit of CHP.
>
> (European Parliament 2002a)

20 European Emission Allowances (EUA), emission credits under the EU ETS, accounts for one tonne of CO_2 emitted (see Commission 2015, p. 97).

21 During the legislative process on the revision, the European Economic and Social Committee (2008, p. 2) drew the attention to the need to eliminate "[p]otential disincentives which may limit the contribution and growth of cogeneration ... and efficient district heating schemes".

22 According to Article 10a(4), "[i]n each year subsequent to 2013, the total allocation to [high efficiency CHP] installations in respect of the production of that heat shall be adjusted by the linear factor". The linear factor established by Directive 2009/29/EC started a decrease of the Community-wide quantity of allowances issued annually accounting for 1.74% drop in comparison to "the average annual total quantity of allowances issued by Member States in accordance with the Commission Decisions on their national allocation plans for the period from 2008 to 2012", as stated in the revised Article 9 of the EU ETS Directive.

23 Such approach was recommended many times at the European level, e.g. the use of biomass in cogeneration was assessed as a factor which could facilitate better exploitation of CHP — DH & C (see Commission 1997a, p. 7).

24 See Article 3(6) of Directive 2003/54/EC.

25 This refers to the definition of "waste heat and cold", defined in Article 2(1) of the RED II as:

> unavoidable heat or cold generated as by-product in industrial or power generation installations, or in the tertiary sector, which would be dissipated unused in air or water without access to a district heating or cooling system, where a cogeneration process has been used or will be used or where cogeneration is not feasible.

26 According to Article 3(1) of the RED II "Member States shall collectively ensure that the share of energy from renewable sources in the Union's gross final consumption of energy in 2030 is at least 32%".
27 Electricity produced from biomass fuels shall be qualified for those needs only if it meets one or more of the requirements established in Article 29(11) of the RED II. Two of them refer to CHP:

> (b) for installations with a total rated thermal input from 50 to 100 MW, it is produced applying high-efficiency cogeneration technology, or, for electricity-only installations, meeting an energy efficiency level associated with the best available techniques (BAT-AEELs) as defined in Commission Implementing Decision (EU) 2017/1442;
> (c) for installations with a total rated thermal input above 100 MW, it is produced applying high-efficiency cogeneration technology, or, for electricity-only installations, achieving a net-electrical efficiency of at least 36%.

28 The other actions concerned, *inter alia*, further development of the internal energy market, improving decentralised energy production and increasing renewable capacity, as well as promoting energy efficiency in general (Commission 2000a, p. 11).
29 The Directive 2001/77/EC was adopted in September 2001, and the Report (Commission 2001b) is dated October 2001.
30 As the Commission reported (2001b, p. 12), reduction of up to 12 Mt CO_2 could be achieved at a cost ranging from 20 EUR to 50 EUR per tonne of CO_2.
31 Gkarakis and Dagoumas (2016, p. 136) compare guarantees of origin to "a label on a bottle: it carries information telling the consumer facts about the product".
32 A calculation for primary energy savings was defined in the CHP Directive by means of a separated and a coupled energy production (see Pohl & Diarra 2014, p. 287).
33 For example, transmission system operators are designated to issue guarantees of origin for electricity produced in high-efficiency CHP units in Denmark or Finland (see Bröckl et al. 2011, pp. 18, 21).
34 As highlighted in Recital 21 of the preamble to the CHP Directive, the guarantees "do not by themselves imply a right to benefit from national support mechanisms".
35 Similarly, even though Article 6(3) of Directive 2004/8/EC provided a deadline for the first evaluation, no real sanction for non-compliance followed it. Also, its wording (addressing the Commission's "request") confirms a very soft approach applied by the Directive to the issue of evaluating the progress on increasing the usage of high-efficiency CHP in the European Union.
36 The criteria adopted in Annex IV to the CHP Directive left plenty of space for the Member States' decision on what should be included in the evaluation, as

CHP in the EU climate action 131

well as how widely and deeply each criterion should be addressed. This resulted from general clauses included in the Annex. For example, in their evaluations the Member States had to cover "the type of fuels that are likely to be used to realise the cogeneration potentials" or "the type of separate production of heat and electricity or, where feasible, mechanical energy that high-efficiency cogeneration is likely to substitute". This approach did not concern the depth of the provided analysis; in fact, it could be very perfunctory and inconsistent, only briefly addressing the criteria mentioned. By way of exception, the Annex brought some specific provisions, e.g. the evaluation was to specify the potential of high-efficiency CHP in reference to 2010, 2015, and 2020. However, even in this case, it should include appropriate costs estimated for each of these time frames only where feasible.

37 "The end result of Member States' action is dependent on many external factors which influence the behaviour of consumers as regards their energy use and their willingness to implement energy saving methods and use energy saving devices", as highlighted in Directive 2006/32/EC (Recital 12).
38 The Annex contained "examples of areas in which energy efficiency improvement programmes and other energy efficiency improvement measures may be developed and implemented in the context of Article 4".
39 See Annex III, point (f).
40 The Commission (2011, p. 11) estimated that, assuming that the Member States go beyond the target year 2016 for energy efficiency, the primary energy savings resulting from the implementation of the Directive would reach just 50–95 Mtoe in 2020, whereas reaching the 20% savings target required achieving savings at the level of 368 Mtoe.
41 As it was already mentioned, the EU 20% energy goal meant the reduction of primary energy use by 368 Mtoe in 2020. By using PRIMES — an energy system model developed at National Technical University of Athens (by the Energy-Economy-Environment Modelling Laboratory) — the Commission (2011a, p. 21) elaborated on the PRIMES energy efficiency scenario in which, due to the effects of the crisis and policies implemented until December 2009, only 164 Mtoe of the savings objective would be delivered (or 8–9% reduction compared to PRIMES 2007 projections).
42 These were Articles 4(1) — (4) and Annexes I, III, and IV to the Energy Services Directive covering the achievement of an indicative energy saving target of 9% of the final energy consumption of each Member State (by 2017), which "albeit different in scope and level of ambition contributes to the realisation of the EU's 20% energy efficiency target by 2020, and should therefore remain applicable until 2017" (Commission 2011b, p. 2).
43 Under the pessimistic scenario of a forecasted drop in the usage of CHP the consumption of primary energy was expected to increase by about 35 Mtoe (Commission 2011c, p. 58).
44 See Recital 39 of the preamble to Directive 2012/27/EU, as well as its Article 14(10).
45 Recital 38 of its preamble.
46 Cf. Recital 29 of the preamble to Directive 2004/8/EC.
47 Under Article 14(2) of the Energy Efficiency Directive "Member States shall adopt policies which encourage the due taking into account at local and regional levels of the potential of using efficient heating and cooling systems, in particular those using high-efficiency cogeneration".
48 5 June 2014 was the precise date for repealing Directives 2006/32/EC and 2004/8/EC pursuant to Article 27(1) of the Energy Efficiency Directive and a deadline for implementing the new Directive, as stated in its Article 28.

49 According to Article 15(5)(c) of the Energy Efficiency Directive, the cost-benefit analysis covers:

> an industrial installation with a total thermal input exceeding 20 MW generating waste heat at a useful temperature level [which] is planned or substantially refurbished, in order to assess the cost and benefits of utilising the waste heat to satisfy economically justified demand, including through cogeneration, and of the connection of that installation to a district heating and cooling network.

Hence, cogeneration was one of the many technologies addressed by Article 15(5)(c) of Directive 2012/27/EU as those utilising the waste heat in order to meet economically justified demand.

50 For example, this includes specific rules on the system boundary, heat loads, or contributing data for the needs of the assessment of the costs and benefits of each installation.

51 Pursuant to Article 15(5) of Directive 2012/27/EU:

> Member States shall ensure that rules relating to the ranking of the different access and dispatch priorities granted in their electricity systems are clearly explained in detail and published. When providing priority access or dispatch for high-efficiency cogeneration, Member States may set rankings as between, and within different types of, renewable energy and high-efficiency cogeneration and shall in any case ensure that priority access or dispatch for energy from variable renewable energy sources is not hampered.

Nevertheless, starting from the beginning of 2020, these provisions have been deleted by Article 70(5)(a)(i) of Directive (EU) 2019/944 (see Chapter 6 of this book).

52 However, this facilitation was designed to be rather different (more complex) than the simple "install and inform" procedure which was linked to the installation of micro-cogeneration units.

53 Therefore, Annex VIII requires the inclusion of "the share of high-efficiency cogeneration and the potential established and progress achieved under Directive 2004/8/EC" in the analysis regarding the national potential for efficiency in heating and cooling.

54 See e.g. Skorek-Osikowska et al. 2017.

55 E.g. according to Mikhail Chudakov, IAEA Deputy Director General and Head of the Department of Nuclear Energy: "[n]uclear cogeneration is very important, particularly if nuclear power is to expand much more broadly in energy markets to meet the need for clean and sustainable energy, while helping to mitigate climate change through avoidance of carbon emissions" (IAEA 2018).

References

2011/278/EU: Commission Decision of 27 April 2011 determining transitional Union-wide rules for harmonised free allocation of emission allowances pursuant to Article 10a of Directive 2003/87/EC of the European Parliament and of the Council, OJ L 130, 17 May 2011.

Anger, N. 2008, "Emissions trading beyond Europe: linking schemes in a post-Kyoto world", *Energy Economics*, 30(4), pp. 2028–2049.

Atănăsoae, P., Pentiuc, R.D., Popescu, P., & Martin, V. 2018, "Factors which influence the qualification of the electricity production in high efficiency cogeneration for biomass combined heat and power plants", *Procedia Manufacturing*, 22, pp. 651–658.

Badami, M., Gerboni, T., & Portoraro, A. 2017, "Determination and assessment of indices for the energy performance of district heating with cogeneration plants", *Energy*, 127, pp. 697–703.

Banet, C. 2017, "The Paris Agreement to the UNFCCC: underlying dynamics and expected consequences for the energy sector", in *European energy law report, XI*, eds M. Roggenkamp & C. Banet, Intersentia, Cambridge, pp. 71–92.

Bjørnebye, H. 2010, *Investing in EU energy security: exploring the regulatory approach to tomorrow's electricity production*, Kluwer Law International, Alphen aan den Rijn.

Braungardt, S., Bürger, V., Zieger, J., & Bosselaar, L. 2019, "How to include cooling in the EU Renewable Energy Directive? Strategies and policy implications", *Energy Policy*, 129, pp. 260–267.

Calmfors, L., Hassler, J., Nasiritousi, N., Bäckstrand, K., Silbye, F., Sørensen, P.B., Carlén, B., Kriström, B., Greaker, M., Golombek, R., Hoel, M., & Holtsmark, K. 2019, *Nordic economic policy review 2019: climate policies in the Nordics*, Nordic Council of Ministers, Copenhagen.

Capros, P., Mantzos, L., Parousos, L., Tasios, N., Klaassen, G., & Van Ierland, T. 2011, "Analysis of the EU policy package on climate change and renewables", *Energy Policy*, 39(3), pp. 1476–1485.

Carlén, B., Dahlqvist, A., Mandell, S., & Marklund, P. 2019, "EU ETS emissions under the cancellation mechanism – effects of national measures", *Energy Policy*, 129, pp. 816–825.

Celades, I., Monfort, E., Ros-Dosdá, T., & Fullana-i-Palmer, P. 2018, "Environmental profile of Spanish porcelain stoneware tiles", *International Journal of Life Cycle Assessment*, 23(8), pp. 1562–1580.

Cendra de Larragán de, J. 2008. "Too much harmonization? An analysis of the Commission's proposal to amend the EU ETS from the perspective of legal principles", in *Climate change and European emissions trading. Lessons for theory and practice*, eds M. Faure & M. Peeters, Edward Elgar Publishing, Cheltenham, pp. 53–87.

Colmenar-Santos, A., Rosales-Asensio, E., Borge-Diez, D., & Mur-Pérez, F. 2015, "Cogeneration and district heating networks: measures to remove institutional and financial barriers that restrict their joint use in the EU-28", *Energy*, 85, pp. 403–414.

Commission Delegated Regulation (EU) 2019/331 of 19 December 2018 determining transitional Union-wide rules for harmonised free allocation of emission allowances pursuant to Article 10a of Directive 2003/87/EC of the European Parliament and of the Council, OJ L 59, 27 February 2019.

Commission Implementing Decision 2017/1442/EU of 31 July 2017 establishing BAT conclusions, under Directive 2010/75/EU of the European Parliament and of the Council, for large combustion plants, OJ L 212, 17 August 2017.

Commission. 1995, *Commission working paper on the EU climate change strategy: a set of options*, SEC (95) 288 final, 1 March 1995.

134 CHP in the EU climate action

Commission. 1997a, *Communication from the Commission to the Council, the European Parliament, the Economic and Social Committee and the Committee of the regions: the energy dimension of climate change*, COM (97) 196 final, 14 May 1997.

Commission. 1997b, *Communication from the Commission to the Council, the European Parliament, the Economic and Social Committee and the Committee of the regions. A Community strategy to promote combined heat and power (CHP) and to dismantle barriers to its development*, COM (97) 514 final, 15 October 1997.

Commission. 1998a, *Communication from the Commission. Energy efficiency in the European Community – towards a strategy for the rational use of energy*, COM (98) 246 final, 29 April 1998.

Commission. 1998b, *Proposal for a Council Directive amending Directive 88/609/EEC on the limitation of emissions of certain pollutants into the air from large combustion plants*, COM (98) 415 final, 8 July 1998.

Commission. 1998c, *Strengthening environmental integration within Community energy policy. Communication from the Commission*. COM (98) 571 final, 14 October 1998.

Commission. 2000a, *Communication from the Commission to the Council and the European Parliament on EU policies and measures to reduce greenhouse gas emissions: towards a European Climate Change Programme (ECCP)*, COM (2000) 88 final, 8 March 2000.

Commission. 2000b, *Communication from the Commission to the Council, the European Parliament, the Economic and Social Committee and the Committee of the Regions: action plan to improve energy efficiency in the European Community*, COM (2000) 247 final, 26 April 2000.

Commission. 2000c, *Report under Council Decision 1999/296/EC for a monitoring mechanism of Community greenhouse gas emissions*, COM (2000) 749 final, 22 November 2000.

Commission. 2000d, *Green Paper: towards a European strategy for the security of energy supply*, COM (2000) 769 final, 29 November 2000.

Commission. 2001a, *Communication from the Commission. A sustainable Europe for a better world: a European Union strategy for sustainable development (Commission's proposal to the Gothenburg European Council)*, COM (2001) 264 final, 15 May 2001.

Commission. 2001b, *Communication from the Commission on the implementation of the first phase of the European Climate Change Programme*, COM (2001) 580 final, 23 October 2001.

Commission. 2002a, *Directive of the European Parliament and of the Council on the promotion of cogeneration based on a useful heat demand in the internal energy market*, COM (2002) 415 final, 22 July 2002.

Commission. 2002b, *Report from the Commission under Council Decision 93/389/EEC as amended by Decision 99/296/EC for a monitoring mechanism of Community greenhouse gas emissions*, COM (2002) 702 final, 9 December 2002.

Commission. 2003, *Proposal for a Directive of the European Parliament and of the Council on energy end-use efficiency and energy services*, COM (2003) 739 final, 10 December 2003.

Commission. 2004, *Communication from the Commission to the Council and the European Parliament. Commission report in accordance with Article 3 of Directive 2001/77/EC: evaluation of the effect of legislative instruments and other community policies on the development of the contribution of renewable energy sources in the EU and proposals for concrete actions*, COM (2004) 366 final, 26 May 2004.

Commission. 2005a, *Communication from the Commission to the Council, the European Parliament, the European Economic and Social Committee and the Committee of the Regions: winning the battle against global climate change*, 9 February 2005, COM (2005) 35 final.

Commission. 2005b, *Communication from the Commission. Report on demonstrable progress under the Kyoto Protocol (required under Article 5 (3)of Decision 280/2004/EC concerning a mechanism for monitoring Community greenhouse gas emissions and for implementing the Kyoto Protocol)*, COM (2005) 615 final, 1 December 2005.

Commission. 2006a, *Communication from the Commission. Action Plan for energy efficiency: realising the potential*, com (2006) 545 final, 19 october 2006.

Commission. 2006b, *Commission staff working document accompanying document to the Communication from the Commission Action Plan for energy efficiency: realising the potential. Impact Assessment*, SEC (2006) 1174, 19 October 2006.

Commission. 2007, *Communication from the Commission to the Council, the European Parliament, the European Economic and Social Committee and the Committee of the Regions. Limiting global climate change to 2 degrees Celsius. The way ahead for 2020 and beyond*, COM (2007) 2 final, 10 January 2007.

Commission. 2008, *Proposal for a Directive of the European Parliament and of the Council amending Directive 2003/87/EC so as to improve and extend the greenhouse gas emission allowance trading system of the Community*, COM (2008) 16 final, 23 January 2008.

Commission. 2011a, *Commission staff working document: Impact Assessment accompanying document to the communication from the Commission to the European Parliament, the Council, the European Economic and Social Committee and the Committee of the Regions – Commission staff working document. Energy Efficiency Plan 2011*, SEC (2011) 277 final, 8 March 2011.

Commission. 2011b, *Proposal for a Directive of the European Parliament and of the Council on energy efficiency and repealing Directives 2004/8/EC and 2006/32/EC*, COM (2011) 370 final, 22 June 2011.

Commission. 2011c, *Commission staff working paper: Impact Assessment accompanying the document Directive of the European Parliament and of the Council on energy efficiency and amending and subsequently repealing Directives 2004/8/EC and 2006/32/EC*, SEC (2011) 779 final, 22 June 2011.

Commission. 2015, *Commission staff working document: Impact Assessment accompanying the document proposal for a Directive of the European Parliament and of the Council amending Directive 2003/87/EC to enhance cost-effective emission reductions and low-carbon investments*, SWD (2015) 135 final, 15 July 2015.

Commission. 2016a, *Communication from the Commission to the European Parliament and the Council – the road from Paris: Assessing the implications of the Paris Agreement and accompanying the proposal for a Council decision on the signing, on behalf of the European Union, of the Paris Agreement adopted under the United Nations framework convention on climate change*, COM (2016) 110 final, 2 March 2016.

Commission. 2016b, *Communication from the Commission to the European Parliament, the Council, the Economic and Social Committee, the Committee of the regions and the European investment bank: clean energy for all Europeans*, COM (2016) 860 final, 30 November 2016.

Commission. n.d. a, *Kyoto 1st commitment period (2008–12)*. Available from: https://ec.europa.eu/clima/policies/strategies/progress/kyoto_1_en [27 February 2019].

Commission. n.d. b, *Phases 1 and 2 (2005-2012)*, Available from: https://ec.europa.eu/clima/policies/ets_en [27 February 2019].

Commission. n.d. c, *First round of national reports: translated in* English. Available from: https://ec.europa.eu/energy/sites/ener/files/documents/ms_reports_translated.zip [27 February 2019].

Commission. n.d. d, *2030 climate & energy framework*. Available from: https://ec.europa.eu/clima/policies/strategies/2030_en [2 September 2019].

Cornelis, E. 2019, "History and prospect of voluntary agreements on industrial energy efficiency in Europe", *Energy Policy*, 132, pp. 567–582.

Council Decision 2002/358/EC of 25 April 2002 concerning the approval, on behalf of the European Community, of the Kyoto Protocol to the United Nations Framework Convention on Climate Change and the joint fulfilment of commitments thereunder, OJ L 130, 15 May 2002.

Council Directive 88/609/EEC of 24 November 1988 on the limitation of emissions of certain pollutants into the air from large combustion plants, OJ L 336, 7 December 1988.

De Rosa, M., Carragher, M., & Finn, D.P. 2018, "Flexibility assessment of a combined heat-power system (CHP) with energy storage under real-time energy price market framework", *Thermal Science and Engineering Progress*, 8, pp. 426–438.

Directive (EU) 2018/2001 of the European Parliament and of the Council of 11 December 2018 on the promotion of the use of energy from renewable sources, OJ L 328, 21 December 2018.

Directive (EU) 2018/410 of the European Parliament and of the Council of 14 March 2018 amending Directive 2003/87/EC to enhance cost-effective emission reductions and low-carbon investments, and Decision (EU) 2015/1814, OJ L 76, 19 March 2018.

Directive (EU) 2019/944 of the European Parliament and of the Council of 5 June 2019 on common rules for the internal market for electricity and amending Directive 2012/27/EU, OJ L 158, 14 June 2019.

Directive 2001/77/EC of the European Parliament and of the Council of 27 September 2001 on the promotion of electricity produced from renewable energy sources in the internal electricity market, OJ L 283, 27 October 2001.

Directive 2001/80/EC of the European Parliament and of the Council of 23 October 2001 on the limitation of emissions of certain pollutants into the air from large combustion plants, OJ L 309, 27 November 2001.

Directive 2004/8/EC of the European Parliament and of the Council of 11 February 2004 on the promotion of cogeneration based on a useful heat demand in the internal energy market and amending Directive 92/42/EEC, OJ L 52, 21 February 2004.

Directive 2006/32/EC of the European Parliament and of the Council of 5 April 2006 on energy end-use efficiency and energy services and repealing Council Directive 93/76/EEC, OJ L 114, 27 April 2006.

Directive 2009/28/EC of the European Parliament and of the Council of 23 April 2009 on the promotion of the use of energy from renewable sources and amending and subsequently repealing Directives 2001/77/EC and 2003/30/EC, OJ L 140, 5 June 2009.

Directive 2009/29/EC of the European Parliament and of the Council of 23 April 2009 amending Directive 2003/87/EC so as to improve and extend the greenhouse gas emission allowance trading scheme of the Community, OJ L 140, 5 June 2009.

Directive 2010/75/EU of the European Parliament and of the Council of 24 November 2010 on industrial emissions (integrated pollution prevention and control), OJ L 334, 17 December 2010.

Directive 2012/27/EU of the European Parliament and of the Council of 25 October 2012 on energy efficiency, amending Directives 2009/125/EC and 2010/30/EU and repealing Directives 2004/8/EC and 2006/32/EC, OJ L 315, 14 November 2012.

Dziok, T., Grzywacz, P., & Bochenek, P. 2019, "Assessment of mercury emissions into the atmosphere from the combustion of hard coal in a home heating boiler", *Environmental Science and Pollution Research*, 26(22), pp. 22254–22263.

Economic and Social Committee. 2011, Opinion of the European Economic and Social Committee on the "Proposal for a Directive of the European Parliament and of the Council on energy efficiency and repealing Directives 2004/8/EC and 2006/32/EC", 26 October 2011, OJ C 24, 28 January 2012.

Etty, T.F.M., Heyvaert, V., Carlarne, C., Farber, D., Lin, J., & Scott, J. 2012, "Transnational dimensions of climate governance", *Transnational Environmental Law*, 1(2), pp. 235–243.

European Committee of the Regions. 2011, *Opinion of the Committee of the Regions on "Energy efficiency"*, 14 December 2011, OJ C 54, 23 February 2012.

European Council. 2007, *Presidency Conclusions of the Brussels European Council (8/9 March 2007)*, 7224/1/07REV 1, 2 May 2007.

European Council. 2008, *Presidency Conclusions of the Brussels European Council (11 and 12 December 2008)*, 17271/1/08 REV 1, 13 February 2009.

European Council. 2014, *Conclusions of the European Council (23 and 24 October 2014)*, EUCO 169/14, 24 October 2014.

European Economic and Social Committee. 2008, *Opinion on the proposal for a Directive of the European Parliament and of the Council amending Directive 2003/87/EC so as to improve and extend the greenhouse gas emission allowance trading system of the Community*, NAT/399, 9 July 2008.

European Parliament. 2002a, *Report on the proposal for a European Parliament and Council Directive establishing a scheme for greenhouse gas emission allowance trading within the Community and amending Council Directive 96/61/EC*, final A5-0303/2002, 13 September 2002.

European Parliament. 2002b, European Parliament legislative resolution on the proposal for a European Parliament and Council Directive establishing a scheme for greenhouse gas emission allowance trading within the Community and amending Council Directive 96/61/EC, 10 October 2002, OJ C 279E, 20 November 2003.

European Parliament. 2012, *Position of the European Parliament adopted at first reading on 11 September 2012 with a view to the adoption of Directive 2012/ … /EU of the European Parliament and of the Council on energy efficiency, amending Directives 2009/125/EC and 2010/30/EU and repealing Directives 2004/8/EC and 2006/32/EC*, 11 September 2012, EP-PE_TC1-COD(2011)0172.

Filippini, M., Hunt, L.C., & Zorić, J. 2014, "Impact of energy policy instruments on the estimated level of underlying energy efficiency in the EU residential sector", *Energy Policy*, 69, pp. 73–81.

Gambini, M., Vellini, M., Stilo, T., Manno, M., & Bellocchi, S. 2019, "High-efficiency cogeneration systems: the case of the paper industry in Italy", *Energies*, 12(3), 335, pp. 1–21. doi:10.3390/en12030335 [27 February 2019].

Geiss, J. 2013. "From agreement via legislation to implementation – will the Cimate and Energy Package deliver until 2020?" in *Sustainable energy policies for Europe: towards 100% renewable energy*, ed. R. Hinrichs-Rahlwes, CRC Press, Boca Raton, FL, pp. 44–62.

Gkarakis, K., & Dagoumas, A. 2016. "Assessment of the implementation of guarantees of origin (GOs) in Europe", in *Power systems, energy markets and renewable energy sources in South-Eastern Europe*, eds F. Mavromatakis & K. Siderak, Trivent Publishing, Budapest, pp. 132–143.

Gvozdenac, D., Gvozdenac Urošević, B., Menke, C., Urošević, D., & Bangviwat, A. 2017, "High efficiency cogeneration: CHP and non-CHP energy", *Energy*, 135, pp. 269–278.

Hitchin, P. 2011, "Is Europe ready for the IED and willing?" *Power Engineering International*, 19(10), pp. 40–45.

IAEA. 2018, *Towards more sustainable nuclear energy with non-electric applications: opportunities and challenges*. Available from: www.iaea.org/newscenter/news/towards-more-sustainable-nuclear-energy-with-non-electric-applications-opportunities-and-challenges [27 February 2019].

Ibáñez-Forés, V., Bovea, M.D., & Azapagic, A. 2013, "Assessing the sustainability of best available techniques (BAT): methodology and application in the ceramic tiles industry", *Journal of Cleaner Production*, 51, pp. 162–176.

Jakubcionis, M., & Carlsson, J. 2017, "Estimation of European Union residential sector space cooling potential", *Energy Policy*, 101, pp. 225–235.

Jansen, J., Gialoglou, K., & Egenhofer, C. 2005, *Market stimulation of renewable electricity in the EU: what degree of harmonisation of support mechanisms is required?* Centre for European Policy Studies, Brussels.

Jansen, J.C., & Uyterlinde, M.A. 2004, "A fragmented market on the way to harmonisation? EU policy-making on renewable energy promotion", *Energy for Sustainable Development*, 8(1), pp. 93–107.

Kaldellis, J.K., Vlachos, G.T., Paliatsos, A.G., & Kondili, E.M. 2005, "Detailed examination of the Greek electricity sector nitrogen oxides emissions for the period 1995–2002", *Environmental Science & Policy*, 8(5), pp. 502–514.

Kliucininkas, L., Zieniute, I., & Mockuviene, J. 2005, "An assessment of the cogenerated electrical energy potential for Lithuania", *Management of Environmental Quality: An International Journal*, 16(5), pp. 398–406.

Knoop, K., & Lechtenböhmer, S. 2017, "The potential for energy efficiency in the EU Member States – a comparison of studies", *Renewable and Sustainable Energy Reviews*, 68, pp. 1097–1105.

Kulovesi, K., Morgera, E., & Muñoz, M. 2011, "Environmental integration and multi-faceted international dimensions of EU law: unpacking the EU's 2009 Climate and Energy Package", *Common Market Law Review*, 48(3), pp. 829–891.

Lecomte, T., de, F., la Fuente, J.F., Neuwahl, F., Canova, M., Pinasseau, A., Jankov, I., Brinkmann, T., Roudier, S., & Delgado Sancho, L. 2017, *Best Available Techniques (BAT) reference document for large combustion plants*, Publications Office of the European Union, Luxembourg.

Leurent, M., Jasserand, F., Locatelli, G., Palm, J., Rämä, M., & Trianni, A. 2017, "Driving forces and obstacles to nuclear cogeneration in Europe: lessons learnt from Finland", *Energy Policy*, 107, pp. 138–150.

Lise, W., Timpe, C., Jansen, J.C., & ten Donkelaar, M. 2007, "Tracking electricity generation attributes in Europe", *Energy Policy*, 35(11), pp. 5855–5864.

Makowska, D., Strugała, A., Wierońska, F., & Bacior, M. 2019, "Assessment of the content, occurrence, and leachability of arsenic, lead, and thallium in wastes from coal cleaning processes", *Environmental Science and Pollution Research*, 26(9), pp. 8418–8428.

Mortensen, B.O.G. 2004, "The EU emission trading directive", *European Energy and Environmental Law Review*, 13(10), pp. 275–284.

Pacala, S., & Socolow, R. 2004, "Stabilization wedges: solving the climate problem for the next 50 years with current technologies", *Science*, 305(5686), pp. 968–972.

Pereira, G.I., & Pereira da Silva, P. 2017, "Energy efficiency governance in the EU-28: analysis of institutional, human, financial, and political dimensions", *Energy Efficiency*, 10(5), pp. 1279–1297.

Piacentino, A., Barbaro, C., & Cardona, F. 2014, "Promotion of polygeneration for buildings applications through sector- and user-oriented 'high efficiency CHP' eligibility criteria", *Applied Thermal Engineering*, 71(2), pp. 882–894.

Pohl, E., & Diarra, D. 2014, "A method to determine primary energy savings of CHP plants considering plant-side and demand-side characteristics", *Applied Energy*, 113, pp. 287–293.

Polders, C., Van den Abeele, L., Derden, A., & Huybrechts, D. 2012, "Methodology for determining emission levels associated with the best available techniques for industrial waste water", *Journal of Cleaner Production*, 29, pp. 113–121.

Raadal, H.L., Dotzauer, E., Hanssen, O.J., & Kildal, H.P. 2012, "The interaction between electricity disclosure and tradable green certificates", *Energy Policy*, 42, pp. 419–428.

Rende, K., Ercan, Ö., Hilmioğlu, B., Ergenekon, P., & Sadıkoğlu, H. 2018, "Assessment of CO_2 reduction techniques of cement production in Turkey", *International Journal of Global Warming*, 16(1), pp. 18–38.

Ruzzenenti, F., & Bertoldi, P. 2017, "Energy conservation policies in the light of the energetics of evolution", in *Complex systems and social practices in energy transitions: framing energy sustainability in the time of renewables*, ed. N. Labanca, Springer International Publishing, Cham, pp. 147–167.

Schiavo, G. 2013, "The new EU directive on energy efficiency: critical view", *Maastricht Journal of European and Comparative Law*, 20(2), pp. 321–326.

Skorek-Osikowska, A., Remiorz, L., Bartela, Ł., & Kotowicz, J. 2017, "Potential for the use of micro-cogeneration prosumer systems based on the Stirling engine with an example in the Polish market", *Energy*, 133, pp. 46–61.

Sokołowski, M.M. 2016, *Regulation in the European electricity sector*, Routledge, Abingdon and New York, NY.

Sokołowski, M.M. 2018, "Burning out coal power plants with the industrial emissions Directive", *The Journal of World Energy Law & Business*, 11(3), pp. 260–269.

Streimikiene, D., Burneikis, J., & Punys, P. 2005, "Review of renewable energy use in Lithuania", *Renewable and Sustainable Energy Reviews*, 9(1), pp. 29–49.

Vajda, P. 2016, "The role of the industrial emissions Directive in the European Union and beyond", *ERA Forum*, 17(4), pp. 487–499.

Verbruggen, A., Dewallef, P., Quoilin, S., & Wiggin, M. 2013, "Unveiling the mystery of combined heat & power (cogeneration)", *Energy*, 61, pp. 575–582.

Wettestad, J., Eikeland, P.O., & Nilsson, M. 2012, "EU climate and energy policy: a hesitant supranational turn?" *Global Environmental Politics*, 12(2), pp. 67–86.

Whiteley, M. 2001, "Cogeneration's European future: cogeneration in a post-Kyoto world", *Cogeneration and On-Site Power Production*, 2(4), pp. 25–28.

Woerdman, E., & Nentjes, A. 2019, "Emissions trading hybrids: the case of the EU ETS", *Review of Law & Economics*, 15(1), pp. 1–32. doi:10.1515/rle-2014-0054 [2 September 2019].

Wojdyga, K., Chorzelski, M., & Rożycka-Wrońska, E. 2014, "Emission of pollutants in flue gases from Polish district heating sources", *Journal of Cleaner Production*, 75, pp. 157–165.

Yukseler, H., Uzal, N., Sahinkaya, E., Kitis, M., Dilek, F.B., & Yetis, U. 2017, "Analysis of the best available techniques for wastewaters from a denim manufacturing textile mill", *Journal of Environmental Management*, 203, pp. 1118–1125.

Zangheri, P., Economidou, M., & Labanca, N. 2019, "Progress in the implementation of the EU Energy Efficiency Directive through the lens of the national annual reports", *Energies*, 12(6), 1107. pp. 1–16.

Ziębik, A., & Gładysz, P. 2012, "Optimal coefficient of the share of cogeneration in district heating systems", *Energy*, 45(1), pp. 220–227.

Ziębik, A., & Gładysz, P. 2013, "Complex analysis of the optimal coefficient of the share of cogeneration in district heating systems", *Energy*, 62, pp. 12–22.

Ziemele, J., Cilinskis, E., & Blumberga, D. 2018, "Pathway and restriction in district heating systems development towards 4th generation district heating", *Energy*, 152, pp. 108–118.

5 European CHP
The EU countries review

The 1970s were a time of changes brought to many European countries and their cogeneration industries. Like the USA, a pro-cogeneration trend has sparked again in some Western European countries. Driven by the postulate of energy savings – not wasting energy but saving it instead – the move on CHP found a fertile land in such countries as Denmark, the Netherlands, and West Germany. Cogeneration has also developed on the other side of the Iron Curtain, being a vital element of energy sectors in Hungary, Poland, and other Central and Eastern European countries. This derived from the heat demand, which steered the growth in cogeneration; accordingly, inadequate demand for heat hindered the investment in heating systems in southern Europe.

At the turn of the 1980s and 1990s, CHP was addressed as one of the tools of energy policy for CEE countries during their democratisation. However, its strengths could not have been utilised everywhere (e.g. Romania). Correspondingly, despite the attention offered by the European countries to combined heat and power (see Chapter 2 of this book), the situation of CHP in 1990s was – as seen from the EU's perspective – "disappointing". In 1994, only a minor share (just 9%) of the Community's electricity was generated in CHP units (see Commission 1997, p. 3, 10).

This improved a few years later. In the late 1990s the cogeneration's share in the electricity generation of the EU-15 reached almost 11%. The major producers were the Netherlands, Italy, and Germany, but the biggest share of CHP use in the generation of electricity was recorded in Denmark (more than 62%), while in terms of heat production Italy took the lead (touching the barrier of 400 PJ of heat produced in CHP). When comparing 1994 to 1998, we can see that the total EU-15 installed cogeneration capacity in 1998 (heat and power) grew by less than 15%, reaching about 72 GW installed in heat and 170 GW in power. Regarding the fuel mix, in most of the EU-15's Member States, the predominantly used fuel was natural gas whose use was growing; the same applied to renewable fuels. However, the use of solid fuels like coal, decreased (see Chapter 2 of this book). This Chapter gives me the opportunity to elaborate on those changes, including those after the subsequent enlargement of the European Union.

As discussed in the preceding parts of the book, the situation of combined heat and power in European countries has been varied. However, to some extent, certain similarities can be observed. This allows for the grouping of Member States in certain categories to review the cogeneration sector. The criteria used for this selection derive from the scale of cogeneration. Factors such as generation of electricity and heat in CHP, as well as the installed capacities (in heat and power) enable to distinguish three groups of countries: big, medium, and minor CHP users. By referring to the statistics discussed in the previous Chapters of this book (including Chapter 2) and providing further data on each Member State, the EU-28 was divided into three categories presented in the following subchapters (cf. Knoop & Lechtenböhmer 2017; Saint Akadiri et al. 2019; Stankeviciute & Krook Riekkola 2014). Figure 5.1 depicts this division.

The aforementioned data includes that presented in the progress reports elaborated on by the Member States under Article 6(3) of the CHP Directive; accordingly, the First Progress Report (FPR) and the Second Progress Report (SPR).[1] The deadline for delivering the first reports was February 2007, while the second deadline was to be elaborated on four years later. The legislative and regulatory framework on the procedures

Figure 5.1 Scale of CHP in the European Union (EU-28)

applicable to high-efficiency cogeneration was discussed in the structure of FPRs and/or SPRs. Wherever necessary, the framework was supplemented by the current developments reported in the draft integrated National Energy and Climate Plan (NECP), delivered by the Member States under Regulation (EU) 2018/1999 on the Energy Union (see Chapter 6 of this book).[2]

Big CHP players

Within the EU, eight big players in combined heat and power can be distinguished; these are Finland, France, Germany, Italy, the Netherlands, Poland, Spain, and the United Kingdom.[3] Germany occupies the top position with respect to the scale of CHP both within this group and in the whole of the EU. Contrasting German cogeneration with the remaining seven Member States, one may find that Germany single-handedly accounts for about one third of the overall production of the group – both in electricity and gas (see Eurostat 2019a). The selection for this group was made on the basis of recent production of electricity and heat by the European CHP (Eurostat 2019b). Member States which produced more than 20 TWh, and/or significantly overcame 100 PJ in produced heat, were qualified as big CHP players.[4]

Finland

In Finland, a significant part of the heated building stock in urban areas is connected to the DH network, and the country exploits the CHP potential (FI NECP 2018, p. 31, cf. Korhonen & Savolainen 2001, p. 146). After the peak in the generation of electricity in 2010, when CHP units produced almost 30 TWh, the production of power from cogeneration in Finland declined; in 2016, it reached the level comparable to production in 1994. The same applies both to the share of energy produced from CHP in total gross electricity generation, and to total heat produced by cogeneration (which differ slightly). In contrast to 1994, the capacity (both in heat and power) has increased, although between 2010 and 2016 a minor drop was recorded (see Table 5.1). However, as reported at the beginning of the 2010s, progress has been made with respect to high-efficiency cogeneration, supported, *inter alia*, by legally guaranteed equal access to the market (FI SPR 2011, p. 2). Some changes in the CHP capacity are also forecasted for the mid-2020s when several CHP plants are likely to be decommissioned (FI NECP 2018, p. 31, 99).[5]

The structure of Finnish fuel mix has been characterised by a high share of renewables for a long time (cf. Salomón et al. 2011). In the 1990s, Finland already had a developed subsidy scheme to support domestic fuels in the DH, and several CHP plants fired by wood-chip were up and running by then (Sandberg, Møller Sneum, & Trømborg 2018, p. 108). In

144   European CHP

Table 5.1 CHP portfolio of Finland between 1994–2016

	1994	1998	2005	2010	2016
CHP electricity generation [TWh]	20.31	25.13	27.46	29.24	21.83
share of CHP in total gross electricity generation	30.9%	35.8%	38.9%	36.2%	31.8%
total CHP installed capacity in electricity [GW]	4.09	5.10	5.83	6.17	5.86
total CHP installed capacity in heat [GW]	12.67	14.78	NA	15.95	14.59
total heat produced in CHP [PJ]	256.40	269.44	249.98	272.84	241.63

Source: Eurostat 2001, Eurostat 2019a.

1998, renewables accounted for more than 40%, reaching 60% in 2016. This was accompanied by a reduction in the use of natural gas, which decreased about two and a half times between 2010 and 2016. As presented in Table 5.2, solid fossil fuels and peat maintained an over 25% share of this mix. However, there are plans to change this under the regulatory framework to be discussed.

What has been changing the Finnish fuel mix are the adopted policies and legislation. First, one should mention energy taxation. In 2011, Finland reformed it: the tax rates for all energy products (with some exceptions) were increased (transport fuels) and a new energy tax, based on the energy content and CO_2 emissions, was introduced (FI SPR 2011, p. 11). New energy taxes have weakened the competitiveness of DH (especially fuelled by natural gas, oil, and coal), although heat from cogeneration obtained some preferential tax treatment (FI SPR 2011, p. 11). Tax has also been included in the new framework presented by Finland in its draft integrated NECP. Energy taxation is targeted there as a tool for stimulating the use of forest chips and forest industry by-products in CHP production. This should make sure that peat will be less competitive than these fuels on the one hand, and more cost-effective than coal and imported fossil fuels on the other hand (FI NECP 2018, p. 47).[6]

Table 5.2 Fuel used in cogeneration in Finland between 1998–2016

	fuel used for CHP [PJ]	solid fossil fuels and peat	oil and oil products	natural gas	renewables	other fuels
1998	440.85	27%	2%	24%	43%	3%
2005	466.87	27.2%	2.3%	23.3%	44.6%	2.7%
2010	450.94	25.3%	1.8%	23.7%	46.5%	2.7%
2016	387.97	25.1%	0.6%	9.5%	60.8%	4.1%

Source: Eurostat 2001, Eurostat 2019a.

Second, in 2018 the Finnish government decided that the use of coal in energy production will be legally prohibited by 2029 (Ministry of Economic Affairs and Employment 2018); in February 2019, the Finnish parliament approved this proposal of banning the use of coal to produce energy from 1 May 2029 (Reuters 2019). This will ensure significant changes in the country's energy industry, including cogeneration. Coal-fired CHP units will be chiefly replaced by heat only boilers using biomass and the CHP capacity will decrease by about 300 MW (FI NECP 2018, p. 99).

However, cogeneration is included in the framework of Finnish policies, measures, and programmes to achieve the energy efficiency goals for 2030. Here, Finland envisages keeping the preconditions for efficient CHP units operating and competing with other generators in an open energy market. This refers to the measures offered to efficient cogeneration for improving the overall efficiencies of primary energy use and of energy production under energy efficiency agreement activities (FI NECP 2018, p. 53).

France

Between 1994 and 2006–2007 the generation of electricity in French CHP units doubled, or even tripled; in 2009 it reached almost 24 TWh, which accounted for a 4.3% share in total gross electricity generation (Eurostat 2019a). Consequently, in 2009 the production of heat in CHP was about to break 200 PJ (Eurostat 2019a). However, the growing trend has not been maintained and in 2016 cogeneration in France in comparison to 2010 noticed a drop with the exception of installed heat and power capacities (see Table 5.3).

Two general comments describe the French CHP sector and its fuels. These are a relatively small share of fossil fuels like coal or oil, and a big proportion of cleaner (in terms of CO_2 emissions) natural gas and renewables (more than 50% and about 30% respectively). In terms of the latter, i.e. renewables, when

Table 5.3 CHP portfolio of France between 1994–2016

	1994	1998	2006[7]	2010	2016
CHP electricity generation [TWh]	8.51	12.66	18.42	15.69	14.96
share of CHP in total gross electricity generation	1.8%	2.5%	3.2%	2.8%	2.7%
total CHP installed capacity in electricity [GW]	2.92	3.49	5.78	4.61	6.07
total CHP installed capacity in heat [GW]	11.19	18.84	NA	13.33	14.86
total heat produced in CHP [PJ]	116.57	170.67	187.39	173.95	163.91

Source: Eurostat 2001, Eurostat 2019a.

146 *European CHP*

Table 5.4 Fuel used in cogeneration in France between 1998–2016

	fuel used for CHP [PJ]	solid fossil fuels and peat	oil and oil products	natural gas	renewables	other fuels
1998	277.99	7%	13%	38%	33%	9%
2006	367.15	4.9%	3.0%	57.7%	21.0%	13.4%
2010	281.23	5.9%	2.6%	56.5%	23.0%	11.9%
2016	260.02	4.7%	4.8%	50.3%	27.7%	12.5%

Source: Eurostat 2001, Eurostat 2019a.

comparing 1998 to 2016, its share decreased (see Table 5.4); however, taking into account 2010 and 2016 the use of renewables has grown and natural gas has dropped. This was in line with the French energy policy objectives aimed at developing combined heat and power based on biomass (see Sergent 2014, p. 498), which would gradually replace the existing natural gas-fired units (FR SPR 2011, p. 3).

In terms of biomass, in 2018 the French "National Biomass Mobilisation Strategy" (*La Stratégie Nationale de Mobilisation de la Biomasse*) was passed (see Ministry of Ecological and Solidarity Transition 2018). Aimed at developing domestic production of biomass, it also targets CHP industry (FR NECP 2019, p. 224). According to the Strategy, as biomass is a scarce resource (and will continue to be scarce until 2050), France prioritises its use for the needs of heating only (so not cogeneration), with some preferences for high-efficiency CHP (see FR NECP 2019, p. 74, 225). In this light, biomass cogeneration is being offered a support mechanism – tendering schemes with remuneration for 20 years, established under the legislation from 2016 (Ministry of Ecological and Solidarity Transition 2018). The same legislation repealed an earlier (2011) feed-in tariff with guaranteed purchase (see Cruciani 2017, p. 319).

Apart from the tender mechanism and tools provided by the CHP Directive, France has established other pro-cogeneration measures (cf. Mauger 2018, p. 502). As reported in 2011, this included: the possibility to use micro-cogeneration powered by liquid or gaseous fuels as an alternative to the obligation of using renewable energy in one-family house; placing micro- and small-scale cogeneration in the system of energy saving certificates; offering tax credit for gas-fired micro-CHP (FR SPR 2011, p. 2).

Germany

Combined heat and power is a firm element of the German energy sector. On the on hand, it was developed over a long time, with the help of different policy measures and financial sources. On the other hand, it faced some issues like in the case of former East Germany (see Chapter 2 of this book), or more recently, when in the twenty-first century the pace of investment in large CHP plants generally slowed down in the country. This slowdown was a result of regulatory framework and emissions trading (see DE SPR 2012, p. 2). In this context, the German government has introduced the 2020 goal to achieve 25% share of electricity generated in CHP in the country's total electricity generation (see Westner & Madlener 2011, p. 5301–5302; Jacobs 2012, pp. 226–227). To facilitate that, the CHP Act of 2002 (*KraftWärme-Kopplungsgesetz 2002*) was amended (see DE SPR 2012, p. 1–2; Jacobs 2012, pp. 227–228). However, the 25% goal has been altered by more moderate targets with the effect from 1 January 2016 (Gailfuß n.d.). The change was brought by the new CHP Act (*KraftWärme-Kopplungsgesetz 2016*) setting the CHP goal for 2020 (together with the goal for 2025) as follows: 110 TWh of electricity to be generated from CHP plants by 2020 and 120 TWh by 2025; also extending the funding scheme for cogeneration till 2022 (Federal Ministry for Economic Affairs and Energy n.d.).

Irrespective of these issues, the German CHP industry is the biggest in the EU. Moreover, Germany is one of the very few EU countries where the scale of the usage of cogeneration has grown. Between 1998 and 2016 CHP recorded a gradual growth in all of the evaluated fields – they have either doubled (electricity generation, total heat production), almost doubled (share of CHP in electricity production, installed capacity in electricity), or almost tripled (installed capacity in heat). This made Germany the biggest cogeneration market in the EU, producing almost 90 TWh of electricity and about 700 PJ of heat in the CHP fleet, accounting for approximately 90 GW of installed capacity in heat and power (see Table 5.5).

The growth in cogeneration observed in Germany has been accompanied by a change in the fuel mix. Comparing 1998 to 2016, a significant share in the use of solid fossil fuels was reduced (from 43% to 13.5%; the latter includes peat), while the use of renewables grew from 2% in 1998 to more than 23% in

Table 5.5 CHP portfolio of Germany between 1994–2016

	1994	1998	2005	2010	2016
CHP electricity generation [TWh]	47.75	41.77	77.85	83.20	87.94
share of CHP in total gross electricity generation	9.0%	7.5%	12.6%	13.2%	13.5%
total CHP installed capacity in electricity [GW]	26.18	22.16	20.84	26.61*	37.21
total CHP installed capacity in heat [GW]	46.56	35.87	NA	63.93	94.60
total heat produced in CHP [PJ]	446.89	340.76	652.53	675.82	697.97

* Data for 2011.
Source: Eurostat 2001, Eurostat 2019a.

Table 5.6 Fuel used in cogeneration in Germany between 1998–2016

	fuel used for CHP [PJ]	solid fossil fuels and peat	oil and oil products	natural gas	renewables	other fuels
1998	606.75	43%	5%	42%	2%	9%
2005	1,204.79	31.0%	5.2%	50.6%	5.3%	7.9%
2010	1,268.71	27.4%	4.0%	49.6%	9.3%	9.6%
2016	1,351.52	13.5%	4.3%	45.6%	23.3%	13.3%

Source: Eurostat 2001, Eurostat 2019a.

2016. This is also due to additional tariffs for CHP production from biomass (see Scheftelowitz, Becker, & Thrän 2018). Apart from that, during the evaluated period natural gas has maintained its share, accounting for about one half of German fuel mix. Table 5.6 presents these trends.

Future development in the field of cogeneration in Germany cover the funding of mini cogeneration plants – maximally 20 kW units, supplying energy to residential and non-residential buildings. It also applies to the implementation of pilot projects of modernised CHP plants aimed at increasing their flexibility under a call for proposals announced by the Federal Ministry of Economic Affairs and Energy (DE NECP 2018, p. 70, 86). The latter derives from an assumption that modernised CHP units "are likely to play a key role in GHG reduction between now and 2030 and even beyond that date" – under the condition that cogeneration power plants reduce their emissions and respond in a flexible way to fluctuations of renewables in the market (DE NECP 2018, p. 86, cf. Stadler 2008, pp. 94–98). By exploiting the experience of the "Use It, Don't Curtail It" (*Nutzen statt Abregeln*) scheme, established under §13(6a) of the Energy Industry Act (*Energiewirtschaftsgesetz*), the pilot innovative CHP projects will test how cogeneration can operate with dual flexibility – by providing both renewable heat and renewable electricity (see DE NECP 2018, p. 86).[8]

Italy

The portfolio of Italian cogeneration can be divided into two parts: the 1990s and post 2005, with the turn of the 1990s/2000s as the borderline of the two phases of growth in CHP. As juxtaposed in Table 5.7, after a rise in the 1990s, driven by the increased tariffs provided for energy-saving plants (see Chapter 2 of this book), combined heat and power in Italy declined. Later on growth picked up, generally maintaining the gradual increase (see Eurostat 2019a). Between 2005 and 2016, the assessed fields increased, achieving about 6 TWh in electricity generation, 2.5 GW of power installed in electricity, and producing about 27 PJ more. Moreover, cogeneration in Italy recorded an increase in efficiency, especially between 2012 and 2013, also due to more efficient CHP technologies (see IT SPR 2011, pp. 188–189).[9]

Table 5.7 CHP portfolio of Italy between 1994–2016

	1994	1998	2005	2010	2016
CHP electricity generation [TWh]	26.48	44.86	27.39	34.71	40.34
share of CHP in total gross electricity generation	11.4%	17.3%	9.0%	11.5%	13.9%
total CHP installed capacity in electricity [GW]	6.33	9.52	5.89	7.35	8.51
total CHP installed capacity in heat [GW]	17.51	23.34	NA	13.87	14.01
total heat produced in CHP [PJ]	253.68	397.80	193.07	202.51	219.77

Source: Eurostat 2001, Eurostat 2019a.

The growth in Italian CHP has been steered by different regulatory drivers. Among them, one may find, for example, support offered via energy efficiency certificates (white certificates) representing the equivalent of annual primary energy savings (see Stede 2017; Aldrich & Koerner 2018, pp. 58–59; Franzò et al. 2019). Further drivers included such facilitations as simplified grid connection procedure, and reduced costs of this connection (IT SPR 2011, pp. 2–3). Moreover, since 2007, Italy has been offering tax deductions for measures which improve energy efficiency in existing buildings such as the replacement of heating installations with micro-cogeneration (IT NECP 2018, p. 123). However, when comparing the tax deduction with the white certificate scheme, one may find the latter much more cost effective considering the ratio of the annual cost of the support with energy savings achieved (see Franzò et al. 2019, p. 425).

In terms of fuel used, for a long time, Italy has been among those EU countries which consumed the biggest volume of fuel for the needs of CHP. In 2010 it exceeded 1,000 PJ, and natural gas was the major fuel used, accounting for over 70% of fuel mix (followed by almost 17% of oil). The situation changed between 2010 and 2016 – mainly due to the growth in the usage of renewable, which in 2016 reached almost 16%, although a switch from oil to natural gas could also be noticed (see Antonelli, Desideri, & Franco 2018, p. 3095). The Italian fuel mix is presented in Table 5.8.

Table 5.8 Fuel used in cogeneration in Italy between 1998–2016

	fuel used for CHP [PJ]	*solid fossil fuels and peat*	*oil and oil products*	*natural gas*	*renewables*	*other fuels*
1998	783.23	1%	15%	68%	NA	16%
2005	887.83	0.8%	18.8%	67.4%	3.5%	9.5%
2010	1,004.78	0.2%	16.7%	70.5%	4.3%	8.3%
2016	451.71	3.2%	8.7%	65.2%	15.6%	7.3%

Source: Eurostat 2001, Eurostat 2019a.

Netherlands

In 1998, combined heat and power generated more than half of total gross electricity produced in the Netherlands, benefiting from pro-cogeneration changes in legislation as well as policies which enabled development of CHP (see Chapter 2 of this book). Currently, despite the fact that "the government does not have a specific incentive policy for CHP", cogeneration is supported by the Energy-Saving Investment Credit. Moreover, natural gas used by CHP units is exempted from energy tax, while operating grants are offered through the Sustainable Energy Production Incentive for CHP units powered by renewable fuels like biomass or CHP (NL NECP 2018, p. 86).

However, in 2016, production of electricity by CHP in the Netherlands was much lower than in the late 1990s when it produced nearly 48 TWh (compared to around 31 TWh in 2016). Between 2007–2010 the installed capacity, both in heat and power, grew again (Eurostat 2019a). Following this rise (mainly in agriculture and horticulture) hardly any new CHP units have been introduced to the Dutch energy system (NL NECP 2018, p. 85), despite the financing available for high-efficiency cogeneration (see NL SPR 2011, p. 6). Furthermore, taking into account 2010 and 2016, the trend has been reversed (see Table 5.9), dropping slightly – in the case of power capacity (around 200 MW less), or more noticeably – with respect to heat (lower by about 2.6 GW).

Regardless of the changes discussed, the Dutch fuel mix has preserved its major structure maintaining the leading position of natural gas; in 2016, its share accounted for 81%. Other types for fuels oscillated around 4% (like solid fossil fuels, oil) or 6% (renewables). However, one should notice a decline in the of usage solid fossil fuels – which decreased from 16% in 1998 to 3.8% in 2016 (see Table 5.10).

The structure of fuels used in cogeneration (the reliance on natural gas) and the price ratio of natural gas and electricity, have resulted in limited

Table 5.9 CHP portfolio of the Netherlands between 1994–2016

	1994	1998	2005	2010	2016
CHP electricity generation [TWh]	31.54	47.84	29.47	39.24	30.78
share of CHP in total gross electricity generation	39.5%	52.6%	29.4%	33.2%	26.7%
total CHP installed capacity in electricity [GW]	6.15	8.50	7.16	9.30	9.08
total CHP installed capacity in heat [GW]	12.05	16.91	NA	18.56	15.98
total heat produced in CHP [PJ]	171.03	238.77	220.28	233.61	174.26

Source: Eurostat 2001; Eurostat 2019a.

Table 5.10 Fuel used in cogeneration in the Netherlands between 1998–2016

	fuel used for CHP [PJ]	solid fossil fuels and peat	oil and oil products	natural gas	renewables	other fuels
1998	561.27	16%	0%	71%	2%	10%
2005	597.50	14.1%	2.4%	69.5%	2.1%	11.9%
2010	467.74	4.8%	0.8%	79.6%	3.1%	11.7%
2016	338.81	3.8%	3.8%	81.0%	5.8%	5.5%

Source: Eurostat 2001, Eurostat 2019a.

production from cogeneration as shown in Table 5.9 (NL NECP 2018, p. 85). Moreover, further decline in the Dutch CHP industry is predicted in the future, driven by the price uncertainty of natural gas and electricity – as a result, the replacement of depreciated CHP units with new ones will not be carried out. Additionally, preferences will be offered for production of electricity and heat from renewables (NL NECP 2018, p. 86). In such market conditions only flexible CHP units, like those equipped with heat storage facilities, will be able to operate cost-effectively (NL NECP 2018, p. 86, cf. Franco & Versace 2017).

Poland

Among the EU Member States, Poland joins those countries which attach certain significance to the usage of combined heat and power in their energy sector. As a result of post-war investments, the share of total electricity produced in CHP in Poland has grown from about 6% in 1970 to 8% in 1980 (see Chapter 2 of this book), exceeding the limit of 10% in the following years; between 2005–2016 this share remained at around 16%. In general, during this period, Polish cogeneration has remained relatively stable. The changes that occurred at that time were rather small – the increase in electricity generation reaching more than 1 TWh, or 400 MW installed in the power capacity. A more visible change occurred in heating where, between 2010 and 2016, the installed capacity was reduced by about 1 GW and the production decreased by more than 30 PJ (see Table 5.11).

For a long time, the vast majority of cogeneration in Poland was powered by fossil fuels, with a dominant share of coal in the production of heat (see Żmijewski & Sokołowski 2010). In 2005 this share was higher than 92%. However, the Polish fuel mix in cogeneration has evolved, reaching about 70% share for fossil fuels in 2016 and making space for renewables and natural gas; in 2016, both accounted for around 10%. Further changes in this mix are forecasted, as investments in gas-powered

152 *European CHP*

Table 5.11 CHP portfolio of Poland between 2005–2016

	2005	2010	2016
CHP electricity generation [TWh]	26.30	27.71	27.60
share of CHP in total gross electricity generation	16.8%	17.6%	16.6%
total CHP installed capacity in electricity [GW]	8.31	8.69	8.72
total CHP installed capacity in heat [GW]	NA	24.83	23.78
total heat produced in CHP [PJ]	275.43	277.10	246.47

Source: Eurostat 2019a.

CHP units are planned (see Gawlik & Mokrzycki 2019, p. 9) and a more widespread usage of biomass and biogas in cogeneration is being considered (see PL NECP 2019, pp. 71–72, 118; Gawlik 2018, p. 235, cf. Dzikuć & Piwowar 2016, p. 861). Apart from that, a significant decrease in the amount of fuel used by Polish CHP industry should be noted. Juxtaposing 2005 and 2016 shows that it dropped three and a half times, as depicted in Table 5.12.

The Polish CHP industry has been addressed by dedicated regulatory measures. In 2007, the tool for promoting energy from high-efficiency cogeneration, a certification scheme, entered into force (cf. Kotowicz & Bartela 2011, pp. 330–331). It imposed an obligation on entities selling electricity to end customers, either to buy certificates or to pay a substitution fee instead – in proportion to the volume of energy offered by these entities (PL SPR 2012, p. 8, cf. Sołtysik & Mucha-Kuś 2015). Under the scheme, which expired at the end of 2018, three types of certificates (yellow, purple, and red) were available for CHP units, depending on their capacity and the fuel used (see Commission 2016). Yellow certificates were for high-efficiency CHP fired by gaseous fuels or those with total installed electrical capacity below 1 MW; while purple certificates were for units powered by methane or by gas obtained from biomass (Energy Regulatory Office 2011, pp. 3–5, see Muras 2011). Red certificates were for all CHP sources with total installed capacity above 1 MW or units fired with fuels used in installations covered by

Table 5.12 Fuel used in cogeneration in Poland between 2005–2016

	fuel used for CHP [PJ]	solid fossil fuels and peat	oil and oil products	natural gas	renewables	other fuels
2005	1,489.79	92.1%	2.9%	2.7%	1.0%	1.2%
2010	459.53	74.3%	8.8%	6.5%	7.6%	2.8%
2016	421.24	70.8%	7.5%	10.1%	10.6%	1.0%

Source: Eurostat 2019a.

yellow or purple certificate (Energy Regulatory Office 2011, pp. 3–5, see Muras 2011). From 2019, combined heat and power in Poland[10] (high-efficiency units connected to DH, new or refurbished and existing gas-powered) is supported under a new mechanism–annual budget of 500 million EUR, available until the end of 2028. It is based on a premium on top of the market price, i.e. a cogeneration premium set as a rule in a competitive bidding (as an exception determined in an administrative way). This premium is delivered until the CHP plant is fully depreciated in a maximal time frame of 15 years (Commission 2019a).

Apart from the support scheme, Poland was providing financial assistance for high-efficiency CHP projects offered by the National Fund for Environmental Protection and Water Management (*Narodowy Fundusz Ochrony Środowiska i Gospodarki Wodnej*) between 2009–2015 and 2014–2020, with an extension until 2023 (see PL SPR 2012, p. 23; PL NECP 2019, p. 102). High-efficiency combined heat and power has also been addressed by governmental programmes aimed at improving air quality – by being an element of energy-efficient heating systems, along with both renewables, and waste heat from industrial installations (PL NECP 2019, p. 102).

Spain

Spain is one of the EU countries where the CHP sector – with small deviations (see Eurostat 2019a) – notices an increase of production of electricity. Between 1994 and 2016 it has grown almost three times. However, when generation of electricity has risen, the production of heat has fallen (about 70 PJ, when comparing 2005 to 2016). When we take into account the early 1990s, though, the recent production of heat in Spain was bigger (see Table 5.13).

The same tendency as shown here, applies also to installed capacity – the 2016 level is higher than the one from the 1990s; however, between 2005

Table 5.13 CHP portfolio of Spain between 1994–2016

	1994	1998	2005	2010	2016
CHP electricity generation [TWh]	8.54	21.92	23.21	22.42	27.48
share of CHP in total gross electricity generation	5.3%	11.2%	4.0%	7.4%	10.0%
total CHP installed capacity in electricity [GW]	1.53	3.56	6.60	3.38	4.16
total CHP installed capacity in heat [GW]	4.70	5.31	NA	10.30	6.40
total heat produced in CHP [PJ]	91.51	141.32	209.21	153.31	138.82

Source: Eurostat 2001, Eurostat 2019a.

154 *European CHP*

Table 5.14 Fuel used in cogeneration in Spain between 1998–2016

	fuel used for CHP [PJ]	solid fossil fuels and peat	oil and oil products	natural gas	renewables	other fuels
1998	291.87	3%	24%	51%	9%	13%
2005	407.54	5.0%	4.3%	53.5%	23.2%	14.0%
2010	322.14	1.3%	5.6%	84.8%	0.0%	8.3%
2016	302.48	2.3%	8.3%	79.2%	1.7%	8.6%

Source: Eurostat 2001, Eurostat 2019a.

and 2016 some decline was recorded (see Eurostat 2019a). Nevertheless, all the newly installed cogeneration units were high-efficiency CHP, as stipulated by Royal Decree No 661/2007 which set minimum efficiency requirements for all cogeneration installations. The Decree also established an extra payment (based on the increased efficiency) for those CHP units which exceed those minimum requirements (ES SPR 2011, p. 3). In addition, Spanish law required conducting pro-efficiency improvements in existing CHP units to achieve high efficiency (ES SPR 2011, p. 3).

However, as drafted in the ES NECP (2019, p. 116), a large volume (2,400 MW) of existing (mainly industrial) gas-fired CHP units, which would reach the end of their lifetime by 2030, will not be renewed or replaced (see Commission 2019c, p. 10). As one may notice, natural gas is the main fuel used in Spanish cogeneration; its share, with minor changes, has grown from around 50% in 1998 to nearly 80% in 2016 (however, in 2010 it reached almost 85%) – see Table 5.14.

To conduct (or continue) the transition of cogeneration units accounting for 1,200 MW to high-efficiency cogeneration between 2021–2030, Spain has offered a new regulatory measure based on the competitive tendering procedure (ES NECP 2019, p. 116). It covers a multi-annual tender schedule to establish a cost-effective remuneration system for the use of public funds, supported by the necessary administrative tools (ES NECP 2019, p. 116).

United Kingdom

In the past, cogeneration in the UK went through different phases of growth and decline, and had various stakeholders (see Chapter 2 of this book). In 2016, cogeneration in the UK produced the volume of electricity comparable to the late 1990s – in both periods this share accounted for around of 5% of the country's total gross electricity generation. However, when juxtaposing the capacities, as provided in Table 5.15, in 2016 the scale of cogeneration was bigger than in the 1990s

Table 5.15 CHP portfolio of the United Kingdom between 1994–2016

	1994	1998	2005	2010	2016
CHP electricity generation [TWh]	11.62	18.64	27.24	23.64	19.80
share of CHP in total gross electricity generation	3.6%	5.2%	6.8%	6.2%	5.8%
total CHP installed capacity in electricity [GW]	2.52	3.72	5.44	6.10	4.57
total CHP installed capacity in heat [GW]	13.20	15.35	NA	7.81	7.12
total heat produced in CHP [PJ]	174.91	225.17	185.24	155.52	129.78

Source: Eurostat 2001, Eurostat 2019a.

(850 MW added), but when taking 2010 into account, this scale decreased. Regarding the heat production between 1998 and 2016, in 2016 cogeneration produced about a half of the amount from 1998 (in the fleet of installations smaller by half). The decline of the 2000s and 2010s has been driven by several factors. Among them were: increased production efficiency and so reduced demand for heat, and the economic situation in the UK (and the recession) which affected manufacturing, resulting in the reduction of CHP production. Yet another factor was the difference between the price of electricity and the cost of generation in cogeneration – it was inadequate to ensure a satisfactory return on investment (see UK SPR 2011, pp. 4–5).

As presented in Table 5.16, the major fuel of the UK cogeneration has been natural gas. With some deviations, natural gas accounted for about 70% in the country's fuel mix for combined heat and power. Another fuel, though not as extensively used as natural gas, was oil which in 2015–2016 came back to the 1990s level (see Eurostat 2019a). Additionally, over the years the amount of fuel used in CHP has declined by about 120 PJ.

In the UK, high-efficiency cogeneration, meeting the requirements set down for such types of CHP units in the Energy Efficiency Directive, is

Table 5.16 Fuel used in cogeneration in the United Kingdom between 1998–2016

	fuel used for CHP [PJ]	solid fossil fuels and peat	oil and oil products	natural gas	renewables	other fuels
1998	370.60	12%	13%	48%	2%	26%
2005	343.36	3.0%	4.0%	71.7%	1.9%	19.3%
2010	301.86	3.8%	1.9%	68.7%	5.0%	20.5%
2016	250.28	1.6%	14.2%	73.9%	6.6%	3.7%

Source: Eurostat 2001, Eurostat 2019a.

certified as "Good Quality CHP" through the "CHP Quality Assurance Programme" (UK NECP 2018, p. 108, see UK SPR 2011, p. 7). The certificates make it possible to obtain the Climate Change Levy exemption (Department for Business, Energy & Industrial Strategy 2018). Since 2010, the UK has established a feed-in tariff scheme for micro-cogeneration; however, these installations have not seen a sustained level of deployment – between 2010–2016 only about 500 such units have been deployed (Department of Energy & Climate Change 2016, p. 6). Moreover, since 1 April 2019 this feed-in tariff scheme has been closed to new applicants (see Office of Gas and Electricity Markets 2019, p. 5). Additionally, the uncertainties related to Brexit poses certain threats to the CHP industry in the UK.

Medium CHP sectors

Austria, Belgium, Bulgaria, the Czech Republic, Denmark, Hungary, Portugal, Romania, Slovakia, and Sweden can be labelled as medium CHP sectors. This category derives from the following production levels: recent generation of electricity lower than 20 TWh and/or production of heat lower (or oscillating around) 100 PJ while accordingly bigger than 3 TWh and 20 PJ (see Eurostat 2019a).

Austria

In the 1990s Austria managed to increase the amount of electricity generated in combined heat and power. Between 1994 and 1998 this production accounted for more than 2.5 TWh growth, and the share of CHP in total gross electricity generation reached almost 25% in 1998 (Eurostat 2001). The country's installed capacity in CHP also grew slightly in that period– in terms of electricity (just 170 MW), and noticeably – in terms of heat capacity which reached 1.35 GW of new units installed during those four years (Eurostat 2001). This increase led to a growth jump in heat produced in CHP, which in 1996 was approximately 22.5 PJ bigger than in 1994. However, only in 1998 it decreased to a level comparable with 1994 – about 79 PJ in 1994 compared to almost 81.5 PJ in 1998 (Eurostat 2001). The statistics are presented in Table 5.17.

In terms of the fuel structure, for just over 223 PJ of fuel used in cogeneration in 1998, the majority was based on natural gas (46%), followed by renewables (16%) and liquid fuels (14%). Hard coal and lignite along with other fuels accounted for 12%.[11] In almost 20 years, the structure moved towards renewables; all the other elements of the energy mix, including natural gas, decreased, while the use of renewables gradually increased – from 16% (1998) to more than 38% (2016). Moreover, even a more widespread usage of high-efficiency CHP powered by biomass is expected (AT NECP 2018, p. 91). Additionally, one should also notice

Table 5.17 CHP portfolio of Austria between 1994–2016

	1994	1998	2005	2010	2016
CHP electricity generation [TWh]	11.72	14.27	10.13	10.96	10.90
share of CHP in total gross electricity generation	21.4%	24.8%	15.4%	15.4%	16.0%
total CHP installed capacity in electricity [GW]*	3.25	3.42	3.25	3.16	3.43
total CHP installed capacity in heat [GW]*	6.00	7.35	NA	8.60	8.85
total heat produced in CHP [PJ]*	79.18	81.47	95.85	110.61	114.94

* Starting from 2005 these are total amounts.
Source: Eurostat 2001, Eurostat 2019a.

a decrease in the fuel used in combined heat and power. It fell from the level of about 253 PJ (2010) to approximately 185 PJ (2016); in 2015 it was even lower, reaching about 159 PJ (Eurostat 2019a). The data is presented in Table 5.18.

In terms of regulatory framework, in June 2006, Austria notified the transposition of the CHP Directive; in the same month the country's state aid scheme for existing/modernised and new cogeneration units was approved (AT FPR n.d. a, p. 1). Generally, the system has been based on two different schemes: operational aid for existing cogeneration plants (2003–2010) granted in order to maintain their operation, and investment aid (2007–2012/2014) for new CHP units (AT SPR n.d., pp. 5–6, cf. Blumberga 2019, p. 192). Investment grants to support new high-efficiency CHP plants have also been addressed in NECP proposed by Austria (AT NECP 2018, p. 41).

Building new CHP plants in the Austrian energy system has been assessed as still technically feasible (cf. scenarios for the expansion of CHP plants using wood offered by Stocker et al. 2011, p. 6084). In practice, however, the development of cogeneration faced problems of an

Table 5.18 Fuel used in cogeneration in Austria between 1998–2016

	fuel used for CHP [PJ]	*solid fossil fuels and peat*	*oil and oil products*	*natural gas*	*renewables*	*other fuels*
1998	223.30	12%	14%	46%	16%	12%
2005	252.57	14.9%	9.3%	45%	20.2%	10.6%
2010	179.98	4.5%	8.9%	45.3%	33.7%	7.7%
2016	184.52	7.8%	9.6%	37.6%	38.1%	7%

Source: Eurostat 2001, Eurostat 2019a.

informative character (see E-Bridge 2005, p. 9). Other issues included: time-consuming procedures deriving from, for example, limited personnel, lack of the relevant expertise of the engaged authorities, or different legal possibilities aimed at delaying the CHP project by its opponents (AT FPR n.d. b, p. 8).[12] CHP in Austria was facing yet another issue – the electricity prices hindering the utilisation of its economic potential for new cogeneration plants has emerged (cf. Büchele et al. 2016, pp. 16–17; AT NECP 2018, p. 134).[13]

Belgium

In 2016, the CHP sector in Belgium was about four times bigger than 22 years previously; in some cases (like electricity generation) it was four times bigger than in 1994 – see the Table 5.19. However, the generation of electricity and heat in CHP (steered by public support, see BE SPR 2012, pp. 7–8), which peaked around 2010, decreased in the following years, oscillating around the level of 100 PJ produced in CHP. A significant drop in this production was recorded in 2013, when cogeneration in Belgium generated just over 27 PJ of heat (Eurostat 2019a).

Traditionally, combined heat and power in Belgium has been fuelled by natural gas – Belgium offered various schemes to develop natural gas in electricity generation; they were also applied to CHP (see Chapter 2 of this book). Nevertheless, over the years this share decreased from 72% in 1998 to about 60% in 2016, but, as explained, the cogeneration sector has grown in the country (when comparing 1998 to 2016). Additionally, Belgium faced some infrastructural issues related to the potential for developing natural gas cogeneration.[14] Natural gas is followed by other fuels, which constitute a significant share in Belgian CHP fuel mix (of more

Table 5.19 CHP portfolio of Belgium between 1994–2016

	1994	1998	2005	2010	2016
CHP electricity generation [TWh]	2.44	3.41	7.36	15.20	12.19
share of CHP in total gross electricity generation	3.4%	4.1%	8.5%	16.0%	14.2%
total CHP installed capacity in electricity [GW]	0.73	0.80	1.89	2.58	2.21
total CHP installed capacity in heat [GW]	3.1	3.19	NA	4.79	5.04
total heat produced in CHP [PJ]	38.97	38.03	75.86	93.72*	104.39

* Data for 2011; accordingly, in 2011, 14,46 TWh of electricity was generated in CHP units in Belgium.
Source: Eurostat 2001, Eurostat 2019a.

than 20%); in the third place are renewables, accounting for about 16% (2016). Table 5.20 presents these statistics.

When discussing the situation of CHP in Belgium, an important legal remark should be made. Belgium is a federal state consisting of three linguistic communities and three regions (Flanders, Wallonia, and Brussels-Capital). Each region has its own powers and duties – also with respect to energy policy which is covered by both federal and regional authorities. However, in terms of the promotion of cogeneration it's the regions that are responsible for it (BE FPR n.d., p. 2). In this context, one should mention that even before passing the CHP Directive, the Belgian regions established support mechanisms applying to cogeneration. Looking at the Walloon Region we can see that it provided certificates, guarantees of origin, and different types of support for the investments. Created in 1997 the "Cogeneration Facilitator" also offered other forms of promotion and technical support e.g. advice on administrative difficulties (BE SPR 2012, pp. 5, 10). This concerned "high-quality cogeneration" – defined in the Walloon legislation – whose scope differed from high-efficiency cogeneration introduced by the CHP Directive (BE SPR 2012, p. 5).

Regarding the problems faced by combined heat and power in Belgium, as presented in the Belgian Second Progress Report (2012, p. 8–12), these issues were noticed at two levels. One was the individual regional level (e.g. the uncertainty about industry in Wallonia, as cogeneration has not been treated as a core business, or the lack of possibilities for new connections of decentralised producers in some parts of the country like West Flanders); the other occurred regardless of regional borders. The latter concerns, *inter alia*, the time-consuming procedures; delays between the investment decision and the commissioning of the plant; administrative burdens put on micro-cogeneration, like the impossibility of selling electricity within one building, to its different units (see BE SPR 2012, pp. 8–12). In Flanders, the legislation has not been fully adjusted to the presence of DH networks as the rules have been fragmented or missing, resulting in legal uncertainty (see Deyne 2016, p. 11).

Table 5.20 Fuel used in cogeneration in Belgium between 1998–2016

	fuel used for CHP [PJ]	solid fossil fuels and peat	oil and oil products	natural gas	renewables	other fuels
1998	63.13	6%	12%	72%	8%	2%
2005	141.09	1.8%	3.2%	60.4%	1.4%	33.1%
2010	203.19	1.3%	0.5%	59.8%	14.0%	24.4%
2016	167.66	1.2%	1.4%	59.3%	16.2%	21.9%

Source: Eurostat 2001, Eurostat 2019a.

160 *European CHP*

In February 2018, the Commission approved the certificates schemes for high-efficiency cogeneration (and also for renewable electricity) implemented in Flanders to comply with the EU State aid rules (Commission 2018). In the framework of the scheme two types of certificates are distinguished: for renewables (green certificate) and for cogeneration (CHP certificate). Under the latter, the high-efficiency cogeneration units receive one certificate for each MWh of energy saving achieved (see Righini & Catti De Gasperi 2019, p. 57). Moreover, Flanders plans to develop micro-cogeneration; the same applies to Wallonia (see BE NECP 2018, p. 31, 96).

Bulgaria

When comparing 2005–2016 data on CHP in Bulgaria (see Table 5.21), one should note a decrease in the produced electricity and heat, despite the priority being given to cogeneration during its transformation (see Chapter 2 of this book). With some peaks – like in 2007 and 2008 (especially the latter is noteworthy, as CHP units in Bulgaria produced almost 59 PJ of heat and 4.5 TWh of electricity) – the country records a falling tendency in terms of production of heat and electricity. Moreover, just about a half of the CHP capacity in electricity was certified as high efficiency cogeneration (BG NECP 2019, p. 127).

The Bulgarian CHP mix consists mainly of a combination of conventional solid fuels and natural gas: about 42% to 39% in 2016. However, between 2010 and 2016 it changed from 50% to less than 30% (parenthetically, the rising trend in gas prices was addressed as "a serious barrier to building combined systems" in Bulgaria, see BG SPR n.d., p. 8); and starting from 2016, the country notes the usage of renewables (see Table 5.22). Additionally, high efficiency gas-fired CHP units are planned (see BG NECP 2019, p. 128). Consequently, (with some minor changes in 2007 and 2013), the volume of fuel used for CHP in Bulgaria is decreasing (Eurostat 2019a).

Table 5.21 CHP portfolio of Bulgaria between 2005–2016

	2005	2010	2016
CHP electricity generation [TWh]	7.36	3.72	3.64
share of CHP in total gross electricity generation	8.5%	8.0%	8.0%
total CHP installed capacity in electricity [GW]	1.89	1.02	1.49
total CHP installed capacity in heat [GW]	NA	3.92	4.73
total heat produced in CHP [PJ]	50.45	40.43	39.35

Source: Eurostat 2019a.

Table 5.22 Fuel used in cogeneration in Bulgaria between 2005–2016

	fuel used for CHP [PJ]	solid fossil fuels and peat	oil and oil products	natural gas	renewables	other fuels
2005	110.02	55.3%	8.2%	30.5%	0.0%	6.0%
2010	67.97	51.4%	9.0%	39.6%	0.0%	0.0%
2016	64.72	42.3%	1.5%	39.1%	5.3%	11.9%

Source: Eurostat 2019a.

Regarding the regulatory framework on CHP, there were certain measures of supporting cogeneration, as listed in the country's Second Progress Report (BG SPR n.d., p. 5). Some of them, for example the mandatory purchase of all energy produced in high efficiency CHP (with some exceptions, like own use by CHP unit), and preferential rates for this type of energy. Another measure was a cogeneration investment obligation (new installations with an output exceeding 5 MW and powered with natural gas were to be CHP, if the need for heat was declared). Yet another measure was a connection priority for high-efficiency CHP units of power installed equal to or lower than 10 MW. With respect to the barriers to high efficiency energy cogeneration (during the time reported under the CHP Directive), Bulgaria identified several. Among them were, *inter alia*, the lack of incentives to use CHP by producers of renewable energy, and unfavourable conditions for connecting new units to the grid (BG SPR n.d., p. 8). To tackle these problems, different measures have been adopted within the framework of the Energy from Renewable Sources Act (ZEVI). They included e.g. the support for (and the implementation of) the construction of heat networks and small decentralised heating/cooling systems; these measures will be applied after 2020 and aimed at developing high efficiency cogeneration (BG NECP 2019, p. 60).

Czech Republic

Despite almost doubling the installed CHP capacity in electricity (from 4.6 GW in 2015 to just over 9 GW in 2016), the amount of electricity produced in cogeneration in the Czech Republic in 2016 was lower than in 2005 (when this capacity accounted for about 5 GW). Moreover, heat produced in CHP has recorded a falling trend (with small deviations, see Eurostat 2019a) – 2016 registered the lowest level of total heat produced in CHP in the Czech Republic, as surveyed by Eurostat (2019a). The CHP portfolio of the Czech Republic is depicted in Table 5.23.

The major fuels used in the Czech cogeneration are solid fossil fuels. In 2016 this category accounted for almost 70% in the fuel mix of CHP; however, it has fallen by about 10% (2005 to 2016). One should also note

162 *European CHP*

Table 5.23 CHP portfolio of the Czech Republic between 2005–2016

	2005	2010	2016
CHP electricity generation [TWh]	13.87	12.24	8.38
share of CHP in total gross electricity generation	16.8%	14.2%	10.1%
total CHP installed capacity in electricity [GW]	5.20	4.79	9.03
total CHP installed capacity in heat [GW]	NA	20.55	20.79
total heat produced in CHP [PJ]	150.67	135.67	101.56

Source: Eurostat 2019a.

a growing share of renewables (16% in 2016), as well as a big drop in the volume used in cogeneration: from more than 431 PT in 2005 to around 166 PJ in 2016 (see Table 5.24).

Regarding the regulatory framework, the Czech Republic adopted a legal environment for cogeneration in the 1990s. The first law regarding cogeneration – Act No. 222/1994 Sb. – obliged the suppliers of electricity to buy it (if technically possible) from CHP (CZ SPR 2012, p. 6). In 2012, an integrated approach concerning the support of renewables and cogeneration was adopted (Act No. 165/2012 Sb. effective from the beginning of 2013). The support for cogeneration included a system of bonuses for electricity generated in high-efficiency CHP but no direct state aid for cogeneration was provided – a universal support within the system of price regulation was also offered to the industry (CZ SPR 2012, pp. 9–10). Among several problems related to the development of CHP (identified in 2012), one may find: permit processes for the construction of energy-related facilities; blocking grid capacity for other electricity generators (including CHP units) by not implementing renewable projects; emissions trading systems being economically unfavourable for bigger cogeneration units – with heat input of more than 20 MW (CZ SPR 2012, p. 16). The proposed legislation was to solve these issues (see CZ SPR 2012, p. 16).

Moreover, the Czech Republic has set a goal of supplying 60% of heat from cogeneration by 2040, which – although currently achieved – depends

Table 5.24 Fuel used in cogeneration in the Czech Republic between 2005–2016

	fuel used for CHP [PJ]	*solid fossil fuels and peat*	*oil and oil products*	*natural gas*	*renewables*	*other fuels*
2005	431.35	79.1%	1.7%	9.2%	5.0%	5.0%
2010	268.79	75.9%	2.0%	7.4%	7.3%	7.4%
2016	165.76	68.1%	0.7%	13.0%	16.0%	2.3%

Source: Eurostat 2019a.

on the post-2020 support for combined heat and power (CZ NECP 2018, p. 42). The Czech government plans to continue supporting CHP plants, on the basis of fuel neutrality, in a division of sources below and over 1 MW of power, which will determine the form of the aid distribution: a decision by energy regulators (for smaller sources) or (for bigger units), offering the support for 15 years (CZ NECP 2018, p. 68).

Denmark

Denmark has a long tradition of developing combined heat and power. Special attention was given to this industry during the time of the oil crisis of the 1970s, when the Heat Supply Act was adopted. It imposed an obligation to designate specific areas supplied with district heat produced by CHP; this pro-cogeneration approach was continued in the 1980s, when the Danish government provided financing for the investment in DH (see Chapter 2). The legislation has established a rule to promote cogeneration "as much as possible", and so the law has steered its development (DK SPR 2011, p. 7). In the 1990s, the Danish CHP sector was responsible for more than 60% of electricity produced – almost 26 TWh (cf. Mortensen & Overgaard 1992). Over the years this has fallen, reaching less than 40% in 2016 (approximately 12 TWh produced in cogeneration). The installed capacity in power was rather stable, having a certain technical potential for development (see DK SPR 2011, pp. 3–4); between 2005–2016 it kept the level of about 5–6 GW (see Eurostat 2019a). Danish CHP units also recorded a decline with respect to production of heat; in contrast to electricity generation this decrease was not as big, but still significant – lower by about a quarter in relation 2010 to 2016 (see Table 5.25).

Cogeneration in Denmark has made a transition towards renewable energy – from 7% in 1998 to more than 43% in 2016. Consequently, the share of solid fossil fuels was reduced. In 2016, it accounted for less than 30% (compared with 55% of hard coal and lignite in 1998). Another type of fuel which has been reduced in the Danish CHP fuel mix is natural gas – about 10% lower in 2016 than it was in 1998 (see Table 5.26).

Table 5.25 CHP portfolio of Denmark between 1994–2016

	1994	1998	2005	2010	2016
CHP electricity generation [TWh]	21.87	25.59	18.89	19.10	12.03
share of CHP in total gross electricity generation	54.5%	62.3%	52.1%	49.2%	39.4%
total CHP installed capacity in electricity [GW]	5.21	7.03	5.69	5.81	5.86
total CHP installed capacity in heat [GW]	9.18	11.00	NA	10.18	8.79
total heat produced in CHP [PJ]	92.39	119.72	118.98	124.74	94.95

Source: Eurostat 2001, Eurostat 2019a.

164 *European CHP*

Table 5.26 Fuel used in cogeneration in Denmark between 1998–2016

	fuel used for CHP [PJ]	solid fossil fuels and peat	oil and oil products	natural gas	renewables	other fuels
1998	364.27	55%	4%	24%	7%	10.0%
2005	299.17	46.4%	4.6%	29.1%	16.9%	3.0%
2010	321.62	49.2%	2.1%	23.8%	20.0%	4.8%
2016	155.04	29.6%	2.4%	14.9%	43.2%	10.0%

Source: Eurostat 2001, Eurostat 2019a.

In the framework of pro-cogeneration legislation different regulatory tools were delivered to the sector. As reported under the CHP Directive (DK SPR 2011, pp. 8–9) this included, *inter alia*, priority grid access; financial support required to cover the necessary investment costs and operating aid (subsidies, price supplements); tax exemptions (heat produced in biomass-powered cogeneration). In recent years there has been a strong drive for substituting coal and gas (DK NECP 2018, p. 51); it was powered by a tax exemption on biomass fuels for heat production, along with a fixed premium scheme (electricity production from the use of solid biomass supported with 2 EUR cent per kWh under the scheme covering existing and new biomass CHP plants that has run for ten years until 2019). In June 2018, under a policy agreement between the government and other Parties of the Danish Parliament, the post-2019 support was established (see DK NECP 2018, p. 6, 51).[15]

Hungary

In the given period (2005–2016) cogeneration in Hungary decreased in all of the evaluated areas (cf. Zsebik 2008). The biggest drop has been recorded in total heat production; this volume has declined almost two times, from more than 47 PJ in 2005 to around 25 PJ in 2016. Other values have also fallen, but not so notoriously (see Table 5.27). These adverse tendencies could be a result of the economic crisis which began in 2008, bringing negative impact on investments as well as production (see HU SPR 2011, p. 1).

Hungarian CHP has recorded high use of natural gas (around 80%) which has been substituted for renewables; between 2010 and 2016 the use of gas fell by about 18% while renewables grew by around 15%. In that period, one should also notice a drop in the volume of the fuel used, as well as an increase of the share of solid fossil fuels and peat in the Hungarian fuel mix (see Table 5.28). Parenthetically, according to governmental plans, by 2030 coal-fired power generation in Hungary will be possible only in case of industrial heat and DH installations (HU NECP 2018, p. 38).

Table 5.27 CHP portfolio of Hungary between 2005–2016

	2005	2010	2016
CHP electricity generation [TWh]	6.84	7.31	4.82
share of CHP in total gross electricity generation	19.1%	19.6%	15.1%
total CHP installed capacity in electricity [GW]	2.05	1.86	1.47
total CHP installed capacity in heat [GW]	NA	3.44	2.82
total heat produced in CHP [PJ]	47.42	42.18	24.65

Source: Eurostat 2019a.

Table 5.28 Fuel used in cogeneration in Hungary between 2005–2016

	fuel used for CHP [PJ]	*solid fossil fuels and peat*	*oil and oil products*	*natural gas*	*renewables*	*other fuels*
2005	97.68	7.0%	1.7%	79.6%	1.2%	10.5%
2010	87.34	3.7%	0.1%	81.2%	6.9%	8.1%
2016	58.39	10.1%	0.1%	63.0%	21.5%	5.3%

Source: Eurostat 2019a.

With respect to the legal environment for CHP, Hungary has provided a simplified licensing procedure for small units (0.5 to 50 MW) in a combined form, both for the construction and production of electricity. It is applicable when minimum energy efficiency requirements have been met by these units (cf. Elek 2010), and the micro-cogeneration has been exempted from the licencing procedure (HU SPR 2011, p. 2).

Portugal

Between 2008–2013 combined heat and power in Portugal was under pressure from the global financial crisis and the eurozone crisis which was affecting the country (see Blanchard & Portugal 2017, p. 154–156). On the one hand, the recorded decline has not been so significant with respect to the power part of the industry CHP; on the other hand, installed capacity in heat has suffered a bigger drop (see Table 5.29). In general, the decline was gradual (year-to-year) – in total around 1 GW (2016), which accounts for one fifth of 2010's level. Parenthetically, thermal energy in Portugal is produced exclusively by CHP plants (PT NECP 2018, p. 76).

As previously observed, the crisis affected the demand for useful heat. It influenced the potential of high-efficiency CHP and resulted in the need to review its support scheme (PT SPR n.d., p. 2). Pursuant to the amendment to support the system, adopted in 2010, the reference tariff had to be non-

166 *European CHP*

Table 5.29 CHP portfolio of Portugal between 1994–2016

	1994	1998	2005	2010	2016
CHP electricity generation [TWh]	3.11	3.29	5.42	6.36	6.25
share of CHP in total gross electricity generation	9.9%	8.4%	11.6%	11.8%	10.4%
total CHP installed capacity in electricity [GW]	0.99	0.97	1.08	1.31	1.19
total CHP installed capacity in heat [GW]	4.19	3.98	NA	4.85	3.76
total heat produced in CHP [PJ]	46.92	50.80	59.61	67.22	61.69

Source: Eurostat 2001, Eurostat 2019a.

Table 5.30 Fuel used in cogeneration in Portugal between 1998–2016

	fuel used for CHP [PJ]	solid fossil fuels and peat	oil and oil products	natural gas	renewables	other fuels
1998	93.92	NA	53%	1%	38%	8%
2005	103.71	0.0%	37.1%	21.0%	36.8%	5.1%
2010	113.87	0.0%	16.4%	41.1%	38.3%	4.3%
2016	108.30	0.0%	7.9%	45.6%	46.0%	0.6%

Source: Eurostat 2001, Eurostat 2019a.

discriminatory in terms of the fuel basis (any preference given to specific fuel), although it had to reflect the environmental benefits. It was also designed to be correlated with market drivers, including the developments of fuel prices (globally) and the consumer price index (PT SPR n.d., p. 4).

Apart from the modification of the tariff (where fuel was an issue), the Portuguese CHP fuel mix has also changed. This concerns mainly one element – oil, which, although previously used extensively (more than 50% in the 1990s) has now been substituted by natural gas and renewable energy. In 2016, they were quite balanced, both reaching around 46%, while oil accounted for less than 8%. With respect to renewable fuels the country has been using mainly biomass, and has plans to promote renewables in heating and cooling (see PT NECP 2018, p. 34, 76). Additionally, Portugal is one of the EU countries which does not use solid fossil fuels and peat in its CHP fuel mix (having a tradition of not doing so – see Table 5.30).

Romania

Cogeneration in Romania encountered certain issues which appeared after the country's transformation (see Chapter 2 of this book). As a result (with minor exceptions), every year the market for cogeneration in Romania has been getting smaller and smaller (see Eurostat 2019a). Table 5.31 adduces this negative trend which, in general, covers all of the analysed fields related to cogeneration (see Tofan, Şerbănoiu, & Burlacu 2015, pp. 148–149). When comparing 2005 to 2016, the generation of electricity in CHP units, the share of production in cogeneration in total gross electricity generation, and total CHP installed capacity in electricity have fallen about three times. Similarly, total CHP installed capacity in heat and total heat produced in CHP have fallen twice (see Table 5.31). The installed CHP capacity has been underutilised – the units were designed to meet the seasonal demand for heat. However, many of them (especially those installed before 1998) were oversized and not adapted to the new conditions of a reduced market of industrial and urban customers (RO SPR n.d., p. 4). Over the years the disconnections from the centralised systems have been continued, and the Romanian heat market has maintained a high level of instability (RO SPR n.d., p. 5).

Notwithstanding the general decline in CHP – as discussed, in the given period combined heat and power in Romania has evolved (see Table 5.32). The use of solid fossil fuels and oil has decreased, but that of natural gas with renewables has grown. These were not very radical changes; however, a fall in the use of solid fossil fuels should be noted (almost 17% between 2010 and 2016).

Table 5.31 CHP portfolio of Romania between 2005–2016

	2005	2010	2016
CHP electricity generation [TWh]	15.55	6.54	5.29
share of CHP in total gross electricity generation	26.2%	10.8%	8.1%
total CHP installed capacity in electricity [GW]	5.25	4.58	1.85
total CHP installed capacity in heat [GW]	NA	10.77	6.28
total heat produced in CHP [PJ]	95.39	69.00	45.88

Source: Eurostat 2019a.

Table 5.32 Fuel used in cogeneration in Romania between 2005–2016

	fuel used for CHP [PJ]	solid fossil fuels and peat	oil and oil products	natural gas	renewables	other fuels
2005	265.42	45.5%	10.5%	42.9%	0.0%	1.1%
2010	117.30	38.5%	5.6%	50.8%	1.9%	3.2%
2016	82.17	28.7%	4.8%	59.8%	6.4%	0.4%

Source: Eurostat 2019a.

168   European CHP

To tackle the negative tendency Romania has adopted various measures to promote cogeneration. This covers, *inter alia*, a monthly-bonus for each MWh of electricity produced in high-efficiency cogeneration based on a demand for useful heat together and regulated price values (aid scheme implemented in 2011, granted to each beneficiary for a maximum period of 11 consecutive years by 2023), or an additional green certificate granted for high-efficiency biomass-powered CHP units, together with grid facilitations (priority access) provided for micro-cogeneration (see RO SPR n.d., pp. 6–8). Recently, an idea to introduce a new mechanism to support high-efficiency CHP in Romania has been proposed (RO NECP 2018, p. 95).

Slovakia

CHP in Slovakia, despite the changes in installed capacity (each falling by around a half during the evaluated periods), has managed to keep a comparable level of produced electricity and heat (or even a very similar one, especially from 2005 to 2016). From this perspective (as shown in Table 5.33), in 2016, the five-times smaller capacity (in electricity) generated nearly 3 TWh (compared to 4.8 TWh in 2005), while the capacity in heat – though smaller by half (in 2010) produced almost twice as much heat. Naturally, apart from technical possibilities, one should take into account weather conditions and other market issues related to heat demand.

The preceding figures are supplemented by Table 5.34. It shows three major trends in Slovak cogeneration. One of them was a big drop in the amount of fuel used in CHP – in 2016 its scale was nearly six times smaller than in 2005. Second, another decline concerns the usage of other fuels (like industrial waste and coal gases) which decreased from about 60% (2005) to less than 6% (2016). Third, in 2016 the CHP in Slovakia was more balanced than it used to be in the past. This balance was based on almost equal shares of renewables and solid fossil fuels with peat, and the 10% difference between them and natural gas (see Table 5.34). In terms of renewable fuels, since 2007 a gradual rise in the proportion of wood chips,

Table 5.33 CHP portfolio of Slovakia between 2005–2016

	2005	2010	2016
CHP electricity generation [TWh]	4.80	4.43	3.01
share of CHP in total gross electricity generation	15.3%	15.9%	11.1%
total CHP installed capacity in electricity [GW]	5.41	2.82	1.00
total CHP installed capacity in heat [GW]	NA	9.21	4.02
total heat produced in CHP [PJ]	33.68	20.06	34.42

Source: Eurostat 2019a.

Table 5.34 Fuel used in cogeneration in Slovakia between 2005–2016

	fuel used for CHP [PJ]	solid fossil fuels and peat	oil and oil products	natural gas	renewables	other fuels
2005	327.71	25.7%	4.5%	8.2%	0.2%	61.4%
2010	89.44	32.5%	15.1%	20.6%	3.4%	28.5%
2016	56.45	24.1%	12.7%	33.7%	23.9%	5.6%

Source: Eurostat 2019a.

has been recorded; it was driven by a requirement to support the production of electricity from biomass only in CHP units (SK SPR 2011, pp. 6–7).

Among measures which have been provided for cogeneration in Slovakia one may find grid preferences (including access to the grid, or preferential transmission, distribution, and supply of electricity), fixed price (tariff) for electricity produced by high-efficiency CHP units (usually offered for 15 years) together with supplement covering the difference between the fixed price and the loss-making price of electricity, or exemption for electricity produced by high-efficiency cogeneration from the excise duty (SK SPR 2011, pp. 10–12). As announced in the draft integrated NECP, the support system for cogeneration (together with renewable energy sources) will be covered by a reform aimed at ensuring the system's cost-effectiveness and minimising the impact on end-uses (SK NECP 2018, p. 179). Besides these measures, high-efficiency combined heat and power has been offered investment assistance under the structural funds, both in 2004–2006 and 2007–2013 programming periods as well as currently, in a framework of Operational Programme "Quality of the Environment" 2014–2020[16] (SK SPR 2011, p. 12–13; SK NECP 2018, p. 88, 161).

Sweden

A large share of hydro and nuclear power along with relatively low electricity prices have resulted in rather a slow development of the CHP sector in Sweden (Sandberg, Møller Sneum, & Trømborg 2018, p. 108). When discussing the statistics on CHP, one may notice two main issues (see Table 5.35). First, some similarities between its scale in 1994 and 2016; the data is quite similar regarding almost all of the evaluated fields. The difference concerns heat produced in cogeneration (around 30 PJ less produced in 2016 than 1994). Even though the installed capacity in electricity in 2016 was bigger than in 1994, the generation of power was almost the same – due to high-efficiency technologies applied. Such units have been operating in Sweden for more than a decade. As reported under the CHP Directive, all Swedish cogeneration units have been high-efficiency

170 European CHP

Table 5.35 CHP portfolio of Sweden between 1994–2016

	1994	1998	2005	2010	2016
CHP electricity generation [TWh]	9.26	9.54	10.67	18.53	9.21
share of CHP in total gross electricity generation	6.4%	6.0%	6.7%	12.5%	5.9%
total CHP installed capacity in electricity [GW]	2.81	3.21	3.49	5.10	3.89
total CHP installed capacity in heat [GW]	8.48	12.44	NA	12.29	8.42
total heat produced in CHP [PJ]	124.47	155.75	132.73	187.20	91.07

Source: Eurostat 2001; Eurostat 2019a.

plants, and the CHP Directive has not affected their already achieved high-efficiency (SE SPR n.d., pp. 1–2). Second, Swedish cogeneration has produced less (by about a half) electricity and heat in 2016 than in 2010.

What should be clarified in this context, is that Sweden does not provide priority dispatch or the prioritising of electricity produced on the basis of energy source (e.g. high-efficiency cogeneration), "since such a procedure distorts competition in the market" (SE NECP 2019, p. 42). Moreover, the country has not provided any direct investment aid dedicated to CHP – there were other, indirect support measures including a certificate scheme for renewables introduced in May 2003 (see SE SPR n. d., pp. 13–14). The previously mentioned renewables have been the top fuel powering Swedish cogeneration; over the years their share has oscillated around 60% (cf. Bernotat & Sandberg 2004, p. 521–523). To some extent, the Swedish fuel mix has been supplemented by three categories of fuels (as in Table 5.36), with the major share of other fuels (industrial waste); this category reached 24% (2016).

Fuels used for heat production in the CHP plants in Sweden are liable to two taxes: on CO_2 and energy (see Börjesson, Hansson, & Berndes 2017, pp. 22–23). However, cogeneration benefits from a reduced rate of tax

Table 5.36 Fuel used in cogeneration in Sweden between 1998–2016

	fuel used for CHP [PJ]	solid fossil fuels and peat	oil and oil products	natural gas	renewables	other fuels
1998	241.63	12%	16%	5%	55%	12%
2005	211.40	9.6%	11.2%	4.2%	65.6%	9.4%
2010	306.12	6.6%	7.2%	10.0%	67.6%	8.5%
2016	145.17	9.1%	0.6%	7.4%	58.7%	24.1%

Source: Eurostat 2001; Eurostat 2019a.

which differs for installations in and outside the EU ETS. Installations within the EU ETS pay an 11% rate (as of 2018) of the CO_2 tax and 30% rate of the energy tax. Units not covered by the EU ETS, pay full CO_2 tax rate on fuels used to produce heat (from 1 January 2018), but still have the reduced rate (30%) of the energy tax (SE NECP 2019, p. 18).

Smaller markets for cogeneration

For the needs of this division, a barrier of 3 TWh of electricity and 20 PJ of heat produced in combined heat and power (see Eurostat 2019a) is applied to distinguish small CHP sectors in the EU. In this context, small markets for cogeneration can be found in those Member States whose CHP sectors have not reached this ceiling either in terms of producing electricity or heat. Therefore, the proposed distinction applies to Croatia, Cyprus, Estonia, Greece, Ireland, Latvia, Lithuania, Luxembourg, Malta, and Slovenia. This whole block is discussed in this subchapter.

Croatia

In Croatia, a significant share of cogeneration belongs to the DH systems of bigger cities like Zagreb and Osijek, while several "heating only" DH systems exist in other towns of overland Croatia (Lončar, Duić & Bogdan 2009, p. 141). As for 2016, generation of electricity from CHP in Croatia was not as big as around 2012 and 2011, when it broke the barrier of 2 TWh. As the installed capacity in heat is growing (with a drop in 2015 – see Eurostat 2019a), so is the volume of heat produced in CHP (see Table 5.37).

The level of fuel used in cogeneration is relatively stable in Croatia (see Table 5.38) – although, as mentioned earlier, in 2015 it noticed a decrease in heat production – just over 15 PJ were used (see Eurostat 2019a). In terms of the Croatian CHP fuel structure, the main fuel has been natural gas, followed by oil (which noted over 50% decrease since 2009), and a growing share of renewables (almost 9% in 2016).

Table 5.37 CHP portfolio of Croatia between 2009[17]–2016

	2009	2012	2016
CHP electricity generation [TWh]	1.62	2.10	1.47
share of CHP in total gross electricity generation	12.7%	19.9%	11.5%
total CHP installed capacity in electricity [GW]	0.55	0.69	0.75
total CHP installed capacity in heat [GW]	1.47	1.72	2.16
total heat produced in CHP [PJ]	12.80	14.04	16.27

Source: Eurostat 2019a.

172 European CHP

Table 5.38 Fuel used in cogeneration in Croatia between 2009–2016

	fuel used for CHP [PJ]	solid fossil fuels and peat	oil and oil products	natural gas	renewables	other fuels
2009	22.70	2.8%	23.1%	74.0%	0.0%	0.0%
2012	26.96	2.4%	6.9%	89.6%	1.1%	0.0%
2016	27.27	2.5%	10.7%	78.0%	8.8%	0.0%

Source: Eurostat 2019a.

A legal framework for supporting cogeneration in Croatia has been established by the Act on renewable energy sources and highly efficient cogeneration of 2015. The Act, which entered into force in January 2016, regulates, *inter alia*, the planning and promoting of generation and consumption of electricity from high-efficiency CHP, and defining incentives for these type of units, including a tariff scheme (HR NECP 2018, pp. 15, 17, see Beus et al. 2018). Earlier, (since 2007), the feed-in tariff system provided a fixed price on the basis of a ten year period-if electricity was generated by natural gas-fired CHP units (Uran & Krajcar 2009, p. 844). The tariff was additionally supplemented by other measures, such as the minimum share of electricity from cogeneration in the electricity supply or a fee for the promotion of cogeneration (see Lončar, Duić & Bogdan 2009, p. 136). Apart from these tools, Croatia is currently planning to develop new heating and cooling systems based on high-efficiency cogeneration or renewables, also with the support of the European structural and investment funds in the next programming period 2021–2027 (see HR NECP 2018, pp. 89–90).

Cyprus

Cogeneration plays a minor role in Cyprus. Its share in total gross electricity generation accounts for less than 1%, as the CHP installations do not even reach the level of 50 MW (2016). The same concerns the volume of fuel used for the needs of combined heat and power (less than 1 PJ); however, since 2015 the vast majority (about 90%) of fuels comes from renewables (Eurostat 2019a). The statistics on Cyprus are presented in the following tables (Table 5.39 and Table 5.40).

As reflected in the Second Progress Report, prepared under the CHP Directive (CY SPR n.d., p. 3), no noteworthy administrative barriers were noticed in Cyprus. However, some other significant barriers to the development of combined heat and power were identified. One of the barriers discussed were fuel prices – the absence of natural gas resulted in high CHP fuel prices being deterrent to investing in cogeneration (CY SPR

Table 5.39 CHP portfolio of Cyprus between 2005–2016

	2005	2010	2016
CHP electricity generation [TWh]	0.01	0.06	0.03
share of CHP in total gross electricity generation	0.3%	1.0%	0.6%
total CHP installed capacity in electricity [GW]	0.01	0.02	0.01
total CHP installed capacity in heat [GW]	NA	0.04	0.01
total heat produced in CHP [PJ]	0.07	0.14	0.12

Source: Eurostat 2019a.

Table 5.40 Fuel used in cogeneration in Cyprus between 2005–2016

	fuel used for CHP [PJ]	solid fossil fuels and peat	oil and oil products	natural gas	renewables	other fuels
2005	0.28	0.0%	100.0%	0.0%	0.0%	0.0%
2010	0.68	0.0%	61.9%	0.0%	38.1%	0.0%
2016	0.30	0.0%	7.0%	0.0%	93.0%	0.0%

Source: Eurostat 2019a.

n.d., p. 3). However, as presented in Table 5.40, the evaluation of the Cypriot fuel mix towards renewables made it possible to tackle the issue.

Apart from that, "soft" matters consistent with the policy character were identified. This concerns e.g. the lack of national financial sources to provide incentives for the potential CHP investors combined with the lack of information, training, or technical knowledge regarding CHP systems (see CY SPR n.d., pp. 3–4). However, these could be easily provided by the country – especially the latter. Nevertheless, in 2017, a self-consumption (of the electricity produced) support scheme for the installation of CHP powered by biomass/biogas was announced in Cyprus (CY NECP 2019, p. 80).

Estonia

Despite a significant drop in CHP capacity, both in heat and power, decreasing about by 44% and approximately 90% respectively, (2010 to 2016, and 2005 to 2016) cogeneration in Estonia managed to produce a comparable amount of electricity (about 1 TWh). This has not been maintained in terms of production of heat, which decreased between 2005 and 2016 by about three and a half times (see Table 5.41). Among several reasons driving these trends one may find changes in the Estonian CHP

Table 5.41 CHP portfolio of Estonia between 2005–2016

	2005	2010	2016*
CHP electricity generation [TWh]	1.04	1.34	0.94
share of CHP in total gross electricity generation	10.2%	10.3%	7.7%
total CHP installed capacity in electricity [GW]	1.60	0.45	0.19
total CHP installed capacity in heat [GW]	NA	1.47	0.65
total heat produced in CHP [PJ]	11.46	12.32	3.25

* Open validation issues.
Source: Eurostat 2019a.

sector, including the closure of old, oil-shale fuelled CHP plants or the dwindling heat market (EE SPR n.d., p. 2)

As one may find in Table 5.42, Estonia is one of those EU countries with the biggest share of renewables in their fuel mix; in 2016 it accounted for more than 60% (cf. Bernotat & Sandberg 2004, p. 528; Volkova, Hlebnikov, & Siirde 2010). Nevertheless, as the Estonian installed capacity in combined heat and power has dropped, so the relation between solid fossil fuels and renewables has improved in favour of the latter (see Table 5.42). Recently, the share of oil in the fuel mix of Estonia has grown. Interestingly, a decade ago, oil was a barrier to investments in cogeneration in the Estonian electricity market. The regulatory priority offered to electricity generated from oil-shale was listed among the factors hindering the development of CHP in the country (Tallinn University of Technology 2007, p. 19). Recently, electricity generation in the efficient cogeneration – powered by peat or retorting gas of the oil shale processing – has been subsidised in Estonia (see EE NECP 2018, pp. 52, 107).

The significant fuel issue was also discussed by Estonia in its progress report under the CHP Directive; the fuel barrier covered no competition in the Estonian gas market and energy security with the reliance on the Russian supplier – Gazprom (EE SPR n.d., p. 3, cf. Belyi 2019). The administrative procedures were not distinguished as significant barriers in Estonia; some

Table 5.42 Fuel used in cogeneration in Estonia between 2005–2016

	fuel used for CHP [PJ]	solid fossil fuels and peat	oil and oil products	natural gas	renewables	other fuels
2005	21.75	49.1%	0.4%	43.3%	7.1%	0.0%
2010	22.04	35.5%	0.3%	28.7%	35.6%	0.0%
2016*	7.65	11.6%	24.5%	0.1%	61.2%	2.6%

* Open validation issues.
Source: Eurostat 2019a.

minor issues concerned the disputes between market participants. Fortunately, the intervention of authorities and open exchange of information enabled the tackling of those issues (EE SPR n.d., pp. 2–3). Recently, the support for efficient cogeneration has been addressed as one of the cross-sectoral measures for GHG reduction in Estonia; efficient CHP projects will be commissioned in the near future (EE NECP 2018, p. 42, 91, 126).

Greece

The penetration of cogeneration in Greece has been rather limited; CHP units have been operated mainly by Greek refineries or food industry, with the domination of non-high-efficiency cogeneration (EL SPR 2011, pp. 8, 33). Nevertheless, in the period discussed (see Table 5.43) both heat and electricity produced by the Greek cogeneration have progressively increased (by about three times), reaching around 19 PJ and approximately 3 TWh in 2016. The only one of the evaluated fields which noticed a small drop, was the total installed power capacity (0.59 GW in 2010 to 0.53 GW in 2016).

These trends are shown in Table 5.43. To a certain extent they were influenced by a mixture of regulatory tools; however, when assessing the situation of the installed power capacity, one may question their efficiency. As expressed in the progress report under the CHP Directive (see EL SPR 2011, pp. 28–30), the guaranteed tariffs have been evaluated as the "key tool" of supporting the investments in Greek cogeneration. Apart from the tariffs, cogeneration has been offered: income tax exemptions, state subsidies covering some expenditures (e.g. instalments paid for equipment), and opportunities for financing the construction of high-efficiency plants under operational programmes, such as "High efficiency cogeneration of heat and power in hospitals" (EL SPR 2011, pp. 30–32).

Table 5.43 CHP portfolio of Greece between 1994–2016

	1994	1998	2006[18]	2010	2016[**]
CHP electricity generation [TWh]	0.82	0.98[*]	1.05	2.48	2.59
share of CHP in total gross electricity generation	2.0%	2.1%	1.7%	4.3%	4.8%
total CHP installed capacity in electricity [GW]	0.22	0.26[*]	0.25	0.59	0.53
total CHP installed capacity in heat [GW]	0.55	0.71	NA	0.96	1.32
total heat produced in CHP [PJ]	5.49	7.47	8.28	12.71	18.92

* Eurostat estimate.
** Open validation issues.
Source: Eurostat 2001, Eurostat 2019a.

176 European CHP

Table 5.44 Fuel used in cogeneration in Greece between 1998–2016

	fuel used for CHP [PJ]	solid fossil fuels and peat	oil and oil products	natural gas	renewables	other fuels
1998	56.61	76%	5%	2%	NA	17%
2006[19]	90.78	85.7%	1.9%	3.0%	0.3%	9.1%
2010	27.97	10.5%	3.6%	47.2%	1.0%	37.7%
2016*	26.75	13.5%	30.7%	29.6%	14.0%	12.2%

* Open validation issues.
Source: Eurostat 2001, Eurostat 2019a.

Among many regulatory solutions offered in Greek legislation, one may find an interesting facilitation for high-efficiency CHP. This concerns the exemption from the obligation to obtain the authorisation for generation or any other certification decision. This privilege was given to small-scale high-efficiency units (less than 1 MW$_e$ or 5 MW$_e$) established by educational or research organisations in the public or private sector (EL SPR 2011, pp. 13–14). The exemption, established by Law 3851/2010, has applied in these cases for as long as the CHP plants have been operated only for educational or research reasons (EL SPR 2011, p. 14).

Finally, regarding the fuel used in the Greek CHP industry, the following observation can be made: in different periods, different fuel has constituted a major share in the Greek fuel mix in combined heat and power (from solid fossil fuels and peat in 2006, through natural gas in 2010, to oil in 2016). Regarding the volume of fuel used in cogeneration, apart from the peak between 2006 and 2008, when Greece used around 100 PJ for the needs of its CHP sector (see Eurostat 2019a), in the recent years this level oscillated around 30 PJ (see Table 5.44).

Ireland

In Ireland, CHP has not been commercially applicable at a large scale (see Chapter 2 of this book); however, despite minor deviations, the Irish cogeneration sector has kept growing over the evaluated period (see Table 5.45). This was due mainly to the policy and legal solution dedicated to cogeneration such as the feed-in-tariff for biomass CHP and anaerobic digestion CHP, or relief from tax for electricity produced from high-efficiency cogeneration (see Howley & Holland 2016, pp. 10–12). Still, in comparison to other EU countries, Ireland's scale is small, due to the fact that heat demand in Ireland is generally low density (see IR NECP 2018, p. 215). It maintains the level below 13 PJ of produced heat and around 2 TWh of electricity (see Eurostat 2019a).

The small-scale CHP system which operates in Ireland is fuelled mainly by natural gas. As presented in Table 5.46, Ireland transformed its cogeneration,

Table 5.45 CHP portfolio of Ireland between 1994–2016

	1994	1998	2005	2010	2016
CHP electricity generation [TWh]	0.26	0.40	1.02	1.92	2.17
share of CHP in total gross electricity generation	1.5%	1.9%	1.7%	6.7%	7.1%
total CHP installed capacity in electricity [GW]	0.07	0.11	0.24	0.29	0.31
total CHP installed capacity in heat [GW]	0.34	0.46	NA	0.66	0.59
total heat produced in CHP [PJ]	3.93	4.86	9.69	11.96	11.24

Source: Eurostat 2001, Eurostat 2019a.

Table 5.46 Fuel used in cogeneration in Ireland between 1998–2016

	fuel used for CHP [PJ]	solid fossil fuels and peat	oil and oil products	natural gas	renewables	other fuels
1998	7.30	31%	7%	55%	0%	7%
2005	85.26	82.9%	3.3%	3.8%	0.4%	9.7%
2010	22.31	4.6%	0.1%	91.6%	1.4%	2.3%
2016	23.82	3.6%	1.3%	92.1%	2.9%	0.1%

Source: Eurostat 2001, Eurostat 2019a.

moving to natural gas from solid fossil fuels. As of 2016, natural gas was the major fuel in the Irish fuel mix; it accounted for just over 92% (see Table 5.46). To optimise the country's fuel mix in heating by increasing production from renewables, in 2018 Ireland launched a Support Scheme for Renewable Heat. The scheme had an operational support component, including the support for high-efficiency CHP heating systems powered by biomass or biogas (see IR NECP 2018, pp. 250–251). Just to mention – between 2006 and 2010, Ireland offered support (capital grants) to, *inter alia*, small scale fossil-fired and biomass-powered CHP units (see IR SPR 2011, p. 4).

As the identified economic potential for heat networks in Ireland is relatively low, certain programmes and support mechanisms at the national and local level would be necessary to develop DH (IR NECP 2018, p. 216). These circumstances create opportunities for providing more cost-effective heat solutions than heat networks – as highlighted in the draft integrated NECP. Future Irish priorities in this field could be focused on deployment and promotion of building scale installations, including building scale cogeneration (IR NECP 2018, p. 216).

Latvia

Since 2000, the share of high-efficiency cogeneration in Latvia's energy sector has increased. This was steered by an energy policy whose aims were: improving energy efficiency and removing any significant regulatory barriers to the development of CHP. The latter could be achieved, for example, by shortening the time of some administrative procedures (LV SPR 2011, pp. 10–11, 14–15). As presented in Table 5.47, combined heat and power maintained its gradual growth between 2005 and 2016 in all of the given fields. In this period, the installed power capacity and generation of electricity in CHP doubled. What should be highlighted here is the fact that combined heat and power produced almost half of all electricity generated in Latvia.

At the beginning of the 2010s natural gas constituted a vast majority of fuel used in Latvian combined heat and power. This started to change around 2012, when the share of renewables began to grow (see Eurostat 2019a). In 2016, the fuel mix of Latvia was much more balanced than it used to be between 2005 and 2011. As presented in Table 5.48, in 2016, the structure of Latvian fuel mix was divided mainly between natural gas, accounting for approximately 63%, and renewables reaching 37%.

Changes in the CHP fuel structure of Latvia are linked to rapid installation of biomass-powered cogeneration units observed since 2011 (Prodanuks et al. 2016, p. 375). The background for this rapid growth is the biomass-potential of Latvia – forests cover 52% of the country's

Table 5.47 CHP portfolio of Latvia between 2005–2016

	2005	2010	2016
CHP electricity generation [TWh]	1.51	2.98	3.12
share of CHP in total gross electricity generation	30.7%	45.0%	48.5%
total CHP installed capacity in electricity [GW]	0.59	0.87	1.29
total CHP installed capacity in heat [GW]	NA	0.85	1.21
total heat produced in CHP [PJ]	11.91	10.45	14.51

Source: Eurostat 2019a.

Table 5.48 Fuel used in cogeneration in Latvia between 2005–2016

	fuel used for CHP [PJ]	*solid fossil fuels and peat*	*oil and oil products*	*natural gas*	*renewables*	*other fuels*
2005	21.87	0.0%	2.4%	91.9%	5.7%	0.0%
2010	25.46	1.2%	0.8%	95.2%	2.7%	0.0%
2016	31.56	0.2%	0.0%	62.8%	37.0%	0.0%

Source: Eurostat 2019a.

territory which is around 64,500 square kilometres in total (see Ministry of Agriculture 2018, p. 3). This potential could be used more widely for the needs of local cogeneration (see Lund et al. 1999, cf. Bernotat & Sandberg 2004, p. 529). To promote the development of CHP units powered by renewables, Latvia has offered investment grants along with other support mechanisms such as the compulsory procurement of electricity or guaranteed payment for installed capacity in power, applicable to cogeneration (LV SPR 2011, p. 13). Nevertheless, the support for fossil fuel consumption in Latvia – including payments to natural gas-fired CHP units – hovered around 25% of energy tax revenue in 2006–2016 (OECD 2019, p. 27). In this context, as mentioned in the draft version of the NECP, Latvia has been working to improve the mandatory procurement system for electricity produced in renewable energy sources and high-efficiency cogeneration (LV NECP 2018, p. 45, 48).

Lithuania

When analysing Lithuanian cogeneration, one may observe that around 2010 it started decreasing (see Eurostat 2019a). When comparing 2005 to 2016, the country's installed capacities as well as the production of heat and power have fallen. However, Lithuania has improved its share of electricity produced from high-efficiency combined heat and power; e.g. in 2010 around 31% (1.77 TWh) of electricity was produced in high-efficiency CHP (LT SPR 2012, p. 6). In this context, as presented in Table 5.49 the share of CHP in total gross electricity generation has remained relatively high (more than a quarter).

Similarly to Latvia, natural gas used to be the major fuel in Lithuania (the share of almost 87% in 2005). For a long time it was supplied from a single source – Russia – making it difficult to forecast any variations in price and posing a risk to energy security by possible disruptions in supplies (LT SPR 2012, p. 7, cf. Bernotat & Sandberg 2004, p. 529). The construction of a liquefied natural gas (LNG) terminal in Klaipėda in 2014

Table 5.49 CHP portfolio of Lithuania between 2005–2016

	2005	2010	2016
CHP electricity generation [TWh]	2.30	1.99	1.11
share of CHP in total gross electricity generation	15.5%	34.6%	25.9%
total CHP installed capacity in electricity [GW]	1.04	1.10	0.59
total CHP installed capacity in heat [GW]	NA	2.49	1.19
total heat produced in CHP [PJ]	19.90	19.34	9.54

Source: Eurostat 2019a.

Table 5.50 Fuel used in cogeneration in Lithuania between 2005–2016

	fuel used for CHP [PJ]	solid fossil fuels and peat	oil and oil products	natural gas	renewables	other fuels
2005	45.00	0.0%	12.6%	86.9%	0.5%	0.0%
2010	32.56	0.0%	16.1%	75.5%	8.4%	0.0%
2016	16.00	0.0%	12.8%	35.5%	40.4%	11.2%

Source: Eurostat 2019a.

enabled Lithuania to diversify its supplies by breaking the Russian monopoly (see Schulte & Weiser 2019; Gucma, Bąk, & Chłopińska 2018; Valionienė & Strakauskaite 2015). However, between 2005 and 2016 the use of natural gas was significantly reduced, falling to around 35% in 2016. Simultaneously, Lithuania increased the usage of renewables in cogeneration. As a result, in 2016 renewables became the major fuel used in the CHP sector (see Table 5.50). The change in the fuel structure has been driven by unlocking the biomass potential steered by public policies (see Gaigalis et al. 2016, p. 845), and the use of wastes for the energy needs (see Katinas et al. 2019).

Lithuania offered cogeneration support via public service obligations, granted to power plants supplying heat to DH, and regulating the annual purchase quotas for electricity generated in cogeneration and electricity feed-in tariffs (LT SPR 2012, pp. 8–9). The support applied to CHP units powered by fossil fuels was to be reduced gradually, while the support for biomass-fired cogeneration was to be gradually increased (LT SPR 2012, pp. 9–10). Lithuania institutes further development of high-efficiency solid biomass CHP along with the use of non-recyclable municipal waste, so that the share of DH powered by renewables will reach 70% by 2020 and 90% by 2030 (LT NECP, pp. 12, 18). This is driven by fixed prices for CHP-generated electricity under determined production quota CHP units, built within the framework of the "National Programme for Heat Sector Development in 2015–2021"[20] (see LT NECP, p. 91, 108).

Luxembourg

Luxembourg's installed capacity is less than 0.2 GW in power and 0.2 GW in heat, making it a minor CHP market even despite having some biomass-fired CHP project in the implementation phase (LU NECP 2019, p. 51). In spite of being a small market, Luxembourg is a stable one. The generation of electricity in cogeneration oscillates around 0.5 TWh and the production of heat (which notices some peaks) swings from 1 to 3 PJ (see Table 5.51).

European CHP 181

Table 5.51 CHP portfolio of Luxembourg between 1994–2016

	1994	1998	2005	2010	2016
CHP electricity generation [TWh]	NA	0.32	0.42	0.44	0.35
share of CHP in total gross electricity generation	NA	22.5%	10.1%	9.6%	15.7%
total CHP installed capacity in electricity [GW]	NA	0.10	0.10	0.12	0.12
total CHP installed capacity in heat [GW]	NA	0.20	NA	NA	0.20
total heat produced in CHP [PJ]	NA	2.20	1.19	3.21	2.28

Source: Eurostat 2001, Eurostat 2019a.

Like in other smaller CHP markets, in Luxembourg natural gas is also the major fuel used in combined heat and power (2016). However, its share is not as big as it used to be before 2014, since when more renewables have been introduced to the country's fuel mix (see Eurostat 2019a). As of 2016, the relation between natural gas and renewables accounted for the ratio 75% to 25% (see Table 5.52).

The evolution of the fuel mix was possible due to the changes in the country's policies and legislation. Between 1994 and 2014 Luxembourg remunerated electricity produced by gas-fired CHP units (CODE2 2014a, p. 6). As declared in 2012, "the focus in future will no longer be on cogeneration based on fossil energy sources but on cogeneration based on renewable energy sources" (LU SPR 2012, p. 5). In this context, from 1st July 2014, the feed-in tariff was abolished in favour of new fossil CHP plants. The existing fossil-fuelled units maintained this scheme for a period of 20 years after they had started generating electricity to the grid (CODE2 2014a, p. 6). Apart from this remuneration, the fund for the protection of the environment offered investment grants of up to 30% to municipalities willing to install a local heating installation based on renewables (Ministry of the Economy 2016, p. 19).

Table 5.52 Fuel used in cogeneration in Luxembourg between 1998–2016

	fuel used for CHP [PJ]	solid fossil fuels and peat	oil and oil products	natural gas	renewables	other fuels
1998	4.58	NA	0%	100%	NA	NA
2005	4.78	0.0%	0.0%	100%	0.0%	0.0%
2010	5.50	0.0%	0.1%	90.0%	9.9%	0.0%
2016	4.26	0.0%	0.0%	74.1%	25.4%	0.5%

Source: Eurostat 2001, Eurostat 2019a.

Malta

Until 2013 Malta's usage of combined heat and power in its energy system was not officially reported by Eurostat (2019a); nevertheless, Malta's first CHP unit (1.7 MW$_e$) was licensed in 2011 (see CODE2 2014b, pp. 5–6). The limited potential for cogeneration was not utilised even when in 2009 and 2010 the government offered 15 million EUR for improving energy efficiency in the industrial sector – only one proposal was related to cogeneration but it has not been accomplished (MT SPR 2011, p. 5).

Nonetheless, after some minor developments, as of 2016 the country had nearly 0.15 GW of installed power capacity and only 2 MW (0.02 GW) of heat capacity. In 2016, these minor developments enabled the production of around 0.25 TWh of electricity and about 0.1 PJ of heat. Nonetheless, generated electricity accounted for more than 28% of total gross electricity in Malta – these statistics are presented in Table 5.53. To encourage the use of high-efficiency cogeneration, in 2016 the government issued a programme granting aid in the form of tax credits (MT NECP 2018, p. 135). However, the country's final energy consumption for heat and cool is relatively low compared to what is needed to establish favourable conditions for improving CHP and DH, or even promoting micro-cogeneration (MT NECP 2018, p. 135).

In 2016, the cogeneration in Malta used approximately 2 PJ of fuel (see Table 5.54). In terms of its structure these were mainly other fuels (almost

Table 5.53 CHP portfolio of Malta between 2005–2016

	2005	2010	2016
CHP electricity generation [TWh]	0.0	0.0	0.24
share of CHP in total gross electricity generation	0.0%	0.0%	28.3%
total CHP installed capacity in electricity [GW]	0.0	0.0	0.14
total CHP installed capacity in heat [GW]	NA	0.0	0.02
total heat produced in CHP [PJ]	0.0	0.0	0.09

Source: Eurostat 2019a.

Table 5.54 Fuel used in cogeneration in Malta between 2005–2016

	fuel used for CHP [PJ]	solid fossil fuels and peat	oil and oil products	natural gas	renewables	other fuels
2005	0.0	0.0%	0.0%	0.0%	0.0%	0.0%
2010	0.0	0.0%	0.0%	0.0%	0.0%	0.0%
2016	1.98	0.0%	0.0%	0.0%	3.3%	96.7%

Source: Eurostat 2019a.

97%) – waste and sewage (MT NECP 2018, p. 127, see Psomopoulos et al. 2017). However, due to the fact that Malta has practically no own and accessible resources of biomass or biogas, and no natural gas distribution network, CHP is only a marginal option in the next decade (MT NECP 2018, p. 135).

Slovenia

Slovenian cogeneration is a small industry which has been producing around 1 TWh and 10 PJ of power and heat (however, in 2005 heat production was bigger, reaching 15 PJ). The country's installed CHP capacity is a stable one, maintaining the level of around 350 MW in electricity and 800 MW in heat (Table 5.55). This quite stable situation of CHP does not change the fact that the sector has been facing some barriers to investments, including the cost of connection to the grid or related to the connection land acquisition issues (SI SPR, n.d., p. 6).

The major fuels used in Slovenian combined heat and power are solid fossil fuels and peat. This category accounts for more than half of the country's fuel mix. However, as adduced in Table 5.56 its share fell from almost 85% in 2005 to about 50% in 2016. Consequently, natural gas together with renewables have started to play a more significant role; in 2016 both of them had a share of more than 20% in the CHP fuel mix of Slovenia.

Table 5.55 CHP portfolio of Slovenia between 2005–2016

	2005	2010	2016
CHP electricity generation [TWh]	1.10	1.14	1.21
share of CHP in total gross electricity generation	7.3%	6.9%	7.3%
total CHP installed capacity in electricity [GW]	0.34	0.33	0.35
total CHP installed capacity in heat [GW]	NA	0.84	0.81
total heat produced in CHP [PJ]	15.00	11.60	10.76

Source: Eurostat 2019a.

Table 5.56 Fuel used in cogeneration in Slovenia between 2005–2016

	fuel used for CHP [PJ]	*solid fossil fuels and peat*	*oil and oil products*	*natural gas*	*renewables*	*other fuels*
2005	64.02	84.0%	1.8%	8.6%	5.5%	0.2%
2010	20.32	59.2%	0.1%	25.6%	14.5%	0.6%
2016	18.40	50.3%	0.2%	27.0%	20.6%	2.0%

Source: Eurostat 2019a.

The support for high-efficiency CHP in Slovenia included guaranteed purchase of electricity, irrespective of the market price. An established centre has been buying electricity for which CHP guarantees of origin have been granted – i.e. the electricity produced in high-efficiency CHP is supported via these legally established prices, tariffs – so a market for it is created. In other words, if someone has this certificate his/her electricity will be bought for this guaranteed price (SI SPR, n.d., pp. 10–12, see Al-Mansour, Sucic, & Pusnik 2014, p. 76). As declared in the draft integrated NECP, Slovenia will deliver a proposal on the tools provided for the needs of the country's policies in the area of renewables, addressing the DH based on renewable energy sources and high-efficiency CHP (see SI NECP 2018, p. 46).

***

The review of all of the EU-28 Member States is thus concluded at this point. However, it does not conclude this book, as at least two more elements are needed. The first concerns the summary of the regulatory review on combined heat and power delivered in this chapter. The second relates to a general conclusion of the issues raised in this book. To fulfil these needs, let us move on to the final part of this work – Chapter 6.

Notes

1 The Member States of the European Union are presented with a two-letter country code, written in capital letters, as used by the Eurostat (n.d.). In terms of the collected data, it is sometimes limited – e.g. when validation issues occur. The category "other fuels" includes, among others, industrial waste and coal gases. In 1998 – the category "solid fossil fuels and peat" was distinguished as "hard coal and lignite", while "oil and oil products" represented "liquid fuels".
2 National Energy and Climate Plan, abbreviated NECP means a concrete Plan elaborated on by each Member State, whereas "integrated national energy and climate plan", as used in Chapter 6 of this book, refers to this plan in general, as a policy tool. As of 2019 these are still draft versions. However, judging by the Commission's evaluations, delivered in June 2019 (see Commission 2019b), one may assume that in many fields related to combined heat and power the solutions offered by the Member States at the stage of proposing their national integrated plans will be maintained in the final versions.
3 At the time of writing this book, the UK is still a Member State of the EU; however, the process of the UK's withdrawal from the EU (Brexit) should be kept in mind.
4 That is why France – which in 2017 generated around 17 TWh of electricity and produced about 178 PJ of heat – has been placed within this group, whereas the Czech Republic, with less than 8 TWh and just over of 100 PJ ended up in the medium category (see Eurostat 2019b); same applies to Denmark with almost 40% share of CHP in total gross electricity generation but production of electricity and heat lower than this threshold.
5 200 MW between 2025–2030 (see FI NECP 2018, p. 99).

European CHP 185

6 What is underlined in the Finnish draft integrated plan "[t[he taxation of peat is a key steering instrument, especially in separate heat production", while renewable fuels are not liable to tax in the field of heat production (FI NECP 2018, p. 47).
7 Due to a statistical issue, data on France is offered for 2006 (instead of 2005 when the fuel used for CHP was reported as reaching just 8.4 PJ, see Eurostat 2019).
8 The "Use It, Don't Curtail It" scheme obliges CHP units operated in grid expansion areas of risk of congestion to limit the feed-in of cogenerated power on an order of transmission system operators issued in an event of congestion in the system, and to generate heat for a power-to-heat facility – due to this heat production CHP plants can flexibly move between the supply and demand side of the electricity market, thus, the whole system becomes more flexible (see DE NECP 2018, p. 86, cf. Stadler 2008, p. 95). As assumed, through the CHP modernisation programme, thanks to the applied technology, enabling to reduce production of heat or power during the periods of renewable loads in electricity or heat, the flexible energy demand system will substitute the rigid and heat-dependent minimum energy production (see DE NECP 2018, p. 86).
9 As reported in the draft integrated NECP it was possible due to the predominant operation of combined-cycle and condensation CHP units which were substantial in size and more efficient (IT SPR 2011, pp. 188–189).
10 Nevertheless, the Polish scheme is open to generators in other Member States (Commission 2019a).
11 Derived gases like refinery gas, coke oven gas, and blast furnace gas make up the majority of the "other fuels".
12 The latter issue was also addressed in SPR. As reported there "objections to the planned plants raised by local residents almost inevitably lead to high-level proceedings usually lasting several years. A solution to this problem has yet to be found" (AT SPR, n.d., p. 3).
13 E.g. Büchele et al. (2016, pp. 16–17) assess that despite a high technical potential due to low electricity prices there is no additional economic potential for CHP (gas-fired) in Austria where "[o]nly in the scenario with low gas price or high CO_2 price of 100 EUR/t CO_2 new CHP plants are economically feasible".
14 Access to the natural gas network is not possible in every part of Belgium as the distribution network in southern Belgium is not as extensive as in the north (BE FPR, n.d., p. 41).
15 As reported in the Denmark's draft integrated NECP (2018, p. 51) the new support framework is divided into three categories:

   1) Existing non depreciated installations will continue with a fixed premium of 2 EUR cent/kWh in the entire depreciation period.
   2) Depreciated installation will be supported by a fixed premium calculated on the basis of the difference in operating cost in using biomass compared to an alternative fossil reference.

   For new installations after 1 April 2019 a grant pool is established, which would give the possibility of aid for new capacity for the production of electricity using biomass, biogas and other green gasses after application.
16 This concerns building high-efficiency CHP units or renovating and upgrading existing plants to upgrade them to high-efficiency cogeneration – of a maximum installed thermal capacity of 20 MW (see SK NECP 2018, p. 88, 161).
17 2008 is the first year in which when Croatia appears in the discussed statistics (Eurostat 2019a); as it is too close to 2010, 2012 is evaluated instead.

18 Due to a statistical issue, data on Greece is offered for 2006 (instead of 2005 when heat produced in CHP units was reported as accounting for 192.50PJ, see Eurostat 2019a).
19 Due to a statistical issue, data on Greece is offered for 2006 (instead of 2005 when fuel used in CHP was reported as accounting for 406.26PJ, see Eurostat 2019a).
20 By implementing the National Programme, units such as high-efficiency biofuel- and municipal waste-fired Vilnius CHP plant (229 MW$_t$ and 92MW$_e$), a waste-fired Kaunas CHP plant (70 MW$_t$ and 24 MW$_e$) are expected to be built, satisfying about 40% of Vilnius and Kaunas DH needs (LT NECP, p. 91).

References

Act No. 165/2012 Sb. Zákon 165/2012 Sb. ze dne 31. ledna 2012 o podporovaných zdrojích energie a o změně některých zákonů [Act of 31 January 2012 on promoted energy sources and amending certain laws].

Act No. 222/1994 Sb. Zákon 222/1994 ze dne 2. listopadu 1994o podmínkách podnikání a o výkonu státní správy v energetických odvětvích a o Státní energetické inspekci [Act of 2 November 1994 on business conditions and performance of state administration in the energy sectors and on the State Energy Inspection].

Act on renewable energy sources and highly efficient cogeneration of 10 September 2015 [Zakon o obnovljivim izvorima energije i visokoučinkovitoj kogeneraciji, 10. rujna 2015], Official Gazette 100/2015.

Aldrich, E.L., & Koerner, C.L. 2018, "White certificate trading: a dying concept or just making its debut? Part I: market status and trends", *The Electricity Journal*, 31 (3), pp. 52–63.

Al-Mansour, F., Sucic, B., & Pusnik, M. 2014, "Challenges and prospects of electricity production from renewable energy sources in Slovenia", *Energy*, 77, pp. 73–81.

Antonelli, M., Desideri, U., & Franco, A. 2018, "Effects of large scale penetration of renewables: the Italian case in the years 2008–2015", *Renewable and Sustainable Energy Reviews*, 81(2), pp. 3090–3100.

AT FPR. n.d. a, *Progress report according to Article 6 (3)of Directive 2004/8/EG. Combined heat and power. Austria*. Available from: https://ec.europa.eu/energy/sites/ener/files/documents/ms_reports_translated.zip [2 September 2019].

AT FPR. n.d. b, *Austria. Report on the results of the analysis and evaluations carried out in accordance with Article 9 of Directive 2004/8/EC – cogeneration Directive*. Available from: https://ec.europa.eu/energy/sites/ener/files/documents/ms_reports_translated.zip [2 September 2019].

AT NECP. 2018, *Draft Integrated National Energy and Climate Plan for Austria 2021–2030* [courtesy translation in English provided by the translation services of the European Commission]. Available from: [2 September 2019].

AT SPR. n.d., *Report in accordance with Articles 6 (3) and 10 (2) of Directive 2004/8/EC: Austria*. Available from: https://ec.europa.eu/energy/sites/ener/files/documents/second_progress_reports_enversion.zip [2 September 2019].

BE FPR. n.d., *Report by Belgium to the European Commission pursuant to Article 10 (1) of Directive 2004/08/EC; Brussels-Capital Region; Walloon Region*. Available from: https://ec.europa.eu/energy/sites/ener/files/documents/ms_reports_translated.zip [2 September 2019].

BE NECP. 2018, *Draft Belgium's Integrated National Energy and Climate Plan 2021–2030* [courtesy translation in English provided by the translation services of the European Commission]. Available from: https://ec.europa.eu/energy/sites/ener/files/documents/ec_courtesy_translation_be_necp.pdf [2 September 2019].

BE SPR. 2012, *Belgium's written report in accordance with Articles 6 (3) and 10 (2) of Directive 2004/8/EC of the European Parliament and of the Council on the promotion of cogeneration based on a useful heat demand in the internal energy market and amending Directive 92/42/EC*. Available from: https://ec.europa.eu/energy/sites/ener/files/documents/second_progress_reports_enversion.zip [2 September 2019].

Belyi, A. 2019, *Stepping on the gas: future-proofing Estonia's energy market and security*, International Centre for Defence and Security, Tallinn. Available from: https://icds.ee/wp-content/uploads/2019/05/ICDS_Report_Stepping_on_the_Gas_Belyi_May_2019.pdf [2 September 2019].

Bernotat, K., & Sandberg, T. 2004, "Biomass fired small-scale CHP in Sweden and the Baltic States: a case study on the potential of clustered dwellings", *Biomass and Bioenergy*, 27(6), pp. 521–530.

Beus, M., Pavić, I., Štritof, I., Capuder, T., & Pandžić, H. 2018, "Electricity market design in Croatia within the European electricity market – recommendations for further development", *Energies*, 11(2), pp. 1–20, 346. Available from: 10.3390/en11020346 [2 September 2019].

BG SPR. n.d., *Report on: the request of the Commission for a report in accordance with Article 6 (3) and Article 10 (2) of Directive 2004/8/EC of the European Parliament and of the Council on the promotion of cogeneration based on a useful heat demand in the internal market*. Available from: https://ec.europa.eu/energy/sites/ener/files/documents/second_progress_reports_enversion.zip [2 September 2019].

Blanchard, O., & Portugal, P. 2017, "Boom, slump, sudden stops, recovery, and policy options. Portugal and the euro", *Portuguese Economic Journal*, 16(3), pp. 149–168.

Blumberga, D. 2019, "Mandatory procurement lessons. Phenomena of external initiator factor", *Environmental and Climate Technologies*, 23(1), pp. 188–213.

Börjesson, P., Hansson, J., & Berndes, G. 2017, "Future demand for forest-based biomass for energy purposes in Sweden", *Forest Ecology and Management*, 383, pp. 17–26.

BG NECP. 2019, *Draft Integrated Energy and Climate Plan of the Republic of Bulgaria* [courtesy translation in English provided by the translation services of the European Commission]. Available from: https://ec.europa.eu/energy/sites/ener/files/documents/ec_courtesy_translation_bg_necp.pdf [2 September 2019].

Büchele, R., Kranzl, L., Müller, A., Hummel, M., Hartner, M., Deng, Y., & Bons, M. 2016, "Comprehensive assessment of the potential for efficient district heating and cooling and for high-efficient cogeneration in Austria", *International Journal of Sustainable Energy Planning and Management*, 10, pp. 3–19.

CHP Act of 2002. KraftWärme-Kopplungsgesetz 2002 [Combined Heat and Power Act of 2002], BGBl I 2002, p. 1092.

CHP Act of 2016. KraftWärme-Kopplungsgesetz 2016 [Combined Heat and Power Act of 2016], BGBl I 2015, p. 2498.

CODE2. 2014a, *D5.1 – final Cogeneration Roadmap. Member State: Luxembourg*. Available from: www.code2-project.eu/wp-content/uploads/CODE2-CHP-Roadmap-Luxembourg.pdf [2 September 2019].

CODE2. 2014b, *D5.1 Final Cogeneration Roadmap non pilot Member State: Malta*. Available from: www.code2-project.eu/wp-content/uploads/CODE2-D5.1-Road map-Malta-Dec14.pdf [2 September 2019].

Commission. 1997, Communication from the Commission to the Council, the European Parliament, the Economic and Social Committee and the Committee of the regions. A Community strategy to promote combined heat and power (CHP) and to dismantle barriers to its development, COM (97) 514 final, 15 October 1997.

Commission. 2016, *State aid: commission approves Polish scheme to support high-efficiency co-generation of heat and power*. Available from: https://europa.eu/rapid/press-release_IP-16-3214_en.htm [2 September 2019].

Commission. 2018, *State aid: commission approves Belgian certificates schemes for renewable electricity and high-efficiency cogeneration in Flanders*. Available from: https://europa.eu/rapid/press-release_IP-18-821_en.htm [2 September 2019].

Commission. 2019a, *State aid: commission approves €5 billion Polish support for cogenerated electricity and surcharge reductions for large energy consumers; opens in-depth investigation into reductions in capacity mechanism surcharge*. Available from: https://europa.eu/rapid/press-release_IP-19-2150_en.htm [2 September 2019].

Commission. 2019b, *National Energy and Climate Plans (NECPs)*. Available from: https://ec.europa.eu/energy/en/topics/energy-strategy-and-energy-union/governance-energy-union/national-energy-climate-plans [2 September 2019].

Commission. 2019c, *Commission staff working document: assessment of the draft National Energy and Climate Plan of Spain accompanying the document Commission Recommendation on the draft integrated National Energy and Climate Plan of Spain covering the period 2021–2030*, SWD(2019) 262 final, 18 June 2019.

Cruciani, M. 2017, "Marketing renewable energy in France", in *Marketing renewable energy: concepts, business models and cases*, eds C. Herbes & C. Friege, Springer International Publishing, Cham, pp. 303–330.

CY NECP. 2019, *Cyprus' Draft Integrated National Energy and Climate Plan for the period 2021–2030*. Available from: https://ec.europa.eu/energy/sites/ener/files/documents/cyprus_draftnecp.pdf [2 September 2019].

CZ NECP. 2018, *Draft Integrated National Energy and Climate Plan of the Czech Republic* [courtesy translation in English provided by the translation services of the European Commission]. Available from: https://ec.europa.eu/energy/sites/ener/files/documents/ec_courtesy_translation_cz_necp_0.pdf [2 September 2019].

CY SPR. n.d., *Report submitted to the European Commission in accordance with Article 6 (3) and Article 10 (2) of Directive 2004/8/EC of the European Parliament and of the Council on the promotion of cogeneration based on a useful heat demand in the internal market, drafted following the template provided by the Commission*. Available from: https://ec.europa.eu/energy/sites/ener/files/documents/second_progress_reports_en version.zip [2 September 2019].

CZ SPR. 2012, *Progress report on the cogeneration of electricity and heat in the Czech Republic according to Directive 2004/8/EC*. Available from: https://ec.europa.eu/energy/sites/ener/files/documents/second_progress_reports_enversion.zip [2 September 2019].

DE NECP. 2018, *Germany's Draft Integrated National Energy and Climate Plan* [courtesy translation in English provided by the translation services of the European Commission]. Available from: https://ec.europa.eu/energy/sites/ener/files/documents/ec_courtesy_translation_de_necp.pdf [2 September 2019].

DK SPR. 2011, *Report submitted by Denmark in accordance with Articles 6(3) and 10(2) of Directive 2004/8/EC of the European Parliament and of the Council on the promotion of cogeneration based on a useful heat demand in the internal energy market and amending Directive 92/42/EEC.* Available from: https://ec.europa.eu/energy/sites/ener/files/documents/second_progress_reports_enversion.zip [2 September 2019].

DE SPR. 2012, *Report from the German government pursuant to Article 6 (3) and Article 10 (2) of Directive 2004/8/EC of the European Parliament And Of The Council on the promotion of cogeneration based on a useful heat demand in the internal energy market and amending Directive 92/42/EEC.* Available from: https://ec.europa.eu/energy/sites/ener/files/documents/second_progress_reports_enversion.zip [2 September 2019].

Department for Business, Energy & Industrial Strategy. 2018, *Combined heat and power quality assurance programme.* Available from: www.gov.uk/guidance/combined-heat-power-quality-assurance-programme [2 September 2019].

Department of Energy & Climate Change. 2016, *Review of support for anaerobic digestion and micro-combined heat and power under the feed-in tariffs scheme.* Available from: www.gov.uk/government/uploads/system/uploads/attachment_data/file/535842/FITs_ADmCHP_consultation_document_May_2016_1_-_14_July_deadline.pdf [2 September 2019].

Deyne, L.D. 2016, "Legal framework on district heating networks in Belgium and the Netherlands: competition, unbundling and reasonable prices?", *European Energy and Environmental Law Review*, 25(1), pp. 11–24.

Directive 2012/27/EU of the European Parliament and of the Council of 25 October 2012 on energy efficiency, amending Directives 2009/125/EC and 2010/30/EU and repealing Directives 2004/8/EC and 2006/32/EC, OJ L 315, 14 November 2012.

DK NECP. 2018, *Denmark's Draft Integrated National Energy and Climate Plan 2018.* Available from: https://ec.europa.eu/energy/sites/ener/files/documents/denmark_draftnecp.pdf [2 September 2019].

Dzikuć, M., & Piwowar, A. 2016, "Ecological and economic aspects of electric energy production using the biomass co-firing method: the case of Poland", *Renewable and Sustainable Energy Reviews*, 55, pp. 856–862.

E-Bridge Consulting. 2005, *Studie über KWK-Potentiale in Österreich* [Study on CHP potential in Austria]. Available from: https://ec.europa.eu/energy/sites/ener/files/documents/ms_reports_translated.zip [2 September 2019].

EE NECP. 2018, *Estonian national energy and climate plan (NECP 2030)* [courtesy translation in English provided by the translation services of the European Commission]. Available from: https://ec.europa.eu/energy/sites/ener/files/documents/ec_courtesy_translation_ee_necp.pdf [2 September 2019].

EE SPR. n.d., *Report by the Republic of Estonia in accordance with Articles 6 (3) and 10 (2) of Directive 2004/8/EC of the European Parliament and of the Council on the promotion of cogeneration based on a useful heat demand in the internal energy market and amending Directive 92/42/EC.* Available from: https://ec.europa.eu/energy/sites/ener/files/documents/second_progress_reports_enversion.zip [2 September 2019].

EL SPR. 2011, *National report under Articles 6 (3) and 10 (2) of Directive 2004/8/EC, of the European Parliament and of the Council, on the promotion of cogeneration based on a useful heat demand in the internal market and amending Directive 92/42/EEC.* Available from: https://ec.europa.eu/energy/sites/ener/files/documents/second_progress_reports_enversion.zip [2 September 2019].

Elek, L. 2010, "Energy efficiency policies and measures in Hungary", *International Journal of Global Energy Issues*, 34(1–4), pp. 42–67.

Energy Industry Act, Energiewirtschaftsgesetz vom 7. Juli 2005 [Energy Industry Act of 7 July 2005], BGBl I 2005, p. 1970.

Energy Regulatory Office. 2011, *Polish support schemes for renewable and cogeneration sources*. Available from: www.ure.gov.pl/download/2/241/Polish_support_schemes_for_renewable_and_cogeneration_so.pdf [2 September 2019].

ES NECP. 2019, *Spain draft of the integrated National Energy and Climate Plan 2021–2030* [courtesy translation in English provided by the translation services of the European Commission]. Available from: https://ec.europa.eu/energy/sites/ener/files/documents/ec_courtesy_translation_es_necp.pdf [2 September 2019].

ES SPR. 2011, *Promotion of cogeneration based on a useful heat demand in the internal energy market (Directive 2004/8/EC) – report*. Available from: https://ec.europa.eu/energy/sites/ener/files/documents/second_progress_reports_enversion.zip [2 September 2019].

Eurostat. 2001, *Combined heat and power production (CHP) in the EU. Summary of statistics*, Office for Official Publications of the European Communities, Luxembourg.

Eurostat. 2019a, *Combined heat and power (CHP) data*. Available from: https://ec.europa.eu/eurostat/documents/38154/4956229/CHPdata2005-2016.xlsx/dd19ad9f-4074-4dd5-86b2-5b24a949a47c [15 March 2019].

Eurostat. 2019b, *Combined heat and power (CHP) data*. Available from: https://ec.europa.eu/eurostat/documents/38154/4956229/CHPdata2005-2017.xlsx/871cc151-5733-423f-ae38-de9b733aa81e [2 September 2019].

Eurostat. n.d., *Glossary: country codes*. Available from https://ec.europa.eu/eurostat/statistics-explained/index.php/Glossary:Country_codes [15 March 2019].

Federal Ministry for Economic Affairs and Energy. n.d., *Combined heat and power*. Available from: www.bmwi.de/Redaktion/EN/Artikel/Energy/modern-power-plant-technologies.html [2 September 2019].

FI SPR. 2011, *Report FI 2011 in accordance with Articles 6(3) and 10(2) of Directive 2004/8/EC of the European Parliament and of the Council on the promotion of cogeneration based on a useful heat demand in the internal energy market and amending Directive 92/42/EC*. Available from: https://ec.europa.eu/energy/sites/ener/files/documents/second_progress_reports_enversion.zip [2 September 2019].

FI NECP. 2018, *Finland's integrated National Energy and Climate Plan: draft version submitted to the European Commission*. Available from: https://ec.europa.eu/energy/sites/ener/files/documents/finland_draftnecp.pdf [2 September 2019].

FR NECP. 2019, *Projet de Plan National Integre Energie-Climat de la France* [Draft of integrated National Energy and Climate Plan of France]. Available from: https://ec.europa.eu/energy/sites/ener/files/documents/france_draftnecp.pdf [2 September 2019].

FR SPR. 2011, *Report of the French authorities pursuant to Article 6 (3) and Article 10 (2) of Directive 2004/8/EC on the promotion of cogeneration based on a useful heat demand in the internal energy market and amending Directive 92/42/EC – in reply to Commission letter ENER/PL/jma/pc/S-309427 of 11 April 2011*. Available from: https://ec.europa.eu/energy/sites/ener/files/documents/second_progress_reports_enversion.zip [2 September 2019].

Franco, A., & Versace, M. 2017, "Multi-objective optimization for the maximization of the operating share of cogeneration system in district heating network", *Energy Conversion and Management*, 139, pp. 33–44.

Franzò, S., Frattini, F., Cagno, E., & Trianni, A. 2019, "A multi-stakeholder analysis of the economic efficiency of industrial energy efficiency policies: empirical evidencefrom ten years of the Italian White Certificate Scheme", *Applied Energy*, 240, pp. 424–435.

Gaigalis, V., Skema, R., Marcinauskas, K., & Korsakiene, I. 2016, "A review on heat pumps implementation in Lithuania in compliance with the National Energy Strategy and EU policy", *Renewable and Sustainable Energy Reviews*, 53, pp. 841–858.

Gailfuß, M. n.d., *CHP Act 2016 – summary of regulations within the new CHP Act*. Available from: www.bhkw-infozentrum.de/rechtliche-rahmenbedingungen-bhkw-kwk/chp-act-2016-summary-of-regulations-within-the-new-chp-act.html [2 September 2019].

Gawlik, L. 2018, "The Polish power industry in energy transformation process", *Mineral Economics*, 31(1–2), pp. 229–237.

Gawlik, L., & Mokrzycki, E. 2019, "Changes in the structure of electricity generation in Poland in view of the EU Climate Package", *Energies*, 12(17), pp. 1–19, 3323. Available from: 10.3390/en12173323 [2 September 2019].

Gucma, M., Bąk, A., & Chłopińska, E. 2018, "Concept of LNG transfer and bunkering model of vessels at South Baltic Sea Area", *Annual of Navigation*, 25(1), pp. 79–91.

Howley, M., & Holland, M. 2016, *Combined heat and power in Ireland: 2016 update*, Energy Policy Statistical Support Unit, Sustainable Energy Authority of Ireland, Cork. Available from: www.seai.ie/publications/Combined%20Heat%20and%20Power%20in%20Ireland%20Update%202016 [2 September 2019].

HR NECP. 2018, *First draft of the Integrated Energy and Climate Plan for the period from 2021 to 2030*. Available from: https://ec.europa.eu/energy/sites/ener/files/documents/croatia_draftnecp_en.pdf [2 September 2019].

HU NECP. 2018, *National Energy and Climate Plan of Hungary (Draft)* [courtesy translation in English provided by the translation services of the European Commission]. Available from: https://ec.europa.eu/energy/sites/ener/files/documents/ec_courtesy_translation_hu_necp.pdf [2 September 2019].

HU SPR. 2011, *Report on the implementation of Articles 6(3) and 10(2) of Directive 2004/8/EC of the European Parliament and of the Council on the promotion of cogeneration based on a useful heat demand in the internal energy market and amending Directive 92/42/EEC*. Available from: https://ec.europa.eu/energy/sites/ener/files/documents/second_progress_reports_enversion.zip [2 September 2019].

IR NECP. 2018, *Draft National Energy & Climate Plan (NECP) 2021–2030*. Available from: https://ec.europa.eu/energy/sites/ener/files/documents/ireland_draftnecp.pdf [2 September 2019].

IR SPR. 2011, *Directive 2004/8/EC promotion of cogeneration: Ireland reporting under Article 6 (3)*. Available from: https://ec.europa.eu/energy/sites/ener/files/documents/second_progress_reports_enversion.zip [2 September 2019].

IT NECP. 2018, *Draft Integrated National Energy and Climate Plan* [courtesy translation in English provided by the translation services of the European Commission]. Available from: https://ec.europa.eu/energy/sites/ener/files/documents/ec_courtesy_translation_it_necp.pdf [2 September 2019].

IT SPR. 2011, *Report on cogeneration in Italy in response to request ENER/PL/jma/pc/S-309427 by the European Commission*. Available from: https://ec.europa.eu/energy/sites/ener/files/documents/second_progress_reports_enversion.zip [2 September 2019].

Jacobs, D. 2012, "The German Energiewende – history, targets, policies and challenge", *Renewable Energy Law and Policy Review*, 3(4), pp. 223–233.

Katinas, V., Marčiukaitis, M., Perednis, E., & Dzenajavičienė, E.F. 2019, "Analysis of biodegradable waste use for energy generation in Lithuania", *Renewable and Sustainable Energy Reviews*, 101, pp. 559–567.

Knoop, K., & Lechtenböhmer, S. 2017, "The potential for energy efficiency in the EU Member States – a comparison of studies", *Renewable and Sustainable Energy Reviews*, 68, pp. 1097–1105.

Korhonen, J., & Savolainen, I. 2001, "Cleaner energy production in industrial recycling networks", *Eco-Management and Auditing: The Journal of Corporate Environmental Management*, 8(3), pp. 144–153.

Kotowicz, J., & Bartela, Ł. 2011, "The influence of the legal and economical environment and the profile of activities on the optimal design features of a natural-gas-fired combined heat and power plant", *Energy*, 36(1), pp. 328–338.

Law 3851/2010, N.3851 «Επιτάχυνση της ανάπτυξης των Ανανεώσιμων Πηγών Ενέργειας για την αντιμετώπιση της κλιματικής αλλαγής και άλλες διατάξεις σε θέματα αρμοδιότητας του Υπουργείου Περιβάλλοντος, Ενέργειας και Κλιματικής Αλλαγής» ["Speeding up the development of Renewable Energy Sources with a view to dealing with climate change, and other provisions falling within the scope of responsibility of the Ministry of the Environment, Energy and Climate Change"], Government Gazette No 85, 4 June 2010.

Lončar, D., Duić, N., & Bogdan, Ž. 2009, "An analysis of the legal and market framework for the cogeneration sector in Croatia", *Energy* 34(2), pp. 134–143.

LT NECP. 2018, *Integrated National Energy and Climate Plan of the Republic of Lithuania: draft version*. Available from: https://ec.europa.eu/energy/sites/ener/files/documents/lithuania_draftnecp_en.pdf [2 September 2019].

LT SPR. 2012, *Report of the Republic of Lithuania in accordance with Articles 6 (3) and 10 (2) of Directive 2004/8/EC of the European Parliament and of the Council on the promotion of cogeneration based on a useful heat demand in the internal energy market and amending Directive 92/42/EEC*. Available from: https://ec.europa.eu/energy/sites/ener/files/documents/second_progress_reports_enversion.zip [2 September 2019].

LU NECP. 2019, *Draft Integrated National Energy and Climate Plan for Luxembourg* [courtesy translation in English provided by the translation services of the European Commission]. Available from: https://ec.europa.eu/energy/sites/ener/files/documents/ec_courtesy_translation_lu_necp.pdf [2 September 2019].

LU SPR. 2012, *Report on progress towards increasing the share of high-efficiency cogeneration in accordance with Article 6 (3) and Article 10 (2) of Directive 2004/8/EC of the European Parliament and of the Council on the promotion of cogeneration based on a useful heat demand in the internal energy market and amending Directive 92/42/EEC*. Available from: https://ec.europa.eu/energy/sites/ener/files/documents/second_progress_reports_enversion.zip [2 September 2019].

Lund, H., Hvelplund, F., Kass, I., Dukalskis, E., & Blumberga, D. 1999, "District heating and market economy in Latvia", *Energy*, 24(7), pp. 549–559.

LV NECP. 2018, *National Energy and Climate Plan of Latvia 2021–2030. Draft for submitting to the European Commission for evaluation* [courtesy translation in English provided by the translation services of the European Commission]. Available from: https://ec.europa.eu/energy/sites/ener/files/documents/ec_courtesy_translation_lv_necp.pdf [2 September 2019].

LV SPR. 2011, *Regular report by the Republic of Latvia on increasing the share of high-efficiency cogeneration pursuant to Articles 6(3) and 10(2) of Directive 2004/8/EC of the European Parliament and of the Council of 11 February 2004 on the promotion of cogeneration based on a useful heat demand in the internal energy market and amending Directive 92/42/EEC*. Available from: https://ec.europa.eu/energy/sites/ener/files/documents/second_progress_reports_enversion.zip [2 September 2019].

Mauger, M. 2018, "The voluminous energy transition legal framework in France and the question of its recognition as a branch of law", *Energy Policy*, 122, pp. 499–505.

Ministry of Agriculture. 2018, *Latvian forest sector in facts & figures 2018*. Availabfe from: www.zm.gov.lv/public/ck/files/skaitlifakti_ENG_19.pdf [2 September 2019].

Ministry of Ecological and Solidarity Transition. 2018, *Biomasse énergie* [Biomass energy]. Available from: www.ecologique-solidaire.gouv.fr/biomasse-energie [2 September 2019].

Ministry of Economic Affairs and Employment. 2018, *Minister Tiilikainen: Finland to ban coal in 2029–incentives package for faster phase-out*. Available from: https://tem.fi/en/article/-/asset_publisher/ministeri-tiilikainen-kivihiilen-kielto-2029-kannustepaketti-nopeille-luopujille [2 September 2019].

Ministry of the Economy. 2016, *Assessment of the potential for the application of high-efficiency cogeneration and efficient district heating and cooling. Report by the Ministry of the Economy, Luxembourg*. Available from: https://ec.europa.eu/energy/sites/ener/files/documents/lu_cogeneration_report_en.pdf [2 September 2019].

Mortensen, H.C., & Overgaard, B. 1992, "CHP development in Denmark: role and results", *Energy Policy*, 20(12), pp. 1198–1206.

MT NECP. 2018, *Malta's 2030 National Energy and Climate Plan. Draft 2018*. Available from: https://ec.europa.eu/energy/sites/ener/files/documents/malta_draftnecp.pdf [2 September 2019].

MT SPR. 2011, *Malta's replies with regard to the report in accordance with Articles 6 (3) and 10 (2) of Directive 2004/8/EC of the European Parliament and of the Council on the promotion of cogeneration based on a useful heat demand in the internal energy market and amending Directive 92/42/EC*. Available from: https://ec.europa.eu/energy/sites/ener/files/documents/second_progress_reports_enversion.zip [2 September 2019].

Muras, Z. 2011, "'Kolorowy zawrót głowy' – czyli specyfika polskich systemów wsparcia OZE i kogeneracji" ['rainbow vertigo' – or a description of Polish support schemes for renewable and cogeneration sources], Czysta Energia [Clean Energy], 5, pp. 12–14.

NL NECP. 2018, *Draft Integrated National Energy and Climate Plan 2021–2030*. Available from: https://ec.europa.eu/energy/sites/ener/files/documents/netherlands_draft necp_en.pdf.pdf [2 September 2019].

NL SPR. 2011, *Report in accordance with Articles 6 (3) and 10 (2) of Directive 2004/8/EC of the European Parliament and of the Council on the promotion of cogeneration based on a useful heat demand in the internal energy market and amending Directive 92/42/EC*. Available from: https://ec.europa.eu/energy/sites/ener/files/documents/second_progress_reports_enversion.zip [2 September 2019].

OECD. 2019, *OECD environmental performance reviews: Latvia 2019 (abridged version)*. Available from: www.oecd.org/environment/country-reviews/OECD-EPR-Latvia-2019-Abridged-Version.pdf [2 September 2019].

Office of Gas and Electricity Markets. 2019, *Feed-in tariffs: essential guide to closure of the scheme*. Available from: www.ofgem.gov.uk/system/files/docs/2019/03/guide_to_closure.pdf [2 September 2019].

PL NECP. 2019, *Draft National Energy and Climate Plan (NECP) – version 3.1* [courtesy translation in English provided by the translation services of the European Commission]. Available from: https://ec.europa.eu/energy/sites/ener/files/documents/ec_courtesy_translation_pl_necp_part_1.pdf [2 September 2019].

PL SPR. 2012, Available from: https://ec.europa.eu/energy/sites/ener/files/documents/second_progress_reports_enversion.zip [2 September 2019].

Prodanuks, T., Cimdina, G., Veidenbergs, I., & Blumberga, D. 2016, "Sustainable development of biomass CHP in Latvia", *Energy Procedia*, 95, pp. 372–376.
Psomopoulos, C.S., Kaminaris, S.D., Ioannidis, G.C., & Themelis, N.J. 2017, "Contribution of WTE Plants in EU's targets for renewables. A review until 2014", *Proceedings of the 5th International Conference on Sustainable Solid Waste Management*, Athens, pp. 21–24.
PT NECP. 2018, *Portugal: integrated National Energy and Climate Plan 2021–2030* [courtesy translation in English provided by the translation services of the European Commission]. Available from: https://ec.europa.eu/energy/sites/ener/files/documents/ec_courtesy_translation_pt_necp.pdf [2 September 2019].
PT SPR. n.d., *Report in accordance with Articles 6 (3) and 10 (2) of Directive 2004/8/EC of the European Parliament and of the Council on the Promotion of cogeneration based on a useful heat demand in the internal energy market and amending Directive 92/42/EEC.* Available from: https://ec.europa.eu/energy/sites/ener/files/documents/second_progress_reports_enversion.zip [2 September 2019].
Reuters. 2019, *Finland approves ban on coal for energy use from 2029.* Available from: https://uk.reuters.com/article/finland-energy-coal/finland-approves-ban-on-coal-for-energy-use-from-2029-idUKL5N20N6QV [2 September 2019].
Righini, E., & Catti De Gasperi, G. 2019, "Survey – the application of EU State aid law in the energy sector", *Journal of European Competition Law & Practice*, 10(1), pp. 53–68.
RO NECP. 2018, *Integrated National Energy and Climate Change Plan for 2021–2030.* Available from: https://ec.europa.eu/energy/sites/ener/files/documents/romania_draftnecp_en.pdf [2 Septemebr 2019].
RO SPR. n.d., *Report of Romania in accordance with Articles 6 (3) and 10 (2) of Directive 2004/8/EC of the European Parliament and of the Council on the promotion of cogeneration based on a useful heat demand in the internal energy market and amending Directive 92/42/EC.* Available from: https://ec.europa.eu/energy/sites/ener/files/documents/second_progress_reports_enversion.zip [2 September 2019].
Royal Decree No 661/2007, Real Decreto 661/2007, de 25 de mayo, por el que se regula la actividad de producción de energía eléctrica en régimen especial [Royal Decree 661/2007, of May 25, which regulates the activity of production of electricity under a special regime], Boletín Oficial del Estado 126/2007.
Saint Akadiri, S., Alola, A.A., Akadiri, A.C., & Alola, U.V. 2019, "Renewable energy consumption in EU-28 countries: policy toward pollution mitigation and economic sustainability", *Energy Policy*, 132, pp. 803–810.
Salomón, M., Savola, T., Martin, A., Fogelholm, C.J., & Fransson, T. 2011, "Small-scale biomass CHP plants in Sweden and Finland", *Renewable and Sustainable Energy Reviews*, 15(9), pp. 4451–4465.
Sandberg, E., Møller Sneum, D., & Trømborg, E. 2018, "Framework conditions for Nordic district heating – similarities and differences, and why Norway sticks out", *Energy*, 149, pp. 105–119.
Scheftelowitz, M., Becker, R., & Thrän, D. 2018, "Improved power provision from biomass: a retrospective on the impacts of German energy policy", *Biomass and Bioenergy*, 111, pp. 1–12.
Schulte, S., & Weiser, F. 2019, "LNG import quotas in Lithuania – economic effects of breaking Gazprom's natural gas monopoly", *Energy Economics*, 78, pp. 174–181.
SE NECP. 2019, *Sweden's draft integrated national energy and climate plan.* Available from: https://ec.europa.eu/energy/sites/ener/files/documents/sweden_draftnecp.pdf [2 September 2019].

SE SPR. n.d., *Template concerning the report in accordance with Articles 6 (3) and 10 (2) of Directive 2004/8/EC of the European Parliament and of the Council on the promotion of cogeneration based on a useful heat demand in the internal energy market and amending Directive 92/42/EEC*. Available from: https://ec.europa.eu/energy/sites/ener/files/documents/second_progress_reports_enversion.zip [2 September 2019].

Sergent, A. 2014, "Sector-based political analysis of energy transition: green shift in the forest policy regime in France", *Energy Policy*, 73, pp. 491–500.

SI NECP. 2018, *Draft Integrated National Energy and Climate Plan for Slovenia* [courtesy translation in English provided by the translation services of the European Commission]. Available from: https://ec.europa.eu/energy/sites/ener/files/documents/ec_courtesy_translation_si_necp.pdf [2 September 2019].

SI SPR. n.d., *Report of the republic of Slovenia in accordance with Articles 6 (3) and 10 (2) of Directive 2004/8/EC of the European Parliament and of the Council on the promotion of cogeneration based on a useful heat demand in the internal energy market and amending Directive 92/42/EC*. Available from: https://ec.europa.eu/energy/sites/ener/files/documents/second_progress_reports_enversion.zip [2 September 2019].

SK NECP. 2018, *Proposal for an Integrated National Energy and Climate Plan*[courtesy translation in English provided by the translation services of the European Commission]. Available from: https://ec.europa.eu/energy/sites/ener/files/documents/ec_courtesy_translation_sk_necp.pdf [2 September 2019].

SK SPR. 2011, *Report on progress towards increasing the share of high-efficiency cogeneration Article 6 paragraph 3 of Directive 2004/8/EC*. Available from: https://ec.europa.eu/energy/sites/ener/files/documents/second_progress_reports_enversion.zip [2 September 2019].

Sołtysik, M., & Mucha-Kuś, K. 2015, "High-efficiency gas cogeneration – an assessment of the support mechanism", *Acta Energetica*, 3(24), pp. 97–102.

Stadler, I. 2008, "Power grid balancing of energy systems with high renewable energy penetration by demand response", *Utilities Policy*, 16(2), pp. 90–98.

Stankeviciute, L., & Krook Riekkola, A. 2014, "Assessing the development of combined heat and power generation in the EU", *International Journal of Energy Sector Management*, 8(1), pp. 76–99.

Stede, J. 2017, "Bridging the industrial energy efficiency gap – assessing the evidence from the Italian white certificate scheme", *Energy Policy*, 104, pp. 112–123.

Stocker, A., Großmann, A., Madlener, R., & Wolter, M.I. 2011, "Sustainable energy development in Austria until 2020: insights from applying the integrated model 'e3.at'", *Energy Policy*, 39(10), pp. 6082–6099.

Tallinn University of Technology. 2007, *Potential for efficient cogeneration of heat and power in Estonia*, Tallinn. Available from: https://ec.europa.eu/energy/sites/ener/files/documents/ms_reports_translated.zip [2 September 2019].

Tofan, B.A., Șerbănoiu, I., & Burlacu, A. 2015, "Environmental and financial assessment for a CCHP district plant in a city in Romania", *Bulletin of the Polytechnic Institute of Jassy*, LXI (LXV), 4, pp. 147–156.

UK NECP. 2018, *The UK's draft integrated National Energy and Climate Plan (NECP)*. Available from: https://ec.europa.eu/energy/sites/ener/files/documents/unitedkingdom_draftnecp.pdf [2 September 2019].

UK SPR. 2011, *Template concerning the report in accordance with Articles 6 (3) and 10 (2) of Directive 2004/8/EC of the European Parliament and of the Council on the promotion of cogeneration based on a useful heat demand in the internal energy market and* amending Directive 92/42/EC. Available from: https://ec.europa.eu/energy/sites/ener/files/documents/second_progress_reports_enversion.zip [2 September 2019].

Uran, V., & Krajcar, S. 2009, "Feed-in tariff and market electricity price comparison: the case of cogeneration units in Croatia", *Energy Policy*, 37(3), pp. 844–849.

Valionienė, E., & Strakauskaite, A. 2015, "Evaluation of bunkering services attractiveness at Klaipeda seaport after establishment of LNG terminal", *Journal of Maritime Transport and Engineering*, 4(2), pp. 32–33.

Volkova, A., Hlebnikov, A., & Siirde, A. 2010, "Defining of eligible capacity for biomass cogeneration plants in small towns in Estonia", *Proceedings of International Conference on Renewable Energies and Power Quality*, Granada, pp. 714–718.

Westner, G., & Madlener, R. 2011, "Development of cogeneration in Germany: a mean-variance portfolio analysis of individual technology's prospects in view of the new regulatory framework", *Energy*, 36(8), pp. 5301–5313.

Żmijewski, K., & Sokołowski, M.M. 2010, "Ciepłownictwo – przegląd uwarunkowań i problemów" [District heating – overview of conditions and problems], *Ciepłownictwo, Ogrzewnictwo, Wentylacja* [District Heating, Heating, Ventilation], 11, pp. 395–399.

Zsebik, A. 2008, "Implementation of CHP plants: the best investment possibilities in Hungary", *Cogeneration and Distributed Generation Journal*, 23(1), pp. 65–79.

6 Cogenclusion
Cogeneration in conclusion

Cogeneration, in principle, is a mature technology remembering the times of the nineteenth century and early electrification run by Thomas Edison and other energy champions of this era. Due to its features giving it its pro-efficiency character, which – as its name suggests – derives from a joint energy process of producing heat and electricity (principally), it has awakened different interests. Apart from the investors, including public ones, it has been noticed by countries and their governments, and so has been addressed in national energy policies and legislation. As discussed in the preceding chapters, this has happened in Europe, where the usage of cogeneration has a long tradition.

However, at different times, European CHP has gone through various levels of interests, experiencing retreats and comebacks. The gamechanger was the oil crisis which made Member States and the European Community move towards wider exploitation of the potential laying in cogeneration. Initially, this has been driven by its pro-efficient nature, resulting in energy savings. Soon, however, with more attention being paid to the reduction of emissions and the decentralisation of the energy sector, some other fields for the usage of combined heat and power appeared. This was also possible due to policy approaches offered in the EU for the liberalisation of the energy market and climate action along with legislation brought by these frameworks.

Nowadays, combined heat and power still has its place in the regulatory framework of the EU and its Member States. The policy attitude to this industry has evolved, just as cogeneration itself has changed, driven by technological development. However, the internal energy market at the turn of the decades (2010s/2020s) is not the same as it was in the 1990s/2000s. The challenges and opportunities implied by energy security, cyber risks, artificial intelligence, climate change, energy storage, energy prosumers, and electric vehicles reshape the legal environment for the European energy sector. This also affects cogeneration – which, to survive on the energy market, has to adapt to the changing circumstances.

In this context, this chapter is aimed at highlighting the current regulatory framework provided by the EU for combined heat and power.

It complements the remarks on the national approaches offered by the Member States to cogeneration made in Chapter 5, by presenting a European perspective established in 2018 and 2019 under the umbrella of the Clean Energy Package and the Energy Union. Apart from the analysis of the current status of cogeneration – with respect to European law concerning it, as well as state-of-the-art CHP depicted by European statistics, this chapter summarises the deliberations presented in this book. This way, Chapter 6 is a *cogenclusion* – the conclusion formed for the needs of combined heat and power discussed from different angles throughout this book.

Cogeneration in the EU: where we are now

In December 2018, the Energy Efficiency Directive was amended. This step, achieved by the passing of Directive (EU) 2018/2002, is part of a wider legislative action undertaken within the framework of the Clean Energy Package. This new initiative of the European Union is aimed at modernising the European economy and boosting investments in clean energy related areas. Apart from energy efficiency, the package also covers such fields as energy consumers and renewable energy sources (Commission 2016). Without depreciating any of these three pillars, at a declarative level, energy efficiency is given a clear priority. The concept of "putting energy efficiency first" reflects the pro-efficiency approach of the European Union where "the cheapest and cleanest source of energy is the energy that does not need to be produced or used" (Commission 2016, p. 4, see Fawcett & Killip 2019). It also strengthens the role of renewable energy to become a global leader as well as enhancing the position of energy consumers (Sokołowski 2018b, p. 60). In this context, energy efficiency has been set as the crucial element of the entire energy system, which actively manages and optimises energy demand and consumption, decreases costs for consumers, and reduces import dependence (Commission 2016, p. 4). Therefore, let us look at how these declarations translate into European Union law and whether they address cogeneration.

As discussed in Chapter 4, the RED II – just like the 2018 amendment of the Energy Efficiency Directive – is an element of the Clean Energy Package. Not only does it maintain the approach introduced by previous legislation on renewable energy sources, but also extends the provisions on combined heat and power. Under RED II, cogeneration is used e.g. for the needs of the EU 2030 renewable target (for qualifying electricity produced from biomass), or for the rules on calculating the greenhouse gas impact (with respect to biofuels, bioliquids and their fossil fuel equivalents). In comparison, the 2018 amendment of the Energy Efficiency Directive seemingly does not deliver any new specific regulatory approach in terms of CHP. Directive (EU) 2018/2002 keeps the provisions established for combined heat and power under the Energy Efficiency Directive in 2012.

This concerns definitions listed in Article 2 (30) – (39) and (41), including "cogeneration", "high-efficiency cogeneration", or "small-scale" and "micro-scale cogeneration unit". Those provisions are meant to encourage Member States to adopt policies in favour of high-efficiency cogeneration (Article 14(2)), or the grid and market issues related to high-efficiency CHP (Article 15(5)). The energy efficiency priority, declared in 2016, tends to omit cogeneration when it comes to introducing new regulatory tools or applying a stronger approach to the support of high-efficiency CHP, at least on the grounds of the Energy Efficiency Directive, as amended in 2018. However, it is a wrong impression which may emerge if the Energy Efficiency Directive is not seen through the prism of the EU's new 32.5% energy efficiency goal, as a part of a bigger European energy agenda. With some exceptions – when a direct reference limits the possibilities for pro-CHP approach (as under Directive (EU) 2019/944 and Regulation (EU) 2019/943), an interpretation of the provisions of the Clean Energy Package allows to deduce a more cogeneration-oriented legal environment.

The Clean Energy Package and cogeneration within the Energy Union: energy efficiency first

What Directive 2018/2002 maintained, has been altered by another legislation put into the framework of the new legislative package of the European Union – Clean Energy Package. First, despite not amending the Energy Efficiency Directive in terms of cogeneration, high-efficiency combined heat and power has been influenced by the provisions of Regulation (EU) 2018/1999 on the Energy Union, just like Directive 2018/2002 enacted in December 2018. Second, the changes to the legal environment on cogeneration have been brought quite quickly by other, initially postponed elements of the Clean Energy Package – the new Electricity Directive and the Electricity Regulation (which were passed in June 2019). Due to the time-division of adopting the legislation included in the Clean Energy Package, some amendments in the existing legislation on the energy sector were delivered six months later, in mid-2019. This applies, *inter alia*, to the grid matters addressed in Article 15(5) of the Energy Efficiency Directive.

The postponed legislation on the EU internal energy market includes Directive (EU) 2019/944 (Fourth Electricity Directive) and Regulation (EU) 2019/943 (Third Electricity Regulation). Both the Directive and the Regulation are subsequent elements of the broader energy agenda, the previously mentioned Clean Energy Package (cf. Gauthier & Lowitzsch 2019; Ludwig 2019).[1] The Fourth Electricity Directive is aimed at ensuring "affordable, transparent energy prices and costs for consumers, a high degree of security of supply and a smooth transition towards a sustainable low-carbon energy system". It addresses traditional energy fields such as generation, transmission, and distribution of electricity; recognises new areas (e.g. storage of electricity), and enhances those already recognised, like the situation of energy consumers, energy poverty, etc. (see Sokołowski et al. 2020). In this context, the Directive establishes key rules on the EU electricity sector, being based on the classic drivers of the European energy market: consumer protection, market integration, third-party access, unbundling, and the independence of the national regulatory authorities (see Sokołowski 2016, pp. 220–221). In the same way, as expressed in its Article 1(b) the Third Electricity Regulation is designed to:

> set fundamental principles for well-functioning, integrated electricity markets, which allow all resource providers and electricity customers non-discriminatory market access, empower consumers, ensure competitiveness on the global market as well as demand response, energy storage and energy efficiency, and facilitate aggregation of distributed demand and supply, and enable market and sectoral integration and market-based remuneration of electricity generated from renewable sources.
>
> Regulation (EU) 2019/943

Apart from being the pillars of the Clean Energy Package, both the Fourth Electricity Directive and the Third Electricity Regulation are the executive components of the Energy Union. They are needed to achieve the five main dimensions of the Energy Union founded in Regulation (EU) 2018/1999. These are (i) energy security; (ii) internal energy market; (iii) energy efficiency; (iv) decarbonisation; (v) research, innovation, and competitiveness. Before moving on to the discussion on the amendments in the European law on cogeneration, brought by the Directive and the Regulation, one should note that the Energy Union with its dimensions influences combined heat and power. This concerns the energy efficiency dimension (iii) providing the space for high-efficiency cogeneration.

Under the Regulation on the Energy Union, by the end of 2019 each Member State was obliged to notify the Commission of an integrated national energy and climate plan (Article 3). They are the long term-planning tools designed for a ten-year period (the next integrated national plans are to be presented to the Commission by the beginning of 2029, and so on); however, the initial plans – which range from 2021 to 2030 – should also consider the long-term prospects. The Regulation on the Energy Union establishes the structure of national plans, listing its main sections – such as an overview of the process. It is followed by elaborations on the plan (including information on the public consultations or stakeholders involved), or different types of energy policy descriptions – like the status quo of the five dimensions of the Energy Union, or of national efforts to implement the dimensions of the Energy Union along planned policies and measures relating to them (see Article 3(2)).[2] The integrated plans are national platforms for establishing and making public the objectives, targets and contributions for the five dimensions of the Energy Union. Under Article 4 of the Regulation on the Energy Union, each Member State sets those targets in an integrated plan, dividing them into the Energy Union's dimension. Is there a place for cogeneration? Where could/should the Member States address it?

The energy efficiency dimension is a natural reference point for cogeneration within the Energy Union. As stated in Article 4(b) of Regulation (EU) 2018/1999, the integrated national energy and climate plan in terms of this dimension (energy efficiency), except the part on the renovation of buildings,[3] has to include specific information. This includes the indicative national energy efficiency contribution to reaching the EU's 2030 energy efficiency goal of 32.5%, and the cumulative amount of end-use energy savings between 2021–2030, as provided by the revised Directive 2012/27/EU. Moreover, the energy efficiency dimension is strengthened by separate provisions on the Member States' contribution setting process (the same applies to the renewable energy dimension).[4] According to Article 6(1) of the Regulation on the Energy Union, during the setting process in the area of energy efficiency, the EU Member States have to take several factors into account. These are: the energy consumption ceiling for 2020 and 2030 (the latter is set as maximum consumption of 1,273 Mtoe of primary energy and/or no more than 956 Mtoe of final energy); measures provided for in the Energy Efficiency Directive; and other measures promoting energy efficiency at the national and European level. This approach indirectly links combined heat and power with the concept of the Energy Union, as high-efficiency cogeneration can be used for its needs.

Furthermore, as already discussed, the integrated national plans – apart from drawing the shape of future energy system – must deliver the description of current energy situation in each Member State. What is important, is that those plans have to contain "an analytical basis". This refers to the description of the current situation for each of the Energy Union's dimensions. The description should be made in line with the structure and format established in Annex I to Regulation (EU) 2018/1999. In Section B of the said Annex, one may find details related to the scope of the analytical basis which the Member States should use for the needs of their integrated national plans. A direct reference to high-efficiency cogeneration appears in the dimension energy efficiency (4.3) of a national plan. One of the building blocks of the analytical basis of the energy efficiency dimension of the Energy Union (see Chapter 4 of this book) is the analysis of the current potential for the application of high-efficiency cogeneration and efficient district heating and cooling.

In the previously discussed context, cogeneration meets the Energy Union. Despite the lack of an explicit reference, the adopted provisions of Regulation 2018/1999 allow for high-efficiency CHP to be attached to the scope of activities aimed at implementing the priority energy efficiency first (cf. Rosenow et al. 2017, p. 77). In Recital 5 of the preamble to this Regulation it is called an "overarching theme". Further, Recital 64 and Article 2(18) highlight the practical and legal significance of the energy efficiency first principle. Under the Regulation on the Energy Union, the principle is "the treatment of energy efficiency as a crucial element and a key consideration in future investment decisions on energy infrastructure in the Union" (see Bartoszewicz-Burczy et al. 2018, pp. 93–94). Taking into account "cost-efficient, technically, economically and environmentally sound alternative energy efficiency measures" before conducting any other action related to the energy sector, such as energy planning, decisions on energy policies and investments – is an obligation (as this is how the principle ought to be read, despite the use of the word "should").[5] Hence, the Member States have to consider whether a pro-efficiency action can substitute, entirely or partially, the other action ("the envisaged planning, policy and investment measures") – while – and this is the crux – still being able to achieve the objectives of these decisions, although reached via different means, i.e. by applying energy efficiency.

What applies to cogeneration (high-efficiency) concerns an open catalogue of the cost-efficient alternatives to the planning, policy and investment measures. The catalogue covers "measures to make energy demand and energy supply more efficient, in particular by means of cost-effective end-use energy savings, demand response initiatives and more efficient conversion, transmission and distribution of energy". Both the open nature of the catalogue ("in particular") and its wording ("more efficient conversion") create a space allowing to include high-efficiency CHP among these measures. Nevertheless, let us contrast this interpretation with the current regulatory regime established for combined heat and power.

The new legal nexus for CHP: regulatory consequences of the Clean Energy Package

With passing the last elements of the Clean Energy Package, a new regulatory framework for cogeneration has been established. Its core consists of the revised (in 2018 and 2019) Energy Efficiency Directive encompassed by the Fourth Electricity Directive (see Milčiuvienė et al. 2019, pp. 6–7), the Third Electricity Regulation (Herrera Anchustegui & Formosa 2019, pp. 7–8), and the previously discussed Regulation on the Energy Union. This is augmented by other legislation, like the already analysed RED II. How much has the legal environment for cogeneration changed – if, at least outwardly, it seems that little has changed?

Addressing the pro-efficiency measures in the Regulation on the Energy Union, while searching for the position of combined heat and power in the recent Package, makes it necessary to analyse the Energy Efficiency Directive. When evaluating its last version, one should notice that, on the one hand, the core legal framework on cogeneration has not been changed. Such basic elements as the definitions relevant for to CHP have been preserved. On the other hand, the legal environment on efficiency has been altered. This includes certain changes on cogeneration introduced by Directive (EU) 2019/944 and Regulation (EU) 2019/943. Furthermore, despite the adoption of the energy efficiency principle, some of those changes limit the possibilities for developing cogeneration, including high-efficiency CHP.

The scope of the amendments modifies the electricity market issues established under the Energy Efficiency Directive and the Third Electricity Directive (Directive 2009/72/EC); the latter was repealed and substituted by Directive (EU) 2019/944 with effect from 1 January 2021. The scope ranges from metering and billing of electricity, through demand response to priority dispatch and grid access for high-efficiency cogeneration. Regarding the priority dispatch and grid access, the Fourth Electricity Directive repeals some pro-cogeneration rules adopted in Article 15 of the Energy Efficiency Directive, in its previous version (see Chapter 4 of this book). From the beginning of 2020, the rules provided in the previous version of Article 15(5) are no longer valid. This applies to bigger CHP sources (neither small-scale nor micro-cogeneration CHP units). Under Article 70(5)(a)(i) of the Fourth Electricity Directive, the first two subparagraphs of Article 15(5) of the Energy Efficiency Directive have been deleted. On their basis, the EU Member States were to ensure that their transmission and distribution system operators, responsible for dispatching the generating units in their territory, provided facilitation for electricity generated in high-efficiency CHP. This concerned: first, guaranteeing the transmission and distribution; second, providing priority or guaranteed access; and third, providing priority when dispatching electricity generating installations. In effect, deleting these pro-cogeneration rules implied changes in the transparency of rules on access ranking and dispatch priorities (see Chapter 4).

The new rules for grid and market issues for high-efficiency cogeneration, coming into force from 1 January 2020, are set by the amended Article 15 of the Energy Efficiency Directive and relevant provisions of the Fourth Electricity Directive and the Third Electricity Regulation. On the basis of Article 31(4) of Directive (EU) 2019/944 the priority dispatch for high-efficiency cogeneration units has become a remote possibility. In comparison to previous legal frameworks, the Member States are not obliged to ensure the priority dispatch – they may do it, if they so wish. Moreover, as amended in 2019, this possibility applies only to the distribution system operators. In addition, the dispatch priority, defined under Regulation (EU) 2019/943,[6] is limited to some small-scale cogeneration units – those using high-efficiency CHP with the installed capacity lower than 400 kW$_e$ (see Boscán 2019, p. 18). Interestingly, the Third Electricity Regulation does not refer to the category of "small-scale cogeneration unit" defined in the Energy Efficiency Directive where it "means a cogeneration unit with installed capacity below 1 MW$_e$". On the contrary, the Regulation in Article 12(4) introduces its own category within the small-scale cogeneration – called a "priority dispatch small-scale cogeneration unit".[7] An exception is provided for high-efficiency CHP units commissioned before 4 July 2019, which have been granted the priority dispatch under the previous rules (repealed provisions of Article 15(5) of Directive 2012/27/EU). Pursuant to Article 12(6) of the Third Electricity Regulation, high-efficiency CHP units commissioned before 4 July 2019, maintain the priority dispatch until these units are significantly modified. This applies to situations when a new connection agreement is needed, or the generation capacity of high-efficiency cogeneration units is increased.

The reasons to limit the possibilities for high-efficiency CHP have not been explained in the proposal on the electricity market, i.e. the Directive or the Regulation, delivered by the Commission in 2016. The drafted version of the Directive, apart from a brief reference to the disclosure of electricity from high-efficiency cogeneration (Commission 2016b, p. 21), delegates this matter to the proposal of the Regulation.[8] Moreover, this document does not provide any answers, as the wording of Explanatory Memorandum in terms of high-efficiency CHP is the same as in the proposal for the Directive (cf. Commission 2016a, p. 20). In both cases, the two Memorandums refer to the explanation of the specific provisions of the Regulation.

What justifies the reasoning on the legislation offered for combined heat and power is the other documentation elaborated on by the Commission, i.e. the Impact Assessment (Commission 2016c) and the Evaluation Report (Commission 2016e), which accompany the Clean Energy Package. As discussed in the Impact Assessment, unconditional dispatch incentives could result in positive variable production costs in CHP (Commission 2016c, p. 44). Moving from the priority dispatch to full merit order-based dispatch for high-efficiency cogeneration, changes these circumstances significantly; under the merit order, it is unlikely that cogeneration will be dispatched first (Commission 2016c, p. 44). However, operating high-efficiency cogeneration under merit order will enable the Member States "to use flexibility resources to their maximum extent, creating e.g. incentives for CHP to use back-up boilers or heat storage to satisfy heat demand in case of low electricity demand" as assessed by the Commission (2016c, p. 44). The lack of priority dispatch forces a change in the market behaviour of high marginal cost technologies like biomass or some CHP units[9] ("incentivized to making best use of the inherent flexibility that their technology can provide to a power system"). The change is enforced by bringing those technologies closer to the role performed by gas-fired power plants operating in periods of high prices – high residual load (Commission 2016d, pp. 11–12). This results in the competition between gas-fired units and marginal cost technologies, including certain cogeneration units like oil-fired or waste-fired CHP (cf. Difs & Trygg 2009, pp. 613–614).[10]

This micro-dimension of flexibility has another macro-effect related to energy systems. Growing production of electricity from renewable energy sources, mainly wind and solar power, makes it necessary to establish solutions in case of minor, or very minor, hourly or daily generation. The answer to this challenge may be a more flexible electricity system (see Commission 2016c, p. 93). To reach it, three types of policy options were offered at the stage of initial works on the Clean Energy Package (cf. Commission 2016a, p. 110). One could call them "zero scenario", "mix cascade scenario", and "max scenario". In the "zero scenario" the rules on priority dispatch are maintained, as under the Energy Efficiency Directive (2012 version). The "max scenario" includes deleting the priority dispatch and access to the grid. Finally, the "mix cascade scenario" is a mixture of three step-by-step sub-options: (a) "level playing field"; (b) "strengthening short-term markets"– including sub-option (a); and (c) "demand response/distributed resources"– covering sub-options (a) and (b) (see Commission 2016a, p. 110). These scenarios reflect "a different degree of ambition to change the market, as well as the different views expressed among stakeholders on how strong the proposed interventions should be" (Commission 2016a, p. 94).

The "zero" and "max" scenarios are quite clear. The "mix" scenario – due to its step-by-step character – may need further comments. Apart from the measures on short-term markets (b)[11] and the tools for demand response and distributed resources (c),[12] the basis for the "mix" option included abolishing the priority dispatch for renewables, indigenous fuels, and cogeneration. The aim was to create "a level playing field" and tackling "barriers preventing demand response from participating in the energy and reserve markets" (Commission 2016a, p. 93). In this area, the following possibilities were discussed: "Option 0: do nothing"; "Option 0+: Non-regulatory approach"; "Option 1: Abolish priority dispatch and priority access"; "Option 2: Limit priority dispatch and/or priority access to emerging technologies and/or small plants"; and "Option 3: Abolish priority dispatch and introduce clear curtailment and re-dispatch rules to replace priority access" (Commission 2016d, pp. 9–11). The first three options ranged from pure theory (Option 0) to a kind of theory (Options 0+ and 1). The last two options, however, seemed to be preferable as their close links and interdependence made it possible to combine them (when implemented). The adopted legislation, included in the framework of the Clean Energy Package, confirms it.

The established provisions of the Third Electricity Regulation show that, in general, the priority dispatch has been abolished (with some exceptions), as proposed under Option 2. Apart from the emerging technologies – where a possibility of granting the priority dispatch is justified by the need of gaining experience for the non-mature technologies (Commission 2016d, p. 10), the Regulation introduced another category. This was the priority dispatch small-scale cogeneration unit, shadowed by small renewable energy sources, also having this possibility. However, in terms of renewable, the Member States "shall ensure" the priority dispatch, whereas with respect to high-efficiency cogeneration they "may provide" it. The aim of this concession derives from a postulate of reducing the administrative burdens, and facilitating technical matters related to dispatching power units operated by unprofessional owners or local entities (see Commission 2016d, p. 10). Their market-power and influence on the market is minor and incomparable to the scale of power and impact that professional medium and large energy utilities have on the electricity sector.

Providing the exemption for small-scale capacity required setting the ceiling for the needs of qualification of units. Regarding combined heat and power, this finally reached 400 kW$_e$ (priority dispatch small-scale cogeneration unit); however, while working on the Third Electricity Regulation, different levels have been evaluated. The initial version of the proposal provided the possibility of granting priority dispatch for high-efficiency CHP units with the installed electricity capacity lower than 500 kW (Commission 2016a). This early proposal was juxtaposed with the Council's provisional position offering 250 kW in this regard (see Council 2017), subsequently increased to 350 kW (Council 2018), and finally to the (adopted) European Parliaments' proposal of 400 kW (European Parliament 2018). Additionally, in the initial proposal of the Commission (2016a) it was the transmission system operators who were responsible for giving the priority when dispatching high-efficiency cogeneration units (drafted Article 11 (2)).

Due to their correlations, discussing Option 2 makes it necessary to also analyse Option 3. As the final legislation is a hybrid option, consisting of priority dispatch for small capacity – including cogeneration and the rules on redispatching with curtailment, provided by the amended law[13] – a few remarks on this subject are necessary. This option moves the market – so market-based energy units are used first.[14] Accordingly, pursuant to Article 13(2) of Regulation (EU) 2019/943 "[t]he resources that are redispatched shall be selected from among generating facilities, energy storage or demand response using market-based mechanisms and shall be financially compensated". Then, if no such market-based units are available, the minimum compensation rules are introduced to provide repayment either related to additional costs – if higher, or to a relevant proportion (high) of lost revenues. The compensation limits the additional investment risk associated with the loss of priority access, and so reduces the increase of capital costs (Commission 2016d, p. 11). As a result, system operators should be motivated to conduct a cost-based assessment of the alternatives available to solve basic grid problems ("situations of system stress", e.g. congestion of grid), thus making space for more innovative solutions like energy storage (Commission 2016d, p. 11). In terms of the costs of compensation for curtailment under Option 3, they are to be covered by system operators. However, total system costs should remain at the level of the pre-Option, as they are combined with the current subsidy schemes for certain types of energy technologies (see Commission 2016d, p. 11).[15]

To limit discrimination of smaller units (including high-efficiency cogeneration), examples of which are excessive curtailment or not-fully equal compensation, more transparency should be provided (Commission 2016d, p. 11). This postulate is reflected in Article 13(1) of the Third Electricity Regulation, where both types of redispatching (of generation and of demand response) have to be subject to objective, transparent, and non-discriminatory criteria; redispatching must also be open to all kinds of technologies covering energy generation, storage and demand response, regardless of the localisation within the EU ("unless technically not feasible").

Moreover, system operators are obliged to guarantee the capability of the grid to transfer electricity produced from high-efficiency cogeneration with minimum possible redispatching (the same applies to electricity produced from renewable energy sources).[16] According to Article 13(5) of the Third Electricity Regulation this approach depends on the maintenance and safety issues of the grid; to some extent this limits the guarantee's scope (cf. Nouicer & Meeus 2019, p. 53). However, the occurrence of arbitrary requirements related to these issues (which could limit the guaranty) is minimised by transparent and non-discriminatory criteria introduced by energy regulators and system operators. Apart from guaranteeing the minimum possible redispatching, the criteria have to cover grid- and market-related operational tools aimed at reducing the downward redispatching of electricity generated in high-efficiency CHP and renewables (e.g. digitalisation of the grid). These criteria also have to safeguard the flexibility of the grid. The tools for reducing the previously mentioned downward redispatching and the services to improve the flexibility of the grid are then reported to the national energy regulators on an annual basis.[17] This may entail a regulatory action. Pursuant to Article 13(4) of Regulation (EU) 2019/943, the regulators submit the report to the Agency for the Cooperation of Energy Regulators, publish a summary of the data included in the report, and present their recommendations for necessary improvements (if needed).

Finally, the Regulation also establishes provisions for applying non-market-based downward redispatching of generation, energy storage, and demand response. This may happen, when no other market-based alternative is available; all the available market-based resources have been used up or are too low in certain situations of grid congestion.[18] Where this type of redispatching could occur with respect to combined heat and power, the following principles apply. First, electricity generated in high-efficiency CHP can be subjected to downward redispatching only when there are no other alternative solutions (apart from downward redispatching of renewable energy sources), or when other solutions would result in disproportionate costs or cause serious threats to grid security. Second, regarding the self-generated electricity in renewables and high-efficiency CHP (which is not transmitted into the grid) it is not subject to downward redispatching, unless no other solution would solve the issues related to grid security. Moreover, the conducted redispatching – regardless of the one giving priority to renewables (as in first), or concerning the self-generated electricity (second) – has to be "duly and transparently justified" (Article 13(6)(d) of the Third Electricity Regulation). The justification has to be included in the previously-mentioned reports.

In general, using non-market redispatching results in financial compensation (as shown in Option 3) – except for those producers who have a connection agreement which does not guarantee reliable energy supply. The compensation has to, at the very least, meet the higher one of the elements listed in Article 13(7) of the Third Electricity Regulation (or their combination – "if applying only the higher would lead to an unjustifiably low or an unjustifiably high compensation"). These elements include: additional operating cost resulting from redispatching (e.g. additional fuel cost, or backup heat in terms of the high-efficiency CHP), and lost net revenues from the day-ahead sale of electricity.

The proposed – and later passed – legislative changes on the legal environment relevant to cogeneration, have been discussed with different stakeholders. Among them one should list: the institutional EU platforms for deliberation as the European Economic and Social Committee, the European Committee of the Regions, as well as branch organisations like COGEN Europe. In this context, the European Economic and Social Committee (2017) underlined the importance of cogeneration in future energy markets based on flexibility and balancing (thanks to its high efficiency). The Committee evaluated CHP's characteristics alongside renewables, noting that they:

> give rise to specific advantages, which the European Commission mentions to some extent in its proposals for the new market design ... [but], the Commission's proposal could be more coherent and concise when it comes to orient the market rules around these advantages.
> (European Economic and Social Committee 2017)

This comment should be supplemented with an assessment by COGEN Europe, which emphasised technical possibilities that allow reaching a higher level of flexibility in the operation of CHP units. According to COGEN Europe this concerns "a significant fraction of the CHP fleet", which could be designed or redesigned to improve its flexibility by such means as partial load capabilities, enhancing electrical components, or adding heat storage facilities (Commission 2016d, p. 15). However, achieving this flexibility "may come at the expense of the site efficiency and industrial productivity" warned COGEN Europe (Commission 2016d, p. 15).

Apart from the matter of flexibility, followed by a possibility of improving market liquidity with the use of combined heat and power (as being one of the dispersed energy sources), cogeneration was also acknowledged in the European Economic and Social Committee's assessment (2017). Here, cogeneration was presented as the technology enabling energy consumers to become energy producers, while in the new energy market "[m]aking consumers more active participants plays a vital role". This bottom-up approach was enhanced by another body – the European Committee of Regions (2017). In its assessment it went a step further, urging the European Commission to grant the Member States "more flexibility in relation to ... the protection of small-scale projects, including combined heat and power plants that are connected to local district heating and cooling networks".

The Committee's call should be juxtaposed with a specific comment coming from the cogeneration sector. Its representatives emphasised the need to link the legal approach offered for combined heat and power with the regulatory framework designed for renewable energy sources. COGEN Europe insisted on creating (at the European level) at least a "CHP – RES parity" regarding the solution proposed on the electricity market, given that "there are no additional policy measures that would compensate for the loss in optimal operation ensured through priority of dispatch for certain types of CHP [units]" (Commission 2016d, p. 15). How has the EU addressed this issue? The following quote explains the rationale behind it:

> [t]he [CHP] parallelism to RES is maintained in all options, whereas the additional costs and possible loss of efficiency [of cogeneration] have to be balanced with the economic cost of significant amounts of inflexible conventional [CHP] generation in a high-RES system.
> (Commission 2016d, p. 15)

The question which could be posed concerns the reality of this parity, i.e. to what extent does the CHP – RES parallelism exist? There are many indications that cogeneration – following the path of development of renewable energy sources – begins to lag behind RES with every step towards the common energy market; slightly, but noticeably. This concerns the priority still attached to renewables at the European level, contrasted with the weakening EU attitude to combined heat and power (with some exceptions offered for high-efficiency CHP). This disparity stems also from different grounds on which these two elements have been constructed out of the EU climate-energy policy. In fact, improving the situation of renewable energy sources is a goal of a long-standing tradition, whereas the promotion of cogeneration – (in general, not taking into account 18% target for 2010 because of its non-binding character) – has been rather a measure (as for the needs of enhancing energy efficiency) than a goal for the European Union.

Cogeneration unpacked: current legal regime on CHP in the EU

The current regulatory environment – the legal nexus on combined heat and power, established by the legislation which brought the Clean Energy Package in 2018 and 2019, is built on the cornerstone of the Energy

Efficiency Directive (2012). Cogeneration – just to remind the reader – defined there as "the simultaneous generation in one process of thermal energy and electrical or mechanical energy" is nowadays seen not only through the prism of its features. Naturally, its pro-efficient nature, embodied by high-efficiency units meeting the criteria of Directive's Annex II, is still vital – as proven by recent legal changes. In many cases, operations other than high-efficiency cogeneration units on the EU internal energy market will be limited or phased-out (see Sokołowski 2018a). However, in line with the revision provided by the Clean Energy Package apart from its high efficiency, also the scale of cogeneration plays an increasingly important role. Here, what really matters is meeting the levels provided for small-scale cogeneration (installed capacity below 1 MW_e), priority dispatch small-scale cogeneration units (installed capacity below $400kW_e$) or micro-cogeneration units (installed capacity below 50 kW_e). This enables, e.g. applying the simple procedure of the "install and inform" type, still available under Article 15(5) of the Energy Efficiency Directive (maintained in the revised version). It allows the Member States to offer this type of procedure for connecting micro-cogeneration; just as before, the Article empowers them to facilitate the grid connection for high-efficiency CHP of small-scale.

As previously discussed, cogeneration is also an element of the Energy Union. The comprehensive assessment of the potential for the application of high-efficiency cogeneration in each Member State, as presented under Article 14(1) of the Energy Efficiency Directive (see Chapter 4 of this book), is one of the key elements of the analytical basis of the Member States' integrated national energy and climate plans prepared under Regulation (EU) 2018/1999. The integrated national plans reach as far as to the regime established by the previous CHP Directive (2004/8/EC); they are indirectly related to the analysis of the national potentials for high-efficiency cogeneration conducted under the CHP Directive.[19] Apart from taking this analysis into account, the linkage to the comprehensive assessment referred to in Article 14(1) of the Energy Efficiency Directive, incorporates identification (and also estimation in terms of identification conducted on-site in residential and service sites) of heating and cooling supply, presented in GWh per year, into the analytical basis of the integrated national plans. Regardless of whether cogeneration is the primary or secondary element of the comprehensive assessment (see Chapter 4), the assessment should be divided by technology, including high-efficiency heat and power cogeneration; in practice shown within residential, services, industry, and any other energy-consuming sectors,[20] and where possible, categorised into conventional (fossil) and renewable sources.

Moreover, as discussed in Chapter 4, the comprehensive assessment may be a dynamic document. This depends on the Commission's request that Member States update their assessments (such an update should be done on a five-year basis). As the provisions enabling such action have neither been repealed nor amended in the recent revision of the Energy Efficiency Directive, this kind of request is still possible. The Commission should submit such a request at least one year ahead of schedule, i.e. the five-year period. Furthermore, the request – and thus the update of the assessments – could be useful for the needs of the integrated national energy and climate plans in terms of this dimension (energy efficiency) and the indicative national energy efficiency contribution to reaching the EU's 2030 energy efficiency goal of 32.5%. This, obviously, would only be possible if the scheduled timing is respected.[21] In the same way, under the current legal regime the Member States are still obliged to conduct the cost-benefit analysis of installing high-efficiency CHP. Article 15(5) and the following paragraphs – relevant in this field – have not been altered by the last revision of the Energy Efficiency Directive. This concerns both the obligation to the cost-benefit analysis as well as the exemptions from this duty (see Chapter 4).

As one may notice, the current regulatory framework on cogeneration combines the 2012 legislation with the reform conducted in 2018–2019. On the on hand, as widely analysed in the previous subchapter, the priorities and guarantees offered for high-efficiency CHP in the 2012 version of the Energy Efficiency Directive (in terms of access to the grid, dispatch, and transmission of the distribution of electricity) are no longer available. They have been replaced by new provisions on priority dispatch small-scale cogeneration units (installed capacity below 400 kW_e) as well as the legal regime on redispatching, established by the Third Electricity Regulation. On the other hand, system operators still have to follow the requirements adopted in Annex XII to the Directive (see Chapter 4). Despite slight changes, its range and general approach presented there have not been revised. Under Annex XII the operators have to publish their standard rules on the cost of technical adaptations of their gird, including the connection. They also have to inform new producers of electricity in high-efficiency CHP wishing to be connected about the costs (complex and detailed estimation) and timing (max 24 months), providing them with standardised and simplified procedures of the connection.

Another element not changed by the 2019 revision, was the matter of public support for cogeneration. As before, under Article 14(11) of Directive 2012/27/EU the Member States may provide public support for high-efficiency cogeneration achieving primary energy savings effectively. Public support, covering cogeneration, district heating generation, and network infrastructure (where applicable), falls under the regime of the EU rules on state aid (see Ezcurra 2014; Flåm 2009; Hancher & Salerno 2011). In these terms, one should refer to the Guidelines on State aid for environmental protection and energy 2014–2020 (Commission 2014), intended to be prolonged until the end of 2022 (Commission 2019).[22] Established pursuant to Article 107(3)(c) of the Treaty on the Functioning of the European Union, the Guidelines are aimed at facilitating the development of selected economic activities in the EU in a way which does not negatively impact internal trade to the extent of conflicting common interest.

With respect to their scope, the Guidelines are applied to public aid provided for environmental or energy reasons ("environmental protection or energy objectives") in all fields covered by the Treaty – if such are listed in the Guidelines' Section 1.2. Among the acknowledged environmental and energy measures – for which state aid may comply with the EU rules on the internal energy market – one may find "aid for energy efficiency measures, including cogeneration and district heating and district cooling". The possibility of granting this type of aid to cogeneration derives from the EU's energy saving goals, contained within the framework of the Climate and Energy Package; nevertheless, by referring to the Energy Efficiency Directive it also goes beyond it. All together they "pave the way for further energy-efficiency improvement beyond 2020" (Commission 2014), which accordingly enables extending the duration of the Guidelines (cf. Commission 2019).

The aid stems from the need to tackle negative externalities, "the market failures hampering an increased level of environmental protection or a well-functioning secure, affordable and sustainable internal energy market" (Paragraph 35 of the Guidelines). These failures hinder the environmental effects that can be reached with the help of cogeneration: the environmental goals for energy efficiency and reduction of emissions.[23] Just like in the Energy Efficiency Directive, public aid granted for cogeneration by the Member States is steered by reaching high efficiency in the CHP sector. Hence, under Paragraph 139 of the Guidelines only investments in high-efficiency CHP can be qualified as compatible with the internal market (if they were financed by state aid). Additionally, state aid offered for cogeneration and district heating using waste has to comply with the waste hierarchy principle. It is based on the following steps: waste prevention, readiness for re-use of waste, recycling, other recovery (e.g. energy recovery), and finally – waste disposal (see Article 4(1) of Directive 2008/98/EC). High level of efficiency reflects an environmental contribution achieved as the effect of the aid when applying high-efficiency CHP. To cap it, the Guidelines accept different measurable indicators whose core is the volume of saved energy; the volume may result from various actions ranging from lower energy performance and higher energy productivity or lower energy consumption and reduced fuel usage.[24]

The form of state aid may differ. However, among different ways of supporting energy efficiency, there is a repayable advance directly addressed in the Guidelines; as emphasised in Paragraph 147, this type of aid "may be considered as an appropriate State aid instrument in particular if the revenues from the energy-efficiency measure are uncertain" (Commission 2014). If the aid has the character of an investment, the level of aid intensities – provided in the Guidelines' Annex 1 – applies. In terms of the aid for cogeneration installations, regardless of their scale (small, medium-sized, or large enterprise) these levels account for 100% of eligible costs, i.e. "the extra investment costs in tangible and/or in intangible assets which are directly linked to the achievement of the common objective" (Paragraph 72 of the Guidelines). The way of granting the aid is based on a competitive bidding process which must be "clear, transparent and non-discriminatory".[25]

The Guidelines also allow granting the operating aid to high-efficiency combined heat and power. Pursuant to Paragraph 151 this applies to two types of situations (Commission 2014). First, the aid may cover CHP units producing electricity and heat if these production costs are higher than the market price. Second, it concerns industrial CHP units where – in comparison with the market price of one unit of conventional energy – higher production cost of one unit of energy in cogeneration can be demonstrated. Moreover, when granting the operational aid for high-efficient combined heat and power, the Member States shall refer to the conditions provided for granting this type of aid for electricity produced in renewable energy sources.

This concerns Section 3.3.2.1 of the Guidelines; for the needs of cogeneration it should be interpreted in a suitable way. Generally, the rules are offered for renewables, and they gradually replace feed-in tariffs by competitive bidding. The application includes three steps (see Mäntysaari 2015, p. 154). The 2015–2016 transitional period (first phase) set up aid granted in a bidding process for 5% of the planned renewable capacity as the minimum. Leaving this period aside, from the beginning of 2016 (second phase) all new aid schemes and measures on renewables (so also on high-efficiency cogeneration) – except units with an installed electricity capacity of less than 500 kW or demonstration projects – have been based on the rules listed in Paragraph 124:

(a) aid is granted as a premium in addition to the market price (premium) whereby the generators sell its electricity directly in the market;
(b) beneficiaries are subject to standard balancing responsibilities, unless no liquid intra-day markets exist [but outsourcing balancing responsibilities to other companies is possible]; and
(c) measures are put in place to ensure that generators have no incentive to generate electricity under negative prices.

(Commission 2014)

Finally, from 1 January 2017 (third phase), the aid for renewables and high-efficiency cogeneration shall be granted via a clear, transparent, and non-discriminatory bidding process. However, some exceptions to the obligatory bidding are provided by the Guidelines. This refers to certain situations: where there is a limited number of eligible projects; where the competitive process would be accompanied by very high or very low bidding (to avoid strategic bidding or underbidding).[26] The exceptions also apply to units with the installed capacity lower than 1 MW_e, or demonstration projects.[27] If the competitive bidding is exempted, according to Paragraph 128 of the

Guidelines, then the rules provided for phase two apply. The competitive bidding process affects one more field: notifying the Commission about individual aid. Pursuant to Paragraph 20 of the Guidelines, if such bidding was not applied, and the aid was granted under the aid scheme as operating aid for cogeneration of a capacity bigger than 300 MW$_e$,[28] this aid has to be proclaimed according to Article 108(3) of the Treaty.

Apart from state aid, another field where cogeneration meets renewables is the RED II, which extends the provisions on CHP (see Chapter 4 of this book), particularly in terms of renewable energy in heating and cooling. RED II addresses this field in Article 23 (heating and cooling in general) and Article 24 (DH & C). The first (Article 23) provides a pathway for increasing the share of renewable energy in this regard. It obliges Member States to reach 1.3% growth,[29] divided between two periods, 2021–2025, and 2026–2030, with the 2020 share of renewables in heating and cooling as the starting point. The latter (Article 24) establishes specific framework for the promotion of DH & C. Within this framework, under Article 24(4), Member States have to implement measures necessary to achieve the heating and cooling goal discussed earlier, choosing either of them. These are the "measures that can be expected to trigger that average annual increase in years with normal climatic conditions". Other measures include a duty imposed on DH & C operators to connect preferable suppliers (using renewables as well as waste heat and cold), and an obligation to buy heat and cold from third-party suppliers (again, using renewables or waste heat). Within this scope, RED II institutes an exemption from these duties being possible due to the usage of high-efficiency cogeneration. It concerns a situation in which "the system lacks the necessary capacity due to other supplies of ... heat or cold produced by high-efficiency cogeneration", or when "efficient district heating and cooling ... exploits high-efficiency cogeneration". The first (Article 24(5)) results in a possible refusal to exercise the duties of operators aimed at supporting third-party suppliers, whereas the second (Article 24(6)) releases from the application of the aforementioned duty in general.

Finally, when discussing current legal environment on combined heat and power, the recent revision of the EU ETS Directive should be addressed. It includes new rules for distribution of free allowances for CHP delivered by Directive (EU) 2018/410 (see Massai & Beyet 2018). The amendment introduces a procedure for dealing with the remaining allowances which resulted from not achieving the maximum level of possible free allocation. Pursuant to the new wording of Article 10a(5) of Directive 2003/87/EC, if the maximum amount (ceiling) which respects the auctioning share, is not reached by the sum of free allocations on an annual basis, the prevention (or limitation) of the reduction of free allocations to respect the auctioning share in later years will be applied. This will be done by using the remaining allowances up to that amount. If that ceiling is reached, free allocations shall be adjusted in a uniform manner. Moreover, the free allocation for DH is exempted from the decrease of free allowances granted to sectors considered to be at low or no risk of carbon leakage.[30]

Directive (EU) 2018/410 is followed by Delegated Regulation (EU) 2019/331 adopted by the Commission in December 2018. Due to the need for "clarity as regards the rules applicable between 2021 and 2030",[31] it repeals the Benchmarking Decision of 2011 due to substantial changes in the EU ETS. In contrast to the Benchmarking Decision, Delegated Regulation (EU) 2019/331 addresses combined heat and power in a more complex way. This pertains to the rules for assigning fuels and emissions of CHP adopted in Annex VII "Data monitoring methods" of the Regulation. Pursuant to Section 8 of the Annex, the rules apply when the operator of cogeneration units and sub-units attributes inputs, outputs, and emissions coming from combined heat and power for the needs of updating benchmark values. For this purpose, Annex VII contains six equations, enabling to determine emissions, energy input, or attribution factors related to CHP.[32]

To sum up these circumstances, one may try to "unpack" the regulatory regime on cogeneration, i.e. all legislative and policy steps conducted by the European Union, or earlier – the European Community. In doing so, the following two diagrams may be of help. They show the main legislation targeting cogeneration in the EU, categorised into four areas of impact (Figure 6.1) and presented as elements of subsequent packages established by the EU (Figure 6.2).

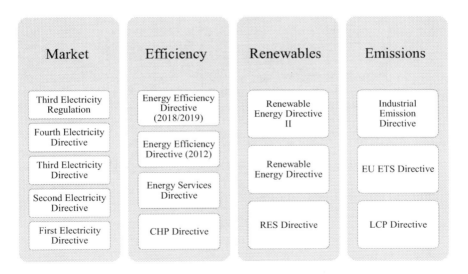

Figure 6.1 Main EU legislation on CHP in the four energy areas of impact

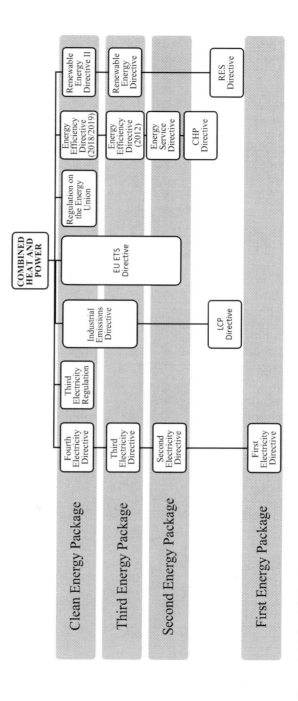

Figure 6.2 Main EU legislation on CHP within the European legislative packages

Recent developments: a follow-up to the statistics on cogeneration

As the regulatory framework aggregated in the preceding subchapter, the statistics on combined heat and power (for 2016 and 2017) highlight the current state-of-the-art CHP in the European Union (cf. Stankeviciute & Krook Riekkola 2014). The data summarises the review delivered in Chapter 5. It shows recent developments in the CHP industry from a different perspective – from a position where seeing the big picture is necessary.

EU-28 CHP: year-to-year report, decade-to-decade comments

According to Eurostat (2019a), in 2016 almost 120 GW of CHP units produced around 360 TWh of electricity in the European Union (accounting for 11% of total gross electricity generated in the EU-28). The installed thermal capacity was more than twice as big (almost 273 GW), producing over 2,812 PJ of heat in the EU. By country, the largest total CHP capacity (electrical and heat) was noted in Germany: 37.21 GW and 94.60 GW, Poland: 8.72 GW and 23.78 GW, the Czech Republic 9.03 GW and 20.79 GW, and the Netherlands 8.97 GW and 15.98 GW. The biggest production in cogeneration was reported in Germany, Italy, and Poland which generated respectively around 88 TWh (DE), 40 TWh (IT), and 28 TWh (PL) of electricity along with 698 PJ (DE), 220 PJ (IT), and 246 PJ (PL) of heat. The Netherlands, Finland, and Spain can also be included among the leaders of electricity and heat produced by CHP units.[33] With respect to the share of cogeneration in the total gross electricity production, three top positions were taken by Latvia: 48.5%, Denmark: 39.4%, and Finland: 31.8% (Eurostat 2019a).[34] Table 6.1 shows this data in each of the EU-28 countries.

When looking at the year-to-year developments (2016 to 2017), CHP in Europe recorded small growth (Eurostat 2019a, 2019b).[35] When analysing how the European cogeneration has changed over ten years, one should highlight its constant share in total gross electricity generation, which has been oscillating around 11% in recent years. The levels related to the production of electricity in CHP and its installed capacity (in electricity) between 2006 (EU-27) and 2016 (EU-28) differ slightly, noting a minor decrease.[36] In contrast, the production of heat in cogeneration accounted for a bigger drop, reaching almost 300 PJ in a ten-year period (see Eurostat 2019a).

EU-28 CHP fuel mix (2016)

In terms of the fuel structure, in 2016, the majority of Member States (15 out of 28) used natural gas as the main fuel for CHP units, with Ireland

Table 6.1 Production of electricity and heat in cogeneration in the European Union in 2016–2017 (EU-28)

Member State	CHP electricity generation [TWh] 2016	2017	share of CHP in total gross electricity generation 2016	2017	total CHP electrical capacity [GW] 2016	2017	total CHP heat production [PJ] 2016	2017	total CHP heat capacity [GW] 2016	2017
Belgium	12.19	12.49	14.2%	14.4%	2.21	2.32	104.39	108.66	5.04	5.11
Bulgaria	3.64	3.53	8.0%	7.7%	1.49	1.23	39.35	40.14	4.73	4.58
Czech Rep.	8.38	7.99	10.1%	9.2%	9.03	8.03	101.56	103.52	20.79	22.07
Denmark	12.03	11.82	39.4%	38.1%	5.86	5.85	94.95	94.42	8.79	8.81
Germany	87.94	94.36	13.5%	14.4%	37.21	39.63	697.97	703.16	94.60	101.34
Estonia	0.94	1.09	7.7%	8.4%	0.19	0.00	3.25	13.60	0.65	0.52
Ireland	2.17	2.16	7.1%	7.0%	0.31	0.32	11.24	11.78	0.59	0.62
Greece	2.59	2.15	4.8%	3.9%	0.53	0.33	18.92	14.61	1.32	0.94
Spain	27.48	28.77	10.0%	10.4%	4.16	4.62	138.82	139.20	6.40	9.81
France	14.96	16.64	2.7%	3.0%	6.07	6.28	163.91	177.59	14.86	15.30
Croatia	1.47	2.00	11.5%	16.7%	0.75	0.84	16.27	18.81	2.16	2.16
Italy	40.34	40.96	13.9%	13.8%	8.51	8.43	219.77	219.89	14.01	13.24
Cyprus	0.03	0.03	0.6%	0.6%	0.01	0.01	0.12	0.14	0.01	0.01
Latvia	3.12	2.84	48.5%	37.7%	1.29	1.28	14.51	14.20	1.21	1.25
Lithuania	1.11	1.10	25.9%	26.2%	0.59	0.60	9.54	10.42	1.19	1.55
Luxembourg	0.35	0.35	15.7%	15.5%	0.12	0.11	2.28	2.64	0.20	0.21
Hungary	4.82	4.65	15.1%	14.1%	1.47	1.48	24.65	25.21	2.82	2.91
Malta	0.24	0.21	28.3%	12.6%	0.14	0.14	0.09	0.07	0.02	0.02
Netherlands	30.78	31.41	26.7%	26.8%	8.97	9.40	174.33	180.47	15.98	16.60

Austria	10.90	9.53	16.0%	13.4%	3.43	2.89	114.94	116.04	8.85	8.96
Poland	27.60	28.43	16.6%	16.7%	8.72	9.18	246.47	253.30	23.78	24.17
Portugal	6.25	6.40	10.4%	10.8%	1.19	1.17	61.69	60.04	3.76	3.74
Romania	5.29	5.79	8.1%	9.0%	1.85	1.82	45.88	46.99	6.28	5.47
Slovenia	1.21	1.26	7.3%	7.7%	0.35	0.37	10.76	11.12	0.81	0.85
Slovakia	3.01	3.46	11.1%	12.5%	1.00	1.67	34.42	36.88	4.02	3.38
Finland	21.83	21.68	31.8%	32.1%	5.86	6.47	241.63	246.53	14.59	16.86
Sweden	9.21	9.01	5.9%	5.5%	3.89	3.04	91.07	91.98	8.42	7.87
United Kingdom	19.80	21.63	5.8%	6.4%	4.57	4.46	129.78	139.79	7.12	7.45
European Union (EU-28)	**359.66**	**371.71**	**11.0%**	**11.3%**	**119.77**	**121.99**	**2,812.54**	**2,881.17**	**272.99**	**285.78**

Source: (Eurostat 2019a, 2019b).

Table 6.2 Fuel used in cogeneration in the European Union (EU-28) in 2016

Member State	fuel used for CHP [PJ]	solid fossil fuels and peat	oil and oil products	natural gas	renewables	other fuels
biggest share: natural gas						
Ireland	23.82	3.6%	1.3%	92.1%	2.9%	0.1%
Netherlands	338.81	3.8%	3.8%	81.0%	5.8%	5.5%
Spain	302.48	2.3%	8.3%	79.2%	1.7%	8.6%
Croatia	27.27	2.5%	10.7%	78.0%	8.8%	0.0%
Luxembourg	4.26	0.0%	0.0%	74.1%	25.4%	0.5%
United Kingdom	250.28	1.6%	14.2%	73.9%	6.6%	3.7%
Italy	451.71	3.2%	8.7%	65.2%	15.6%	7.3%
Hungary	58.39	10.1%	0.1%	63.0%	21.5%	5.3%
Latvia	31.56	0.2%	0.0%	62.8%	37.0%	0.0%
Romania	82.17	28.7%	4.8%	59.8%	6.4%	0.4%
Belgium	167.66	1.2%	1.4%	59.3%	16.2%	21.9%
France	260.02	4.7%	4.8%	50.3%	27.7%	12.5%
Germany	1,351,52	13.5%	4.3%	45.6%	23.3%	13.3%
Portugal	108.30	0.0%	7.9%	45.6%	46.0%	0.6%
Slovakia	56.45	24.1%	12.7%	33.7%	23.9%	5.6%
biggest share: renewables						
Cyprus	0.30	0.0%	7.0%	0.0%	93.0%	0.0%
Estonia	7.65	11.6%	24.5%	0.1%	61.2%	2.6%
Finland	387.97	25.1%	0.6%	9.5%	60.8%	4.1%
Sweden	145.17	9.1%	0.6%	7.4%	58.7%	24.1%
Denmark	155.04	29.6%	2.4%	14.9%	43.2%	10.0%
Lithuania	16.00	0.0%	12.8%	35.5%	40.4%	11.2%
Austria	184.52	7.8%	9.6%	37.6%	38.1%	7.0%
biggest share: solid fossil fuels and peat						
Poland	421.24	70.8%	7.5%	10.1%	10.6%	1.0%
Czech Republic	165.76	68.1%	0.7%	13.0%	16.0%	2.3%
Slovenia	18.40	50.3%	0.2%	27.0%	20.6%	2.0%
Bulgaria	64.72	42.3%	1.5%	39.1%	5.3%	11.9%
biggest share: oil and oil products						
Greece	26.75	13.5%	30.7%	29.6%	14.0%	12.2%
biggest share: other fuels						
Malta	1.98	0.0%	0.0%	0.0%	3.3%	96.7%

Source: (Eurostat 2019a).

(92.1%), the Netherlands (81%), Spain (79.2%), and Croatia (78%) having the biggest shares of natural gas in their energy mixes for cogeneration (Eurostat 2019a). According to Eurostat (2019a), seven EU countries used mainly renewables in their CHP units; these were Cyprus (93%), Estonia (61.2%), Finland (60.8%), Sweden (58.7%), Denmark (43.2%), as well as Lithuania (40.4%) and Austria (38.1%). However, the last two had a comparable share of gas used for the needs of cogeneration (Greece also had quite a big share of natural gas, but instead of renewables it was balanced with oil). Solid fossil fuels and peat were the major energy fuels in Poland (70.8%), the Czech Republic (68.1%), Slovenia (50.3%) and Bulgaria (42.3%), whereas other fuels were used almost exclusively in Malta (Eurostat 2019a). A juxtaposition of the Member States' fuel energy mixes in cogeneration is provided in Table 6.2 and on Figure 6.3.

Additionally, fuel portfolios of the Member States have changed slightly when comparing 2016 to 2017. Despite minor reductions in the usage of renewables noticeable in the annual survey in a few Member States, a more general growing tendency of renewable fuels used in cogeneration should be recorded (Eurostat 2019b).[37] There are many indicators that this trend will be maintained, steered by the policies and legislation – moving the European Union towards its goals on the usage of renewable energy sources.

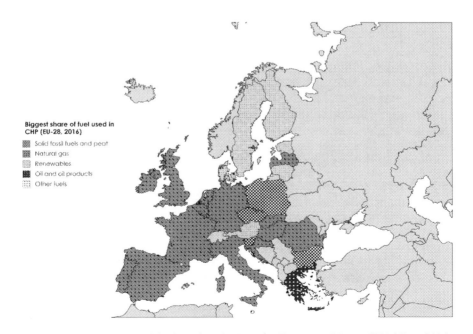

Figure 6.3 Biggest share of fuel used in CHP in the European Union (EU-28) in 2016

Finally, one cannot omit the data on primary energy savings achieved by the European cogeneration, as its contribution to the European climate action. Measured since 2016 (Eurostat 2019a), in that year they accounted for about 1,297 PJ. In 2017, this value was even higher – it reached almost 1,350 PJ (Eurostat 2019b).[38] Accordingly, this resulted in nearly 31 Mtoe (2016) and more than 32 Mtoe (2017) saved. In comparison, 2007's projection for the European Union in 2020 was for the primary energy consumptionto reach 1,842 Mtoe. At the same time, the 20% goal under the energy efficiency pillar of the EU climate action will require a reduction of 368 Mtoe. Thus the EU's 2020 energy consumption must not overcome 1,474 Mtoe of primary energy as provided in Article 3(1) of the Energy Efficiency Directive.

A regulatory box – the outcomes of the European action on combined heat and power

All the legislation and policies on cogeneration – combined with regulatory measures and tools to support and promote CHP – could be collected in one *regulatory box* – a joint category of European laws and policies on combined heat and power. Let us "unpack" it in the following sections. Additionally, by referring to its different elements – main measures and tools – let us recapitulate to conclude the topic of cogeneration (*cogenclude*). This will also involve a discussion on how the regulatory regime dedicated to combined heat and power evolved in the EU. In doing so – by referring to Freiberg's classification of the tools of regulation (Freiberg 2010, pp. 84–85) – let us divide this box into six practical categories: (i) economic tools; (ii) transactional regulation; (iii) authorisation as regulation; (iv) structural regulation; (v) informational regulation, and (vi) legal regulation.

Economic tools

Economic tools involve the allocation or use of resources of a tangible character like money or property (in all forms) – this includes, *inter alia*, tenders, tradable permits along with "cap and trade" schemes, price regulation, taxes, charges and levies, or bounties and subsidies (see Freiberg 2010, pp. 84–85, cf. Sokołowski 2016, pp. 85–86). One may find many examples of their use in the energy sector as a whole, as well as in the CHP industry. What varies here is the scale of the use of specific types of tools along with detailed solutions.

Let us start with tenders – discussed in the 1990s in terms of RWC producers joining tenders for new capacities. Tenders came back in the regime delivered by the Guidelines on State aid for environmental protection and energy 2014–2020 (Commission 2014), becoming the main way for granting aid for high-efficiency cogeneration support, which by rule has to be distributed through a clear, transparent, and non-discriminatory bidding process. The French tendering scheme for biomass-fired CHP, the Spanish measure for cogeneration with multi-annual tender schedule, or the new Polish "pay as bid" scheme dedicated to combined heat and power are all examples of the practical application of this tool.

Nevertheless, for a long-time price regulation for the European cogeneration has been steered by tariffs and certificates (quota systems) selected by the Member States as the operational support schemes for the CHP industry. The former (tariff/pricing schemes), in terms of their characteristics, are linked to the price of electricity delivered to the grid, offering a fixed price for it (feed-in tariff). They are also related to electricity market price with a fixed bonus on the market price of electricity (price premium scheme). The latter (certificates), are based on a two-step duty of electricity suppliers. The first step is to obtain a volume of certificates – bought either from the operators of cogeneration or on the certificate market. The second step is an alternative – to submit the certificates to the energy market regulator, or to pay a buy-out fee to fulfil their obligation. Regarding the application of this systems, the pro-CHP tariffs have been steering the development of the sector even before the era of energy market liberalisation (the Netherlands) or at its early stage (Italy). At different stages of the EU market reform in the energy sector, the tariffs have been used by Bulgaria, Cyprus, the Czech Republic, Denmark, Estonia, France, Germany, Greece, Hungary, Latvia, Lithuania, Luxembourg, Portugal, Slovakia, Slovenia, Spain, and the UK. With respect to certificate schemes for CHP (different from renewable certificates) such operational support has been offered to cogeneration in Belgium, Italy, and Poland.

Aside from bidding, tariffs, and certificates, traditional fiscal tools such as taxes have been used for the needs of combined heat and power in Europe. Being of an operational character, these tools allow for the tackling of risks related to fuel prices, and are quite stable in their nature (as a rule, tax regimes are rather rigid instruments). However, in the case of the CHP industry the role of these tools has not been a decisive market driver. Nevertheless, tools like tax write-offs for connecting buildings to DH (which existed in West Germany before the German reunification of 1990) or the Energy Taxation Directive (Directive 2003/96/EC) with the exemptions or reduced levels of taxation with respect to the energy used and produced by high-efficiency cogeneration, could be listed here. Energy tax exemptions have been applied for cogeneration in Finland, France, Germany, Italy, the Netherlands, Slovenia, Sweden, and the United Kingdom, whereas France and the United Kingdom (together with Denmark) have offered business tax exemption for CHP. Additionally, among other economic tools used for the development of CHP, one may find accelerated fiscal allowance for investments which have been adopted in Belgium, France, Ireland, the Netherlands, and the UK.

This wide category of economic tools includes other means, too, just to mention the EU ETS based on cap and trade mechanism with cogeneration as its element. Charges are related to accessing the grid (charges for connection of a CHP unit), while the rules on their costs were introduced at the EU level (Annex XII to the Directive 2012/27/EU). To some extent they correlated with the already-mentioned incentives (taxes and levies, see Climate Change Levy adopted in the UK). Eventually, one may find a common denominator – subsidies. However, in terms of their form they should not be confused with the tools of transactional regulation.

Transactional regulation

Regarding transactional regulation such tools as contract, procurement, or grant are the basis for distinguishing this category (Freiberg 2010, pp. 84–85, cf. Sokołowski 2016, pp. 85–86). Among the examples of their application in cogeneration initiatives such as financial grants offered in West Germany for constructing CHP plants or for conversing oil-fired heating systems to DH, grants for CHP feasibility studies established in the UK in 1970s could be mentioned. Capital grants to develop investments in the CHP sector have also been available in other Member States including Austria, Belgium, Cyprus, the Czech Republic, Denmark, Finland, Greece, Hungary, Ireland, Italy, the Netherlands, Latvia, Lithuania, Luxembourg, Poland, Portugal, Slovakia, Slovenia, and Spain.

Apart from grants, transactional regulation contains such tools as energy conservation loans and standby contracts – examples of their application may be found in the history of developing combined heat and power in the Netherlands. Moreover, transactional regulation includes the framework of standard contracts for RWC auto-producers and public utilities, voluntary environmental agreements concluded for the needs of cogeneration, and contracts financed under the Community's initiatives like the Joule, Thermie, or SAVE programmes.

Furthermore, the European regulatory framework on utilities' procurement in the field of electricity and heat, brought by Directive 93/38/EEC and subsequent legislation on this matter, also represents the category of transactional regulation. The same concerns the proposal to introduce a mandatory procurement system for electricity generated by renewables and high efficiency CHP in Latvia.

Authorisation as regulation

Authorisation as regulation combines such tools as licences, registrations, permissions, certificates, and accreditations – all these tools derive from the exclusive power of the authorities to approve certain forms of conduct (Freiberg 2010, pp. 84–85, cf. Sokołowski 2016, pp. 85–86). In terms of combined heat and power these tools exist in correlation with other regimes, like the framework on industrial emissions (determining possible exemptions, as under the LCP Directive of 2001), They are also addressed in an anti-barrier movement resulting in mitigating the regulatory barriers, including time-consuming bureaucracy with expensive procedures to obtain operating licences.

In this anti-barrier approach, the regulatory tools (authorisation as regulation) in terms of cogeneration consist of: streamlining procedures by reducing the time and costs of obtaining necessary permits; exempting entities using micro-CHP from authorisation procedures e.g. by providing them with a dedicated simple procedure like "install and inform"; and also elaborating on guidelines for authorisation of CHP units. This dimension of the regulatory tools also includes calls for reviewing the administrative procedures for small and medium-sized CHP addressed by the Energy Efficiency Directive.

Structural regulation

The possibility to influence physical, environmental, and process design defines structural regulation (Freiberg 2010, pp. 84–85, cf. Sokołowski 2016, pp. 85–86); this category is represented by guidelines on the energy efficient design of CHP units. In practice, this refers to BAT conclusions (2017 LCP BAT conclusions) setting the energy efficiency levels associated with BAT-AEELs along with monitoring and emission values (linked with the conclusions) set for cogeneration. Additionally, BAT conclusions distinguish between general levels for all combustion units of a given type, such as coal-fired units with separate provisions on CHP. They also introduce separate types of cogeneration units, like different categories of CHP CCGT. The structural regulation includes such tools as providing fast-track planning procedures for CHP power plants or considering the development of CHP units in grid planning provided by system operators.

Informational regulation

Informational regulation includes disclosure, performance indicators, and credit ratings – all the tools related to the access to knowledge and information (Freiberg 2010, pp. 84–85, cf. Sokołowski 2016, pp. 85–86). A mixture of different examples of their use can be listed here. Among them are such initiatives as the recommendation to develop expert dialogue on CHP, the establishment of advisory panels to promote combined heat and power (announced as early as the 1970s), or actions on the information about CHP and DH & C. Other examples include technical advice and training conducted under the SAVE and SAVE II programmes, along with a pro-consumer approach expressed by steps proposed with respect to energy bills (which could address energy and heat produced in cogeneration). Moreover, the whole system of guarantees of origin containing specific data on electricity and heat represents this type of regulation.

Finally, informational regulation also has a dimension directed towards cogeneration itself (so, it does not apply only to informing other participants of the market transactions – mainly customers or investors – about cogeneration). In this light, the measures contained in Annex XII to the Energy Efficiency Directive – designed to make system operators act transparently and fairly with respect to high-efficiency CHP – can be qualified as informational regulation. The operators are obliged to share certain information with the new producers of electricity from high-efficiency CHP willing to be connected to the grid. The information relates to such issues as the costs related to the connection to the grid, or the timetable of the grid application.

Legal regulation

Legal regulation represents the ability to use other regulatory tools by a legitimate authority, those tools being applied via the mechanisms of the legal apparatus – primary law, delegated law, quasi-legislation soft law (Freiberg 2010, pp. 84–85, cf. Sokołowski 2016, pp. 85–86). In comparison to the preceding regulatory tools, law performs a dual role. It is one of the means of regulation itself, traditionally providing the ultimate sanction when the systems fail; it is also used as a conduit for the needs of other tools (Freiberg 2010, p. 84). This makes legal regulation a meta-regulatory tool, where law propels the aforementioned regulatory tools. This way, taxes, levies, charges, bounties and subsidies (economic tools), bidding rules and guidelines on contractor grant expenditures (transactional regulation), licences, certificates, permits, accreditation systems and registration mechanisms (authorisation as regulation), technology and design used, impact on the environment (structural regulation), recipients, catalogue, and ways of sharing the information (informational regulation) – are created, established and delegated, influenced by law (see Freiberg 2010, p. 84, cf. Sokołowski 2016, pp. 85–86).

All these circumstances highlight the complex nature of law, which in all of its forms transcends the classic scheme of command and control to reach the shape and influence approach. Moreover, these circumstances emphasise the legal nature of public regulation (Sokołowski 2016, p. 86). Within public law regulation, I notice two main categorises (Sokołowski 2016, pp. 218–219). They are: its narrow and broad sense, defined as "the activity of the national regulatory authorities conducted on the basis of public law, where regulation is regulator" (regulation *sensu stricto*, narrow sense, with a notion of *day-watchman state*) and "any mechanism of control and influence" (regulation *sensu largo*, broad sense). Regulation is conducted by the state, although in the European Union it gains a broader meaning: it includes action at the national levels well as a pan-European move, as climaxed in this book.

CHP: where were we – where will we be?

After more than 20 years since the adoption of PURPA (the late 1990s), the US non-utility generating capacity, mainly CHP, has doubled (Dismukes & Kleit 1999, p. 154). Between 1980 and 2000, the installed cogeneration capacity in the USA increased from about 12 GW to over 66 GW – according to the US government it was possible due to the implementation of PURPA and tax incentives offered (EPA & DOE 2012, p. 12). In the early 2000s, the restructuring of the wholesale markets for electricity in several US states (which enabled independent power producers to sell directly to the market – the status of qualifying facility was no longer needed) caused a market uncertainty. It resulted in delayed energy investments, also in the area of cogeneration (EPA & DOE 2012, p. 12).

In practice, the deregulation process (beginning with the passing of the 1992 Energy Policy Act and continuing with the 2005 Energy Policy Act) made the contracts that had been established under PURPA, by qualified CHP facilities, less attractive (Chittum & Kaufman 2011, p. 2). The negative effects for cogeneration deriving from the changes in the regulatory framework (especially, from the Energy Policy Act of 2005), were aggravated by rising natural gas prices. As a result, CHP development slowed precipitously between 2004 and 2005, leading to a steep decline in the new cogeneration installations which persisted until the 2010s (Hedman, Hampson, & Darrow 2013, p. 7). In the 2010s, its level was around 82 GW of CHP units installed at over 4,400 industrial and commercial facilities across the USA, representing 8% of the US generating capacity, and producing over 12% of total electricity generated annually (Hampson et al. 2016, p. 5).[39] In comparison, in the mid-1980s CHP units accounted for about 7% of the US electricity production capacity (Charo, Stearns, & Mallory 1986, pp. 461–462).

This PURPA's postscriptum shows the link between the development of combined heat and power and the regulatory framework dedicated to CHP, established by relevant policies and legislation. Let us recapitulate the regulatory road of combined heat and power, assessing the past (and to some extent current – as some of the solutions adopted on this regulatory road are still valid) as well as future possible developments of the legal environment offered for combined heat and power (high-efficiency CHP).

What was – the past EU regulatory framework on CHP

The European regulatory framework with its laws and policies established on CHP – the legal environment created for the needs of cogeneration – is a firm element of the energy policy of the EU. In different phases of the European integration it has been addressed in various ways, noticed by different countries, having its leaders in the East, West, North, and South. However, it is still very heterogeneous, as its development, and the scale of application depend on many factors, including climate, infrastructure, behaviour of energy consumers, as well as policies and legislation offered.

Due to its pro-efficiency benefits, CHP has been acknowledged as the technology of "a more rational use of energy, since the 1970s combined heat and power has been of interest to Europe. Being under pressure from oil, the European Community wanted to reduce its energy-dependence on the rest of the world. In contrast to the USA, CHP has not been given as a direct approach as in the case of PURPA. However, different characteristics and the legal situation of the Community and the USA at that time have to be taken into account (a pan-European organisation of countries and a federal country). Nevertheless, this resulted in an expert discussion on the promotion of combined heat and power conducted as a cooperative and informative approach.

However, cogeneration – facing problems of different nature – economic, technical, and legal – needed a multilevel action: local, regional, and national if the usage of combined heat and power (with its measurable energy savings potential) was to be utilised to a greater extent. Reaching this target required resolving the obstacles to the development of CHP which existed in the majority of Community countries. In the 1980s, actions to tackle those obstacles were sped-up, driven by the Community's agenda on the rational use of energy. These concerned the RWC framework to the building of which the Council encouraged the Member States in Recommendation 88/611/EEC as well as the financial coverage launched at the turn of the 1980s and 1990s by the Joule, Thermie, and SAVE programmes.

Another driver for the European cogeneration was the liberalisation of the energy market, carried out in different stages, from the zero-phase to the fourth one conducted recently. The market opening for new entities gave a possibility for investments at a smaller, local scale. However, it also brought competition which forced the existing CHP units to adapt to the new conditions, including the costs of their operation in two markets: electricity and heat. To mitigate the risks brought by the liberalisation and to utilise the strengths and benefits of cogeneration deriving from its overall efficiency, the CHP sector was offered certain regulatory tools – which evolved during the following phases of the market reform. These interventions were conducted at the national level – and initially, at the

Cogenclusion 229

European level a soft approach was applied. This was under the First Electricity Directive, where a space was left for the Member State's decision (e.g. instead of granting the priority – as a national duty – Member States could require that system operators give priority to cogeneration when dispatching generating installations).

This approach was further confirmed in 1997, with the passing of the Strategy on CHP; however, cogeneration was addressed there in a more comprehensive way. The Strategy highlighted the economic, regulatory, and institutional barriers to this development; it also offered a vision of doubling the 9% share of CHP in the total gross electricity generation in the coming years, to reach at least 18% by 2010). Despite this assumption, the Strategy confirming the indirect (coordinative) role of the EU in the field of development of cogeneration at the European level, provided a rather non-regulatory approach to the development of CHP, leaving the promotion of it to the Member States' evaluation.

In this light, the 1990s' action on combined heat and power, as delivered by the First Energy Package, one should notice the intention to improve the situation of CHP. On the one hand, this was to be done with the use of the initial legislation, action programmes bringing financial sources, and a strategic framework offering an 18% goal for CHP in 2010. On the other hand, this agenda was inconsistent in action, as highlighted by the case of the First Gas Directive creating barriers for the development of CHP.

However, the energy market reform did not stop after the first step made through the First Energy Package. What this legislation started was an unfinished construction with not enough regulatory capacity to move cogeneration at the Community's level, as well as boundaries and limitations of the current framework of the First Energy package and the Strategy on CHP. A new impetus was needed, both for the energy sector in the EU and for combined heat and power. This came in the early 2000s with the passing of the Second Energy Package, followed by the Energy Taxation Directive and the CHP Directive. However, their regulatory push on cogeneration was not as strong as it could be.

In contrast to the First, the Second Energy Package with its Second Electricity Directive, was a step forward towards a broader regulatory regime for the electricity sector. Nevertheless, the framework for CHP was filled with examples of soft regulatory attitude. There were some exceptions, though – a stricter approach emerges from a narrow sense of regulation (regulation *sensu stricto*) where the Member States where obliged to designate an independent energy regulator responsible for monitoring the market condition for new producers of electricity, including cogenerates. Apart from that, a certain pro-cogeneration treatment was adopted in the Energy Taxation Directive, which has allowed exemptions to be applied, or levels of taxation to CHP to be reduced.

The soft approach to combined heat and power was also applied in the CHP Directive. Its regulatory arsenal, no matter how pro-CHP it was, was loaded rather with blank cartridges than the real regulatory ammo which could create investment security, lower the administrative burdens, and create a level field for CHP and its operators. The statistics on the development of combined heat and power in the EU clearly prove it. Instead, Directive 2004/8/EC offered the "business as usual" approach at the European level – and cogeneration was supported only where it was supposed to be supported. Despite the pan-European benefits of CHP, no real European focus was attached to the sector, such was the attitude that was directed towards renewable energy sources and reduction of emissions. The 18% goal for 2010 has vanished like the emissions coming from a power plant's chimney. The Member States could adopt – or not – their own CHP goals. They could also give and retrieve financial support for CHP, as well as establish and delete their policies on cogeneration; only in Romania and Bulgaria the CHP Directive had a direct result of the introduction of some measures on cogeneration. The growth or decline of cogeneration in the European countries was in general driven by specific national policies and conditions – the European cap under the CHP Directive had rather a marginal (if any) effect. It was a soft failure of the CHP Directive, as I call it; its soft wording was among the reasons of the ineffectiveness of the Directive.

This approach has not been changed with the passing of the Third Energy Package, with its Third Electricity Directive. In comparison to CHP, more space in the internal energy market was given to renewable energy sources, while the regulatory framework on cogeneration has not been extended (to some degree, it was even limited). Combined heat and power was still facing problems hampering the utilisation of its potential – including its pro-efficiency nature – which could have benefitted the targets of the European energy policy. The barriers existing in various Member States ranged from the competition from depreciated power plants, fuel price pressure, unstable heat demand, problems with accessing the grid, limited financial sources for the renewal of capacity, and regulatory and policy uncertainty.

The soft regulatory framework introduced by the Energy Packages: the First, Second, and Third was, in general, neutral to the development of CHP – apart from anti-cogeneration as presented in the First Gas Directive. The cogeneration was recognised in the European market reform – but the real support for it was delivered at the national level. However, taking into account the European action on rationalisation of energy usage, energy savings, and energy efficiency, and comparing this attitude to the EU's approach towards renewable energy sources and action on reduction of emissions, cogeneration was in a much worse position.

To some extent this approach derives from an early poor relation of the three elements of the European climate action, i.e. enhancing energy efficiency – the promotion of renewable energy sources and reduction of emissions. The climate agenda of the EU was sped-up in the late 2000s by the Climate and Energy Package. The EU flagship "3 x 20%" goals for 2020 in these three fields have not been equal. Energy efficiency was treated differently from renewables and emissions, which were both confirmed and strengthened by a binding legislation, while the 2020 goal on energy efficiency was non-binding. As cogeneration has been linked with the energy efficiency pillar – it has indirectly been hindered by the limitations existing within this goal until the adoption of the Energy Efficiency Directive.

Nevertheless, due to the features of technologies applicable to the CHP industry, cogeneration has found its place within the EU action on renewables and emissions; both frameworks have recognised CHP in the internal energy market, offering different regulatory tools for combined heat and power. However, in both of these fields of the EU climate-energy policy, cogeneration stands in the second row. Although, for quite some time CHP has been linked to the promotion of renewable energy sources, where many EU policy documents and legislation have addressed these fields together in quite a fair way. Nevertheless, over the years a preponderance of renewables over cogeneration could be noticed – therefore the development of CHP has turned towards renewable fuels. The same concerns the move on other low-emission solutions – but this results from the European action on reduction of emissions.

In this light, the pillar of the climate-energy policy of the EU in which cogeneration moves into the first row is energy efficiency. The poor relation between the three pillars of the EU climate-energy agenda has been mitigated. It was accomplished by regulatory framework to ensure the promotion of energy efficiency within the EU to achieve the 20% target on energy efficiency in 2020 (established in 2012 with the adoption of the Energy Efficiency Directive). This also involved a clear switch to high-efficiency cogeneration – a regulatory form in which CHP has evolved throughout all the years of being targeted by the EU. However, this time also, in certain fields the Directive has been insufficient to adopt the European coverage over the promotion and growth of cogeneration to exploit its pro-efficiency potential in the EU.

With the finalised legislative process on the Clean Energy Package – it being a regulatory platform for realising EU goals for the climate and energy policy for 2030 – the European Union once more came back to the legal environment on combined heat and power. This concerns the revision of the Energy Efficiency Directive – the legal nexus evaluated in the opening subchapter of this part of the book. Here the discussion on the CHP in the past stops. Taking these circumstances into account, as being an important lesson learnt, let us move on to the very last part of this book – the comments on the future of cogeneration and its regulatory regime.

What will be – the future legal environment for MCFlexSHE CHP: Micro-Collective-Flexible-Smart-High-Efficiency CHP

The issues examined in this book show how combined the European law on CHP is; it covers cogeneration with different attitudes and levels of attention: European, national, regional, and local. Much indicates that the last two, and/or especially the last one (local approach) will be among the most important regulatory directions for the development of the CHP industry. This results from the drive to move energy generation closer to energy consumer (as in terms of renewable energy sources, also with respect to combined heat and power) with the use of modern technologies – decreasing its scale and reaching the level of micro-generation (micro-cogeneration) is possible. As this micro-scale needs a more regulatory attention, it requires certain regulatory tools; those which provide access to the electricity grid and heating network, non-discriminatory treatment, measures enabling the creation of a clear prosumer model of micro-cogeneration. These tools also include other regulatory instruments (applicable in both the grid/network and prosumer model) such as access to information, regulatory surveillance and intervention (if needed), and financial initiatives – both of an investment and operational character. All these taken together create the regulatory future of this sector.

By applying the micro-scale of combined heat and power, the technology comes back to Pearl Street. However, it does not come alone. It is brought by its unprofessional users – energy consumers becoming energy producent – prosumers. They are important stakeholders of the move already commenced in renewables. With the support of the state – as progress in building this micro-scale needs regulatory attention with a clear offer of regulatory tools, including incentives – prosumers can develop this technology. It would be a vibrant contribution to the assumptions and goals delivered in the Clean Energy Package with its energy efficiency first and a fair deal for consumers on its banners, placing consumers in the position of active and central players on the energy markets (see Sokołowski 2018b). Moreover, under this framework – with its pro-cooperative character (see Sokołowski 2018b, cf., 2019), the prosumers' individual action can evolve into a collective move – where cogeneration cooperatives/cogeneration communities (*cogenatives/cogenmunities* as I call them), will be established.

Furthermore, apart from market issues, the future of the European CHP – or rather high-efficiency CHP – will be driven by global and European policies and legislation on renewables, emissions, and energy efficiency even more than before (every day we know more about the European Green Deal – time will show what kind of a deal the Green Deal brings us). Therefore, the fuel mix in CHP industry will continue its evolution towards reaching low-emission/zero-emission, retiring fossil fuel over-capacity and increasing the share of renewable fuels in heating and cooling, at the same time addressing the issue of solid biomass (to limit pressure on wood). As CHP will be applied according to the new approach – seen through the prism of the EU principle of energy efficiency first – further optimisation of the energy demand and consumption, decrease of costs for consumers, or reduction of import dependence will have its impact on the CHP industry.

Another change in the operation of combined heat and power will concern the improvement of its flexibility in the energy market, changing the market behaviour (or leading to losing the market position) of certain CHP units. Without the priority dispatch those units will move to the role performed by peak power operating in the period of high prices (high residual load). This requires increasing the flexibility of the CHP units to their maximum to speed-up their smooth move between the supply and demand of the electricity market. Further changes are implied by applying the solution of dual flexibility concerning the operation of renewable heat and renewable electricity in CHP units. To reach this flexibility, further incentives to install and operate back-up boilers or heat storage facilities – to meet heat demand and to tackle low power demand – are needed in cogeneration.

The flexibility of combined heat and power moves the old technology of cogeneration closer to the already quite well-rooted (in the energy sector) postulate of "smart energy solutions". This links to the current and future obligation of energy technologies, and also cogeneration, to be smart. Rapid changes in the world around us – ranging from climate change and climate strikes, through energy storage and electric vehicles, to cyber risks and artificial intelligence, or energy prosumers and robotics in the energy sector – will not leave combined heat and power aside. These issues do not knock on Edison's door on Pearl Street, they storm them. What should the owner of a CHP plant do then? One might answer: "Make cogeneration great again"! Another might reply: "OK, but how"? In my view, CHP has to change – the future belongs to Micro-Collective-Flexible-Smart-High-Efficiency cogeneration – *MCFlexSHE CHP* is my answer.

Finally, in the case of the law on combined heat and power in Europe there are at least three options to tackle this dilemma. First, legal solutions can steer the move on *MCFlexSHE cogeneration* by facilitating the development of those types of solutions and supporting their stakeholders. The European Green Deal is a perfect chance to address law on CHP, while deciding on the future of cogeneration in the EU. Second, the law can do nothing. Under the model of "business as usual" these matters can be left as they are. Third, the regulatory framework can block this transition, intentionally or unknowingly.

For now, my thoughts on cogeneration end here. I hope you the reader have found answers on CHP in my book, but just in case you are looking for more, I promise to elaborate further in the future. Now, let them spread further, beyond the pages of this book. It is only possible with your help, reader (#cogeneration).

Notes

1 Apart from the recast Renewable Energy Directive (EU) 2018/2001, the revised Energy Efficiency Directive (EU) 2018/2002, the Fourth Electricity Directive (EU) 2019/944, and the Third Electricity Regulation (EU) 2019/943, the Clean Energy Package includes: the Energy Performance of Buildings Directive 2018/844, as well as the Regulations on Governance of the Energy Union and Climate Action ((EU) 2018/1999), on risk-preparedness in the electricity sector ((EU) 2019/941), and on the European Union Agency for the Cooperation of Energy Regulators ((EU) 2019/942).
2 Besides these elements, as listed in Article 3(2) of the Regulation on the Energy Union, the integrated national energy and climate plans shall also cover other issues. One of them is a description of the regulatory and non-regulatory barriers and hurdles impeding the realisation of, the objectives, targets or contributions with respect to renewables and energy efficiency. Another one covers two types of assessment: of the effects of the planned policies and measures on the objectives of the Energy Union (one including their consistency with the long-term greenhouse gas emission reduction objectives under the Paris Agreement, and the long-term strategies on reducing GHG emissions; the latter related to planned policies and measures on competitiveness concerning the five dimensions of the Energy Union). Yet another issue is an annex on the national methodologies and policy measures for reaching energy savings as set in Article 7 of the Energy Efficiency Directive and Annex V of the Regulation on the Energy Union.
3 In their integrated national plans, the Member States have to include, *inter alia*, the milestones (of an indicative nature) under the long-term strategy for the renovation of public and private residential and non-residential buildings, and the total floor area (or equivalent annual energy savings to be reached in 2021–2030 pursuant to Article 5 of the Energy Efficiency Directive.
4 See Article 5 of Regulation (EU) 2018/1999.
5 The obligation of the Member State refers to "at least" checking the possibility of applying the pro-efficiency actions – in fact, the word "should" refers to the end-result which may be denied after the evaluation. However, one cannot depreciate this obligation. In comparison, a softer attitude within the energy efficiency first principle concerns establishing regional, local, and private cooperation in terms of energy efficiency. Here "Member States should … encourage the spread of that principle" ("should" linked with "encourage" represents a soft regulatory approach).
6 According to Article 2 of the Third Electricity Regulation, the priority dispatch is:

> with regard to the self-dispatch model, the dispatch of power plants on the basis of criteria which are different from the economic order of bids and, with regard to the central dispatch model, the dispatch of power plants on the basis of criteria which are different from the economic order of bids and from network constraints, giving priority to the dispatch of particular generation technologies.

7 Parenthetically, one may also notice minor differences (or small inconsistency) in the wording. In terms of the installed capacity, the Energy Efficiency Directive uses "kW_e" whereas the Third Electricity Regulation refers to "kW" of "an installed electricity capacity".

8   As already mentioned in the Explanatory Memorandum to the Directive (Commission 2016b, p. 21), the proposed Chapter V of the new Regulation on electricity "also incorporates rules on the connection if cogeneration units, previously included in Directive 2012/27/EU of the European Parliament and of the Council of 25 October 2012 on energy efficiency".
9   The calculation of the marginal cost of CHP generation can be complicated due to a possibility to of splitting the joint costs for electricity and heat generation in numerous ways (Difs & Trygg 2009, p. 607).
10 According to the Commission (2016d, p. 12), the removal of priority dispatch can be followed by a significant reduction of the running hours of an energy unit – the studies in this field carried out for the needs of the Impact Assessment have shown 85% lower dispatch for wood-based biomass electricity production mainly in favour of gas-fired power plants (Commission 2016d, p. 12).
11 This concerns better integration of short-term energy markets along with the harmonisation of their gate closure times, bringing them closer to real-time (Commission 2016c, p. 93).
12 As listed in the Impact Assessment this sub-option included "pulling all flexible distributed resources concerning generation, demand and storage, into the market via proper incentives and a market framework better adapted to them, based on active aggregators, roll-out of smart-metering and time-of-use supply tariffs linked to the wholesale prices" (Commission 2016c, p. 94).
13 Under Article 2(26) of the Third Electricity Regulation "redispatching" is defined as:

> a measure, including curtailment, that is activated by one or more transmission system operators or distribution system operators by altering the generation, load pattern, or both, in order to change physical flows in the electricity system and relieve a physical congestion or otherwise ensure system security.

14 "[T]hus curtailing or redispatching first those generators which offer to do this against market-based compensation" (Commission 2016d, p. 11).
15 According to the Commission (2016c, p. 11) "this is the preferred option, in order to ensure that the abolishment of priority grid access has no unwanted negative consequences on the financial framework notably of [renewable energy sources] but also of CHP".
16 Under Article 13(5)(a) of the Third Electricity Regulation the minimum possible redispatching

> shall not prevent network planning from taking into account limited redispatching where the transmission system operator or distribution system operator is able to demonstrate in a transparent way that doing so is more economically efficient and does not exceed 5% of the annual generated electricity in installations which use renewable energy sources and which are directly connected to their respective grid, unless otherwise provided by a Member State in which electricity from power-generating facilities using renewable energy sources or high-efficiency cogeneration represents more than 50% of the annual gross final consumption of electricity.

17 The scope of the reports is wider; in addition to these elements, the reports shall include: the level of development and effectiveness of market-based redispatching, volumes in MWh, and the type of generation source subject to redispatching. What should be noted is the need to include the reasons for conducting redispatching.

236 Cogenclusion

18 See Article 13(3)(a) – (d) of Regulation (EU) 2019/943.
19 This correlation is provided by the Article 14 of the Energy Efficiency Directive.
20 It is a sector different from the other three listed which "individually consumes more than 5% of total national useful heating and cooling demand", as given in the Annex VIII of the Energy Efficiency Directive.
21 Pursuant to Article 14(1) of the Directive 2012/27/EU the comprehensive assessment of the potential for the application of high-efficiency CHP was to be conducted and delivered by the Member States to the Commission by 31 December 2015. At the Commission's request, made at the latest on 31 December 2019, the assessment shall be updated and delivered again by each Member State before 31 December 2020.
22 One may note that by this time some references addressed in the Guidelines (Commission 2014) would be outdated, e.g. the Europe 2020 strategy (Commission 2010).
23 See Paragraph 142 of the Guidelines (Commission 2014).
24 See Paragraph 141 of the Guidelines (Commission 2014).
25 Pursuant to Paragraph 80 of the Guidelines:

> [s]uch a bidding process must be non-discriminatory and provide for the participation of a sufficient number of undertakings. In addition, the budget related to the bidding process must be a binding constraint in the sense that not all participants can receive aid. Finally, the aid must be granted on the basis of the initial bid submitted by the bidder, therefore excluding subsequent negotiations.
>
> (Commission 2014)

26 See Paragraph 126 of the Guidelines (Commission 2014).
27 See Paragraph 127 of the Guidelines (Commission 2014).
28 The electrical capacity applies also to the needs of aid granted for the generation of heat in cogeneration; see Paragraph 20(d) of the Guidelines (Commission 2014).
29 An exception is granted to those Member States not using waste heat and cold – this increase is limited thereto an indicative 1.1%.
30 As stated in the extended Article 10b(4) of the EU ETS Directive:

> [u]nless otherwise decided in the review pursuant to Article 30, free allocations to other sectors and subsectors, except district heating, shall decrease by equal amounts after 2026 so as to reach a level of no free allocation in 2030.

31 See Recital 2 of the preamble to Delegated Regulation (EU) 2019/331.
32 Among them one may find a primary equation, i.e. Equation 8 which allows to figure out the emissions of a CHP unit:

$$Em_{CHP} = \Sigma \, AD_i \cdot NCV_i \cdot EF_i + Em_{FGC}$$

[w]here Em_{CHP} are the annual emissions of the cogeneration unit expressed as t CO_2, AD_i are the annual activity data (i.e. quantities consumed) of fuels i used for the CHP unit expressed in tonnes or Nm^3, NCV_i the net calorific values of fuels i expressed as TJ/t or TJ/Nm^3, and EF_i the emission factors of fuels i expressed in t CO_2/TJ. Em_{FGC} are process emissions from flue gas cleaning expressed in t CO_2.

33 As reported by Eurostat (2019a), in 2016, the Netherlands had electricity generation accounting for around 31 TWh of electricity and 174 PJ of heat,

Finland produced nearly 22 TWh of electricity and around 242 PJ of heat, and Spain generated more than 27 TWh of electricity and almost 139 PJ of heat.
34 High shares were also noticed in Malta (28.3%), the Netherlands (26.7%), and Lithuania (25.9%) – however, some of these shares represented fairly small energy systems, e.g. Malta with 0.14 GW of total cogeneration capacity, or 0.59 GW of CHP installed in Lithuania (Eurostat 2019a).
35 CHP electricity generation: +12.05 TWh, share of CHP in total gross electricity generation: +0.3%, electrical capacity: +2.22 GW, total CHP heat production: +68.63PJ, total CHP heat capacity: +12.79 GW (see Eurostat 2019b).
36 When comparing 2016 (EU-28) and 2006 (EU-27), the CHP electricity generation in 2016 was nearly 7 GWh lower than in 2006, and the CHP electrical capacity decreased by around 14 GW (Eurostat 2019a).
37 Minor drops were recorded in Poland (9.5% of renewables in 2017, compared to 10.6% in 2016) and Romania (5.6% in 2017 to 6.4% in 2016); a bigger change was noticed in Slovakia: 14.1% of renewables in 2017 and 23.9% in 2016 (Eurostat 2019b).
38 It should be clarified that this value contains negative figures (see Eurostat 2019b).
39 As the DOE informs in its release of the CHP Installation Database (2018), at the end of 2017 there were 81.3 GW of combined heat and power installations in the USA, with the following states having the highest numbers of new CHP installations: New York (53), New Jersey (10), California (5), and Pennsylvania (5). The top fuel for new cogeneration units was, in the vast majority of them, natural gas (94) followed by several biomass (13) installations; more than 39% of them were smaller CHP systems using micro-turbines and fuel cells (Department of Energy 2018).

References

Bartoszewicz-Burczy, H., Baumgartner, R.J., Fawcett, T., Fritz, M.M., Killip, G., Valladolid, T., & Violi, C. 2018, "Assessing the intangibles: socioeconomic benefits of improving energy efficiency", *Acta Energetica*, 4, pp. 93–98.

Boscán, L.R. 2019, "European Union retail electricity markets in the green transition: the quest for adequate design", *Wiley Interdisciplinary Reviews: Energy and Environment*, e359, pp. 1–28. doi:10.1002/wene.359 [2 September 2019].

Charo, R.A., Stearns, L.R., & Mallory, K.L. 1986, "Alternative energy power production: the impact of the Public Utility Regulatory Policy Act", *Columbia Journal of Environmental Law*, 11(2), pp. 447–494.

Chittum, A., & Kaufman, N. 2011, *Challenges facing combined heat and power today: a state-by-state assessment*. Available from:www.energy.gov/sites/prod/files/2013/11/f4/ie111.pdf [27 February 2019].

Commission. 2010, *Communication from the Commission. Europe 2020: a strategy for smart, sustainable and inclusive growth*, COM(2010) 2020 final 3 March 2010.

Commission. 2014, *Guidelines on State aid for environmental protection and energy 2014–2020*, OJ C 200, 28 June 2014.

Commission. 2016, *Communication from the Commission to the European Parliament, the Council, the Economic and Social Committee, the Committee of the Regions and the European investment Bank: Clean energy for all Europeans*, COM (2016) 860 final, 30 November 2016.

Commission. 2016a, *Proposal for a Regulation of the European Parliament and of the Council on the internal market for electricity (recast)*, COM(2016) 861 final, 30 November 2016.

Commission. 2016b, *Proposal for a Directive of the European Parliament and of the Council on common rules for the internal market in electricity*, COM(2016) 864 final, 30 November 2016.

Commission. 2016c, *Commission staff working document: Impact assessment accompanying the document: proposal for a Directive of the European Parliament and of the Council on common rules for the internal market in electricity (recast); proposal for a Regulation of the European Parliament and of the Council on the electricity market (recast); proposal for a Regulation of the European Parliament and of the Council establishing a European Union Agency for the Cooperation of Energy regulators (recast); proposal for a Regulation of the European Parliament and of the Council on risk preparedness in the electricity sector*, SWD(2016) 410 final, part 1/5, 30 November 2016.

Commission. 2016d, *Commission staff working document: Impact Assessment accompanying the document: proposal for a Directive of the European Parliament and of the Council on common rules for the internal market in electricity (recast); proposal for a Regulation of the European Parliament and of the Council on the electricity market (recast); proposal for a Regulation of the European Parliament and of the Council establishing a European Union Agency for the Cooperation of Energy regulators (recast); proposal for a Regulation of the European Parliament and of the Council on risk preparedness in the electricity sector*, SWD(2016) 410 final, part 3/5, 30 November 2016.

Commission. 2016e, *Evaluation report covering the Evaluation of the EU's regulatory framework for electricity market design and consumer protection in the fields of electricity and gas; Evaluation of the EU rules on measures to safeguard security of electricity supply and infrastructure investment (Directive 2005/89); accompanying the document: proposal for a Directive of the European Parliament and of the Council on common rules for the internal market in electricity (recast); proposal for a Regulation of the European Parliament and of the Council on the electricity market (recast); proposal for a Regulation of the European Parliament and of the Council establishing a European Union Agency for the Cooperation of Energy regulators (recast); proposal for a Regulation of the European Parliament and of the Council on risk preparedness in the electricity sector*, SWD(2016) 412 final, 30 November 2016.

Commission. 2019, *State aid: Commission to prolong EU State aid rules and launch evaluation*. Available from, https://europa.eu/rapid/press-release_IP-19-182_en.htm [2 September 2019].

Council of the European Union. 2017, *Proposal for a Regulation of the European Parliament and of the Council on the internal market for electricity (recast)*, 15879/17, 20 December 2017.

Council of the European Union. 2018, *Proposal for a Regulation of the European Parliament and of the Council on the internal market for electricity (recast)*, 5834/ 6/18REV 6, 23 November 2018.

Difs, K., & Trygg, L. 2009, "Pricing district heating by marginal cost", *Energy Policy*, 37(2), pp. 606–616.

Directive (EU) 2018/2001 of the European Parliament and of the Council of 11 December 2018 on the promotion of the use of energy from renewable sources. OJ L 328, 21 December 2018.

Directive (EU) 2018/2002 of the European Parliament and of the Council of 11 December 2018 amending Directive 2012/27/EU on energy efficiency, OJ L 328, 21 December 2018.

Directive (EU) 2018/844 of the European Parliament and of the Council of 30 May 2018 amending Directive 2010/31/EU on the energy performance of buildings and Directive 2012/27/EU on energy efficiency, OJ L 156, 19 June 2018.

Directive (EU) 2019/944 of the European Parliament and of the Council of 5 June 2019 on common rules for the internal market for electricity and amending Directive 2012/27/EU, OJ L 158, 14 June 2019.

Directive 2001/80/EC of the European Parliament and of the Council of 23 October 2001 on the limitation of emissions of certain pollutants into the air from large combustion plants, OJ L 309, 27 November 2001.

Directive 2008/98/EC of the European Parliament and of the Council 19 November 2008 on waste and repealing certain Directives, OJ L 312, 22 November 2008.

Dismukes, D.E., & Kleit, A.N. 1999, "Cogeneration and electric power industry restructuring", *Resource and Energy Economics*, 21, pp. 153–166.

Energy Policy Act of 1992, Pub. L. 102 – 486, 106 Stat. 2776, 1992.

Energy Policy Act of 2005, Pub. L. 109 – 58, 119 Stat. 594, 2005.

EPA & DOE. 2012, *Combined heat and power: a clean energy solution*. Available from: www.energy.gov/eere/amo/downloads/chp-clean-energy-solution-august-2012 [27 February 2019].

European Committee of the Regions. 2017, Opinion of the European Committee of the Regions – renewable energy and the internal market in electricity, 13 July 2017, OJ C 342, 12 October 2017.

European Economic and Social Committee. 2017, Opinion of the European Economic and Social Committee on: proposal for a Regulation of the European Parliament and of the Council on the internal market for electricity (recast); Proposal for a Regulation of the European Parliament and of the Council on risk-preparedness in the electricity sector and repealing Directive 2005/89/EC; proposal for a Regulation of the European Parliament and of the Council establishing a European Union Agency for the Cooperation of Energy regulators (recast); proposal for a Directive of the European Parliament and of the Council on common rules for the internal market in electricity (recast), 31 May 2017, OJ C 288, 31 August 2017.

European Parliament. 2018, *European Parliament legislative resolution of 26 March 2019 on the proposal for a regulation of the European Parliament and of the Council on the internal market for electricity (recast)*, P8_TA-PROV(2019)0227.

Eurostat. 2019a, *Combined heat and power (CHP) data*. Available from https://ec.europa.eu/eurostat/documents/38154/4956229/CHPdata2005-2016.xlsx/dd19ad9f-4074-4dd5-86b2-5b24a949a47c [15 March 2019].

Eurostat. 2019b, *Combined heat and power (CHP) data*. Available from https://ec.europa.eu/eurostat/documents/38154/4956229/CHPdata2005-2017.xlsx/871cc151-5733-423f-ae38-de9b733aa81e [2 September 2019].

Ezcurra, M. 2014, "EU state aid and energy policies as an instrument of environmental protection: current stage and new trends", *European State Aid Law Quarterly (ESTAL)*, 4, pp. 665–676.

Fawcett, T., & Killip, G. 2019, "Re-thinking energy efficiency in European policy: practitioners' use of 'multiple benefits' arguments", *Journal of Cleaner Production*, 210, pp. 1171–1179.

Flåm, K.H. 2009, "EU environmental state aid policy: wide implications, narrow participation?" *Environmental Policy and Governance*, 19(5), pp. 336–349.
Freiberg, A. 2010, *The tools of regulation*, Federation Press, Sydney.
Gauthier, C., & Lowitzsch, J. 2019, "Outlook: energy transition and regulatory framework 2.0: insights from the European Union", in *Energy Transition*, ed. J. Lowitzsch, Palgrave Macmillan, Cham, pp. 733–765.
Hampson, A., Tidball, R., Fucci, M., & Weston, R. 2016, *Combined heat and power (CHP) technical potential in the United States*, US Department of Energy, Washington, DC. Available from: www.energy.gov/sites/prod/files/2016/04/f30/CHP%20Technical%20Potential%20Study%203-31-2016%20Final.pdf [27 February 2019].
Hancher, L., & Salerno, F. 2011, "State aid in the energy sector", in *Research handbook on European state aid law*, ed. E. Szyszczak, Edward Elgar Publishing, Cheltenham, pp. 246–276.
Hedman, B., Hampson, A., & Darrow, K. 2013, *The opportunity for CHP in the United States*, ICF International for American Gas Association, Washington, DC. Available from: www.aga.org/sites/default/files/sites/default/files/media/the_opportunity_for_chp_in_the_united_states_-_final_report_0.pdf [27 February 2019].
Herrera Anchustegui, I., & Formosa, A. 2019, "Regulation of electricity markets in Europe in light of the Clean Energy Package: prosumers and demand response". doi:10.2139/ssrn.3448434 [9 September 2019].
Ludwig, G. 2019, "A step further towards a European energy transition: the 'Clean Energy Package' from a legal point of view", in *The European dimension of Germany's energy transition*, eds E. Gawel, S. Strunz, P. Lehmann, & A. Purkus, Springer, Cham, pp. 83–94.
Mäntysaari, P. 2015, *EU electricity trade law: the legal tools of electricity producers in the internal electricity market*, Springer, Cham.
Massai, L., & Beyet, C.M. 2018, "Current developments in carbon & climate law European Union", *Carbon & Climate Law Review: CCLR*, 12(3), pp. 272–273.
Milčiuvienė, S., Kiršienė, J., Doheijo, E., Urbonas, R., & Milčius, D. 2019, "The role of renewable energy prosumers in implementing energy justice theory", *Sustainability*, 11(19), pp. 1–16, 5286.
Nouicer, A., & Meeus, L. 2019, *The EU Clean Energy Package (ed. 2019)*, European University Institute, Florence. Available from: http://hdl.handle.net/1814/64524 [12 October 2019].
Public Utility Regulatory Policies Act, Pub. L. 95 – 617, 92 Stat. 3117, 1978.
Regulation (EU) 2018/1999 of the European Parliament and of the Council of 11 December 2018 on the governance of the Energy Union and climate action, amending Regulations (EC) No 663/2009 and (EC) No 715/2009 of the European Parliament and of the Council, Directives 94/22/EC, 98/70/EC, 2009/31/EC, 2009/73/EC, 2010/31/EU, 2012/27/EU and 2013/30/EU of the European Parliament and of the Council, Council Directives 2009/119/EC and (EU) 2015/652 and repealing Regulation (EU) No 525/2013 of the European Parliament and of the Council, OJ L 328, 21 December 2018.
Regulation (EU) 2019/941 of the European Parliament and of the Council of 5 June 2019 on risk-preparedness in the electricity sector and repealing Directive 2005/89/EC, OJ L 158, 14 June 2019.
Regulation (EU) 2019/942 of the European Parliament and of the Council of 5 June 2019 establishing a European Union Agency for the Cooperation of Energy Regulators, OJ L 158, 14 June 2019.

Regulation (EU) 2019/943 of the European Parliament and of the Council of 5 June 2019 on the internal market for electricity, OJ L 158, 14 June 2019.

Rosenow, J., Cowart, R., Bayer, E., & Fabbri, M. 2017, "Assessing the European Union's energy efficiency policy: will the winter package deliver on 'efficiency first'?", *Energy Research & Social Science*, 26, pp. 72–79.

Sokołowski, M.M. 2016, *Regulation in the European electricity sector*, Routledge, Abingdon and New York, NY.

Sokołowski, J., Lewandowski, P., Kiełczewska, A., & Bouzarovski, S. 2020, "Measuring energy poverty with the multidimensional index: application to Poland", *Energy sources, Part B: Economics, planning, and Policy*, special issue on "Energy Poverty Alleviation: Effective Policies, Best Practices and Innovative Schemes".

Sokołowski, M.M. 2018a, "Burning out coal power plants with the industrial emissions Directive", *The Journal of World Energy Law & Business*, 11(3), pp. 260–269.

Sokołowski, M.M. 2018b, "European law on the energy communities: a long way to a direct legal framework", *European Energy and Environmental Law Review*, 27(2), pp. 60–70.

Sokołowski, M.M. 2019, "Renewable energy communities in the law of the EU", Australia, and New Zealand", *European Energy and Environmental Law Review*, 28(2), pp. 34–46.

Stankeviciute, L., & Krook Riekkola, A. 2014, "Assessing the development of combined heat and power generation in the EU", *International Journal of Energy Sector Management*, 8(1), pp. 76–99.

Index

18% cogeneration goal 6, 62, 69, 209, 229–230; *see* Strategy on CHP of 1997
27% energy efficiency goal 99–100, 127
3 x 20% goals 99, 231; *see* Climate and Energy Package
30% energy efficiency goal 127
32.5% energy efficiency goal 99–100, 199–201, 211

Action Plan for energy efficiency of 2006 6, 116–117
administration 21, 31, 34, 37, 47n30, 47n32, 57–58, 64, 66–67, 85, 86n2, 103, 114, 158–159, 175, 200, 222–227
administrative barriers 13, 33, 72, 77, 90n39, 91n42, 112, 118, 159, 172, 205–206, 230; *see also* regulatory tools
administrative procedures 7, 37–39, 69, 72, 77, 79–80, 85, 88n11, 90n39, 91n42, 112–114, 118, 120, 123, 153, 159, 174, 178, 206, 225, 230
Agency for the Cooperation of Energy Regulators 207, 234n1
ALTENER programme 62
Arab embargo of 1973 31; *see* oil crisis
artificial intelligence 197, 233; *see* smart energy
Austria 27–30, 45n14, 73, 78, 81, 83, 89n25, 142, 156–158, 185n13, 219–221, 224
Austrian School 55
authorisation 58–59, 65–67, 77, 90n36, 119, 125–126, 176, 222, 224–225, 226; *see also* regulatory tools

base load 11
Belgium 21, 24, 27–30, 73, 78, 81, 83, 142, 156, 158–160, 185n14, 218, 220, 223, 224; Cogeneration Facilitator 159
Benchmarking Decision of 2011 109, 215
benchmarking 107, 215; *see also* regulatory tools
Best Available Techniques 102–103, 106–107, 128n9, 128n12–15, 130n27, 225; *see* Industrial Emissions Directive
Brexit 156, 184n3
Bulgaria 25, 73, 78, 80, 81, 83, 85, 142, 156, 160–161, 218, 220, 221, 223, 230; Energy from Renewable Sources Act 161
burden-sharing agreement 129n16

carbon leakage 215
Cecchini report 57; *see also* energy market
certificates 72, 74, 75, 146, 149, 152–153, 156, 159–160, 223–224; green certificates 89n31, 114, 160, 168; red certificates 152–153; white certificates 74, 149, 89n31; *see also* regulatory tools
certification 112, 116, 176, 226
CHP Directive 3, 6, 8, 14n1–n2, 89n29, 89n32, 90n37–n38, 108, 116, 118–122, 130n32, 130n34–n36, 131n46, 132n48, 132n53, 142, 146, 157, 159, 161, 164, 169–170, 172, 174, 175, 210, 215–216, 229–230; evaluation 6, 79–86, 117–118, 126–127, 230; proposal 68–72, 112–113; tools 72–79, 114–115
CHP-RES parity 68–79, 90n38, 110, 112, 209

Index   243

Clean Energy Package 3, 127, 198–211, 214, 213, 231–232, 234n1; Fourth Electricity Directive 7, 132n51, 199–200, 202–203, 206–207, 215–216; Third Electricity Regulation 7, 199–200, 202–208, 211, 215–216, 234n6–n7, 235n13, 235n16, 236n18; *see also* European Green Deal

Climate and Energy Package 4, 99–100, 110, 117, 212, 231; *see* 3 x 20% goals

climate 37, 71, 228; climate awareness 101; climate change 99–101, 112, 115, 132n55, 197; climate strikes 233; European Climate Change Programme of 2000 112; United Nations Framework Convention on Climate Change 129n16; *see also* integrated national energy and climate plans

CO_2 emissions 15n10, 62, 100–101, 104, 108–109, 112–113, 115, 129n17–n20, 130n30, 144, 145, 170, 185n13, 236n32; CO_2 allowances 12, 109, 111, 129n20, 129n22, 214–215; CO_2 tax 65, 144, 170–171; *see* Benchmarking Decision of 2011

coal ban 145; *see* Finland

cogenatives 6–7, 232; *see* cogenmunities

cogeneration in definitions 6, 9, 68, 70, 113, 121, 123, 199, 203; applications of CHP 9–11, 14n3–n4, 15n12, 20–26, 44n8, 104–105, 112, 127, 175, 213, 232–233; CHP technologies 1, 5, 9, 11–13, 15n13, 34, 36, 38, 40–41, 48n36, 65, 75, 90n39, 101, 108–109, 112, 115, 117, 126, 127, 127n2, 132n49, 148, 169, 204–207, 231–233; cost-benefit analysis of CHP 122, 124, 132n49, 211; economics of cogeneration 1, 5, 13, 61, 104; industrial cogeneration 8–9, 11, 13, 20, 23–25, 36, 39, 89n28, 89n34, 90n39, 112, 124, 153, 164, 213, 227; large-scale CHP 9, 22; micro-CHP 8, 10, 62, 66, 76, 88n20, 89n30, 117, 125–126, 132n52, 146, 149, 156, 159–160, 165, 168, 182, 199, 203–204, 210, 225, 232–233, 237n39; small-scale CHP 8–9, 14n2, 25, 41, 112, 126, 146, 176, 199, 203–206, 209–211

cogenmunities 6–7, 232; *see* cogenatives

combined-cycle gas turbine 8, 12, 103, 105–107, 225

command and control 226; *see also* regulatory tools

common market 31–32

competition 4, 24, 29, 44n5, 35, 56, 59, 64, 66, 68, 70, 72, 79, 80, 86n2–n3, 109, 170, 174, 204, 228, 230

consumers 20, 23, 34, 36, 37, 42, 47n30–n31, 55, 59, 66, 110, 114, 131n37, 198–200, 228; active consumers 1, 209, 232–233; *see* prosumers

Croatia 142, 171–172, 185n17, 218, 220–221; Act on renewable energy sources and highly efficient cogeneration of 2015 172

cross-border transit 57

cross-subsidisation 22

cyber risks 197, 233

Cyprus 2, 73, 78, 81, 83, 129n16, 142, 171, 172–173, 218, 220–224

Czech Republic 73, 78, 81, 83, 89n30, 142, 156, 161–163, 184n4, 217–218, 220–221, 223–224

day-watchman type regulation 4, 226–227; *see also* regulatory tools

Decentralisation 8, 23, 34, 37, 43, 44n5–n6, 56, 58, 88, 130m28, 159, 161, 197

de-industrialisation 26

demand-side management 42, 65, 185n8, 198, 233

Denmark 14n7–n8, 21, 23–24, 26–30, 39, 44n7, 73, 78, 81, 83, 130m33, 141–142, 156, 163–164, 184n4, 185n15, 217–218, 220, 221, 223–224; Energy Plan of 1981 23; Heat Supply Act of 1979 22, 163; Nordjylland Power Station 14n7

deregulation 227

derived gases 30, 185n11

Distribution System Operator 60, 87n8, 89n23, 124, 203, 235n13, 235n16; *see also* grid

district heating 11, 14n3, 15n11, 21–26, 37, 39–40, 43, 44n1, 44n4, 44n7, 45n13, 46n26, 59, 71, 90n40, 104–105, 112, 117, 129n21, 130n25, 163, 211–212, 236n30; district heating and cooling 9, 88n11, 129n23, 132n49, 201, 212, 214; major district heating systems 14n8

double efficiency rule 70–71

244 *Index*

Edison, Thomas 20, 197, 233
electric vehicles 197, 233
electricity market 56–57, 59, 63, 70, 72, 75, 87n7, 120, 174, 185n8, 200, 203–204; electricity pool 56; electricity sector 20–21, 35, 55–59, 109, 200, 206, 229
energy bills 66, 225–226
energy consumption 10, 12, 15n10, 31–32, 47n32, 63, 76, 103, 115–116, 118, 130n26, 131n42–n43, 172, 173, 182, 198, 201, 212, 222, 235n16
Energy Efficiency Directive 3, 6, 7, 118, 123–127, 131n47, 132n48–49, 155–156, 198–203, 205, 210–212, 215–216, 222, 225, 226, 231, 234n2–n3, 234n7, 236n19–20, 231; *see also* Clean Energy Package
energy efficiency first 198–202, 232, 234n5; *see also* Energy Union
energy labels 33
energy packages 56–57, 68, 85, 230
energy policy 1, 25, 31–32, 38, 40, 58, 60, 63, 85, 99, 111, 141, 146, 159, 177–178, 228, 230
energy poverty 200
energy savings 5, 9–10, 13, 24, 32–33, 36, 38–39, 40–41, 60, 88n11, 100, 114–119, 121–123, 130n32, 131n37, 131n40, 131n42, 141, 146, 148–149, 150, 197, 201–202, 211–212, 222, 228, 230, 234n2–n3
energy security 4, 62, 67, 72, 79, 111, 174, 179, 197, 200; *see also* energy policy
Energy Service Directive 6, 115–119, 131n37, 132n48, 216; *see also* energy savings
energy storage 11, 197, 200, 206–207, 233, 235n12; heat storage 46n26, 104, 151, 204, 208, 233; electricity storage 200
Energy Union 198–202, 210, 234n2; Regulation on the Energy Union 7, 200–202, 216, 234n2
energy utilities 20–21, 33–34, 39, 61, 70, 206
environmental protection 12–13, 14n6, 21, 37–38, 40–41, 43, 59–60, 62–64, 68, 71, 76, 88n11, 90n39, 100–102, 104, 111, 113, 118, 128n9, 153, 166, 169, 181, 202, 212, 225–226

Estonia 73, 78, 81, 83, 142, 171, 173–175, 218, 220–221, 223
European Green Deal 232–233
European Union Emission Trading System 4, 7, 101, 107–109, 129n18–n20, 171, 215, 224; EU ETS Directive 108–109, 129n19, 129n22, 214–216, 236n30; *see also* CO_2 emissions
externalities 63, 212

Finland 24, 26–30, 45n14, 73, 78, 81, 83, 89n30, 130n33, 142–145, 217, 219–221, 223–224, 237n33; *see also* coal ban
First Energy Package 57–64, 216, 229; First Electricity Directive 3, 58–60, 63–65, 67, 87n8, 88n11, 88n15, 88n19–n21, 215–216, 229; First Gas Directive 58, 63–64, 85, 229–230
First Renewable Energy Directive 90n38, 100, 215–216; *see also* Climate and Energy Package
France 21, 26, 27–30, 61, 73, 78, 81, 83–84, 90n42, 142–143, 145–146, 184n4, 185n7, 218, 220, 223; National Biomass Mobilisation Strategy of 2018 146

gasification of coal 106
Germany 2, 26, 30, 73, 78, 81, 83, 89n25, 141–143, 146–148, 217–218, 220, 223; East Germany 22, 44n5, 146; West Germany 21–22, 141, 223–224; CHP Act of 2002 147; CHP Act of 2016 147; Energy Industry Act 148; Use It, Don't Curtail It scheme 148, 185n8
global financial crisis 165
Greece 27–30, 73, 78, 81, 83, 142, 171, 175–176, 186n18–n19, 218, 220–221, 223–224; Programme high efficiency cogeneration of heat and power in hospitals 175
greenhouse gases emissions 1, 11, 99, 103, 108, 111–112, 115, 127n2, 129n16, 148, 175, 198, 234n2; *see* CO_2 emissions
grid 7, 22, 29, 34, 45n17, 55, 58, 61, 67, 72, 75, 77, 85, 112, 117, 125, 162, 169, 185n8, 199, 206–207, 223, 225, 235n16; grid access 34, 39, 61, 66–67, 70, 76, 80–81, 85, 88n17, 110, 113, 115, 119–120, 124–126, 149, 161, 164, 168, 169, 181, 183, 203, 205, 210–211,

Index 245

224, 226, 230, 232, 235n15; *see also* Third Party Access
guarantees of origin 7, 80, 110, 113–114, 116, 118, 121, 123, 130n31, 130n33–n34, 159, 184, 226; *see also* regulatory tools

harmonisation 31, 107, 116, 121, 125, 235n11
Hayek von, Friedrich August 55; *see* Austrian School
heat demand 11–12, 24, 69–70, 80–83, 90n40, 104, 108, 116, 119, 141, 168, 176, 204, 230, 233
heat network 21–23, 25, 37, 132n49, 143, 159, 161, 177, 183, 209, 232
Hungary 22, 73, 78, 80–81, 83–84, 90n40, 141–142, 156, 164–165, 218, 220, 223–224

Industrial Emissions Directive 102, 106–107, 128n8, 216; *see* Best Available Techniques
integrated national energy and climate plans 143, 184n2, 200–201, 210–211, 234n2-n3; *see also* planning
internal energy market 3, 6, 57, 60, 64–69, 71–72, 108, 111, 130n28, 197, 199–200, 210, 212, 230–231; *see also* common market
investment aid 22–23, 73–76, 157, 163, 169–170, 179, 181, 224, 232; *see also* state aid
Ireland 24, 27–30, 39, 73, 78, 81, 83, 89n30, 142, 171, 176–177, 217–218, 220, 223–224; Support Scheme for Renewable Heat 177
Italy 2, 21, 23–24, 26–30, 39, 61, 74, 78, 81, 83, 141–143, 148–149, 217–218, 220, 223–224; Energy-Saving Investment Credit 150

Joul programme 5, 39–40, 43, 224, 228
Joule-Thermie programme 62

Kyoto Protocol 3, 99, 101, 107–108, 111; *see also* climate

Latvia 74, 78, 81, 83, 89n30, 142, 171, 177–179, 217–218, 220, 223–224
Lawson, Nigel 55

LCP Directive 65, 122, 124, 215–216, 225; *see also* Industrial Emissions Directive
legislative package 67, 199
liberalisation 2–3, 5–6, 43, 55–57, 61, 63, 69–71, 79, 83, 87m10, 197, 223, 228; *see also* internal energy market
licences 61, 102, 165, 224–226; *see also* regulatory tools
Lithuania 74, 78, 81, 83–84, 89n30, 90n42, 142, 171, 179–180, 218, 220–221, 223, 224, 237n34; Ignalina Nuclear Power Plant 90n42; National Programme for Heat Sector Development in 2015–2021 180
Luxembourg 27–30, 74, 78, 83, 142, 171, 180–181, 218, 220, 223–224

Major, John 56
Malta 2, 74, 78, 81, 83, 129n16, 142, 171, 182–183, 218, 220–221, 237n34
market failure 212; *see also* externalities
metering 47n30, 47n32, 203, 235n12; *see also* consumers
Micro-Collective-Flexible-Smart-High-Efficiency cogeneration 8, 232–233

Netherlands 21, 23–24, 26–30, 39, 74, 78, 81, 83, 89n30, 141–143, 150–151, 217–218, 220–221, 223–224, 236n33, 237n34; Electricity Act of 1989 56; Sustainable Energy Production Incentive 150
NO$_x$ emissions 102, 104–105, 127n7; *see* Industrial Emissions Directive

oil crisis 13, 21, 23–24, 36, 163, 197; *see* Arab embargo of 1973

Paris Agreement 100, 234n2; *see also* greenhouse gases emissions
Paris Summit of 1972 31–32; *see* energy policy
planning 42, 48n37, 71, 77, 172, 200, 202, 225, 235n16
Poland 2, 22, 25, 45n10, 74, 78, 81, 83, 141–143, 151–153, 217, 219–221, 223–224, 237n37; National Fund for Environmental Protection and Water Management 153
Portugal 27–30, 74, 78, 80–81, 83, 142, 156, 165–166, 219–220, 223–224

post-war Europe 22, 25, 151
pre-package phase 57; *see also* internal energy market
pricing 13, 33–34, 75, 223; feed-in tariff 73–76, 83, 146, 156, 172, 176, 180–181, 185n8, 213, 223; price premium 75, 153, 164, 185n15, 213, 223; *see also* regulatory tools
priority dispatch 120, 125, 170, 203–206, 210–211, 233, 234n6, 235n10; *see also* regulatory tools
procurement 6, 57–58, 86n3, 179, 224
prosumers 197, 232–233; *see* active consumers
public service obligations 180; *see also* regulatory tools

qualitative and quantitative proposals 64; *see* Second Energy Package

rationalisation of energy usage 31–32, 40, 43, 230; *see also* energy savings
registration 224, 226; *see also* regulatory tools
regulatory authorities 21, 64, 66–57, 114, 200; *see* day-watchman type regulation
regulatory tools 3, 4, 6, 7, 22, 30, 39, 65, 66, 69, 72–79, 85, 113–116, 119, 123–124, 126, 144, 146, 152, 154, 164, 172, 175, 184, 199–200, 205, 207, 228, 231–232; regulatory box 7, 222–227; economic tools 222–224; transactional regulation 224; authorisation as regulation 224–225; structural regulation 225; informational regulation 225–226; legal regulation 226–227
Renewable Energy Sources Directive 69, 76, 89n35, 90n38, 110, 112, 130n29, 215–216; *see also* CHP Directive
Renewable-Waste-Cogeneration 5, 38–39, 59, 222, 224, 228
residual heat 12, 35, 36, 40, 46n24; *see also* heat demand
robotics 233
Romania 25–26, 45n11, 45n13, 74, 78, 80, 82–83, 85, 114, 142, 156, 166–168, 219–220, 230, 237n37; National Strategy on the heating supply of localities through district generation and distribution systems 26, 45n11
Russia 174, 179–180; Gazprom 174

SAVE programme 5, 40–43, 62, 224–226, 228
SAVE II programme 62, 87n11, 225–226
Second Energy Package 5, 64, 57, 216, 229; Second Electricity Directive 3, 64, 67–68, 76–77, 89n35, 90n36, 110, 129n24, 215–216, 229; Second Gas Directive 64, 67
Second Renewable Energy Directive 110–111, 130n25–n27, 198, 202, 214; *see also* Clean Energy Package
Single Buyer model 59; *see also* energy market
Slovakia 74, 78, 80, 82–83, 89n30, 90n39, 142, 156, 168–169, 219, 220, 223–224, 237n37; Operational Programme Quality of the Environment 2014–2020 169
Slovenia 74, 78, 82–83, 142, 171, 183–184, 219–221, 223–224
smart energy 232–233, 235n12; *see also* artificial intelligence
Spain 27–30, 74, 78, 82–83, 142–143, 153–154, 217–218, 220–221, 223–224, 237n33
standards 33–34, 38, 41–42, 47n32, 103, 125, 127n7, 211, 224; *see also* regulatory tools
state aid 2, 35, 65, 121, 157, 162, 212, 212, 214; Guidelines on State aid for environmental protection and energy 2014–2020 211–214, 222, 236n22–n28
Strategy for Sustainable Development of 2001 112; *see also* climate
Strategy on CHP of 1997 60–64, 102, 111, 229; *see also* CHP Directive
subsidiarity 85
subsidies 23, 164, 174–175, 222, 224, 226; *see* state aid
support schemes 72, 75–76, 80, 85, 113–114, 153, 165, 173, 223; *see also* regulatory tools
sustainability 60, 100, 102, 110–111, 113, 132n55, 199, 212; *see also* climate
Sweden 27–30, 45n14, 74, 78, 80, 82–84, 142, 156, 169–171, 219–221, 223

taxation 13, 20, 22, 68, 71–74, 76, 144, 146, 149–150, 164, 170–171, 175–176, 179, 182, 185n6, 222–224, 226, 227, 229; *see also* CO_2 tax
tendering schemes 146, 154, 222–223; *see also* regulatory tools

Index   247

Thatcher, Margaret 55
Thermie programme 5, 40–41, 43, 224, 228
Third Energy Package 5–6, 64, 67, 216, 230; Third Electricity Directive 67–68, 203, 215–216, 230
Third Party Access 59, 87n7; *see also* grid access
Transmission System Operator 60, 123–125, 130n33, 185n8, 203, 206, 235n13, 235n16; *see also* grid
trigeneration 8, 14n3

United Kingdom 21, 24, 27–30, 55–56, 61, 78, 82–83, 87n10, 142–143, 154–156, 184n3, 219–220, 223–224; Central Electricity Generating Board 56; CHP Quality Assurance 156; Climate Change Levy 156, 224; Electricity Act of 1989 56; Energy Survey Scheme 45n9; Good Quality CHP 156; Lead City Scheme 24; *see also* Brexit

United States 2, 5, 14n7, 20–21, 31, 141, 227–228, 237n39; American Electric Power Service Corp. v. FERC 35; Energy Tax Act of 1978 33; FERC v. Mississippi 35; National Energy Act of 1978 33; National Energy Conservation Policy Act of 1978 33; Natural Gas Policy Act of 1978 33; Power Plant and Industrial Fuel Use Act of 1978 33; Public Utility Regulatory Policies Act 2, 5, 21, 33–35, 45n17–n18, 227–228

waste heat 9–10, 36, 46n23, 116, 119, 124, 130m25, 132n49, 153, 214, 236n29; *see also* heat demand
waste hierarchy principle 212
waste to energy 36

Żmijewski, Krzysztof 5

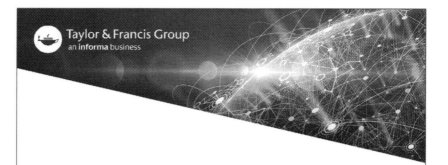

Printed in the United States
by Baker & Taylor Publisher Services